PEMMICAN EMPIRE

In the British territories of the North American Great Plains, food figured as a key trading commodity after 1780, when British and Canadian fur companies purchased ever-larger quantities of bison meats and fats (pemmican) from plains hunters to support their commercial expansion across the continent. *Pemmican Empire* traces the history of the unsustainable food-market hunt on the plains, which, once established, created distinctive trade relations between the newcomers and the native peoples. It also resulted in the near annihilation of the Canadian bison herds north of the Missouri River. Drawing on fur company records and a broad range of Native American history accounts, George Colpitts offers new perspectives on the market economy of the western prairie that was established during this time, one that created asymmetric power among traders and informed the bioregional history of the West where the North American bison became a food commodity hunted to nearly the last animal.

George Colpitts is Associate Professor of History at the University of Calgary.

Studies in Environment and History

Editors

J. R. McNeill, *Georgetown University*
Edmund P. Russell, *University of Kansas*

Editors Emeritus

Alfred W. Crosby, *University of Texas at Austin*
Donald Worster, *University of Kansas*

Other Books in the Series

Micah Muscolino *The Ecology of War in China: Henan Province, the Yellow River, and Beyond, 1938–1950*
John Brooke *Climate Change and the Course of Global History: A Rough Journey*
Emmanuel Kreike *Environmental Infrastructure in African History: Examining the Myth of Natural Resource Management*
Paul Josephson *An Environmental History of Russia*
Gregory T. Cushman *Guano and the Opening of the Pacific World: A Global Ecological History*
Sam White *Climate of Rebellion in the Early Modern Ottoman Empire*
Alan Mikhail *Nature and Empire in Ottoman Egypt: An Environmental History*
Edmund Russell *Evolutionary History: Uniting History and Biology to Understand Life on Earth*
Richard W. Judd *The Untilled Garden: Natural History and the Spirit of Conservation in America, 1740–1840*
James L. A. Webb Jr. *Humanity's Burden: A Global History of Malaria*
Frank Uekoetter *The Green and the Brown. A History of Conservation in Nazi Germany*
Myrna I. Santiago *The Ecology of Oil: Environment, Labor, and the Mexican Revolution, 1900–1938*
Matthew D. Evenden *Fish versus Power: An Environmental History of the Fraser River*
Nancy J. Jacobs *Environment, Power, and Injustice: A South African History*
Adam Rome *The Bulldozer in the Countryside: Suburban Sprawl and the Rise of American Environmentalism*
Judith Shapiro *Mao's War Against Nature: Politics and the Environment in Revolutionary China*
Edmund Russell *War and Nature: Fighting Humans and Insects with Chemicals from World War I to Silent Spring*
Andrew Isenberg *The Destruction of the Bison: An Environmental History*
Thomas Dunlap *Nature and the English Diaspora*
Robert B. Marks *Tigers, Rice, Silk, and Silt: Environment and Economy in Late Imperial South China*

(*continued after Index*)

PEMMICAN EMPIRE

Food, Trade, and the Last Bison Hunts in the North American Plains, 1780–1882

George Colpitts
University of Calgary

CAMBRIDGE
UNIVERSITY PRESS

CAMBRIDGE
UNIVERSITY PRESS

University Printing House, Cambridge CB2 8BS, United Kingdom

One Liberty Plaza, 20th Floor, New York, NY 10006, USA

477 Williamstown Road, Port Melbourne, VIC 3207, Australia

314-321, 3rd Floor, Plot 3, Splendor Forum, Jasola District Centre, New Delhi-110025, India

79 Anson Road, #06-04/06, Singapore 079906

Cambridge University Press is part of the University of Cambridge.

It furthers the University's mission by disseminating knowledge in the pursuit of education, learning and research at the highest international levels of excellence.

www.cambridge.org
Information on this title: www.cambridge.org/9781107622890

© George Colpitts 2015

This publication is in copyright. Subject to statutory exception and to the provisions of relevant collective licensing agreements, no reproduction of any part may take place without the written permission of Cambridge University Press.

First published 2015
First paperback edition 2018

A catalogue record for this publication is available from the British Library

Library of Congress Cataloging in Publication data
Colpitts, George, 1964–
Pemmican empire : food, trade, and the last bison hunts in the North American plains, 1780–1882 / George Colpitts.
    pages   cm. – (Studies in environment and history)
Includes bibliographical references and index.
ISBN 978-1-107-04490-6
1. Bison industry – Great Plains – History.   2. Food industry and trade – Great Plains – History.   3. Pemmican – History.   4. Fur trade – Great Plains – History.   I. Title.   II. Series: Studies in environment and history.
HD9438.B573C65   2014
338.3´72964309034–dc23   2014016433

ISBN 978-1-107-04490-6 Hardback
ISBN 978-1-107-62289-0 Paperback

Cambridge University Press has no responsibility for the persistence or accuracy of URLs for external or third-party internet websites referred to in this publication, and does not guarantee that any content on such websites is, or will remain, accurate or appropriate.

To Francine

CONTENTS

List of Figures		*page* x
Acknowledgments		xi
	Introduction	1
1.	Changing Food Energy Regimes in the Northern Fur Trade, 1760–1790	19
2.	The Pemmican Bioregion, 1790–1810	58
3.	Food Fights and Pemmican Wars, 1790–1816	100
4.	Selling Bison Flesh in the British Market after 1821	148
5.	Commercial War Zones in the Bison Commons, 1835–1850	189
6.	Ending the Pemmican Era	219
	Conclusion	260
Fur Trade Food Glossary		267
Bibliography		281
Index		299

FIGURES

1.1	Plains and prairie people in the late eighteenth century	*page* 23
1.2	Donald McKay's map, 1791	24
1.3	Forts and posts in the Pemmican Empire	50
1.4	Caloric energy of corn, wild rice, and pemmican	54
2.1	Edward Umfreville's 1790 sketch of a pound	67
2.2	John Macdonell's sketch of a pound, 1797	68
2.3	Paul Kane, "A Buffalo Pound"	69
2.4	Winter bison distribution	73
2.5	The fat frontier in the Great Plains	90
2.6	A pemmican bag	95
3.1	"Buffalo Hunting"	125
4.1	Pemmican book prices	156
4.2	Fat book prices, 1811–1871	157
4.3	Dried meat prices, 1811–1871	157
4.4	Quotas, Northern Department	180
4.5	Fur trade districts	182
5.1	Royal Navy pemmican tin	194
5.2	Bison tallow production, 1835–1857	200
6.1	Fresh meat and pemmican, Fort Edmonton, 1860s	230
6.2	The 1869 "Methodist" hunt to Nose Hill	233
6.3	Métis pounded and dried meat trades, Fort Edmonton, 1858–1865	234
6.4	Niitistapi, Nakota, and Cree trade, Fort Edmonton, 1858–1863	235
6.5	Métis fats and pemmican trades, Fort Edmonton, 1858–1863, in pounds	236
6.6	McKay's Character Book at Fort Ellice, 1868 (HBCA)	238
6.7	Excerpts from McKay's Character Book	241

ACKNOWLEDGMENTS

I must acknowledge many people who have generously helped me as I was writing this book. My research began when I wrote a PhD graduate seminar paper for the late Dr. John Foster on provisions trading at Cumberland House, later published in *Prairie Forum*. My project on the fur trade was profoundly influenced by Dr. Foster's instruction and encouragement and I remain in his debt. I've had convivial intellectual feasts from across disciplines, and especially the rich fare offered at the Bison Symposium, hosted by University of Saskatchewan in May 2011. I thank the remarkable environmental and western historians, Bill Waiser and Geoff Cunfer, for their invitation to partake. Special thanks must go, also, to symposium contributors Alwynne Beaudoin, Dan Flores, John Gow, Elizabeth Robertson, Matthew Todd, Ernie Walker, and Gary Zellar. I must single out Ted Binnema, in particular, for our ongoing exchanges over the years, and Gerhard Ens, who has always offered support and help in following up my research. The Network in Canadian History and Environment (NiCHE) and, for that reason, Alan MacEachern deserve great thanks. I must credit, too, anonymous readers of my articles in *Prairie Forum*, and those appearing in *Great Plains Quarterly* and *Western Historical Quarterly*. Cartographer Shawn Mueller, in Calgary, deserves much credit for the maps he has drawn for me. Susan McKee at the University of Calgary Library's spatial and data collection area also helped a great deal with the GIS climatic mapping.

Many archivists and specialists were indispensable. Julie Reid, at the Centre du patrimoine, St. Boniface, guided me through the Provencher and Taché papers and other sources. Chris Kotecki, of the HBC archives, provided great support in my use of that collection, as did the Manitoba Provincial Archives. In Edmonton, the Provincial Archives of Alberta helped, particularly Diane Lamoureux, who led me through the Oblate archives held there. At the Glenbow, Doug Cass, Lindsay Moir, and Susan Kooyman deserve much thanks, as does Hugh Dempsey, who helped at various points on my earliest research questions. Donald B. Smith has always been generous in his help and encouragement. Much appreciated and dearly missed as an extraordinary colleague and Blackfoot specialist is Gerald Conaty.

I am very thankful for valuable conversations with fellow fat enthusiasts from archaeology and biology. Brian Kooyman (University of Calgary), Jack Brink (Provincial Museum of Alberta), and Len Hills (University of Calgary) were all helpful. There was also Mick Price (University of Alberta), Al Shaefer and the lipids experts at the Lacombe laboratory (Agriculture Canada), and Robert Hudson (University of Alberta) who all engaged in my queries. Steven Greyeyes welcomed me to his bison pemmican camp just outside Riding Mountain National Park in November 2011. Jon Proven was greatly appreciated for his butchery experience on that occasion, as were all the camp participants. Red Deer bison handler (if not bison "whisperer") *extraordinaire* and rancher Ivan Smith deserves special thanks, as do the Big Bend's butchers who taught me much about how bison meat comes off the bone. Fellow board members of the Eleanor Luxton Historical Foundation deserve thanks, too, for their support and interest in Western Canada's bison past.

Finally, my family has been terrifically supportive (and patient) with someone almost clinically obsessed with bison fat. Long-suffering and truly inspirational was Francine Michaud. My son, Gabriel, made the road trips to Montana, and then to North Dakota, Minnesota, Manitoba, and Saskatchewan in search of old buffalo haunts. Having my son with me on that occasion, I think, is proof that even the buffalo's memory in the present is as lifegiving as its flesh and fat were in the past.

INTRODUCTION

In 1870, an American Indian Agent visiting Red River remarked on the widespread consumption of "pemmican"– a native foodstuff composed mostly of large quantities of bison fat and dried, pounded meat. It seemed above the 49th parallel in the North American Great Plains, pemmican was forming "the national dish so to speak, of a population composed of many nationalities; and like everything else in this peculiar country, it is a wonderful mixture." Henry M. Rice went on to write that "it is a difficult matter to tell at all times exactly where the half-breed ends and the white man or Indian begins; correspondingly difficult is it to tell where the buffalo terminates and the pemmican begins."[1]

However, what Rice discovered was nothing new: pemmican in the northern latitudes of the Great Plains had been the food stuff supporting, and this for quite a while, British settlers, missionaries, military officers, and merchants. Even prisoners at the Red River jail ate a pound of pemmican a day, plus water. Not many people liked to eat it. Americans dubbed it "Red River Granite," given its high proportion of harder, unsaturated fats. Visitors said it tasted a lot like candle wax and bed feathers, and given its hurried production for commerce, trade pemmican usually offended the palette with admixtures of "hair, stick, bark," as one of its eaters complained.[2] But taste aside, pemmican found a formidable

---

[1] Henry M. Rice (reprinted, 1981), "Pemmican," in *The Minnesota Archaeologist*, 40(2):96.
[2] See July 4, 1839 resolution 20, whereby prisoners unable to "maintain themselves shall be maintained ... at a rate of a pound of pemmican a day or of an equivalent in other provisions." This was later rescinded and prisoners "shall not be allowed to supply himself with any other kind of food or with any luxury whatsoever," than pemmican. Resolution 20, July 4, 1839, and June 23, 26, 1841, Loose Minutes of the Council of Assiniboia, 1837–1862, E.16/3. American terminology is found in Edward N. Wentworth (1956), "Dried Meat: Early Man's Travel Ration," *Agricultural History*, 30(1):4. Robert Kennicott wrote at La Pierre's House in January 1862 that "Pemmican is supposed by the benighted world outside to consist only of pounded meat and grease; an egregious error; for, from some experience on the subject, I am authorized to state that hair, sticks, bark, spruce leaves,

dietary place in the changing circumstances of the British West. As a food source, it fueled the wide-ranging circuits of fur company "York boats" that established a British commercial, missionary, and colonial presence from Hudson Bay to the Arctic Ocean. In the late 1850s, Henry Youle Hind, a Canadian naturalist visiting Rupert's Land, the lands carved out by royal charter for the Hudson's Bay Company (HBC), was struck by the pemmican-fueled transport there – a "vast internal system" operated by the company ran upwards of 200 boats, of 4 tonnes each, and employed no fewer than 1,200 voyageurs in its transportation annually.[3] By 1870 pemmican was so ubiquitous and cheaply procured for commercial, military, and colonial transport that if it was "peculiar to Rupert's Land," as another observer said,[4] the British West was also disconcertingly dependent on this energy source. Troubling to many observers was that bison herds supporting this food supply were quickly disappearing, and, within a decade, this energy "regime" was in effect all but exhausted.

This environmental history examines the nature of the pemmican trade forming by the early nineteenth century. It examines how, in the northern latitudes of the Great Plains, a bioregion shaped by market forces, ideal climatic conditions, and increasingly intensive bison hunting developed and underwent significant change in its historical circumstances. Although it is generally accepted that the pemmican food trade supporting the northern fur companies was responsible for most of the annihilation of the "Canadian" bison herds north of the Missouri, there have been surprisingly few studies of the nature of the social and political dynamics around food exchange and the human responses to the environmental change it fostered.[5] This book attempts to provide

---

stones, sand, etc., enter into its composition, often quite largely, especially if the meat has been pounded by the Indians." Anonymous (1867), "Robert Kennicott" *Transactions of the Chicago Academy of Sciences*, **1**:177. Many thanks to Ted Binnema for sending me Kennicott's remarks.

[3] Henry Youle Hind, *Narrative of the Canadian Red River Exploring Expedition of 1857, and of the Assiniboine and Saskatchewan Exploring Expedition of 1858*, Vol. II (London: Longman, Green, 1860), 103.

[4] Joseph James Hargrave, *Red River* (Alton: Friesen, 1977 [1871]), 168.

[5] Arthur Ray and William Dobak have offered significant studies of the pemmican trade. Arthur J. Ray (1984), "The Northern Great Plains: Pantry of the Northwestern Fur Trade, 1774–1885," *Prairie Forum* **9**:263–280. Ray also provided an overview of the pemmican trade in *Indians in the Fur Trade: Their Role as Trappers, Hunters, and Middlemen in the Lands Southwest of Hudson Bay, 1660–1870* (Toronto: University of Toronto Press, 1998), 125–136; William A. Dobak (Spring 1996), "Killing the Canadian Buffalo, 1821–1881," *Western Historical Quarterly* **27**:39–48. The first significant historical study of pemmican as a critical food energy was pioneered in the work of arctic explorer, Vilhjalmur Stefansson, who championed its use as a U.S. army war ration, *The Fat of the Land* (New

an understanding of how and why pemmican became a driving energy source in the British western territories, and the nature of a society that developed around the trading, use, and distribution of bison fats and meats.

Understanding the fur trade from the perspective of its food supply is timely given the recent historical interest in food as a matter of imperial and colonial history. Jeffry Pilcher has highlighted the centrality of food in world history, and moments when agrarian food surpluses benefited European powers in their global expansion over the course of the eras of exploration and discovery.[6] The development of European food systems, exchanges of new food energy sources from colonial points around the globe, and dietary shifts that drove new orders of muscle power in agricultural improvements, make food history critical to understandings of colonial, economic, and even urban-industrial change.[7]

In North America, Europeans in the 1770s discovered the benefits derived from mass producing bison pemmican which, because of its high fat content, offered fantastic amounts of caloric energy to fur brigades. Because of the way that it was cheapened in mass production and delivered in new food systems, pemmican consumption expanded to underwrite not only greater commercial reach, but also to support sinews of colonial power.

However, pemmican constituted more than the emergence of a new market commodity. Unlike other animal fur and skin trades, food trading between Native people and newcomers created arguably unique relationships based on obligations and rules of reciprocity. New energy also changed relationships between humans and the natural world in America. Certainly, the pemmican trade made for a different history of contact. As Henry Rice suggested, the pemmican-making in the north created an inseparable society of people where food was produced, traded, and consumed between them. No less important was his observation that, in such

---

York: Macmillan, 1957), which was a follow-up and rebuttal to critics of his earlier work, *Not by Bread Alone* (New York: Macmillan, 1946).

[6] Jeffrey M. Pilcher, *Food in World History* (New York and London: Routledge, 2006), 17–18.

[7] Chris Otter (2012), "The British Nutrition Transition and Its Histories," *History Compass*, 10/11:818 [812–825]. David Grigg (1995), "The Nutritional Transition in Western Europe," *Journal of Historical Geography*, 21(3):247–261; also, E. J. T. Collins (1975), "Dietary Change and Cereal Consumption in Britain in the Nineteenth Century," *Agricultural History Review*, 23(2):97–115. Craig Muldrew, *Food, Energy and the Creation of Industriousness: Work and Material Culture in Agrarian England, 1550–1780* (Cambridge: Cambridge University Press, 2011), 260–263, 319.

circumstances, the bison became indistinguishable from the pemmican upon which all depended. Explaining the economic and social characteristics of this emerging food-exchange "pemmican empire," then, becomes the objective of this book.

In environmental and native history, there is a great interest in better understanding why humans are prompted to exhaust natural resource "commons."[8] This is particularly the case with colonial outposts where Europeans or Native people drawn into a market quickly overhunted, extirpated, exterminated, or simply ruined New World fish stocks, game populations, furbearers, and other forms of terrestrial wealth. Although considerable economic analysis has weighed features of Garrett Hardin's model of the "tragedy of the commons," historians have often found the hypothetical commons, as an idea, unmanageable in its simplest terms.[9] It is often hard to locate Hardin's uninformed individualism in historical circumstances. As well, unhampered access to a "commons" rarely existed in historical settings. Resources and the territories they existed within have often been hedged in by proprietary groups, tribal nations or many other claimants to make their access neither free nor remotely "open." The way humans exploit resources, too, cannot be easily reduced to a single human characteristic or predictable behavior. Not all cultures use to their ruin historical commons. Indeed, historians

---

[8] George Colpitts (Summer 2012), "Provisioning the HBC: Market Economies in the British Buffalo Commons in the Early Nineteenth Century," *The Western Historical Quarterly*, 179–181. See Richard H. Grove, *Green Imperialism: Colonial Expansion, Tropical Island Edens and the Origins of Environmentalism, 1600–1860* (Cambridge: Cambridge University Press, 1995). For an overview of the questions posed, see I. G. Simmons, *Changing the Face of the Earth: Culture, Environment, History*, 2nd ed. (Oxford: Blackwell, 1996); on the impact of capitalization on the "world hunt" of the seventeen through eighteenth centuries, including fur, deerskins, whale, and codfish, see John F. Richards, *The Unending Frontier: An Environmental History of the Early Modern World* (Berkeley: University of California Press, 2003).

[9] See, e.g., Theresa A. Ferguson, "Wood Bison and the Early Fur Trade," in Patricia A. McCormack, and R. Geoffrey Ironside, eds., *The Uncovered Past: Roots of Northern Alberta Societies*, Circumpolar Research Series No. 3 (Edmonton: Canadian Circumpolar Institute Press, 1993), 63; Tine de Moor (2009), "Avoiding Tragedies: A Flemish Common and Its Commoners under the Pressure of Social and Economic Change during the Eighteenth Century," *Economic History Review*, 62:1–22; John McKenna, Anne Marie O'Hagan, James Power, Michael Macleod, and Andrew Cooper (June 2007), "Coastal Dune Conservation on an Irish Commonage: Community-based Management or Tragedy of the Commons?" *The Geographical Journal*, 173:157–169; Emily Young (2001), "State Intervention and Abuse of the Commons: Fisheries Development in Baja California Sur, Mexico," *Annals of the Association of American Geographers*, 91:283–306; C. Allen and Ian Keay (2006), "Bowhead Whales in the Eastern Arctic, 1611–1911: Population Reconstruction with Historical Whaling Records," *Environment and History*, 12:89–113

often identify changing modes of production, cultural differences, and evolving economic systems to better explain resource exhaustion, especially in places that, properly speaking, offered "open access resources." Very often, they have pointed to the rise of the market economy, moments of capitalist accumulation and industrialized transformations of the earth – and related energy regimes animating human work –in the history of resource exhaustion.[10]

The open-access killing of the bison raises its own example of a tragic overkill in a North American commons. The near extermination of the animal is usually explained in reference to the skin and robe trade in the United States, where unrestrained competition set Indian and American hunters against herds, especially after the 1850s.[11] The American example offers many perspectives on competitive forces, open access, and the ways groups and individuals weighed short- versus long-term interests in one of the most significant resource annihilations in North American history.[12] But while the American West offers a number of insights into the human choices and strategies of Native people and frontiersmen hunting bison herds for subsistence and the market, a very different commons history played out in the British portions of the Northern Great Plains. There, the fate of the "Canadian" bison herds that ranged north of the Missouri between the Rocky Mountains to the west and the

---

[10] Arthur McEvoy, "The Problem of Environment," in *The Fisherman's Problem: Ecology and Law in the California Fisheries, 1850–1980* (Cambridge: Cambridge University Press, 1986), 9–14; Andrew Isenberg, *The Destruction of the Bison: An Environmental History, 1750–1920* (Cambridge: Cambridge University Press, 2000), 156–159; Henning Bohn and Robert T. Deacon (June 2000), "Ownership Risk, Investment, and the Use of Natural Resources," *American Economic Review*, 90:526–549; Robert Mendelsohn (October 1994), "Property Rights and Tropical Deforestation," *Oxford Economic Papers*, New Ser., 46:750–756; Philippe Jacquin, *Les Indiens blancs: Français et Indiens en Amérique du Nord (XVIe-XVIIIe siècles)* (Montreal: Libre Expression, 1996), 112–114.

[11] On Indian response to the market elsewhere, see Ann M. Carlos and Frank D. Lewis, *Commerce by a Frozen Sea: Native Americans and the European Fur Trade* (Philadelphia: University of Pennsylvania Press, 2010), 114–116, 131–145; Pekka Hämäläinen, *The Commanche Empire* (New Haven: Yale University Press, 2008), 148, 152, 240–243; John Milloy, *The Plains Cree: Trade, Diplomacy and War, 1790–1870* (Winnipeg: University of Manitoba Press, 1990), 21–39; Theodore Binnema, *Common and Contested Ground: A Human and Environmental History of the Northwestern Plains* (Norman: University of Oklahoma Press, 2001), 117–119; Dan Flores (September 1991), "Bison Ecology and Bison Diplomacy," *History*, 78:465–485. Timothy C. Losey and Gabriella Prager (1975), "A Consideration of the Effects of the Demise of Bison on the Subsistence Economy of Fort Victoria: A Late 19th Century Hudson's Bay Post," *Canadian Archaeological Association Bulletin*, 7:162–182.

[12] Isaac Lippincott (April 1916), "A Century and a Half of Fur Trade at St. Louis," *Washington University Studies*, III, Part II (2):221.

Red River Valley to the east formed around different demands for bison commodities, and different social and economic relations between newcomers and Indian hunters.[13]

Across these grasslands, fescue belts and arcs of parkland ecotone – the latter a distinct deciduous-grass transitional ecology spanning between northern boreal forest on the north and plains grasslands on the south – perhaps as many as five to six million animals were sheltered from much of the market hunt for skins and robes, given the slow development of rail transport facilities and other technological lags.[14] Instead, from the 1780s onwards, it was the growing commercial demands for pemmican that became consequential to the bison's long-term and soon unsustainable human use. The food needs of fur traders expanding their commerce in the subarctic incited factory production and standardized food making in the adjacent plains and prairie. In just less than a century, environmental factors such drought, rising plains and Métis hunting populations, and, possibly, introduced bovine diseases, joined with a growing maul of food market hunting to end the buffalo era. More importantly, the "commons" in which these forces converged changed and threw up new opportunities and challenges for humans, especially Native people, who drew from it. Although William Dobak and Arthur J. Ray have both explained how the provisions trade helped kill "the Canadian bison," their work overlooks the particular type of market this food trade supported, and the choices it presented to Native people, Métis, and traders as they concerted their killing of bison, almost to the last animal.[15]

As a comprehensive history of the commercial rivalry and then monopolization of the pemmican trade in the dynamics of climate and shrinking bison populations, this work complements other perspectives on western environmental history provided by Donald Worster, Elliot West,

[13] Ray and Dobak suggested the possibility of bovine diseases impacting the herds, increased plains Indian populations, herd losses to predators, and the impact of climatic change; but ultimately, they single out the wasteful outdoor butchery for provisions trading as the most important factor in the "killing of the Canadian buffalo" northward. Dobak, "Killing the Canadian Buffalo, 1821–1881," 39–48; Ray, "The Northern Great Plains: Pantry of the Northwestern Fur Trade," 263–280. James Daschuk provides an overview of indemic bovine tuberculosis affecting North American bison herds in the pre-contact era, *Clearing the Plains: Disease, Politics of Starvation and the Loss of Aboriginal Life* (Regina: University of Regina Press, 2013), 8–10.

[14] Dobak produced the population estimates for the Canadian herds based on range carrying capacity. Dobak, "Killing the Canadian Buffalo," 36; Ray's analysis is provided in "The Northern Great Plains," 263–280.

[15] Dobak, "Killing the Canadian Buffalo, 39–48; Ray, "Pantry of the Northwestern Fur Trade," 263–280.

Introduction   7

and Richard White. They have situated capitalism, changing modes of production, expanding market economies, and the peculiarities of western ecological regions themselves into the sweep of western history.[16] *Pemmican Empire* tells the history of provisions trading by integrating the fields of Native and Métis history with Northern Plains environmental history. It will become evident that the provisions trade, like other manifestations of the market in the West, unbalanced power between major groups such as the Cree, Blackfoot, and other Plains Native people. The developing provisions trade certainly deflected the history of Métis ethnogenesis and this group's market orientation, as Gerhard Ens' work has already suggested. This study adds the insight that the strategies made by Metis around pemmican, dried meat, and fat trading, especially when prices fell on these commodities after 1821, were significant historical developments. Additionally, this study's emphasis on the interrelations of tribal nations in the specific environment of the Northern Great Plains, and especially the opportunities opening to them in the climate window of the northern latitudes builds on the work of Ted Binnema. In his environmental history of the Northern Great Plains, climate figured centrally in the changing trade relations of the comparatively horse-poor and gun-rich entities in the "northern coalition" and the ecological reality of the northwestern bison frontier. Many of these works draw from, or are informed by the concept of a bioregion, perhaps most effectively applied by environmental historian Dan Flores, who has argued that ecological regions are a good starting point to understanding the economic and social history of even transborder places, especially on the Great Plains. Bioregional approaches have been valuably applied by many Canadian historians;[17] in this work, the specific ecological region

[16] See Donald Worster, *Under Western Skies: Nature and History in the American West* (Oxford: Oxford University Press, 1992), 13–14, 58–59; Donald Worster, "Doing Environmental History," *The Ends of the Earth: Perspectives on Modern Environmental History* (Cambridge: Cambridge University Press, 1988), 289–307; Elliott West, *The Contested Plains: Indians, Goldseekers, and the Rush to Colorado* (University Press of Kansas, 2000); Richard White, *The Roots of Dependency: Subsistence, Environment, and Social Change among the Choctaws, Pawnees, and Navajos* (Norman: University of Nebraska Press, 1988).

[17] Gerhard Ens, *Homeland to Hinterland: The Changing Worlds of the Red River Metis in the Nineteenth Century* (Toronto: University of Toronto Press, 1996); Theodore Binnema, *Common and Contested Ground: A Human and Environmental History of the Northwestern Plains* (Norman: University of Oklahoma Press, 2001); Dan Flores, *The Natural West: Environmental History in the Great Plains and Rocky Mountains* (Noran: University of Oklahoma Press, 2003), in particular, the chapter, "Place: Thinking about Bioregional History," 89–107; See Neil Forkey, *Shaping the Upper Canadian Frontier: Environment, Society and Culture in the Trent Valley* (Calgary: University of Calgary Press, 2003) and Shannon Stunden Bower, *Wet Prairie: People, Land and Water in Agricultural Manitoba* (Vancouver:

spanning most of the British Plains to perhaps the Missouri profoundly impacted, and was impacted upon, by a market economy, the Northern Plains climate and the vicissitudes of the stochastically abundant bison populations found there.[18]

It was not just a quibbling point when visitors distinguished between dried meat, or "jerky" territories south of the 49th parallel, and a pemmican empire in the north. The very nature of the two food forms, north and south, led to very different historical outcomes and market relations. Jerky, or dried meat, was the most elemental product of the chase. When an animal's carcass was flensed, its flesh, if carefully butchered, could be lain on racks and, in twenty-four or forty-eight hours yield to the sun's force and the desiccating effects of prairie breezes. Plains women dried meat with smoke, heat from a fire, or sunlight. They preferred the latter. Solar heat more slowly released enzymes that added distinctive and more pleasant tastes to the meat while it cured. At the end, jerky could have a myriad of flavors. It was, though, a staple food. It could be tied in bales. It held less ceremonial and diplomatic value as a gift given to strangers. Jerky was ultimately a banal cuisine: in long lengths it could veritably serve as a trouser belt.

Pemmican, on the other hand, was comparatively labor intensive and notoriously finicky in its preparation. The critical component in pemmican making was fat, hence the Cree derivative of the word *pemmican* (pronounced *pemigan*) meaning "he makes grease."[19] The very word emphasized the work entailed in pemmican making, as well as suggesting the life-giving caloric energy derived in the process.[20] Pemmican

---

UBC Press, 2011). Other examples of bioregional approaches can be found in William J. Turkel, *The Archive of Place: Unearthing the Pasts of the Chilcotin Plateau* (Vancouver: UBC Press, 2007); and James Murton, *Creating a Modern Countryside: Liberalism and Land Resettlement in British Columbia* (Vancouver: UBC Press, 2007).

[18] The importance of bison scarcity is only recently becoming appreciated as a force in Northern Plains history. See Adam R. Hodge (April 2012), "'In Want of Nourishment for to Keep them Alive,': Climatic Fluctuations, Bison Scarcity, and the Smallpox Epidemic of 1780–82 on the Northern Great Plains," *Environmental History*, 17:365–403.

[19] Edward N. Wentworth, "Dried Meat – Early Man's Travel Ration," Smithsonian Publication No. 4290 (Washington, DC: Smithsonian Institution, 1957), 564; Hodge suggests that the "Cree *ptmtkdn* [derives] manufactured grease, from *piniikeu*, he (or she) makes (or manufactures) grease, that is, by boiling crude fat, *plinu*, in water and skimming off the supernatant oil." He said that the verb was used by the Cree "in the sense of *he makes pemmican*," Smithsonian Institution Bureau of American Ethnology, Bulletin No. 30, *Handbook of American Indians North of Mexico*, Vol. II, Frederick Webb Hodge, ed. (Washington, DC: Smithsonian Institution, 1912), 223–224.

[20] I am grateful for my discussions of the word's etymology and this transformative meaning (and proper pronunciation as "Pimigan") with Cumberland House Cree specialist

fats were traditionally extracted as marrow from the bisons' – or other animals' – long, hollow bones, and "grease" from their large, bulbous cancellous bones. The latter was accomplished by crushing the bones and boiling them. Of all fat on the North American plains bison (*Bison bison*), and, farther north, the wood subspecies (*Bison bison athabascae*), those of its marrows and bone greases held the highest concentrations of white or oleic fatty acids, offering unsaturated, more clean-burning, fat energy.[21] These fats were sought after because they did not leave a waxy, unpleasant aftertaste.[22] But they were also fattier than water-impregnated and lower energy subcutaneous fats (such as the bison's albeit delectable hump fat), intramuscular fat (the marble fats, or "flaky" fats in meat) and interior, or organ leaf fats (sometimes likened to butter for their consistency).

Once joined in a ratio of hard and soft fats – some taken from the marrows, others from the interior – and melted, pemmican makers poured the liquid into sacks filled with dried meat that had been pounded into near powder. The high-fat and protein solid that cooled into a block could offer an astounding 3,200 to 3,500 calories per pound. Commonly fried further in bison fat to make a stew, called *Rughaghan*, pemmican could pack as much as 3,800 calories per pound, easily. Some pemmican

and Cree descendant, Keith Goulet, at the 2010 Rupert's Land Colloquium, Winnipeg, Manitoba.
[21] John D. Speth and Katherine A. Spielmann (1983), "Energy Source, Protein Metabolism, and Hunter-Gatherer Subsistence Strategies," *Journal of Anthropological Archaeology*, 2:1–31. On the issue of selectivity of bone for marrow qualities or quantities, see Kehoe, *The Gull Lake Site*, 145–149, 152. For an in-depth analysis of marrow selection, especially that with high oleic acid concentrations often in the lower extremities of mountain sheep and caribou, see Lewis R. Binford, *Nunamiut Ethnoarchaeology* (New York: Academic Press, 1978), 24–31; on the variety of behavioural, environmental and situational factors that help determine the presence or absence of bone at kill and butchering sites, see Lewis R. Binford and Jack B. Bertram, "Bone Frequencies – And Attritional Processes," in Lewis R. Binford, ed., *For Theory Building in Archaeology: Essays on Faunal Remains, Aquatic Resources, Spatial Analysis, and Systematic Modeling*, (New York: Academic Press, 1977), 77–153. There has been doubt about selectivity of quality over quantity: see J. W. Brink (1997), "Fat Content in Leg Bones of *Bison bison*, and Applications to Archaeology," *Journals of Archaeological Science*, 24:259–274. Speth, however, makes the persuasive claim that selectivity was likely made around changing marrow conditions between sexes, age, and season of the year. See Speth, above, and also discussion by Alice Marie Emerson, "Archaeological Implications of Variability in the Economic Anatomy of *Bison Bison*," PhD thesis, Washington State University, 1990.
[22] Specifically, they "diffuse easily to the circumvallate papilla and foliate papilla" in the oral cavity. See E. Morin (2007), "Fat Composition and Nunamiut Decision-making: A New Look at the Marrow and Bone Grease Indices," *Journal of Archaeological Science*, 34:80.

makers added dried service or other varieties of berries to boost the flavor and nutritional value of the end product. Edward Wentworth's wartime analysis, while investigating the merits of fat-protein pemmican as a K-ration food for American troops, concluded that it came quite close to the ultimate solid fat source – lard – which yields 4,000 to 4,200 calories.[23] Given that pemmican, if sealed from air and kept from moisture, could store indefinitely, this concentrated food energy had terrific military application. It always has. Plains archaeologists trace the first pemmican making to the northern latitudes of the Great Plains some 5–6,000 years ago, a key moment in the cultural history of the region, as pemmican's massive energy stores and durability provided for greater mobility and safeguarding against starvation. Most likely, pemmican boosted the very nature of plains cultures, because it encouraged longer-distance travel, warfare, the elaboration of plains trade patterns and greater food security.[24]

With such a central place in plains cultural development, it is not surprising that pemmican figures in regional origin stories that link people with the bison as a perpetually gifting food source. Pemmican was more than a mere product of the hunt. Its production joined makers with the totality of the animal itself. The manufacture of traditional or "sweet" pemmican required intensive processing of a bison carcass, if not its almost complete disassembly. The manufacture of sweet pemmican, in particular, necessitated a thorough butchery of an animal to yield its most tasty interior organ fats like kidney and intestinal fats – the former often praised for their butter-like quality (John Palliser, as only an aristocratic traveler could, rated Missouri bison butter higher than turtle fat!).[25] Such fats could be accessed only by thoroughly splitting the belly,

[23] Edward N. Wentworth, "Dried Meat – Early Man's Travel Ration," Smithsonian Publication No. 4290 (Washington, DC: Smithsonian Institution, 1957), 567.
[24] J. Michael Quigg (1997), "Bison Processing at the Rush Site, 41TG346, and evidence for Pemmican Production in the Southern Plains," *Plains Archaeologist*, 42:159; and Brian O. K. Reeves, "Communal Bison Hunting on the Northern Plains" in L. B. Davis and B. O. K. Reeves, eds., *Hunters of the Recent Past* (London: Unwin, Hyman, 1990), 169–170. Laura L. Scheiber (2007), "Bison Economies on the Late Prehistoric North American High Plains," *Journal of Field Archaeology*, 32(3):297–313. As Kehoe suggests, despite the increasing efficiency of "edge" area hunting on the Northern Great Plains, Thomas F. Kehoe, *The Gull Lake Site: A Prehistoric Bison Drive Site in Soutwestern Saskatchewan* Publications in Anthropology and History No. 1 (Milwaukee Public Museum, 1973), 2, 87.
[25] "Fat is used instead of butter" among the Osage, according to *Tixier's Travels on the Osage Prairies*, ed. John Francis McDermott, translated from the French by Albert J. Salvan [1844] (Norman: University of Oklahoma Press, 1940), 194–195. John Palliser tasted cow fat at Fort Union of this sort: "peculiarly delicious, and more like that of turtle than

rather than simply harvesting exterior hump and subcutaneous fats. The truly sweet, but comparatively unstable, bone marrows and greases, meanwhile, were extracted only with great effort, by twisting, cracking, and crushing the animal's upper and sometimes mid-section bones.[26] In traditional or "sweet" pemmican, hard interior core fats, then, were mixed with the soft and, often, liquid distal marrows (or those farthest from the body).[27] For the sweetest pemmicans, makers chose the finest brisket, loin, and marbled meat to dry and beat to powder.

In making such pemmican, then, Native people aligned their subsistence needs to the animal in its entirety, if not its very essence in hard and soft fats and its rich offerings of protein. Traditionally, a prime buffalo availed a bag of pemmican, its fats and proteins filling the skin of a bull sewn together. The Arapaho tradition around the buffalo lodge and the sacred bundle suggests how intensive butchery of such an order figured fundamentally in related magico-religious ceremonialism. Arapaho hunters completely dissembled a bison for a people's physical and even spiritual sustenance. In the tradition, the mythical woman origin-figure makes fine pemmican from the bison's sweetest marrow fats and choicest meats. The loaf she makes is finally offered by the chief in his tent to his starving people, and they "came in and took off any amount they wanted and ate it with their children. As the people took cakes of it, it retained its original size."[28] Crow, Blackfoot, and other northern nation

---

beef." "[O]ver [beef] it has a decided superiority in delicacy of flavour, and in not surfeiting those who even feast immoderately upon it." John Palliser, *Solitary Rambles and Adventures of a Hunter in the Prairies* (Edmonton: M.G. Hurtig, 1969), 102. Many thanks to Len Hill for his very useful description of kidney fats.

[26] Wissler all but identified the difference between local fare in Blackfoot cuisine, culture, and mythology, and the stuff that was more standardized for the historical era trade. He drew a distinction between Blackfoot butchery techniques and pemmican making that produced layered pemmican for home use – likely made of superior ingredients including the richest and tastiest fats and meats – and that which the Blackfoot produced to meet the "demand" of fur companies, in which "the Indians supplied a kind of pemmican, packed in large bags sealed with tallow. In buffalo days, the Blackfoot produced a great deal of this material." He went on to say, "For their own use, they often stored buffalo meat, cut into small pieces and mixed with dried and toasted back-fat. Clark Wissler (March 1910), "Material Culture of the Blackfoot Indians," *Anthropological Papers of the American Museum of Natural History*, V, Part I: 24.

[27] Stefansson, *Not by Bread Alone* (New York: Macmillan, 1946), 27–28.

[28] The woman "took the good bones of the buffalo and pounded them and placed them in a kettle to boil for tallow. Then she roasted the best meat (the tenderloin perhaps) and got it very finely beaten, mixing thoroughly the meat and the tallow, and nice sweet pemmican was made...." The legend continued: traveling with this special cake of pemmican, the man journeyed far to his people's camp to find its occupants in a state of starvation. He presented the pemmican to the chief who invited everyone to his tent and

mythologies[29] reference pemmican as a source of life, if not the very beginning point of a tribal nation's origins, such as the myth of the "floating pemmican" also in Arapaho myth.[30] These pemmican stories reinforced thorough practices in food preparation. George Caitlin observed Blackfoot and Crow women along the Missouri drying meat for such fare: they prepared only the "choicest" parts of the bison for their dried meat, "cutting across the grain" to allow alternate layers of fat and meat to dry, and exposing both to the sun "for several days."[31] Another traveler in the Upper Missouri noted roughly the same, that "The choicest cuts of meat are selected and cut into flakes and dried. Then all the marrow is collected and the best of the tallow, which are dissolved together over a slow fire to prevent burning."[32]

As the Cree etymology of the word suggests, pemmican was not so much what it *was*, as *how it came about*. However, in the period of the fur trade, this began to change. Unlike traditional pemmican, the market encouraged the production of a different type of fare. Market hunting encouraged a less exploitative and far more wasteful butchery of the bison carcass. A bag of trade pemmican made in the early 1860s was now made commonly from the meat of three bison and the fat of six.[33] Market pressure tended to rush pemmican production. Native people – especially Métis – selling their products to purchase necessary European goods often harvested only the most accessible fats and meats. Trade pemmican was made almost exclusively with the bulky core fats, which, containing more saturated fat, had higher melting points and preserved longer. Very little, if any, marrow was used and a substitute was found in the easily harvested *dépouillé*, or back fat of the animal. The greatest difference in trade pemmican, however, was in its factory production at trade posts. Native and European labor was joined there for the caloric

---

all "came in and took off any amount they wanted and ate it with their children. As the people took cakes of it, it retained its original size."Dorsey and Kroeber, "Origin of the Buffalo Lodge and the Sacred Bundle," in *Traditions of the Arapaho*, 45–47.

[29] See Clara Ehrlich's analysis of myths which showed the importance of killing fat animals, young women eloping with fine meat, and camp tyrants taking, unjustly, the best meats, selecting "tongues, fine meat and fat; another tyrant selects ten men to get the best meat and skins for him." "Tribal Culture in Crow Mythology," 324.

[30] See "Nihancan pursued by the Rolling Stone," with reference to the floating pemmican, in Dorsey and Kroeber, "Arapaho Traditions," 69.

[31] George Caitlin, in Michael Moody ed., *Letters and Notes on the North American Indians* (New York: Clarkson N. Potter, 1975), 168–169.

[32] Clark Wissler (March 1910), "Material Culture of the Blackfoot Indians," *Anthropological Papers of the American Museum of Natural History*, V, Part I:23.

[33] Henry Lewis Morgan, *The Indian Journals 1859–62*, 141.

needs of the subarctic fur trade. As much as creating different social relations at posts between traders, Native women and hunters, a new use and meaning of the bison emerged in this commercial purpose, bringing to mind White's observation that humans ultimately form their environmental understandings and know their environment through work.[34]

All the same, trade pemmican was still a foodstuff and had different understandings in exchange than other animal commodities such as fur, robes, and skins. Vibert and Ritchie have suggested that food remained a critical designator in the fur trade and shaped relations between gender, class, and race.[35] Anthropology around food exchange makes clear that foodstuffs, even as trade commodities, are rarely given or taken without significant obligations accruing in the hands and stomachs of their receivers. More than any other commodity of exchange, plains foods became the means to an "intimate frontier" where human relations at plains posts, especially between women and men, were joined in pemmican making.[36]

In exploring the pemmican trade, I begin by examining the expanding food needs of the European fur trade by the late eighteenth century. Companies from Montreal and Hudson Bay needed new supplies of food

---

[34] Richard White, "Are You an Environmentalist or Do You Work for a Living?" in William Cronan, ed., *Uncommon Ground: Rethinking the Human Place in Nature* (New York: W.W. Norton, 1996), 171–185.

[35] Elizabeth Vibert, "The Contours of Everyday Life: Food and Identity in the Plateau Fur Trade," in Carolyn Podruchny and Laura Peers, eds. *Gathering Places: Aboriginal and Fur Trade Histories* (Vancouver: UBC Press, 2010), 119–148; Leslie Ritchie (1999), "'Expectations of Grease & Provisions,': The Circulation and Regulation of Fur Trade Foodstuffs," *Eighteenth-Century Life*, 23(2):124–142; I have used "intimate frontier," implying sexual, gender and cultural interactions, from Albert L. Hurtado, *Intimate Frontiers: Sex, Gender and Culture in Old California* (Albuquerque: University of New Mexico Press, 1999).

[36] Food histories suggest how food marked social distinctions, drew together classes or drove great moments in history itself. For examples, see Caroline Bynum, *Holy Feast and Holy Fast: The Religious Significance of Food to Medieval Women* (Berkeley: University of California Press, 1987), 33–44, 67–69; an overview of food historiography is provided by Diane Kirkby Tanja Luckins, eds., *Dining on Turtles: Food Feasts and Drinking in History* (Houndmills, Basingstoke: Palgrave, 2007), 1–14; emerging American culture around food is explored by J. E. McWilliams, *A Revolution in Eating: How the Quest for Food Shaped America* (New York: Columbia University Press, 2005); and the relationship between a food article, its support to human muscle work, and the shaping of civilizations is suggested by W. H. McNeill (1999), "How the Potato Changed the World's History," *Social Research*, LXVI(1):67–83. See Franca Iacovetta, Valerie J. Korinek, and Marlene Epp, eds., *Edible Histories, Cultural Politics: Towards a Canadian Food History* (Toronto: University of Toronto Press, 2012); Jeffrey M. Pilcher, eds., *The Oxford History of Food History* (New York: Oxford University Press, 2012).

energy as they stretched across the low carrying capacity environment of the subarctic. As companies innovated on their transport across the Canadian Shield, they discovered the caloric energy and near superabundance of bison fats to be tapped in the Red River Valleys and the North Saskatchewan catchments. By transferring newly discovered Dene traditions in pemmican making to their commercial operations there, Europeans introduced factory production to create trade pemmican offering energy to drive commercial expansion in the last decades of the eighteenth centuries. Bison fats in pemmican provided significantly greater calories per pound than did the traditional corn-based diets of voyageurs. By the early nineteenth century, European commerce gained pace and a near-transcontinental reach by adopting this energy source.

Just how a European market integrated itself initially in the Red, Assiniboine, Souris, and Saskatchewan River Valleys in the late eighteenth century had much to do with traditions around native pounding and parkland "edge" social adaptations situated in northern latitudes of the plains. Chapter 2 argues that winter pound-making and the first food trading depending on it occurred in ideal environmental circumstances. The prevalence of food sharing traditions proved critical to European trade. The greater winter seasonality in these northern latitudes made bison more predictable in their fall and winter movements, allowing for abundant returns on hunting. Once organized, the great summer market hunts – themselves an aboriginal innovation responding to the market – organized around northern climate favoring the provisions trade. Métis, Blackfoot, Cree, and other Indian hunters exploited the comparatively cooler maximum summer temperatures in the northern latitudes to handle fats, which went rancid less frequently in such conditions and could be produced more easily in surpluses for trade.

Commons themselves have histories, as Chapter 3 makes plain. They change as their natures are transformed and humans invest new meaning and effort into their exploitation. As the market expanded, and especially, as prices rose on provisions to encourage new numbers of hunters, the resulting larger supplies did not in the end satiate demand. This was made evident after 1810, when the first food fighting was sparked in the context of greater demands made by companies for pemmican. The HBC at that date began using larger quantities of pemmican to support its James and Hudson Bay posts; it also expanded provisions trading to underwrite its ambitious gambit in the northern – and calorie-poor – Athabasca district. The Montreal-based North West Company, meanwhile, purchased its own bulk orders to firm up its northern trade and support its continent-wide canoe routes to the Pacific coast, this to support a trade in Canton China. In 1811, the founding of Lord Selkirk's Red River Colony established new demands for bison food, now to support settlers whose crops chronically failed them. However, despite a spate of ideal winters and successful hunting which in fact provided fantastic new quantities of food on hand, any attempt to rationally share pemmican among these various interests failed. This chapter suggests that capitalized companies following "imaginary" needs locked themselves into strategies to obtain limitless supply. The inclination in this stateless "commons" was for parties to beggar their neighbors and attempt to monopolize food resources. This chapter reexamines the resulting scramble and degeneration into the "pemmican wars," as contemporaries called them, between 1814 and 1816 – and the eventual Seven Oaks Massacre in June 1816. Traders and newly organizing market hunters had little interest in sharing food supply. Indeed the "prisoner's dilemma" playing out in pounding areas was clear: companies given the option of sharing smaller portions of the common plenty, or sacrificing their rivals even at their own peril, simply chose the latter.

As Chapter 4 explains, the lock-stock rising costs of provisions became one of the major reasons why, in 1821, all companies in British territories joined together in the monopolized HBC. Across Rupert's Land, and one of the largest swaths of North America, a London-based company regulated the fur trade from Hudson Bay, to the Pacific, to the Arctic Ocean. In the period following, the company used its single-purchaser or monopsony power in the plains to significantly reform the provisions trade to feed the ever-wider circuitry of York boats and crews elsewhere. Unlike the American West where competitive agent-buyers under the banner of the American Fur Company drove commerce, the British territories were controlled by a "factor" trading company. Trade, prices, and profits were directly controlled by London investors. The HBC used standing orders and a quota system to suppress prices each year on pemmican, dried meat, and fats and determine quantities of each from plains districts. This era offered a single, distant, and powerful commercial entity the power to plan in the long term. Immediately after 1821, the company launched the beginnings of the first bison conservation in North America to allow bison, thought already to have been overhunted in certain areas, to "recruit." However, conservation was at odds with the company's interest in commercial expansion. By 1827, the HBC used its advantages to successfully drive pemmican prices to a quarter of their value before the amalgamation, and it continued to suppress prices until the end of the buffalo era. The greater temptation, in the end irresistible, was for the company to increase its use of buffalo food products because of their low prices on the market.

Certainly the cheap and ever larger supplies of food helped the company tighten its commercial grip on not only the Athabasca, Mackenzie, and Caledonian areas, but also, more importantly, its territories vulnerable to American competition and expansion, including the Columbia. Perhaps more importantly, low prices allowed posts to stock far more than their assigned quotas required, and with a wealth of food on hand, traders drew from discretionary funds to support Native people and encourage them to continue and more exhaustively overhunt and overtrap adjacent areas of plains and boreal forests.

The type of market forming then helps explain some of the characteristics of bison hunting in the British territories, suggested in Chapter 5. It also shaped Native strategies, limited their choices, and informed their decision making. Low prices on their product forced Métis hunters in the Red River area to form two annual hunts by 1827, and by the 1850s, a third was often undertaken, both to increase these community's saleable products but also to stock food for specializing winter robe camps. It was, however, the higher orders of waste of summer hunting, carried out over vast distances that likely made the greatest impact. Low prices in the north prompted Métis to continue to use the summer season, despite its disadvantages and vast scale of waste, to produce pemmican for trade. By the 1840s, George Simpson, governor of the company, was confident to call his near-continental trade empire, a "whole machine ... working smoothly and to the entire satisfaction of the classes and descriptions of people in this country."[37] This was a mischaracterization of what had taken place. His company had introduced an unsustainable market that, growing with each decade, encouraged wasteful production, ever greater volumes of consumption and skewed colonial development to maintain an extraordinary dietary dependency on traded bison meat.

Between the 1860s and late 1870s, bison herds rapidly thinned in the Northern Great Plains as market hunting intensified. Ray suggests that the now sizeable Red River Colony, alone, might have been consuming between 7.5 and 15 million pounds of bison meat a year.[38] A Red River newspaper, critical of the Métis in the settlement still making

---

[37] Hudson's Bay Company Archives. George Simpson, Report to the Governor and Committee in London, 1839, D.4/106.
[38] Ray, "Pantry in the Northwest," 95.

annual hunts far to the west, and still fully dependent on wild meat for their subsistence, suggested that in addition to what they returned with to trade, the 600 or 700 settlement buffalo hunters "wasted" enough meat in the field to feed six or seven thousand people in France, Britain, or Germany.[39] By then, robe hunters stocked their winter camps with massive amounts of bison meats; and traveling pemmican making armies could consume upward of 15,000 lbs. of bison simply to support themselves while they made pemmican for trade. No wonder that herds collapsed rather quickly by the end of the 1860s. The last bison hunters were well aware of the herds' imminent destruction.

This book, however, does not attempt to clarify the chronology and unfolding of that overkill. Perhaps the greatest value of Frank Gilbert Roe's classic examination of the North American bison is in challenging historical witness accounts often used to make generalizations of the buffalo herds' whereabouts, population changes, and movements, especially by the end of the era.[40] This work is really about how changes that obviously occurred, especially in the market itself, shaped Native, Métis, and newcomer choices and behaviors. In closer analysis, these groups did not necessarily act as is often presumed. As Chapter 6 suggests, there was less steep decline into chaos described by some western historians. Initially, in the mid to late 1860s, plains Cree, Assiniboine, and Ojibwa joined large hunting cooperatives to cross vast distances to hunt in enemy territories. These multiethnic cooperatives, led in many cases by Cree and Assiniboine warrior societies, now controlled more effectively access to a significantly smaller bison commons. Ironically, Native people benefited from the shrinking resource, at least initially. They could restrict others from hunting or charge tolls for those given limited entry. At least by 1865, collectives of Assiniboine, Cree, and Ojibwa in the Fort Ellice area used their access to the last bison herds to force higher prices on provisions from the company's traders. The greatest bargaining power was enjoyed by Métis, who organized large cooperatives in the Saskatchewan and Red River Valleys and hunted the smaller herds in xeric territories. These hunting brigades had been infiltrating or gaining access via kin-connections Assiniboine, Cree and Saulteaux and even Blackfoot territories, often using large numbers in their contingents to leverage permission or purchase entry. Métis councils formed in Fort Edmonton

---

[39] George Colpitts, *Game in the Garden*, 42.
[40] F. G. Roe, *The North American Buffalo: A Critical Study of the Species in Its Wild State*, 2nd ed. (Toronto: University of Toronto Press 1970), 489–495.

and St. Laurent in the early 1870s to exert native control over the hunt and create hunting rules to stop interlopers and other hunters from dispersing the last animals.

Although there is some evidence that these hunters, knowing the end was near, attempted forms of conservation, they did not for long. When herds thinned and shrank back into a single territory and all parties converged into it, a mêlée ensued. The "fisherman's problem" trumped decision-making in camps having few reasons to conserve animals for other hunters' benefits. When in 1876 and 1877 the last bison herds north of the Missouri migrated eastward, Native and Métis provisions hunters overkilled now to supply themselves for the uncertain future. Ironically, some of the most brisk trading happened in the very last years of the herds when hunters rushed to protect themselves from future want with greater supply, and to sell to the HBC at a loss for much needed goods. The HBC made every effort to purchase everything to safeguard its now precarious transport system. From the last marts in Fort Carlton and Fort Qu'Appelle, the company purchased with abandon.

This work analyzes the history of a bioregion forming within the climate, market economy, and bison hunting traditions converging on the northern latitudes of the Great Plains. As bison meats and fats were transformed for the market and Native people and newcomers joined in the production and exchange of food, an arguably unique society emerged. This was not a peaceable kingdom, by any means. The Canadian West, where the British market held its influence, was no more "mild" as the US West was "wild." As an emergent pioneer society, however, it was clearly stamped by the nature and asymmetries of power in food exchange and the different history of aboriginal–white contact unfolding there. When herds collapsed in Canadian territory in 1879 and the last Blackfoot, Cree, and Métis hunts took place by 1882 in Montana, colonialism in Canadian territories had been significantly imprinted by the relationships, market trading, and power dynamics of the pemmican era. But, whatever those legacies, few colonists and Native people were able to fully anticipate the material, subsistence, and social impoverishment that would accompany the end of the buffalo era.

1

CHANGING FOOD ENERGY REGIMES IN THE NORTHERN FUR TRADE, 1760–1790

These Ojibwa ate "Buffalo Rucheggan mixed with fat": "what may seem surprising they traded most of it from the pedlers who has more of it than they can use, as the fire country through which they pass is so plentiful of that kind of provision."[1]

James Sutherland, traveling in Canadian Shield territories, 1785

In 1792, the London-based Hudson's Bay Company (HBC) ordered servants in three boats and two canoes from Albany House, on James Bay, to join the trade in what was termed the "Little North" deep in the Canadian Shield. From there, some of the men were to build a post in the Red River Valley.[2] Although the company had already built posts far inland on the northern periphery of the Great Plains, the expedition that year marked the beginnings of a chaotic convergence of merchant capital within the tall, swaying grasslands on the sprawling prairie of modern-day Manitoba.

It took two seasons for those leaving Albany House to reach their destination through places "no Europeans or Canadians had ever set their face before," as one of the otherwise experienced traders stated in his journal.[3] John Sutherland, another trader, kept his own journal, mostly

---

[1] Hudson's Bay Company Archives [hereafter "HBCA"] July 25, 1785, Gloucester House Journals, B.78/a/15.

[2] HBCA. A.5/3 London Correspondence Book Outwards – General Series 1788–1796; Fol. 109; May 30, 1793, correspondence acknowledging letters sent from Albany 1791 and 1792, which the committee "read with great satisfaction" the plan suggested. The expansion entailed post building at Portage de l'Isle and Rainy Lake. On these developments, see Victor Lytwyn, *The Fur Trade of the Little North: Indians, Pedlars and Englishmen East of Lake Winnipeg, 1760–1821* (Winnipeg: Rupert's Land Research Center, 1986), 67–83; and Margaret L. Clarke, "Reconstituting the Fur Trade Community of the Assiniboine Basin, 1793–1812," MA thesis, University of Winnipeg, 1997, 2–31.

[3] HBCA. May 24, 1794, Portage de L'Isle Journals, B.166/a/1, reel 1M578.

to lament the difficulty of reaching his posting.[4] By October 1794, when his small bateaux of goods finally arrived at the prairie and he was leading them up the Assiniboine River, the tall grasses at points made it easier to pole and row boats against the current than walk overland. Sutherland could count eighty portages from James Bay to that stretch of the river. The wintering post he finally built at Beaver Creek (later the location of Fort Ellice, near St. Lazaar on the Manitoba–Saskatchewan border) presented its own difficulties. In January, with prairie winds likely howling outside, the trader – probably inebriated at the time – misfired his revolver and shot off one of his own thumbs.[5]

Others in Sutherland's contingent were almost as demoralized as he was. En route to build the larger Brandon House farther downriver on the Assiniboine, the traders there saw their post decline into an alcoholic free-for-all. Brandon's foundations shook the first year with knife fights, shootings, and drunken brawling. Its chief trader (and one of the post's roughest fighters), Donald (aka "Mad") McKay, summed up plains life in his Christmas Eve journal entry: "To be an Indian trader is the meanest and most dangerous business upon the face of the Earth; God grant that I may once more return to my Native country," he wrote, "and all the Buffaloes of the NW [North West] will not induce me leave it."[6]

But the HBC was here to stay, as were Montreal men coming via the Canadian track from the St. Lawrence Valley, and Americans who were using the Upper Mississippi to get into the Red River and Red Lake reaches. In the early 1790s, Duncan M'Gillivray estimated no fewer than twenty-one houses were taking up in the Qu'Appelle, Assiniboine, and Red River Valleys alone.[7] These posts were bartering

[4] Ibid., October 7, 1793. Like most journals of daily occurrence, the Albany, or York, chief factor would check and mark Sutherland's most interesting remarks, these for their own reports home. Given Sutherland's emotional written outbursts, his journals often were marked considerably.

[5] John Sutherland counted the portages in his journal inland in 1793; see HBCA, October 6, 1793, Fort Ellice Post Journals, B.63/a/1. The other HBC route to Lake Winnipeg from York Factory was thirty-two; and from Montreal ninety-eight, see "Diary of John Macdonell," in Charles M. Gates, ed., *Five Fur Traders of the Northwest* (St. Paul: Minnesota Historical Society, 1965), 117–119. John's "alias" according to Archibald Macleod was "Sugar Royall." On a visit to Fort Alexander, Macleod "made him very drunk, of all the stupid Puppies I ever sett eyes on he is the most nonsencicall [sic] & dull." "Diary of Archibald N. McLeod," ibid., 138; Sutherland's accident was recorded in HBCA, Brandon House Journals, May 1, 1794, B.22/a/1.

[6] HBCA. Brandon House Journals, December 24, 1793, B.22/a/1.

[7] There were twenty-one houses in Red River department in 1794, fourteen to oppose, he noted, including those sent by the HBC the previous fall. Arthur S. Morton, ed., *The Journal of Duncan M'Gillivray of the North West Company at Fort George on the Saskatchewan,*

furs, but, more significantly, they were switching their trade into food, in ever larger quantities. Companies were shifting their commercial expansion rapidly into a high-calorie energy regime based on bison flesh.

They really had no choice in the matter. By the time the HBC was following Montreal companies to the prairie steppe of Manitoba, commercial enterprise had reached the limits of an insufficient corn-based diet. Now companies were harnessing a revolutionary new energy source. Many of the posts in the Assiniboine Valley were developing a manufactured, standardized product stored in surpluses, and a rudimentary food system to deliver it the boreal forest areas to feed traders. This type of food did not merely have a different taste. From a metabolic point of view, pemmican offered fantastic new orders of fat energy, and propelled commercial expansion at a far higher pace than corn-based diets had previously.

As any trader knew, food mattered. But while food figured importantly in social and cultural contexts, it was the way that carbohydrates, fats, and proteins actually combusted at a molecular level that made pemmican critical in the fur trade's development.[8] In preindustrial settings, food energy at a basic level animated brute muscle power. In all back-country farming, logging, fishing, and proto-industrial points in North America, colonists gained energy in the hoppy conviviality of countryside taverns, the fatty *tortières* of Lower Canada, or even the seasonal clockwork of

---

1794–5 (Toronto: Macmillan, 1929), 58. Robert Goodwin estimated by 1795 that "we have no less than 23 Canadian Houses in this River and our Servants occupy but three of these...." HBCA. Robert Goodwin Letter to Charles Isham, February 6, 1795, Brandon House Journals, B.22/a/1.

[8] Franca Iacovetta, Valerie J. Korinek, and Marlene Epp, eds., *Edible Histories, Cultural Politics: Towards a Canadian Food History* (Toronto: University of Toronto Press, 2012). Muldrew offers a critical new view of early modern diet and its caloric energy to allow for enclosure and agricultural improvements predating the industrial era. Craig Muldrew, *Food, Energy and the Creation of Industriousness: Work and Material Culture in Agrarian England, 1550–1780* (Cambridge University Press, 2011). Vernon identifies how contemporary changes in food systems and urbanization helped change understandings of hunger as a social rather than an individual failing. James Vernon, *Hunger: A Modern History* (Cambridge, MA: The Belknap Press of Harvard University Press, 2007), 18–21; 42–44; John Burnett, *Plenty and Want: A Social History of Diet in England from 1815 to the Present Day* (London: Thomas Nelson, 1966), 7–13; on food systems, see Kenneth F. Kiple, *A Movable Feast: Ten Millennia of Food Globalization* (Cambridge: Cambridge University Press, 2007), 214–225; and James Belich, *Replenishing the Earth: The Settler Revolution and the Rise of the Anglo-World, 1783–1939* (Oxford: Oxford University Press, 2009). An important perspective on modern food systems is offered by Richard Perren, *Taste, Trade and Technology: The Development of the International Meat Industry Since 1840* (Surrey, UK: Ashgate, 2006).

binge religious feasting. Bursts of caloric energy, in periods of better food production or widened food systems, became in themselves important drivers of economic, commercial, and colonial change.[9] In this context, the fur trade's new reliance on bison flesh signaled a shift occurring in what John McNeill has termed preindustrial "endosomatic" energy regimes animated by human work.[10] As the switch into a new energy source was fundamental to the fur trade's larger expansion, and, ultimately, consequential to the eventual fate of the Canadian bison herds, the discovery and exploitation of buffalo pemmican energy in the eighteenth century constitutes an important, early issue in the market hunt of British buffalo commons.[11]

Moving into the Winnipeg Steppe

Although the HBC had previously expanded inland to Cumberland House in 1774 and then spread a tendril of posts westward toward the North Saskatchewan, establishing sites in the parkland belts at Hudson and then Manchester House, and finally Fort Edmonton by 1795, the plan to expand to the Red River Valley redirected the company toward the pan-flat steppe of Manitoba and the valleys of the Red, Assiniboine, and Souris Rivers. The plan was not really just to trade fur, but also to solve a problem. Food shortages had grown more serious and complex as European commerce stretched westward into the heart of the continent and, specifically, deep within the low biotic carrying capacity of the Canadian Shield.

The map of this country, sketched by Donald McKay in 1791 and sent to London to propose sending men to establish a post inland, provided hints of the interests by companies to find new sources of food. As a snapshot of the interior, it captured the massive geographic extent of the prairie country, as well as the plains tribes ranging from the Siouan Dakota, to the Arikara and Mandan, to the Blackfoot at the foot of the Rocky Mountains (see Figure 1.1). By the mid-nineteenth century, a

---

[9] Vernon, *Hunger: A Modern History*, 84–86; Alain Drouard, "Reforming Diet at the End of the Nineteenth Century in Europe," in Peter Lumnel Atkins and Derek J. Peter Oddy, eds., *Food and the City in Europe Since 1800* (Abingdon, UK: Ashgate, 2008), 216.

[10] J. R. McNeill, *Something New Under the Sun: An Environmental History of the Twentieth Century World* (New York: W. W. Norton, 2000), 11.

[11] W. H. McNeill also suggests the ways that food energy storage sustained civilization and courses of history in the case of the potato: W. H. McNeill (1999), "How the Potato Changed the World's History," *Social Research*, LXVI(1):67–83.

Changing Food Energy Regimes 23

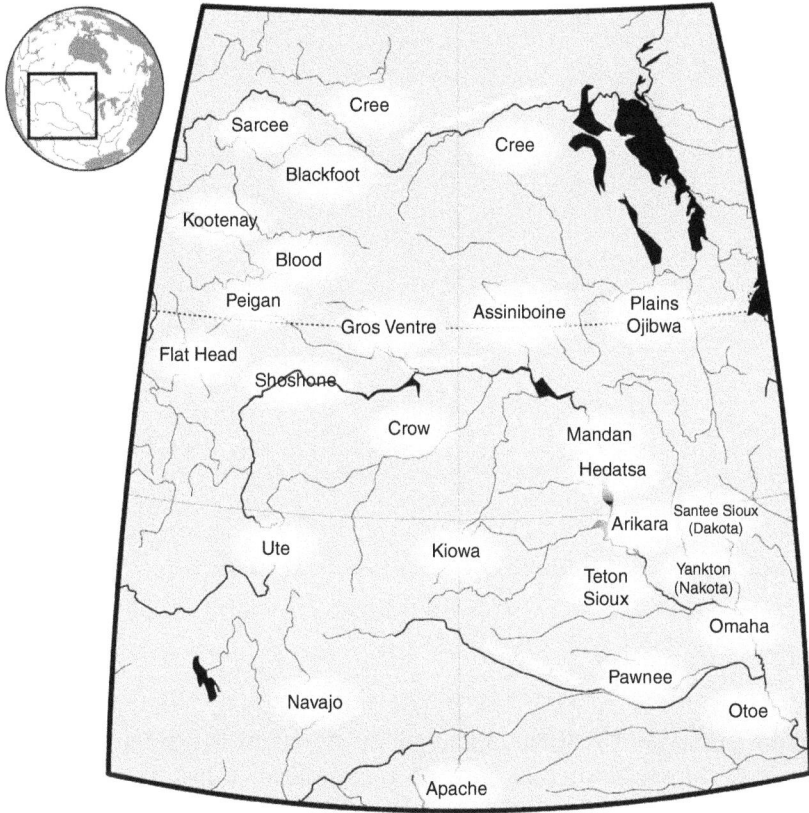

Figure 1.1. Plains and prairie people in the late eighteenth century (map by Shawn Mueller, 2013).

good estimate of only the Blackfoot and Cree, just two of the people appearing in McKay's map, would be around 25,000; in his day, there might have been as many as 65,000 in the Northern Plains as a total.[12]

---

[12] Figure 1.1, Plains and prairie people in the late eighteenth century, map by Shawn Mueller, 2013. Hind used HBC figures, and George Simpson's 1858 census information, as a reliable estimate for plains portions of Rupert's Land, Henry Youle Hind, *Narrative of the Canadian Red River Exploring Expedition of 1857, and of the Assiniboine and Saskatchewan Exploring Expedition of 1858*, Vol. II (London: Longman, Green, 1860), 149. By 1874, W. J. Christie made estimates of the Saskatchewan District, showing 7080 Cree and 9400 Blackfoot and Stoney Assiniboine, with 2000 Métis; with a total of 18,000, 857 of Correspondence in Indian commissioner papers, NWT. One estimate, extrapolated with Blackfoot and Assiniboine, of the Northern Great Plains populations in 1805 was 65,000. Epp and Dyck, "Early Human-Bison Population Interdependence in the Plains Ecosystem," 329.

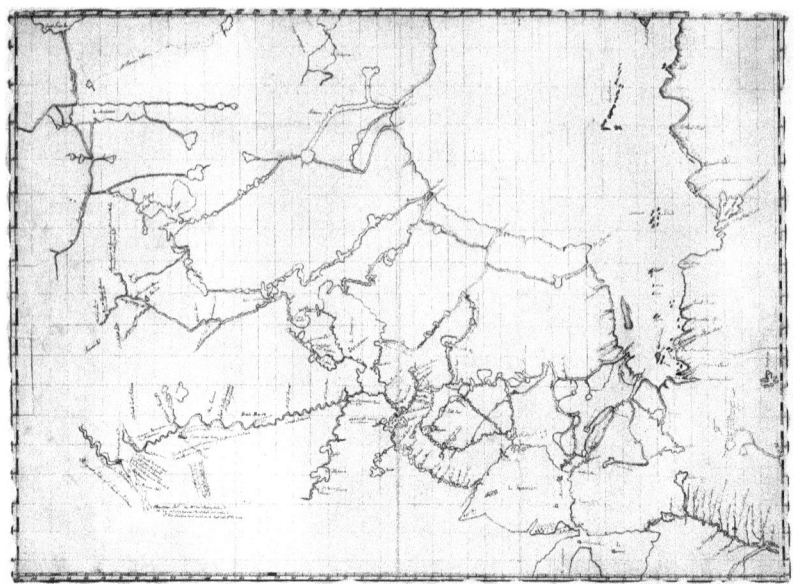

Figure 1.2. Donald McKay's map, 1791 (Source: Hudson's Bay Company Archives, Winnipeg).

It was not accidental that McKay also indicated, prominently, that there were also "Great Plains and plenty of buffalo all this track on both sides of the river" when he showed the Red River Valley. This food supply was also written in his accompanying report on this "river called Red River, who [sic] runs from the Southwest to Northeast and discharges itself in to Lake Ouinipique." McKay praised it almost lyrically: its steady and deep current, for 400 miles uninterrupted by a single portage and providing "good navigation for either canoes or boats." And, beyond the furs to be tapped in the region it was "well provided with buffaloes, deer..." (Figure 1.2)[13]

The HBC London committee reviewing McKay's map and eventually approving his expedition to establish posts, one of which in the breadbasket of the steppe region, was well aware of the significance of these food sources. HBC traders had faced increasingly desperate

[13] Figure 1.2, Donald McKay's map, 1791. "A Map of Hudsons Bay and Interior Westerly particularly above Albany 1791..." by [Edward Jarvis and Donald McKay], [ca. 1791]. Courtesy of the Hudson's Bay Company Archives, Archives of Manitoba, HBCA. G.1/13; HBCA. Edward Jarvis agreement with Donald McKay, 1790, f.167; McKay's overall plan was detailed in Donald McKay to Committee, October 1790, ff. 123–125, in London Correspondence Inward, 1784–1792 A.11/5.

circumstances as they climbed rivers flowing down the Canadian Shield to James and Hudson Bays. Where they left lowlands and then began climbing shield granite, traders faced some of their most difficult paddling against heavy currents, white water rapids, and hernia-bursting portages.[14] In the case of Fort Albany, almost every day's passage inland from the coast made food supply more tenuous. Beginning in the 1760s and over the course of two decades, James Bay traders had moved farther inland to try to compete with Canadians already there. They had realized that the Albany River offered a torturous but travelable route to its source 1000 km inland at headwaters in Cat or Catfish Lake in what is now central-eastern Ontario. McKay, a former Montreal trader who had already been inland, confirmed to Albany employees that, once it reached the river's headwaters, a brigade could portage to water courses on what would become termed the "English track," which could lead, eventually, to Lake Winnipeg and from there to the Missouri, the Rocky Mountains, and a vast concourse of tribal nations. From the salty waters of James Bay, then, traders could reach buffalo grasslands at the forks of the Qu'Appelle and the Red River, as they did in 1794, by about 2042 km of travel.[15]

Raising enough food to feed men along the Albany's crooked and chaotic sections, however, was the nub in the entire plan. Ojibwa and Cree could never provide enough country food at posts like Albany. In general, the Canadian fur trade stretched out over a subarctic ecological biome with some of the lowest biotic carrying capacities in North America. The sparse animal and vegetable life available there could sustain as few as 5 to 10 people per 100 square miles, compared to the Northeastern Woodlands of the present United States, where 50 and 100 could be nourished.[16] Finding enough food became a problem as soon

---

[14] See E. L. Bruce (1939), "The Canadian Shield and Its Geographic Effects," *Geographic Journal*, 16:231. Eric W. Morse, *Fur Trade Canoe Routes of Canada: Then and Now* (Toronto: University of Toronto Press, 1989), 29. On "hubs" see Morris, 30–31; he also vividly describes canoeing these rivers in Eric W. Morse, *Freshwater Saga: Memoirs of a Lifetime of Wilderness Canoeing in Canada* (Toronto: University of Toronto Press, 1987). Harold Innis, *The Fur Trade in Canada: An Introduction to Canadian Economic History*, new edition (Toronto: University of Toronto Press, 1999), 158–159; post-Winsconsinan lake formation is described in R. Cole Harris, ed., *Historical Atlas of Canada: From Beginning to 1800*, Vol. 1 (Toronto: University of Toronto Press, 1987), plate 4.

[15] Sutherland estimated 1,616 miles from Albany to Qu'Appelle, but his measures of a mile, probably accomplished by dead reckoning, seems to have been inconsistent and inaccurate.

[16] Shepard Krech III relies on the lower figure, and, generally, the "delimiting environment" of the subarctic in general. See his "On the Aboriginal Population of the

as HBC traders from Albany reached Marten Falls by 1784, about 150 miles inland as the crow flies. The post there served for years as an always inadequately supplied food depot for crews going farther up the Albany River.[17]

Food problems grew with the geomorphic reality of the Albany and practically all shield rivers that made transporting European foods far inland a logistic nightmare, to say the least. The topographical complexities of these rivers, which moved from frequently shoal lowlands to roiling uplands, were well understood by the Ojibwa and Cree of the region, Algonquian speaking people who did not look at Shield rivers as single entities to travel from one end to another upon, as Europeans did, but as separate rivers within rivers with unique characteristics, identities, and *Okimaws* or proprietary river headmen for each.[18]

These problems had forced technological innovation of sorts at Albany House. By the 1780s, the post's journals make mention of "Mr. Maugenest" (Germain Maugenest), a French Canadian recruit who likely brought some know-how from the Montreal trade and introduced a way to unpack and repack the ungainly fifty-gallon barrels of provisions sent from London (stuffed with fifty "pieces" of salt beef, each weighing six pounds; or sixty of pork, each weighing five), into smaller eight-gallon "rundlets" that could be more easily transported. These were covered with leather, abundantly available nearby. The leather also made them more fireproof, no small consideration considering that many casks also carried lethal quantities of gunpowder.[19]

Kutchin," *Arctic Anthropology*, 15(1):89–104 (1978). His North American estimates are found in Table 3.2, North America, 1500, in Shepard Krech III, *The Ecological Indian: Myth and History* (New York: W. W. Norton, 1999). However, Vale's population densities, factoring in anthropogenic fire, doubled those figures. Thomas Vale, "The Pre-European Landscape in the United States," Thomas Vale, ed., *Fire, Native Peoples and the Natural Landscape* (Washington, DC: Island Press, 2002), 11.

[17] Henry the younger believed that Martin Falls remained the depot by 1800, but, as Gough points out, he was likely unaware that the HBC was now forming its own provisioning depot on the plains themselves, using the newly learnt "art of preserving provisions." Alexander Henry the Younger, August 14, 1800, 16, with Gough's footnote 33. Gough makes use of A. S. Morton's first discussion on the developing provisioning system and the problem of caching, *The History of the Canadian West*, 431.

[18] Victor P. Lytwyn, *Muskekowuck Athinuwick: Original People of the Great Swampy Land* (Winnipeg: University of Manitoba Press, 2002), 10.

[19] On Maugenest, see Alice M. Johnson, *Saskatchewan Journals and Correspondence: Edmonton House 1795–1800; Chesterfield House, 1800–1802* (London: The Hudson's Bay Record Society, 1967), xlii.

More crucial still was the long experimentation in "bateaux" design. It was first undertaken at Albany by Joseph Isbister to deal with the "shoal" sections of the river and get supplies to the first inland post on the Albany, Henley House. Isbister's construction of a distinct boat design in 1745, "ye flatt bottom barge" as he termed it, was built deliberately as an alternative to birch bark canoes, which were expensive to make at James Bay and fragile in shield rivers. "I intent to make triell to build a boat to drawe as little watter as a Canno & Carie more goods," he wrote, summing up, in fact, the best features of the eventual "York boat" emerging in the process.[20] These were soon regularly carrying goods to Henley. By 1781, Albany was fully dependent on these "bateaux," using them to get beyond its Gloucester House and eventually to Sutherland's House. By then, a fully loaded bateau hauling some forty rundlets of provisions drew only thirteen inches of water.[21]

Still, Albany's supply lines were terrifically costly in manpower and food, a situation frustrating Edward Jarvis, Albany's governor, who organized transport by 1786, and had to use a mind-boggling three-season relay system that switched men, provisions, and goods between flotillas of "bateaux," high gun wall "boats," and then large canoes to finally get up the "hill" country of rapids, falls, and portages.[22] Once getting men to the exposed Shield and its difficult upland sections, the system was nearly collapsing. Men fell into line to haul, like in a dirge, large canoes up the angry river sections by lines or poles. Very often men reached the upland sections of present-day Manitoba barefoot, having worn through their moose-skin moccasins on the hard granite.

So bad was the provisioning problem that by 1790, John McNabb, one of Albany's senior officers, sent "private remarks" to London on the logistic problems he was facing feeding men going anywhere beyond Marten Falls. Some fifty men were seasonally stretched out between Henley House, the first inland post, and James Sutherland's hut on distant Seul, or Red, Lake, the farthest point inland. Besides a bit of Indian wild rice, these men still had to be fed almost daily "on European meat," much of it poorly preserved, putrid bacon and barrels of weevil-infested flour that had traveled, amazingly, all the way from London's creosote-soaked wharves.[23] Their Montreal rivals, already

[20] HBCA. September 16, 1745, B.3/a/37 Albany Fort Journal by Jos. Isbister.
[21] HBCA. May 29, 1781 B.3/a/79 Albany Fort Journal by Thomas Hutchins.
[22] HBCA. Edward Jarvis letter to Committee in London, September 3, 1786, A.11/5.
[23] "The expence of provisions hinderance [sic] further inland business and [its] conserving consequence[s] are almost incredible." HBCA. John McNabb, "Private Remarks" to Committee in London, June 2, 1790, A.11/5.

inland, benefited only marginally better on wild rice and Indian corn supplied from Montreal, Detroit, and in present-day Ontario, the Rainy Lakes area.

It was in such complex hydrology that Donald McKay presented to Jarvis the plan to extend the HBC's trade to the Winnipeg steppe, showing in map and report a tantalizing new possibility. Surplus food sources of the plains could in part feed crews moving inland. McKay planned to build up a post – what became Brandon House – on the frontier of buffalo country and use its returns to form a food caching system. While trading whatever furs the plains Cree and Assiniboine might provide, Brandon employees would gather as much of bison meats and fats as possible. Brigades exiting to Osnaburgh House in the fall would then bury bison caches for those who returned in the spring. Incoming crews would, in turn, leave barrels of flour and rum in other locations for their exiting compatriots the next season.

The plan was awkward. It would need much refinement, especially because the HBC was only beginning to learn "the art of preserving provisions," as A. S. Morton said of this formative moment, almost in understatement.[24] The HBC certainly had no clue as to how to make pemmican at this time. Caches themselves proved unworkable. McKay had badly overestimated the altruism of ravenously hungry voyageurs to look after their brother paddlers and, within a year, caches were ransacked or simply not being recharged by departing crews. He was also remiss in thinking that he could sink dried buffalo meats into the perpetually moist and often semi-permafrost boreal soils along the length of the Albany. Many stashes had rotted in the ground by the time they were needed.[25]

McKay's general idea of fully employing bison flesh, too, continued to rely on dearly bought European foods trucked inland. In fact, right up to 1799, the thinking was that European food would have to be sent inland in some form. That year, the London committee went so far as to distribute to all its posts the quite newfangled food "digester" becoming popular in England to feed urban poor. It constituted a small cast iron pot, with a latched lid, designed as a pressure cooker so that any nutrient

---

[24] A. S. Morton, *A History of the Canadian West to 1870–71: Being a History of Rupert's Land (The Hudson's Bay Company's Territory) and of the North-West Territory (including the Pacific slope)* (Toronto: University of Toronto Press, 1973 [1939]), 431.

[25] A. S. Morton, *A History of the Canadian West*, 428.

value could be extracted from bones, and soups made from the resulting "portable cakes" or bouillon cubes that could then be sent inland.[26]

But the important turn in thinking was McKay's focus on the plains as a food source. By 1792 McKay had procured two new Northwest canoes from Ojibwa at Red Lake, Albany's farthest post inland, and by then news returned from London that the company's Committee had seen McKay's proposal, its accompanying map, and read over Jarvis's letters. It warmly encouraged the project to enter the trade in the Winnipeg Steppe.

A Limited Fur Trade Energy Regime

The gaining commercial interest in plains food sources makes better sense by putting it into the context of the limits apparent in the "endosomatic energy regime" constraining Canada's fur trade by the 1780s.[27] Since its inception centuries before, the fur trade had spread inland from the St. Lawrence Valley in what John Jennings characterized as a native European cooperative encounter in a "canoe frontier."[28] The trade's reach enlarged in an environmentally exhausting gambit of classic overreach, as furbearers were overtrapped for commercial purposes. In the trade's earliest manifestation, the French found need for ever larger sources of supply from native people inland. From the viewpoint of colonization, the expanding Canadian fur trade was immediately enabled but in the long term disadvantaged by its emergent culture and geographic expansion. In more southerly areas of the subarctic and the St. Lawrence mixed-forests where French colonization took place, Algonquian-speaking Cree and Ojibwa had perfected canoe building from basic materials of the boreal forest. Their birchbark craft liberated people in the region to rapidly travel far-flung territories in the

---

[26] See the description, HBCA. Letter of London committee to John McNabb, Albany, May 31, 1799, point 19, London Correspondence Book Outwards, 1796–1803, A.6/16; for the use of digesters in England at the time, see their description in soup kitchens, Gordon Bradley Hindle, *Provision for the Relief of the Poor in Manchester, 1754–1826* (Manchester: Oxford University Press, 1975), 94–95.

[27] The expression is J. R. McNeill's, described in *Something New Under the Sun: An Environmental History of the Twentieth Century World* (New York: W. W. Norton, 2000), 11.

[28] See John Jennings, "The Canoe Frontier," in *The Canoe: A Living Tradition* (Toronto: Firefly Books 2002), 27–33; a valuable view of the commercial drive, leading to furbearer exhaustion and further expansion, is offered by John F. Richards, *The Unending Frontier: An Environmental History of the World* (Berkeley: University of California Press, 2003), 463–517.

comparatively short hydrological cycle of the summer season. The broad belt of wide-girthed white birch (paper birch – *Betula papyrifera*) groves, patches of black spruce that offered a canoe gumming material, and stands of Jack pine providing sinew allowed Alonquian Ojibwa, Cree, Nippising, Ottawa, Algonquin, and other boreal people to build a floating engineering marvel: the quite small, but durable and easily portaged, birchbark canoe.

Almost immediately on their arrival, French colonists and traders adopted the canoe. As they depended from the start on traded furs for the colonial staple-oriented economy, they used canoes to move rapidly inland in trading junkets.[29] But despite the military and trading advantages of canoe technology, the expanding frontier depending on this water craft was ultimately unsustainable. It was prohibitively expensive from the start in terms of transport and, especially, manpower costs. Although canoe transport gave the French and later English Montreal traders unrivaled capacity to explore the watery corridors along the edge of the Shield, particularly from three key lake hubs (Superior, Winnipeg, and eventually Athabasca) that provided jumping off points to the continent's further penetration, their canoe transport ultimately depended on the relatively small returns gained from heavy investments of human labor.

These limits were not uncommon in preindustrial settings where relatively small inputs of water and wind power meant that human muscle fiber accounted for up to 70% of all the mechanical energy transforming the environment – perhaps 80% if plant and animal energy inputs are also considered.[30] Before a "massive increase in energetic capacity" was tapped by burning fossil fuels to produce mechanical energy – McNeill's "exosomatic energy regime" – human muscle fiber drove most of the preindustrial workplace.[31] Acting alone or in concert with other laborers, often aided by horse, oxen, or other animals, colonists in the

---

[29] On the makings of the "Ghost Empire," see Philip Marchand, *Ghost Empire: How the French Almost Conquered North America* (Toronto: McClelland and Stewart, 2005); on the nature of the French Empire, see James Pritchard, *In Search of Empire: The French in the Americas, 1670–1730* (Cambridge: Cambridge University Press, 2004); on the geopolitics of empire see William M. Fowler, Jr., *Empire at War: The French and Indian War and the Struggle for North America 1754–1763* (New York: Walker and Company, 2005); and Fred Anderson *Crucible of War: The Seven Years' War and the Fate of Empire in British North America 1754–1766* (New York: Vintage Books, 2001).

[30] Graeme Wynn, *Canada and Arctic North America: An Environmental History* (Santa Barbara: ABC-Clio, 2007) 113.

[31] McNeill, *Something New Under the Sun*, 11.

northeastern spans of America strained and sweated to provide muscle power for pick-and-shovel mining, winter logging, canal digging, and marshland dyke and land reclamation.[32]

But unlike farm economies freed up by breakthroughs in labor-saving devices (the cradle scythe, the fanning mill, or the first seed drills drawn by horse, to name a few)[33] the expanding fur trade reached relatively early the limits of its potential work efficiency. Carolyn Podruchny well describes the heavy, almost inconceivably difficult human effort to drive the fur trade, one giving rise to a distinctive and "manly" voyageur culture.[34] As Claiborne Skinner simply observed, men employed driving canoes "did physically brutal work in an absurdly long work day."[35] Given the enormous food energy needs to maintain it, the costs of canoe transport alone became prohibitively high if not "astronomical" the farther inland it went.[36] One canoeman was required for every 500 lbs. of cargo delivered to the end of the Great Lakes by the late seventeenth century, when a sailing ship, by comparison, needed one man for every ten tons delivered across the Atlantic.[37]

This transport depended almost exclusively on human manpower. A late eighteenth century traveler viewing the fur trade commented that "No men in the world are more severely worked than are these Canadian voyageurs. I have known them to work in a canoe twenty hours out of twenty-four, and go on at that rate during a fortnight or three weeks without a day of rest or any diminution of labour." He added, significantly, that "they lose much flesh in the performance of such journeys, though the quantity of food they consume is incredible."[38]

---

[32] John Clarke, *The Ordinary People of Essex: Environment, Culture, and Economy on the Frontier of Upper Canada* (Montreal and Kingston: McGill-Queen's University Press, 2010), 219–220.

[33] John Clarke, *The Ordinary People of Essex*, 220; J. Sherman Bleakney, *Sods, Soil, and Spades: The Acadians at Grand Pré and Their Dykeland Legacy* (Montreal: McGill-Queen's University Press, 2004).

[34] Carolyn Podruchny, *Making the Voyageur World: Travelers and Traders in the North American Fur Trade* (Lincoln: University of Nebraska Press, 2006), 86–134.

[35] Claiborne Skinner, "The Sinews of Empire: The Voyageurs and the Carrying Trade of the *Pays d'en Haut*, 1681–1754," PhD dissertation, University of Illinois at Chicago, 1991), 232; and Claiborne A. Skinner, *Regional Perspectives on Early America: Upper Country: French Enterprise in the Colonial Great Lakes* (Baltimore: Johns Hopkins University Press, 2008).

[36] Skinner, "The Sinews of Empire," 110.

[37] Ibid., 8.

[38] Carolyn Podruchny, *Making the Voyageur World: Travelers and Traders in the North American Fur Trade* (Lincoln: University of Nebraska Press, 2006), 88.

It is doubtful that the limited cargo capacity of even enlarged canoes could have overcome the chronic caloric deficits growing with the fur trade's expansion, especially after the conquest of Quebec in 1759 and the infusion after 1763 of British capital into the trade. The fur trader Peter Grant estimated northern canoes now spreading farther across the northwest could travel only on average six miles an hour, or up to eight or nine if the men put up a sail to aid them. Based on this, Podrychny estimates that voyageurs in northwest, or "voyageur," canoes might have traveled at best 75 to 125 miles a day, although the frequent portaging would have slowed their rate considerably to perhaps 50.[39]

Even after finessing and enlarging Algonquian canoe technology to the needs of commerce in the seventeenth century, the returns of scale were not impressive. The Montreal cargo canoes emerging in the 1680s were intentionally supersized, but still ungainly and limited to deep water routes. These *canots du maître* plied the St. Lawrence–Great Lakes corridor with crews numbering as few as six but often as many as twelve, and averaging eight to ten; these craft could carry up to 8,000 lbs. Larger canoes by the mid-eighteenth century allowed for the 50-lb. *pièce* to be packed in 100-lb. packs, 60 of which could be hauled in these larger canoes, along with 1,000 lbs. of provisions.[40] When companies spread farther inland on the shield or into the smaller, more difficult waters of the Hudson Bay watersheds, the "north west canoe" was adopted: smaller, carrying about two tons of cargo, perhaps twenty-five feet in length, and manned by an average of five or six men. Even paddling in unison, and well-disciplined by emergent voyageur traditions, the canoe frontier reached the limit of its productivity and geographic extent by the mid-eighteenth century.[41]

Similar to transport problems in the shield facing HBC crews, the insurmountable problem in the canoe frontier, until the full adoption of the York Boat in 1821, was the stout and relatively strong narrow-bladed paddle. It did not displace a great deal of water and voyageurs had to use a short, but monotonous, stroke of forty counts a minute to gain any speed.[42] Given the staggering dead weight of a Montreal

---

[39] Grant is quoted by Podrychny, *Making the Voyageur World*, 100. Skinner suggests the lower figure was in the height of shipping season, and in the end, conditions deteriorated to the point where twelve to fourteen was more realistic. "The Sinews of Empire," 217.

[40] Skinner, "The Sinews of Empire," 208.

[41] Morse, *Fur Trade Canoe Routes of Canada*, 7–9; on the different dimensions and carrying capacity of canoes in the fur trade, see Jennings, *The Canoe: A Living Tradition* (Toronto: Firefly Books, 2002).

[42] Skinner, "The Sinews of Empire," 230.

canoe in water – well over four tons – and the fact that these craft did not glide well, voyageurs paddled almost constantly to keep a canoe in motion. Meanwhile, the relatively short season in northern Canadian latitudes and need to cover sometimes thousands of miles before ice-up forced voyageurs to work almost ceaselessly, 12- to 14-hour days typically. Men, then, would launch canoes often by 4:00 am and put them up at 9:00 or 10:00 pm, or with the sun's final setting. Podrychny points out that in lake country, the working shifts lengthened considerably because ideal voyaging occurred at night when the wind fell and trips became safer on open water. Either to make up for lost time or to speed up the journey, voyageurs paddled throughout the night in such places, and twenty-four-hour voyaging was not uncommon, especially through the dangerous *traverses* of the Great Lakes. A grueling cross-continent voyage, then, awaited many of these men. From Lachine (outside Montreal) to Fort Wedderburn on Lake Athabasca in 1818, Robert Seaborne Miles recorded one day, certainly not atypical, beginning at 5:00 a.m.; the men took breakfast at 7:00 followed by a lunch break at 1:15 p.m., and they resumed paddling at 3:00 until 8:40 pm. Exclusive of rest breaks, the working day stretched twelve hours in length.[43]

No wonder voyageurs consumed enormous quantities of food. Although French fur traders learned from Alonquian speakers to smoke tobacco as an appetite suppressant,[44] they ate ravenously. But with much cargo already given over to provisions and no additional capacity to enlarge supply, crews, simply put, went hungry. The common estimate is that voyageurs burnt between 4,000 and 6,000 calories a day.[45] One researcher evaluating a 155-lb voyageur paddling and portaging fifteen hours a day would expend almost 7,000 calories.[46] Fur traders ran significant caloric deficits and, unlike the stereotypes of 1920s silent movies showing strapping and muscular French Canadian voyageurs, these chronically underfed, overworked laborers were likely underweight, not muscular, and likely debilitated in some ways by personal injuries,

---

[43] Robert Seaborne Miles' diary, 1818, is reproduced in Podrychny, *Making the Voyageur World*, 115–117.

[44] Skinner, "The Sinews of Empire," 224–227.

[45] Morse rates the calories as 4,000 to 5,000, without attribution, *Fur Trade Canoe Routes of Canada*, 24. Skinner counts 4,000 to 6,000 calories, without attribution, "The Sinews of Empire," 59.

[46] Ronald S. Lappage (May 1984), "The Physical Feats of the Voyageur," *Canadian Journal of the History of Sports*, 15(1):34.

bone deformities, and frequently stressed constitutions.[47] The likely beefy Selkirk farmer/settlers sent to colonize Red River and whose enormous appetites amazed Peter Fidler, reveals a contrast with the more typical and quite emaciated fur trader of his time. These were more accustomed to gorging when food was available, starving much of the time, and expending fantastic amounts of energy from wiry-muscled body frames.[48] Probably a good image of what voyageurs looked like physically is hinted in modern-day paddlers on trans-Atlantic rowing competitions – in superior and more energy-efficient craft – and supported by optimally balanced and high energy diets of up to 8,000 calories a day (65 percent carbohydrate, 10 percent protein, and 25 percent fat). They still lose weight with daily calorie deficits ranging from 1,200 to 1,500 kcal; despite their fantastic food intake, these super-athletes shed on average between 20 and 25 lbs. in 58 days of intensive rowing.[49]

The voyageur diet in the St. Lawrence–Great Lakes corridor was limited in a number of other ways. Since the Canadian Shield's carrying capacity was so low these men could not be replenished en route. Brigades took on agricultural product in the colony and then through relay from corn-growing outposts such as Detroit and the southeastern areas of the Great Lakes. The "custom of the voyageur," as their rationed diet was called, was pretty meager, however: in ideal circumstances it consisted of the triumvirate of leached corn (Indian corn first dried for transport and boiled before eating to allow its sugars to be better digested), and/or dried peas, and a portion of fat in the form of lard (the Montreal men going to Grand Portage, hence, were called the "lard" or "pork" eaters). Any additional corn supply from Detroit, however, was prohibitively expensive; as were any tallow pork fats available there.[50] Given that

[47] Ping Lai and Nancy C. Lovell (1992), "Skeletal Markers of Occupational Stress in the Fur Trade: A Case Study from a Hudson's Bay Company Fur Trade Post," *International Journal of Osteoarchaeology*, 2:221–234; and Nancy C. Lovell and Aaron A. Dublenko (1999), "Further Aspects of Fur Trade Life Depicted in the Skeleton," *International Journal of Osteoarchaeology*, 9:248–256.

[48] Peter Fidler also recorded on August 9, 1814 at Red River: "The mowers refused to eat fish. They lately came from the Highlands. They are the worst to please and satisfy of all the people." Fidler remarked on one of their groups consisting of four men, eleven women and boys, eating nine fish for a single meal, an extravagant consumption given that "over 12 men here and all their families use only 12 fish for a meal." Peter Fidler's Journal, Winnipeg Post, B.235/a/3.

[49] Nancy Clark, Cato Coleman, Kerri Figure, Tom Mailhot, and John Zeigler (2003), "Food for Trans-Atlantic Rowers: A Menu Planning Model and Case Study," *International Journal of Sport Nutrition and Exercise Metabolism*, 13:227–242, 229.

[50] Alexander Henry the Younger in 1761 paid 40 livres a bushel for corn at Michilimackinac; and a dollar a pound for tallow, "These high prices for grain and beef led me to be very

corn might avail 132 calories in a 154 g quantity, peas 31 calories in 28 g, and lard 1,849 calories in 205 g, it was, indeed, to the detriment of voyageurs that the latter was often too scarce to procure in great quantities, and diets tended to be seriously balanced to favor carbohydrates over fats. Proteins were almost nonexistent. They were available only if crews fortuitously located native hunters en route who traded fresh meat, or fish.

The cargo of a three-man canoe in 1694 heading for Illinois Country was likely typical, its voyageurs consuming more carbohydrates than fats and very little protein. Their diet was made of a biscuit to grease ratio of 6:1 (120 lbs. of biscuit to 20 lbs. grease), and 2 *minots* of dried peas (a minot was equivalent of a bushel or about 56 lbs.).[51] In these circumstances, a man would have 40 lbs. biscuit, and a little under 7 lbs. of grease and 3 gallons of dried peas for the entire voyage. From a caloric point of view, their diet was woefully, if not dangerously, undernourished. Their feeding is noteworthy, too, for the heavy starch carbohydrate component, striking because modern-day extreme athletes typically crave the high energy of fats. The diet of men going on to Detroit in the same period was much the same: 100 lbs. of biscuit and 25 lbs. of lard per man.[52] How this might have been improved, even if there was not such an onus on cargo space, is not certain. Skinner's estimate of the *livre* cost of a late seventeenth century three-man canoe suggests that provisions already constituted the greatest expenditure for outfitters. Of the 2,430 livres spent purchasing a canoe, the wages, and equipment for one adventure in the late seventeenth century, a full 1,350 livres, or 55 percent of the total expenses, were spent on provisions.[53]

Voyageur bourgeois began to strategize and improvise around this crisis. Initially, it was simply accepted that they could not pack enough food and assumed that something, especially fish, could be purchased en route. But, the farther the destination, the slimmer were the odds on which they could gamble like this. Pig fat was likely the first to disappear in diet, and corn likely predominated as a remaining food

---

industrious at fishing." Alexander Henry, *Travels and Adventures: In Canada and the Indian Territories* (Edmonton: M. G. Hurtig, 1969), 56.

[51] Skinner, "The Sinews of Empire," 61; the lb-weight of corn is derived from US Department of Agriculture data provided in Tad W. Patzek, *Ethanol from Corn: Clean Renewable Fuel for the Future, or Drain on Our Resources and Pockets* (New York: Kluwer Academic, 2003), 3.

[52] Skinner, "The Sinews of Empire," 109.

[53] Ibid., see table, 61.

source. Le Sieur de La Vérendrye, who perhaps moved the fur trade the farthest in the early eighteenth century, left Montreal in 1731 to reach Kaminisquia, the farthest point on the other side of Lake Superior after 79 days, to cover about 1,100 miles.[54] Later, outbound voyages, first to Rainy Lakes, then Lakes of the Woods and finally, Lake Winnipeg, took 104 days, and were slowed considerably by the deteriorating conditions late in the season. In such extremities of the French fur trading empire, traders desperately searched for Ojibwa and Cree to trade meats, fats, and wild rice. The greatest quantities to be added beyond Lake Superior and the Grand Portage were usually the high starch wild rice stocks harvested by Ojibwa near Lake of the Woods. Alexander Henry the Elder, in the mid-1770s, was shocked by how "very expensive" corn was for sale near Michilimackinac; lard was sold at $1 a pound. He learned how critical these supplies were, however, when his crew's travelled beyond the Great Divide. Most of his truly outbound journeys beyond Michilimackinac were made only with corn. On every occasion, he bought what he could of Ojibwa wildfowl and wild rice to add to inventories. At Lac La Pluie, he described trading throughout the night with Ojibwa women for more than a hundred dearly needed sacks of wild rice to continue his journey into the great Northwest.[55]

Henry, who had to pack far more provisions than other cargo in canoes going into the actual northwest in the mid-1770s knew how precious these food supplies now were. In a relatively short voyage for twelve of his men between Michilimackinac and the end point of Lake Superior, of about a month, he purchased fifty bushels of corn. The ration of just over four bushels per man would likely have given about 230 lbs. of corn for each.[56] A generous estimate would give each voyageur, then, about 7 lbs. of corn a day, or about 3,680 calories, likely well below their own energy needs.

These deficits became the more critical given the way the human body consumed food energy in the course of a voyageur's travels. In both the Montreal routes inland, and those now being ascended from James Bay by Donald McKay in 1794, transforming energy into work required the release and combustion of adenosine triphosphate (ATP), which is broken down into chemical energy for muscle contraction. In the fur trade, combinations of muscular contraction dominated work: short-

---

[54] Ibid., 219.
[55] Alexander Henry, *Travels and Adventures*, 54, 241, 243–244.
[56] Ibid., 184.

term anaerobic systems provided energy for short bursts of effort for sudden, short-duration exertions – to respond, for instance, to the sudden, temperamental changes in a river's currents and velocity, to rapids that imperiled life and limb, and, of course, to the *portage*. With a 100-lb. *pièce* suspended on their backs by tumpline, men would make portages in adrenaline-hopped half-mile runs, doubled over – and given that each voyageur was responsible for three *pièces*, one mile of portage in reality translated into a gauntlet of running and stumbling five (for this very reason, the "Grand Portage" at Lake Superior lived up to its name: eight miles in length, it represented forty miles of "triple tracking.")

The anaerobic energy system provided quicker and immediate energy (sometimes about thirty to forty seconds of maximal muscle activity) and used glycogen and phosphates to combine with ADP molecules. The dearly purchased ATP energy, however, left a residue of lactate acid that, if accumulating with too much intensive work, resulted in sore and fatigued muscles and eventually forced an individual to end effort altogether.[57] When James Sutherland, one of McKay's "patroons" leading a separate contingent inland in 1794 earlier travelled with Ojibwa over a fifty-six–day period across shield country, on one day paddling and carrying a canoe during an incredible nineteen-hour stretch, he confessed that night in his journal to being "very unhappy" and "not able to lift my arms," suggesting that this maximal muscle exertion had been reached.[58]

The greatest food energy, however, was more typically released from aerobic metabolism in which ATP was created through the burning of glucose. These oxidative systems, sustaining the greatest part of the voyageur's work day of monotonous but tiring paddling, importantly, took energy from fats and carbohydrates, to create comparatively vast amounts of ATP. It is also worth highlighting that, unlike the sheer high exertion duties that occasionally arose in portaging, most paddling, at forty strokes a minute, would have constituted medium-exertion exercise over, albeit, very long, continuous, periods of time.[59]

---

[57] A. Salim Goktepe, "Energy Systems in Sport," in *Amputee Sports for Victims of Terrorism* NATO Science for Peace and Security Series – E: Human and Societal Dynamics, Vol. 7 (Ankara: Centre for Excellence 2007), 26.

[58] HBCA. On the June 16, 1785, the paddling started before 3 a.m. and ended at 10 pm. See James Sutherland Journal, Gloucester House, B.78/a/15.

[59] On these energy systems, see Mark Hargreaves and Lawrence Spriet, eds., *Exercise Metabolism*, 2nd ed. (Champaign, IL: Human Kinetics, 2006); and Stanley P. Brown, Wayne C. Miller, and Jane M. Eason, *Exercise Physiology: Basis of Human Movement in Health and Disease* (Baltimore: Lippincott Williams & Wilkins, 2006).

Some of the energy needed for such demoralizing work, whether from Montreal or James Bay, was met in liquid form. As fur trade voyageur traditions hardened around difficult labor, quite ritualized and geographically prescribed boozing, if not binge drinking, added critical calories to heavy-labor travel. The albeit bulky but absolutely requisite barrels of "journey brandy" were always given safe passage and lofted above shoulders in portages like holy relics. Woe to the bourgeois or York boat master neglecting to carry enough alcohol to boost the spirits of his men and, in so doing, bolster their very metabolisms. In shield country, the daily reward of a "dram" or "gill" of at least a good couple of shots of brandy was usually forthcoming. Bourgeois carried enough for this frequent imbibing inland, and made sure to cache barrels in places to meet outgoing crews hauling around waterfalls, hacking out new portage routes, or risking their necks on rapids descents.

"Mad" McKay's own first expedition to Brandon House was paced with almost daily regales of alcohol. He seems to have completely disregarded Albany House's policy on moderation (in fact, the master there had ordered that there should be no alcohol on the river, given the numerous social and health problems arising with binge drinking and alcoholism at Bay-side factories).[60] McKay, horrified that his men were supplied only a scant eight bags of flour, no meat, and no "journey brandy" for their plains expedition, immediately rejected such nonsense, "as Brandy is the principle article in the Country where I am going to."[61]

McKay, like all masters, knew that voyageur morale depended on the frequent, almost daily, round of strait brandy, grog (watered down spirits) or "high wines" (or mixed spirits – high wines being double distilled rum carrying up to 80 and 90% alcohol).[62] En route, a difficult ascent of a water fall, portaging, or running of bad rapids, where enormous physical energy was expended, masters rewarded men, immediately and without question, with the energetic boost of booze. Metabolizing as they paddled, they were very likely in various states of inebriation, particularly

---

[60] Edward Jarvis at first planned for the expedition to be a dry one: "And no Brandy rum or any liquor whatever be issued or allowed from the day they will depart from red lake to the day thy return to the said lake," HBCA. Edward Jarvis agreement with Donald McKay, October 1790, A.11/5 London Correspondence Inward from HBC Posts 1784–1791 (Albany), footnote 125.

[61] HBCA. Donald McKay's Journal, July 30, 1793, Brandon House Journals, B.22/a/1.

[62] Gough offers a valuable description of High Wines (90%) and Low Wines (60%). See Barry Gough, ed., Barry M. Gough, *The Journal of Alexander Henry the Younger: 1799–1814*, Vol. I (Toronto: Champlain Society, 1988), 6, footnote 18.

on lake stretches where fine motor skills were really no longer required. French crews had to imbibe frequently. Sometimes they found ways to drink a great deal. When McKay's own expedition from James Bay finally entered the upland portions of the shield in south central Ontario in lake country, his crews began traversing the Montreal brigade routes, particularly the Lac Seul, Red Lake, and the Pigeon River transects. Even Orkney employees had the knack of knowing which lakes they crossed had been previously "purchased" by extravagant Montreal bourgeois. In return for men "naming" the lakes in their honor the bourgeois had returned a pint (termed "grog" and likely generously cut high wines) to their men, with the promise that from that point, all voyageurs and now HBC paddlers and boatsmen, would be treated the same way. McKay, then, found himself needing to give a pint of watered brandy, the equivalent of sixteen shots, to each man at "Mr. Nielson's Lake," and later, at "Mr. Berren's Lake." These generous portions, of course, took a toll on supply, but McKay complied at each place where "the men givin [sic] three cheers, I served the pint of groggg each man ... a customary fee in this country."[63]

The farther the destination, however, the less food and alcohol remained for these crews. Just as McKay feared, given the length of the journey to Winnipeg River, the barrels began to run out. Just beyond Lake Winnipeg and ascending finally the Assiniboine, his heavily worked crew now sobered up and began resenting McKay's short rationing beginning on the 9th of September. This "sett of stubborn ill natured and lazy men," McKay wrote in exasperation. Canoes kept getting "stoved" (seemingly deliberately) on tree roots out of carelessness, and this beyond a ready supply of oak, elm and ash, to repair hulls. The men openly threatened to leave him and his packet of goods on the bald prairie, likely among the strewn buffalo turds. Their arrival to the baptised McNabb's Island, where one last round of *hurrahs* were yelled, further depleted brandy stocks and by October 18, with no more alcohol to spare on such travel, the inland expedition ground to a miserable halt. How "often do I repent that I engaged myself in this Grand and Dangerous enterprise," McKay wrote.[64] The men and goods would go no farther. What became Brandon House and its very foundations were hastily built on the very spot where the journey brandy could be stretched no further.

---

[63] HBCA. Donald McKay's Journal, August 16, 1793, Brandon House Journals, B.22/a/1.
[64] Ibid., September 13, 1793.

All the same, it was quite a feat of bartending: from Osnaburgh to that point on the Assiniboine, McKay had spilled no less than "80 gallons of spirits" on the "men and Indians on my journey in, without any trade or scarce any provisions."[65]

Heavy imbibing was hardly unique for laboring class culture in this period. It figured among males as a means of bonding. Generally speaking, males followed two patterns of consumption, as Craig Heron has pointed out: daily consumption of alcohol at work and at home, coupled with "celebratory imbibing."[66] But as Craig Muldrew has pointed out in the case of English farm labor in the seventeenth and eighteenth centuries, alcohol formed a significant source of food energy, freeing up labor that proved critical in the improvement and enclosure of lands and their greater productivity.[67] The actual alcohol in brandy, or ethanol, is broken down in the liver through the enzyme alcohol dehydrogenase (ADH), and its derivatives are subsequently broken down further by a second enzyme into carbon dioxide and water.[68] As a balance to meagre fur trade diet, frequent rewards of grog and periodic heavy binging of straight brandy were undoubtedly critical for work, or at least adding to one's energy in the circumstances. A single shot of brandy might have availed perhaps 85 calories, with 2 grams of sugar and 2 grams of carbohydrate. Studies suggest that brandy can have significant medicinal and food energy value since "it surpasses starch and sugar in alimentary value, since weight for weight, it contains more energy."[69] It is certainly worth considering the calories offered in periods of voyageur binging. The men en route to Fort Edmonton in 1798, for instance, began one day at 4 a.m. and labored until 8 pm while they portaged goods around a single fall on the Saskatchewan. In camp that night each man was given "one pint of brandy," likely in a very stiff concentration.[70] They did not have to do extraordinary labour, though, to drink a lot. William Tomison found his men complaining if they did not receive 2 gallons of brandy

---

[65] Ibid., June 19, 1794.
[66] Craig Heron, *Booze: A Distilled History* (Toronto: Between the Lines, 2003).
[67] Craig Muldrew, *Food, Energy and the Creation of Industriousness* (Cambridge: Cambridge University Press, 2011), 122–128.
[68] See "Alcohol Metabolism: An Update," published by the National Institute on Alcohol Abuse and Alcoholism, and drawing from P. N. Friel, J. S. Baer, and B. K. Logan (1995), "Variability of Ethanol Absorption and Breath Concentrations during a Large-scale Alcohol Administration Study," *Clinical and Experimental Research*, 19:1055–1060.
[69] Henry Guly (July 2011), "Medicinal Brandy," *Resuscitation*, 82(7–2):951–954.
[70] July 23, 1798, Alice M. Johnson, *Saskatchewan Journals and Correspondence* (London: Hudson's Bay Record Society, 1967), 138.

each to undertake a journey from Fort Edmonton of 10 or 12 days – which would have given them an astounding 16 shots spirits a day.[71]

All the same, as fur traders knew, they could carry only so much booze, and, as seen, they could pack only so many supplies of corn and fats by the time they reached the upland sections of present-day Manitoba. There no way to avoid this cold-sober reality of the expanding commercial fur trade in the late eighteenth century.

Starving Fur Traders

As early as the 1770s, the absolute caloric limits to the canoe frontier were being reached as British merchants took over the fur trade at Montreal after the Conquest and sent much larger contingents beyond the Grand Portage into the great Northwest. Although a western trade had been managed by de la Vérendrye and his sons, and then a series of French commanders at the Postes de l'Ouest, their small numbers allowed men to rely, if only barely, on caches and informal food purchases from plains people.[72] La Vérendrye also encouraged the Assiniboine and Cree in the area to hunt on behalf of his posts – although it is not certain that they did. At least one fort, La Jérémy (its precise location is not known), seems to have served as a provisioning post.

But the British era saw far many more Europeans moving from 1,500 to 2,000 miles inland from Montreal. Given their numbers and the proliferation of posts competing with each other, starvation awaited many of them upon entering the Lake Winnipeg region, representing, really, the end of food supply. Alexander Henry the Younger reached that limit precisely at the Forks of the Red and the Assiniboine, where corn was exhausted and, almost miraculously, his men found bison to feed themselves, likely in wild gluttony. The fur trade, however, was initially not moving in the direction of the plains, but rather, steadily along the rim of the shield, northwest and across the great traverses of Lake Winnipeg into the Saskatchewan drainage for the Athabasca. This was the fur trade's true "Eldorado." But it was just beyond reach. In 1775, Peter Pond and Alexander Henry "barely reached their wintering place" across Lake Winnipeg; their 100 men in 20 canoes came very

---

[71] June 25, 1799, Tomison complained that the men had been "too liberally supplied" in this way and tried to cut the ration to a gallon per man, Johnson, ed., *Saskatchewan Journals and Correspondence*, 173.

[72] Harold Innis, *The Fur Trade in Canada*, 93–111.

close to starving to death just making the lake passage, and they lived miserably on fish during the winter, their corn and wild rice long before exhausted. Another Montreal trader, Thomas Frobisher, led crews that almost starved crossing Lake Winnipeg, and also ended up subsisting only on fish in their push to distant Île-à-la Crosse.[73]

In the 1770s, fur trade journals more commonly reported cases of exhaustion, hunger, starvation, and even cannibalism in the farther extremes of the Canadian shield.[74] Even if they arrived to their wintering camps, Canadians faced horrid conditions during the cold season when food supply virtually ended altogether in the boreal environment. Benjamin Frobisher in 1775 admitted to his HBC rivals the "great Destress he ware in for Provisions, which ware really shocking" in what became known as the English River district, just north and east of Lake Winnipeg. One or two of Frobisher's men starved to death during the winter, one had apparently resorted to cannibalism, and Frobisher himself had survived only by eating the post's moose skins and many of the furs traded from Native people – "and even a few garden seeds" imported from Canada. [75] By the time traders in a last gasp reached Lake Winnipeg, swatting mosquitoes and cursing blackflies, food really figured as their chief concern, as Alexander Henry the Elder's narrative makes clear in the 1770s. The first settlements stuck on the eastern shores of Lake Winnipeg, such as those on Blood River, were in climax forest, often completely vacated by Ojibwa in these worst seasons of the year. Europeans learned in a hurry how to fish the vast but capricious waters of the lake, but hunting in these forests was always difficult, or game populations easily exhausted.[76]

The fur trade historian Harold Innis suggested that a solution to the problem was found as early as 1775 and put into effect in 1778, when Alexander Henry, Thomas and Joseph Frobisher and Peter Pond

---

[73] W. A. Sloan (1979), "The Native Response to the Extension of the European Traders into the Athabasca and Mackenzie Basin, 1770–1814," *Canadian Historical Review*, LX(3):284–285.

[74] See, for instance, the cases of starvation reported by John Long, and the frequent resort to eating *tripe de la roche* as a survival strategy. George Colpitts, *Game in the Garden: A Human History of Wildlife in Western Canada* (Vancouver: UBC Press, 2000), 19.

[75] *Journals of Samuel Hearne and Philip Turnor Between the Years 1774 and 1792*, ed. J. B. Tyrrell (Toronto: Champlain Society, 1934), 190.

[76] HBCA. John Best's illustrative journal at Blood River: "god knows how We are to put over the Winter for there is no fish to be got," he wrote November 8, 1794, and moose were no longer found in the forests on the east shores of Lake Winnipeg, B.254/a/1, Blood River Journal 1794–1795.

pooled their remaining trade goods and food supplies in the spring at the entranceway to the English River district beyond Cedar Lake. Led by Dene guides whom Henry and the Frobishers had previously met, Pond went on alone and used this collected food and goods to go on through the portage – the "La Loche" doorway – what turned out to be a grueling twelve-mile pathway and the single most difficult portage of the entire fur trade. From there they got into Chipewyan territories beyond the Clearwater and onto the Athabasca River.[77] From a commercial point of view, the risk was well worth it: Pond returned triumphantly to Montreal with canoes laden with a fortune in truly cold-weather fine furs for the London markets.

The logistic challenge of linking Montreal merchants to furs now being collected on the rocky shield shores of Lake Athabasca, however, required far more than a simple pooling of food remainders in spring. It was fortunate that, immediately after their arrival in Athabasca territory, Montreal traders made a critical discovery in native food production, eventually transferring what were northern winter pemmican traditions to their business operation. Traders in the Northwest might have seen– although likely not many – had eaten Native pemmican. Here, Europeans in Dene country were making a leap in their thinking, that of joining a northern survival technique to aid commercial expansion. In so doing, they would decisively shift diets from their carbohydrate base on one side of the Grand Portage, to one of protein and fat on the other.

The hint of this breakthrough appears in Alexander Henry's memorial to the British naturalist, Joseph Banks, written in 1781, in which Henry argued the feasibility of an overland passage right to the Pacific "sea" from this new northern toehold of the fur trade. Once they travelled over the La Loche portage into the Arctic drainage and reached the jumping off places to the Pacific from Lake Athabasca, Henry wrote, traders would find their transit grinding to a halt very late in the navigable season. As the deep frosts sealed in and rivers iced up, voyageurs would hurriedly build posts and employ local hunters to take the Athabasca variety of bison. These were the wood buffalo (*Bison bison athabascae*) and though not stating it as such, Henry was suggesting that they would be hunting a herd animal in a winter seasonal round along the Athabasca and Slave Rivers. From these herds the men's winter subsistence would be raised: "mostly flesh, dry'd buffaloe meat, and mouse

---

[77] Innis, *Peter Pond: Fur Trade and Adventurer* (Toronto: Irwin and Gordon, 1930), 135–136.

deer [i.e. 'moose-deer,' or moose], it is not only the provisions for the winter season, but, for the course of the next summer must be provided which is dry'd meat, pounded to a powder and mixed up with buffaloes grease, which preserves it in the warm seasons here." [78]

Because Henry himself had not yet been privy to such intelligence first hand, Innis singled out Peter Pond as the genius behind solving the pemmican puzzle.[79] He even suggested that Pond introduced pemmican-making to plains people whom he said previously relied on dried meat.[80] Here, he was simply in error. More likely, the Nor'westers had appropriated a practice of the subarctic Chipewyan among whom they dwelt and who already used a technique of producing winter pemmican for difficult summer periods before the moose rut and the easier fall hunt. There was a convenient lining up of these northern traditions with the exigencies of a now completely strung-out, commercially driven fur trade that was starving for food. The same technique would help companies taking advantage of the short summer to return furs and take trade goods back and forth across vast distances, without stopping to hunt and gather food. Even better, winter pemmican production took advantage of the seasonal behaviour of herd animals like caribou and buffalo in Dene territories which sheltered, usually, in discrete regions, and were hunted for fat and grease easily handled in the coolest season of the year.

Henry's report, however, implied a cascade of social and cultural obligations accruing in such food production. Europeans would depend solely on Dene to provide them the critical first building blocks: dried and fresh meats, and fats. Then, traders in posts, almost inevitably relying further on Native women to cut and sew bags from bulls' hides, and a variety of other steps in production, would assemble the pieces into pemmican, with recipes initially only vaguely understood. Even though Dene

---

[78] The memorial is quoted by Harold Innis, *Peter Pond*, 83–84.
[79] He does not credit Henry, who never visited the Athabasca district, and spoke only of dried meat from firsthand experience. The memorial was written, as Innis pointed out, after Henry had conversed with Pond, see *Peter Pond*, 87, footnote 1.
[80] "There is some reason to believe that it was a cultural trait [pemmican making] of the Chipewyans or of the northern Indians of Athabasca and that the Plains Indians prior to the coming of the White man had subsisted on dried meat. It is possible that Pond made a valuable contribution in adapting the pemmican which he found in use among the Athabascan Indians to the development of the trade from the Saskatchewan." Harold A. Innis (1928), "Peter Pond and the Influence of Capt. James Cook on Exploration in the Interior of North America," *Transactions of the Royal Society of Canada*, 3rd Ser. Section II, 131–137.

contributed very little "ready-made" pemmican to Europeans, the mere changing hands of food in any form heaped obligations on the part of these European receivers.

The trader Peter Fidler, traveling with Chipewyan traders in 1798, described the nature of such obligations first hand. He noted the hunting and gathering strategies, as well as pemmican making, of northerners on what to modern readers might seem a staggeringly long seasonal round in the dead of winter. As luck has it, Fidler was a careful observer who left meticulously detailed descriptions of this way of life when he traveled with Chipewyan between Fort Chipewyan to the southern shores of Great Slave Lake, before returning in Spring. In some six months, the party canoed, walked and tramped on snowshoes over an astounding 400-mile journey often in bone chilling temperatures and the semidarkness of northern winter daylight. The camp foraged on the move over crusty snow and river ice. They searched for food as they went, or other Indian bands that might help. Fidler's statement that "always with them is either a feast or a famine" accurately caught the tenuous life in this region, ironically, one of the most valuable fur trading areas of Canada. The band ate whatever was available, from beaver, to moose, to wood buffalo. When hunting was successful, they ate well. The anthropologist June Helm carefully studied Fidler's journal and concluded that the group gorged itself on about 6.1 to 6.8 lbs. of meat every day, per person, when it was available. Game was eaten in its entirety. The bison subspecies in the region, the wood buffalo, was hunted and eaten completely – meats, fats, intestines, reproductive organs, fetuses, even skin.[81]

Fidler criticized the Chipewyan for their improvident feasting in good times, when he felt that they should have paid attention to the longer term, that is, eating less and storing more. But the band was traveling mostly on foot and carrying everything they possessed. Although their camp stopped to split and dry meat when there was hunting success, the quantities they could carry were not great. Some were cached. But much had to be eaten in situ, or carried in condensed dried state.

Somewhat counterintuitively, the most common means of carrying food in the subarctic environment was by giving it away. Traditions of food sharing, giving freely to others in distress or sharing it equally with bands, families, or complete strangers who fused themselves temporarily into one's camp, ensured that a lot of otherwise cumbersome food

---

[81] June Helm (1993), "'Always with Them Either a Feast or a Famine' Living off the Land with Chipewyan Indians, 1791–92," *Arctic Anthropology*, 30(2):46–60.

surpluses were transferred into other hands or stomachs.[82] This in turn heaped forms of obligation on the receivers that might return in kind when the givers themselves faced difficult times. Rather than stockpiling surplus food, which imposed on hoarders a precarious sedentary existence, the subarctic tradition was to disperse it, freeing bands for real mobility, and opening up a larger territorial base from which they could mix diets and encourage social and economic exchanges across a number of ecological regions.[83]

On his northern tour with the Chipweyan, Fidler, however, discovered a compact, supercharged food energy source that figured squarely as one of the most important of the northerner's seasonal round. The Chipewyan took advantage of a moment of abundance in the northern winter to store energy for periods of want. In Fidler's experience, pemmican making – drying meat and using the stomach of the bison as a cauldron to melt fats – occurred specifically with the convergence of wood buffalo herds along the Slave and Athabasca Rivers in late December and early January. Although the members of the party were gastronomic generalists, eating a wide variety of fare (they even ate porcupines), their round took them and many other bands strategically to specific winter forest areas where bison sheltered themselves in the coldest months of the year. The band was able to take an astounding 12,000 to 14,000 lbs. of consumable tissue from bison during this small window of opportunity in their journey,[84] when herd animals were within range and easily killed in winter pounds. Despite these frigid circumstances, the party could also handle and store the fats and grease from the bison they killed.

Alexander Mackenzie, the Montreal trader who later stretched British lines of commerce to the Arctic and then on to the Pacific Oceans, soon replaced Pond at Fort Chipewyan. He described the energy source for his eventual Imperial expansion: Chipewyan pemmican. At least this is what he described to the English-reading public. Making pemmican in winter for summer use might seem strange to southerners but as a later

---

[82] Ibid., 54.

[83] The needs for mobility between ecological reasons is well described by Arthur J. Ray, "Periodic Shortage, Native Welfare, and the Hudson's Bay Company," 1670–1930," in K. Coates and W. Morrison, eds., *Interpreting Canada's North: Selected Readings* (Toronto: Copp Clark Pitman, 1989), 94–112.

[84] On "commensal" food sharing traditions, see Helm, "Always with them a feast or a famine," for measurements of consumable flesh, see Helm's table of Animals Killed, which indicate January and February the key months, p. 49. The most numerous number of animal killed, was the beaver, some eighty-four, which likely gave about 1,150 lbs. of consumable tissue, fifty-five.

explorer, Viljalmur Stefansson took pains to highlight, winter was the time for eating fresh meats in these territories. Pemmican was produced for consumption during periods when the hunt failed, or, during the difficult time of traveling in spring and during the scorching, long, summer days in the high north.[85] Mackenzie, thinking of this winter context for food preparation, wrote that the meat was dried "over a slow fire, sometimes in the sun or the frost," and the "inside fat and that of the rump which is much thicker in these wild than our domestic animals, is melted down and mixed in boiling state...."[86] He said that it was on this provision "which the Chepewyans, as well as the other savages of this country, chiefly subsist in their journies."[87]

Already by the 1780s, local Chipewyan, Cree, and Beaver were providing supplies of bison, elk, and deer during the winter to these newcomers in the North. They did so, certainly, for trade goods. But they also were enlarging their social and political connections to these needy newcomers and vastly safeguarding themselves with food sharing traditions by giving and trading food to these posts. It is difficult to say whether they were even trading out of large surpluses, or simply selecting meats they felt they could part with, keeping in mind the frequent periods of want they themselves might well be facing in the near future. They certainly felt that such a food trade gave them a right to a post's commissary, once it was built up, when they themselves faced starvation.[88]

Europeans collected Dene foods at the portal of the La Loche carrying place. There it awaited incoming canoe brigades making the last jump into a nascent system of posts on the Athabasca, Slave, and Mackenzie Rivers. At Fort Chipewyan, Alexander Mackenzie coordinated a relay system between camps of Beaver and Cree at least by 1788, when he sent contingents by the very end of the navigable season up the Peace River to

---

[85] Vilhjalmur Stefansson, *Not by Bread Alone* (New York: Macmillan, 1946), 188–190, 232.

[86] Alexander Mackenzie, Voyages from Montreal, in W. Kaye Lamb, ed., *The Journals and Letters of Sir Alexander Mackenzie* (Cambridge: Cambridge University Press, 1970), 152.

[87] He added that "There is another sort made with the addition of marrow and dried berries, which is of a superior quality," ibid.

[88] Arthur Ray called the phenomenon "fur trade post dependency." See Arthur J. Ray, "Periodic Shortage, Native Welfare, and the Hudson's Bay Company," 1670–1930," 94–112. However, I have used the expression, as fur traders did, as "the custom of the country," since fur traders not only provided food in times of need, but accepted food from Indians and were, therefore, very sympathetic to their periodic bouts of starvation in the subarctic. See my references to fur traders using the term "custom of the country," in Colpitts, *Game in the Garden*, 36–37.

collect "provisions for the canoes in their voyage out in the Spring."[89] A few years later, a single canoe plying the Peace River would collect about two tons of dried meat for that purpose.[90]

Dene Pemmican Traditions in Prairie Commerce

The subarctic biome provided for this system with the work of wood Cree, Chipewyan, and Beaver, and did so throughout the fur trade era. The Slave Lake trader W. F. Wentzel by 1807 described Beaver producing "Taureau or Piimecan" which was "tolerably good when mixed up with grease," which "is our staple article of provisions *when travelling* [his emphasis].[91] In the long term, however, the subarctic could not supply the needs of the fur trade. The critical limitation was fat: companies there came to rely on caribou herds, which availed comparatively too little fat to make requisite quantities of trade pemmican. Subarctic pemmican, then, was often very lean for this reason.[92] A number of factors also began conspiring against northern food production: the devastating impact of crowd infectious diseases on boreal and subarctic populations after 1781 were likely important; so was the common practice of companies creating fur and game "deserts" by deliberately overhunting territories, to rid competitors from boreal forests.[93] These left vast stretches north of the Saskatchewan, the Peace River, territories southeast of James Bay and those around Lake Winnipeg emptied of big game, particularly moose. Probably the most important factor, however, was the exploding numbers of newcomers in these subarctic environments. The North West Company (NWC), alone, had almost 1100 men in the northwest by 1805. With the HBC men spreading into many areas of the subarctic, the numbers of posts weighed heavily on a region with very little food and game.[94]

---

[89] Roderic McKenzie, "Réminiscences," in L. R. Masson, *Les bourgeois de la Compagnie du Nord-Ouest*, Vol. I (New York : Antiquarian Press, 1960), 24.
[90] Sloan, "Native Response to European Traders," 285, footnote 10.
[91] W. F. Wentzel to Roderic McKenzie, March 27, 1807, in Masson, *Les Bourgeois du Nord-Ouest*, 90.
[92] Caribou pemmican could pack with as little as 35:55 to 33:57 fat to pounded meat ratios; see Innis, *Fur Trade in Canada*, 300.
[93] See Ray, "Periodic Shortages," 5–7; George Colpitts, "Moose-Nose and Buffalo Hump: the Amerindian-European Food Exchange in the British North American Fur trade to 1840," Diane Kirkby and Tanja Luckins, eds., *Dining on Turtles: Food Feasts and Drinking in History* (Houndmills, Basingstoke, UK: Palgrave Macmillan, 2007), 64–81.
[94] Innis, *Fur Trade in Canada*, 238.

As a result, fur companies shifted their provisioning southward (Figure 1.3), towards the plains and the plains bison herds (*bison bison*). This happened almost immediately as they found posting nearby, such as in 1774, when the HBC's staff at Cumberland House, likely without protesting much, organized flying visits and finally a wintering house to exploit these herds. In the case of Cumberland House, situated within a boreal environment, their food needs were initially met in moose trades with nearby Basquia and other wood Cree. In fall they offered canoes and in winter sleds filled with dried, half dried and pounded moose meat, with fat. But moose could barely keep the larger contingents at Cumberland House satiated. The post, typical of boreal establishments, went hungry and sometimes risked starvation during three key winter months (late December to early March) when staff usually went on short rations. In 1777, for instance, its 15 men had to divide up a scant 975 lbs. of dried moose meat and a bit of fat over 37 days. That amounted to about 1.75 lbs. of dried meat per person per day. Like other posts, too, Cumberland House stubbornly imposed a sedentary social organization on the area, effectively exhausting nearby forests of moose, deer, bear, and other manner of game. An alarming decline in local moose populations was soon perceived by Matthew Cocking, who saw the need to build an "early Settlement above towards the Buffalo Country" and a trade among the Assiniboine. The Montreal "peddlars," competing with these English traders, were already doing that by 1777, trading as much buffalo flesh higher up the Saskatchewan where the river passed closer to the herds to send food downriver to otherwise destitute "lake" forts.[95] Cocking and John Longmoore finally built Lower and Upper Hudson Houses on the Saskatchewan in large measure to trade bison flesh from the Cree. Cumberland House journals indeed show staff first eating bison by 1778. The dietary switch was made just as moose meat trades dropped significantly, likely because Cree bands nearby had overhunted these animals to support these fur traders and the crews transecting farther afield from there.[96] It may not have been a good moment to adopt the strategy, given what appears to have been a concurrent decline

---

[95] E. E. Rich, *Cumberland House Journals and Inland Journal 1775–1782*, I (London: Hudson's Bay Record Society, 1951), 109–110.

[96] George Colpitts, "'Victuals to Put into our Mouths': Environmental Perspectives on Fur Trade Provisioning Activities at Cumberland House, 1775–1782," in Gregory P. Marchildon, ed., *The Early Northwest* (Regina: Canadian plains Research Center, 2008), figures 9 and 10, and p. 141.

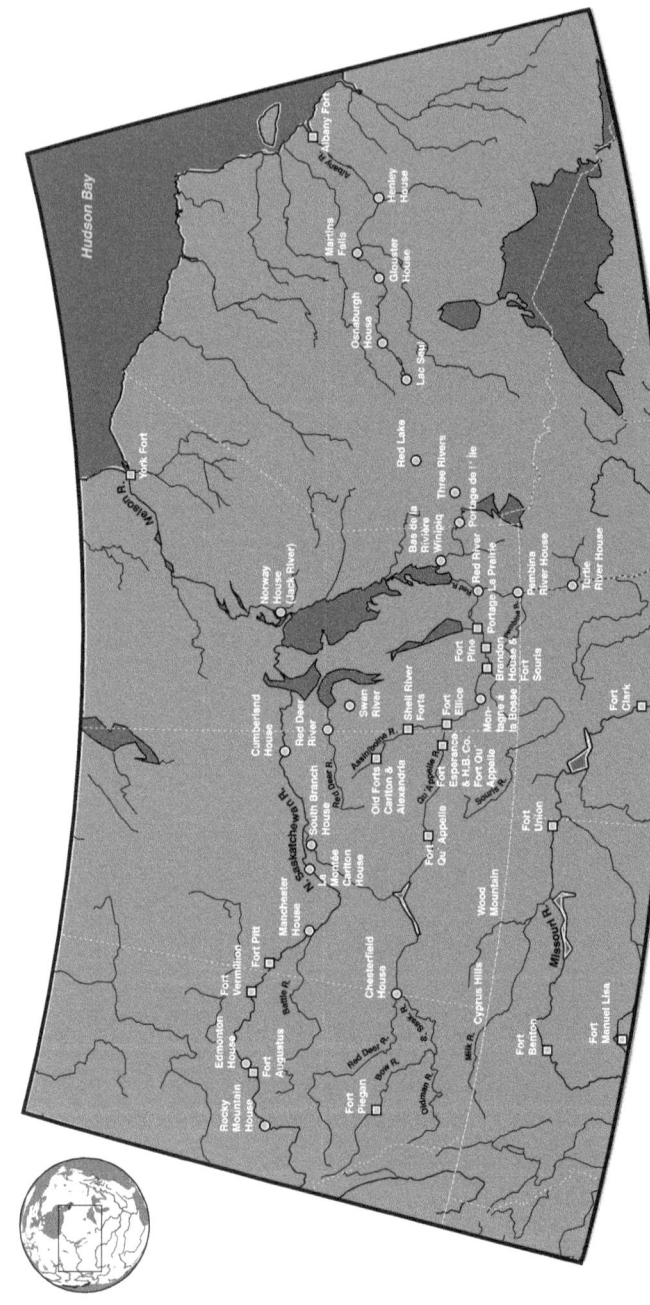

Figure 1.3. Forts and posts in the Pemmican Empire (map by Shawn Mueller, 2013).

in bison populations in that area of the Great Plains anyway in the late 1770s.[97] However, in the long term, the focus on this food source was now established.

As early as 1775, the Montreal trader Alexander Henry the Elder visited the Montreal-supported Fort des Prairies, likely in western Manitoba, in the dead of winter and witnessed firsthand the abundance offered in plains country. Curious to see this "fire country," no doubt because it was always characterized by Indian informants as a superabundantly rich game region, Henry had faced food supply problems almost the entire journey from Montreal. He nearly froze by the time he stumbled into the post hungry and, one suspects, disorientated by the stupendous food stocks before him. "Hospitably entertained by my friends," Henry noted in his journal upon his arrival; the post servants "covered their table with the tongues and marrow of wild bulls. The quantity of provisions, which I found collected here, exceeded every thing of which I had previously formed a notion. In one heap, I saw fifty ton of beef [bison meat], so fat that the men could scarcely find a sufficiency of lean."[98]

The food here changed hands from Cree and Assiniboine. Henry later saw their "pounds" first hand, glimpsing the power of such carefully built enclosures that, as a form of communal hunting, drove animals in lanes toward killing sites, often made out of fallen timber and brush and lined by human hunters. Once they were built, with seemingly little extra effort on the Assiniboine's part, these pounds (or "ponds" as traders called them) generated quantities that more than met their own needs and could support a trading post. This was fortunate because Henry saw that Assiniboine were not motivated by the same needs of forest dwelling boreal forest people. Their bison hunt (at least when it was a success) fulfilled all their dietary and material needs. They wanted to trade only to obtain luxuries. This was certainly the case that winter, where on a single occasion, Henry saw the slaughter of some seventy-two animals in the pound; women efficiently moved the meat to the camp

---

[97] Adam R. Hodge makes this assertion, "'In Want of Nourishment for to Keep them Alive': Climatic Fluctuations, Bison Scarcity, and the Smallpox Epidemic of 1780–82 on the Northern Great Plains," *Environmental History*, 17:376–378 (April 2012). My own quantified research at Cumberland House, suggests not as much an abhorrent climatic disruption in the region as a quite typical boreal forest difficulty when moose populations simply were not sustainable for a nearby post.

[98] Alexander Henry the Elder, *Travels and Adventures in Canada and the Indian Territories between the Years 1760 and 1776* (Edmonton: M. G. Hurtig, 1969), 275–276.

where they separated out bison shoulders, hearts, and tongues, and the rest was consumed as ordinary food or dried "for sale at the fort."

Through this means, the Montreal companies were acquiring so much food at Manitoba posts that they were beginning to exceed even their own immediate needs. By the end of the 1780s, as they directed more of their trade to the prairie, Montreal houses had such surpluses that they were even venting quantities of the pemmican they were producing to boreal forest tribes. James Sutherland, traveling through north central Ontario in a brigade of Ojibwa canoes in 1785 noted that the twelve Ojibwa, led by Newitchcanisium, were using buffalo pemmican to make almost marathon-like passages by canoe over the shield from their visit to HBC posts. Instead of stopping and cooking to eat, they had a little fat "which they mix with Ruahaggan [a form of buffalo pemmican] and eat while they paddle."[99] They were, indeed, canoeing through the daylight hours without pause, their supercharged fuel source "Buffalo Rucheggan mixed with fat" and Sutherland expressed in wonder: "what may seem surprising they traded most of it from the [Montreal] pedlers who has more of it than they can use, as the fire [or plains] country through which they pass is so plentiful of that kind of provision."[100]

Like Fidler had among the Chipewyan, Sutherland noted the ways that the Ojibwa guided themselves according to strict rules of food sharing and generosity. When the brigade finally came to a stop to repair the hulls of its haggard canoes, some of the hunters fanned out to find fresh fare (no one liked to eat the pemmican Europeans produced, even then!). They returned with beavers and a bear and commenced to "destroy more provisions within a 36 hours than would serve Gloucester [House] for a week." Each tent shared its food in common: "they vye with each other who shall give most away," he said. But he also made the particularly important observation: "they share with us [Sutherland and his own European assistant] equally with themselves, making no distinction."[101]

Sutherland, Henry, and Cocking were witnessing a significant shift in food energy sources driving the fur trade both on the plains and, now the boreal forest. The numbers speak for themselves: a single pound of pemmican might have contained as much as 3,200 to 3,500 calories per pound. What became the standard bag of the stuff, weighing

---

[99] HBCA. June 12–17, 1785, Gloucester House Journals, B.78/a/15.
[100] Ibid., July 25, 1785.
[101] Ibid., July 10, 1785.

90 lbs., likely had the caloric value of between 288,000 and 315,000 kilocalories. That almost doubled the food energy value of dried corn or wild rice. Indeed, the "custom of the voyageur," described by Alexander Mackenzie, and driving the almost inconceivably difficult manual work of the fur trade to that date, was clearly insufficient for the trade's further expansion. Voyageurs, he said, "have no other allowance here [at Grand Portage], or in the voyage, than Indian corn and melted fat." Mackenzie rated it "wholesome, palatable food, and easy of digestion… sufficient for a man's subsistence during twenty-four hours; though it is not sufficiently heartening to sustain the strength necessary for a state of active labour."[102] Indeed, at most, 510 calories could be derived from the lard (a 4-ounce ration), and the corn (a daily quart, perhaps 1.43 lbs. in weight), added 2,676, for a total of 3,186, still far below the needs of a man burning 4,000 to 6,000 calories a day. The custom likely declined further in terms of food energy when, in farther stretches from Grand Portage, diets were given over to greater concentrations of corn alone. Put in this perspective, a Montreal canoe usually carrying 1,000 lbs. of provisions could haul corn for about 300 man-days of energy. In an eight-man canoe, that might yield perhaps thirty-eight days of actual journeying. If they were fortunate to take on, like Alexander Henry the Younger did, 100 bags of wild rice, in Lac La Pluie (at about 1,619 cal/lb), the same canoe could carry energy for a further thirty-three days. By contrast, a Montreal canoe hypothetically carrying 1,000 lbs. of pemmican would have the food energy for 533 man-days, in an eight-man canoe, sixty-seven days of journeying (see Figure 1.4).[103]

Comparing so simply carbohydrate-rich diets on the eastern side of the divide to the protein and fat heavy diets, on the other side, however, is fraught with problems from the perspective of physiology. Simply having greater calories of energy available in their food did not necessarily mean that it could be used by muscle tissue to do work. Fats and proteins contain greater calories; however, body metabolism derives that energy less efficiently as it can from carbohydrates. Aerobic exercise probably

---

[102] Mackenzie quoted in Innis, *Fur Trade in Canada*, 224.
[103] Figure 1.4 is derived from "Dried Indian Corn" and "Wild Rice" values provided by the United States Department of Agriculture (USDA) Nutrient Database, Agricultural Research Service of the National Agricultural Library (online resource); the higher pemmican value provided by Edward N. Wentworth (1956), "Dried Meat: Early Man's Travel Ration," *Agricultural History*, 30(1):8, has been adopted here because Wentworth provides a conservative estimate of pemmican energy and voyageurs often mixed pemmican with melted fat to make *Ruchagan* en route, thus increasing its food energy.

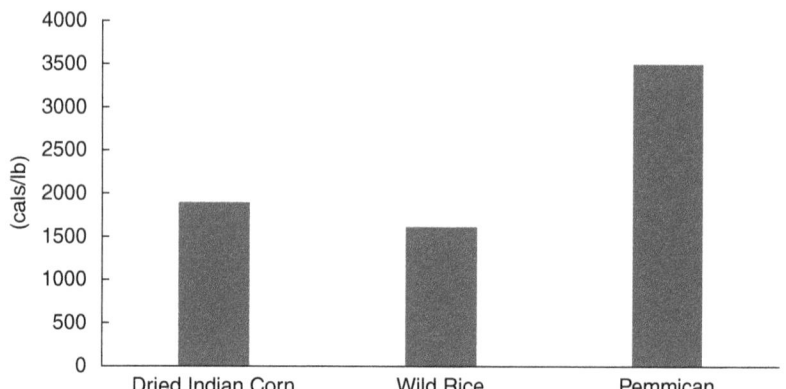

Figure 1.4. Caloric energy of corn, wild rice, and pemmican (cals/lb.) compared (based on USDA Nutrient Database and Wentworth, 1956).

better converts carbohydrates into ATP than it does fat. The fur trade, creating such extremes in diet, for that reason, continues to raise numerous questions about its ultimate sustainability in the present day.[104] The switch from high carbohydrates on one side of the Great Divide into the almost exclusive diet of fat and protein on the other, whatever its long-term effects on voyageur bodies, however, availed significant gains for commercial expansion.[105] One important study in physiology has suggested that carbohydrates provide "most of the energy for short-term maximal endurance exercise, whereas lipid [fat] makes substantial contributions to the energy requirements of more prolonged exercise," essentially making these fats most appropriate for the extraordinary long days and almost unlimited outlays of exercise undertaken by voyageurs. More importantly, exercise physiologists note that modern-day elite athletes, after adapting themselves to a high-fat diet for a number of days, are able to undertake ultra-endurance events with high-fat diets without apparently deleterious effects to the body.[106]

[104] William D. McArdle, Frank I. Katch, and Victor L. Katch *Essentials of Exercise Physiology*, 3rd ed., Vol. I (Baltimore: Lippincott, Williams & Wilkins, 2006), 94.
[105] See the various possible means of ATP production, and different routes to muscle fatigue very germane to this discussion, T. D. Noakes (2000), "Physiological Models to Understand Exercise Fatigue and the Adaptations that Predict or Enhance Athletic Performance," *Scandanavian Journal of Medicine & Science in Sports*, 10:123–145, 134–135.
[106] See John A. Hawley and Will G. Hopkins (1995), "Aerobic Glycolytic and Aerobic Lipolytic Power Systems," *Sports Medicine*, 19(4):240–250; and Estelle V. Lambert, David

It was likely the sheer physiological stress of a high-fat and meat diet in voyaging that made country provisions at posts the more important. Traders like Alexander Henry the Younger made sure to grow whatever he could from potato and vegetable patches. He stored quite large surpluses of potatoes, turnips, carrots, beets, parsnips, cucumbers, melons, squashes, corn, and heads of cabbage from fall harvests.[107] However, in respect to actual voyaging and the reality of meat-heavy diets while in posts, the switch into pemmican energy is a striking feature of the fur trade's longer history. More than simply striking on an alternative food energy source, fats in pemmican were likely revolutionary in terms of commercial expansion. They undoubtedly increased the very pace of voyaging, allowing transport routes to significantly lengthen and quicken now into the farthest reaches of the subarctic. These were likely the very reason why "northwest" men who switched to this energy source commonly jeered at the "pork eaters" they met each year at Grand Portage: the men they met were likely debilitated and poorly served by the corn and wild rice of the long and physically exhausting transects they had endured coming inland from Montreal. Those who ate pemmican were loath to return to corn diets, such as the men moving from northwestern service to the American Fur Company, where the "custom of the voyageur" remained, disappointingly, the typical fare in much of its keelboat service.[108]

Conclusion

The switch to a higher energy food source in the fur trade was apparent in the early days of the 1790s. By 1792, Montreal companies built their

---

P. Speechly, Steven C. Dennis, and Timothy D. Noakes (1994), "Enhanced Endurance in Trained Cyclists during Moderate Intensity Exercise Following 2 Weeks Adaptations to a High Fat Diet," *European Journal of Applied Physiology*, 69:287–293; and discussion in T. D. Noakes (2000), "Physiological Models to Understand Exercise Fatigue and the Adaptations that Predict or Enhance Athletic Performance," *Scandinavian Journal of Medicine & Science in Sports*, 10:123–145.

[107] See Alexander's tabulation of his vegetable returns in 1805, Gough, ed., *Journal of Alexander Henry the Younger*, I, 165.

[108] Henry E. Hamilton, *Incidents and Events in the Life of Gurdon Saltonstall Hubbard 1802–1886* (The Newberry Library, 1997), 20–21. At Mackinaw, the American Fur Company rationed daily to a man one pint of hulled and dried corn, with two to four ounces of tallow. "it was quite sufficient, and generally more than they could consume. It was invariably liked by them, and it was found that they could endure more hardships on this than on a diet of bread and meat." He said that Canadian "pork eaters" were usually "much dissatisfied" with this ration, but were "laughed out of it by the old voyageurs…," 20.

first depots at the head of the Winnipeg River, christened Le Sieur's after its builder, but, more commonly known as Bas de la Rivière Winipic. It became, with Cumberland House, the NWC's key supply base to what was developing as the jumping off to a vast commercial empire. Initially, a modest 100 to 250 bags of pemmican annually were delivered from the Assiniboine and upper Red River posts to this depot.[109] Even this supply represented a significant release of greater quantities of food energy. Brigade travel quickly organized around the compact fuel offered in pemmican. By 1809, Alexander Henry the Younger was mass producing and shuttling it back from Fort Vermillion, near present day Edmonton, and used for a single brigade of eleven canoes (six per canoe) going to the depot a mere sixty-six bags of pemmican – about a single bag allotted to each person for the entire trip. Another forty, going the other way, could get the contingent to the salty airs of the Pacific on the Columbia.[110] Duncan M'Gillivray, keeping a journal at Fort George, stated that bison fats and meats were now the post's chief trading commodities and if their supply was interrupted, it "would prevent progress & stop the Trade," he said. "It is wisely ordered by Providence that this should be so."[111]

The greater footprint and the faster pace of pemmican-fueled fur trading were made manifest at Lake Winnipeg later in the decade. At least by 1800, voyageur crews from Montreal staged annual contests at this traditional starving point in voyageur life. After they had settled in at the food depot, undoubtedly resting and adapting their bodies to the high-fat diets of the Northwest, they joined up with other brigades and set out across the lake's vast surface in a race to the Athabasca district. The first crew arriving won. Around them now were elite voyageurs specially chosen to make annual 4,000-mile round-trip runs between Grand Portage and Lake Athabasca – using pemmican to do so. Sometimes up to a hundred canoes took part in these contests. Now availing themselves of fat energy, voyageurs increased their pace. The forty stroke/minute paddling of corn country was considerably quickened. As historian Marjorie Wilkins Campbell described, voyageurs increased their speed from forty to sixty, then to sixty-five strokes per minute during these contests. Guides in the front of each canoe "hacked off hunks of pemmican for the straining voyageurs who chewed as they paddled till

---

[109] A. S. Morton, *A History of the Canadian West*, 429.
[110] Gough, Barry M., ed., *The Journal of Alexander Henry the Younger, 1799–1814*, Vol. II (Toronto: The Champlain Society, 1988), 395.
[111] Morton, Arthur S., ed. *The Journal of Duncan M'Gillivray of the North West Company at Fort George on the Saskatchewan, 1794–5* (Toronto: Macmillan, 1929), xlviii.

they verged on exhaustion."[112] The record at such speed was forty hours of continuous paddling. On that occasion, the bourgeois finally stopped the contest, fearing for the men's lives.[113]

Pemmican production, then, solved one of the more important problems of the British fur trade. Ironically, pemmican food energy raised others. As food energy increased in availability, so did its use by companies expanding their activities and competing more vigorously against their rivals. There is no coincidence that the most violent, competitive period of the Northwest fur trade, approximately from 1780 to 1821, coincided with the release of comparatively vast amounts of this food energy. Pemmican allowed companies to deliver more goods to Native people, more alcohol, more guns, and, because they were competing with each other, incite more violence, overtrapping and overhunting among nations inland.[114] The shift into this new energy source, then, not only tripped off further commercial expansion, but also changed ways of life forming around a new endosomatic energy regime. This one, based on bison fat, animated a larger, more competitive fur trade now was poised to spread to the very shores of the Pacific and Arctic Oceans.

---

[112] Marjorie Wilkins Campbell, *The North West Company* (Toronto: Macmillan, 1957), 44.
[113] Campbell, *The North West Company*, 44.
[114] An overview of the violent period between 1780 and 1821 is provided by Gerhard J. Ens, "Fatal Quarrels and Fur Trade Rivalries: A Year of Living Dangerously on the North Saskatchewan, 1806–07," in Michael Payne, Donald Wetherell, and Catherine Cavanaugh, eds., *Alberta Formed: Alberta Transformed*, Vol. 1 (Edmonton: University of Alberta Press, 2005), 133–159.

2

THE PEMMICAN BIOREGION, 1790–1810

> *"poor in flesh"* = *1* motion, both hands, as if scraping the chest, from the centre out towards the arm pits.
>
> *"fat"* [animal] = two motions: both hands closed, knuckles up, thumbs against each other (resembling the shape of a buffalo's back), 2nd motion out and rounding as the side of a buffalo
>
> Alexander Culbertson's "Description and meaning of signs among the Indians in Montana"[1]

It was a place categorically and gastronomically different from any other they had encountered in the New World. Europeans arriving to the prairie in the 1780s and 1790s had heard about the "fire country," as it was called by fur traders, but it was the geomorphology and the buffalo biomass sprawling before them that usually confounded newcomers. At the forks of the Assiniboine and Red Rivers in 1793, John Sutherland, who had never seen a prairie, began his mental adjustments to the region, as many did, by eating bison meat: "I reckon it as good as any fresh Beef," he pronounced.[2] There was, though, much for him to learn: beyond the characteristics of fat and lean in buffalo diet, customs around food sharing were entrenched in the steppe areas. Traders already accustomed to some degree to meat-sharing traditions in the boreal forest, were quickly drawn into complex protocols of food exchange that, in turn, shaped economic behaviors here in distinctive ways.

Arguably the defining characteristic of the prairie was its dryness. The prairie was so dry that Europeans first arriving to the region had difficulty mudding chimneys. Their post walls collapsed, sod roofs leaked

---

[1] Montana State Historical Archives, Helena, from SC 586 Correspondence, diary and journal of Alexander Culbertson.

[2] HBCA. September 6, 1793 entry, B.63/a/1, Journal of John Sutherland, at River Kapell [Qu'Appelle, known as Beaver House] 1793–1794.

when it did rain, and most "forts" had to be completely rebuilt every year. Newcomers also learned the reality of plains life. A post's real sustainability depended less on familiar and durable construction materials than it did on extensive Cree and Assiniboine kin-based food sharing networks nearby, the support of bands through intermarriage, and the generosity of hired hunters who helped these posts build their trade. That they succeeded at all in amassing food surpluses for export into the fur trade and, by the end of the century, in reaching what might be termed "peak" production from local winter pounds, constitutes a formidable moment in the transformation of the area into a pemmican bioregion. As this chapter makes clear, the emerging provisions trade benefited from more that the region's seemingly superabundant bison herds. Its parkland/prairie ecology favored food reciprocity, which at posts allowed for trade surpluses to accrue. Almost as critically, the climatic fault line in their Northern Plains latitudes gave greater winter seasonality, affecting bison physiology and fatness, and better drove them into winter shelters frequently for massive, communal killing. More importantly for the market, however, was a fortuitous "fat frontier" in these latitudes that gave Native people and Europeans an advantage handling fats in summer. These conditions encouraged the entry of market exchange into the region and, when posts were built, the development of a mass factory food production. Such historical circumstances, and the ecological realities of the steppe, then, are key considerations in the development of a Northern Plains bioregion. They explain both some defining characteristics and the widespread incidence of trade pemmican in the northern latitudes emerging primarily in British territories by the early nineteenth century.

Making Sense of a Bison Landscape

When fur trade companies began to depend on the food energy of buffalo meats and fat, their traders quickly infiltrated river basins in the "upper" Red River itself and the "Lower" parts of the river, both at the elbow of the L-shaped Assiniboine and up the crooked, leafy tendrils of the eastern portions of the Qu'Appelle Valley (traders at this juncture called the Red River the "Upper" and the Assiniboine the "Lower" Red River). At least by 1795, wintering herds of bison attracted Europeans into the Souris Basin and to a flurry of meat trading that now occurred at Montagne à la Bosse nearby. The Pembina, too, was now hunted for the market by Ojibwa, Cree, Assiniboine, and undoubtedly Missourian and

Upper Mississippi Métis, who moved in and out of the growing economic opportunities offered in trade, as it suited them.[3] Commercial hunting even expanded to the Mandan's very backdoor on the leeside of the Missouri Couteau. Farther east, market hunters were as far as Devils Lake, North Dakota. Specializing for the trade, Ojibwa, fur company freemen, and proto-Métis camps brazenly purloined bison and beaver skins from Sioux territories. At least by 1801, Europeans such as Alexander Henry the Younger led parties of Ojibwa to butcher in the great and bloody war zone separating Ojibwa from Sioux along the Upper Red River in present-day Minnesota.[4]

The quantity of bison flesh consumed, bagged up and shipped out of the Winnipeg Steppe, even by 1798, undoubtedly surpassed a million pounds annually.[5] There always remained an interest in trading prairie beaver but that animal's quick and quite rampant over trapping meant that it was bison meats and fats that "in this part is looked on as useful as ye furs," the Hudson's Bay Company (HBC) trader Robert Goodwin admitted, seeing his own Brandon posting specialize in the stuff by 1795.[6] To the west, older fur trading posts high on the upper Saskatchewan and down the South Branch of the Saskatchewan, hurriedly built in the wave of commercial speculation around prairie beaver skins in the 1780s, were refitted into the far more robust meat trade. Come spring, as they shifted into full pemmican production, Saskatchewan parkland and Winnipeg steppe posts became veritable abattoirs, smelly, fly-besotted, and spilled over with fat and blood.

Europeans and Americans first glimpsing the steppe (the flattened lacustrine bottom of an ancient post–Ice Age Lake Agassiz) expressed wonder at both the fantastic abundance of food and the mesmerizingly flat terrain around them. It was all as "level as a House floor," Daniel

---

[3] On the Missourian Métis, see Martha Harroun Foster, *We Know Who We Are: Métis Identity in a Montana Community* (Norman: University of Oklahoma Press, 2006), 26–28.

[4] On the Assiniboine, Robert Goodwin noted the trade at Brandon being lost to the new "Mountain le boss." He wrote that there were "upwards of 20 houses on this river only." HBCA. January 6, 1795, Brandon House Journals, B.22/a/2. On the Red River game war zone, see Paul S. Martin and Christine R. Szuter (February 1999), "War Zones and Game Sinks in Lewis and Clark's West," *Conservation Biology*, 13(1):36–45.

[5] Arthur Ray estimates that the steppe posts might have consumed 1,323,000 lbs. in a single year, simply to feed their staff and families. Arthur J. Ray, *Indians in the Fur Trade: Their Role as Trappers, Hunters, and Middlemen in the Lands Southwest of Hudson Bay, 1660–1870* (Toronto: University of Toronto Press, 1998), 130.

[6] HBCA. Robert Goodwin, Brandon House Journals, May 9, 1795, B.22/a/2.

Harmon wrote, amazed.⁷ In the social interactions at these posts inland, such as at Alexandria, on a single occasion, "came twelve Families of Crees & Assiniboines from the large Plains and let us have Furs & Provisions & who have been drinking ever since, both Men & Women, which occasions them to make an intolerable noise, for they talk, Sing & cry all at the same time." As for his own men, so well provided for from the plains, Harmon was dismayed that his reprimand to them playing cards on Sunday was met by a reply that "there is no Sabbath in this Country." The men's behavior, he wrote, "but too plainly shews that they think as they speak." Harmon thought "it is a lamentable fact that the most of those who are in this wild part of the World, lay aside the most of Christian and Civilized regulations...."⁸

Alexander Henry the Younger, nephew of a famous uncle namesake and Montreal trader, struggled to describe the geography and plenitude around him: "We have reached the commencement of the great plains of Red River," he wrote on his arrival, "where the eye is lost in one continuous level westward. Not a tree or rising ground interrupts the view."⁹ To Henry, the bison embodied the superabundance and frightening power of the region. Here, bison pounded down hillocks, fertilized soils, churned up trees, and left their wallows like massive potholes, the earth's surface morphing into a ghastly terrain Barry Potyondi characterized as "buffalo landscape."¹⁰ John Macdonell of Garth, arriving the same year as the HBC's first contingents in 1793, joined the Nor'wester's house on the upper waters of the Assiniboine. The animals and their grassy environment surpassed his powers of description, with his writing on a day in fall a single journal entry: "Incredible numbers of Buffaloes to be seen in all directions."¹¹

The Winnipeg or "Agassiz" Steppe stretches across some 7,000 square miles of prairie, a hummocky, poorly drained, and often supersaturated "soup bowl" sitting on the top of the wide rim of the Canadian Shield in

---

⁷ October 23 [22], 1800, Daniel Williams Harmon, *Harmon's Journal 1800–1819*, new edition with Foreword by Jennifer S. H. Brown (Surrey: Touchwood Editions, 2006), 26.

⁸ November 16, Sunday, 1800, *Harmon's Journal*, 27.

⁹ August 26, 1800 entry in Barry M. Gough, ed., *The Journal of Alexander Henry the Younger, 1799–1814*, Vol. 1 (Toronto: The Champlain Society, 1988), 32.

¹⁰ Barry Potyondi, *In Palliser's Triangle: Living in the Grasslands, 1850–1930* (Saskatoon: Purich Publishing, 1995), 11–15.

¹¹ October 7, 1793, "Diary of John Macdonell," in Charles M. Gates, ed., *Five Fur Traders of the Northwest: Being the Narrative of Peter Pond and the Diaries of John Macdonell, Archibald N. McLeod, Hugh Faires, and Thomas Connor* (Minneapolis: University of Minnesota Press, 1933), 115.

much of present-day Manitoba. Tall grass species flourished in the deep soils deposited as the once mucky bottom of this massive lake that had spread from James Bay beyond the present shores of Lakes Manitoba, Winnipeg, and Winnipegosis, extending far into what is now Minnesota and North Dakota. This was classic tallgrass prairie – with a tuberous anchoring deep and wide in the soils and drawing moisture from the insectivorous hemp of roots and subterranean organisms that thrived within it.[12]

Bison herds returned almost incessantly to some area of the prairie steppe to rake and gore the topography. Whether it figured as a keystone or competing entity with other biotic life is a matter of debate.[13] The animal was, however, quintessentially associated with the Great Plains in the historical era, coming to represent the deceptively brutish power and sudden violence of grassland environments.[14] Beyond their impressive physical dimensions as individuals – the dressed weight of a fat male was 1,000 to 1,400 lb, a fat female 700 to 1000 lb[15] – was the bison's presence as a collective entity. Well adapted to its inland grassy niche, the plains species (*Bison bison*) was a fearsome force as a collective biomass. The North American plains species is sometimes said to have numbered between 30 to 60 million across the Great Plains in the historic period. This number, however, is based on a hypothetical estimate of environmental carrying capacity. The herds most likely rarely reached that size in reality, as they constantly expanded and collapsed around changing climatic conditions. Far smaller numbers should be kept in mind, as frequent bouts of drought alone likely closely curtailed populations.[16] At best, the plains were patchy with this life form. The herds "swarmed"

---

[12] Licht, "Ecology & Economics of the Great Plains" 2–5. James E. Sherow, *The Grasslands of the United States: An Environmental History* (Santa Barbara: ABC Clio, 2007), 5–9. On the hydrological characteristics of the "soup bowl" of the steppe, see Shannon Stunden-Bower, *Wet Prairie: People, Land and Water in Agricultural Manitoba* (Vancouver: UBC Press, 2011).

[13] Licht, "Ecology & Economics of the Great Plains," 41.

[14] HBCA. Thomas Henderson's encounter with one of these beasts was notable enough that the Fort Ellice clerk recorded it in the post journal in 1822. November 29, 1822, Fort Ellice Journals, B.63/a/2.

[15] January 15, 1801, *Harmon's Journal* 32.

[16] I have benefited from the observations of Alwynn Beaudoin, as well as discussions taking place at the University of Saskatchewan's Bison Symposium where the issue of carrying capacity was raised. Just on how patchy bison were around scant waterholes is revealed in the diary of Culbertson who nearly died of thirst leaving Fort Benton and traveling across the plains to Red River, "*Journal of a Journey*," July 10, 1870, Culbertson Files, SC 586.

around good forage and, especially, sources of water in ideal climate conditions.[17] In the northern latitudes, impressive herds were seen commonly in winter, such as in February 1793 when fur trader Peter Fidler passed a single herd to the east side of the Red Deer River near the Hand Hills of present-day Alberta. It "numbered some millions ... as no ground could be seen [between] them in that compleat [sic] semicircle and extending at least 10 miles...."[18]

To various degrees, humans and bison had been locked in a reciprocal relationship for millennia. To the west, humans on the plains so adapted themselves to the animal's seasonal movement, herd behavior, and even psychology that in the era before the horse, humans and animals reached one of the most stable ways of life in North American human record.[19] On the western plains in the territories of the Blackfoot, Aitsina, and those of the plains Assiniboine, investments of human tool kits, anthropogenic burning, communal hunting, and magico-religious observances harnessed the animal to humans, and humans to animal in an impressive dynamic. For true plains bison hunting cultures, real meat was bison flesh, and if reduced to eating any other, the Blackfoot, Piikani, and Sioux considered themselves starving.[20] The Blackfoot, one of the plains tribes attaining a veritable socioeconomic synergy with this herd animal, followed a calendar timed according to this movable feast's comings and goings. The Blackfoot two-season year (there was no fall or spring) began with the bison's migration from winter shelter belts; it ended on their return. The "home days" moon not surprisingly coincided with the rut, when the bison was unbelievably dangerous to hunt and a tribal ingathering instead occurred around the Sun Dance, a "world renewal event."[21]

[17] Licht estimates the bison's collective biomass by weight being 50 billion pounds at the beginning of the nineteenth century – heavier than the weight of all Canadian and American human populations in the present day. Daniel S. Licht, *Ecology and Economics of the Great Plains* (Lincoln: University of Nebraska Press, 1997), 5.

[18] George W. Arthur, "An Introduction to the Ecology of Early Historic Communal Bison Hunting Among the Northern Plains Indians," Archaeological Survey of Canada Paper No. 37 (Ottawa: National Museums of Canada, 1975), 56–57.

[19] Trevor R. Peck and J. Rod Vickers, in Michael Payne, Donald Wetherell, and Catherine Cavanaugh, eds., "*Buffalo and Dogs: The Prehistoric Lifeway of Aboriginal People on the Alberta Plains, 1004–1005,*" Vol. I (Edmonton: University of Alberta Press, 2006), 55–79; Walter Hildebrandt and Brian Hubner, *The Cypress Hills: An Island by Itself* (Saskatoon: Purich, 2007), 16–21.

[20] Eleanor Verbicky-Todd, "Communal Buffalo Hunting among the Plains Tribes," Archaeological Survey of Alberta Occasional Paper No. 24, 1984 (Edmonton: Alberta Culture Historical Resources), 7–8.

[21] Peck and Vickers, "Buffalo and Dogs," 69–77.

These plains cultures ordered their relationships with other biotic life and even the ethereal realm in respect to this herd animal's almost perpetual gift of food. The corn growing Pawnee ritualized their annual bison hunts far into the central plains as more than simply a food-gathering mission. Through the human sacrifices of the morning star cult and the priestly bison calling rituals, the Pawnee made their penultimate quest bison flesh and fats, each hunter hoping to return with enough to not only satiate his lodge's needs, but also to pay for the many shaman rituals throughout the rest of the year that, by necessity, began with gifts to priests of bison back fat.[22]

The Blackfoot rapport with wolves had much to do with how humans long observed Canid pack organization for their bison hunting. Close "cooperation" between wolves and their human "brothers" likely informed proto-Blackfoot cultures devising the great bison drives through running lanes to jumps and pounds. As anyone handling live, temperamental and completely wild bison can attest, for humans on foot to drive sometimes thousands of bison hundreds of miles is more than impressive. As Barsh and Marlor have argued, this "science" was most likely inspired by observing wolf behavior in packs, and wolves have remained integral to Blackfoot cosmology ever since.[23] The Siksika (Blackfoot), Piikani (Peigan, or Piegan), and Kainai (Blood) likewise esteemed beaver as one of the underwater grandfather creatures and maintained taboos against their hunting and trapping. This "conservation" had much to do with the animal's capacity to store water in otherwise parching plains streams and rivers, helping direct bison herds more predictably toward watering holes well known by humans. The bison–human–beaver nexus was complete in the Blackfoot beaver bundle ceremonies that aided buffalo callers – men and women – to direct and anticipate the bison herds in their midst.[24]

---

[22] See James F. Brooks, *Captives and Cousins: Slavery, Kinship, and Community in the Southwest Borderlands* (Chapel Hill: University of North Carolina Press, 2002), 10–17; Gene Weltfish, *The Lost Universe* (New York: Basic Books, 1965), 63, 190–195.

[23] See Russel Lawrence Barsh and Chantelle Marlor (December 2003), "Driving Bison and Blackfoot Science," *Human Ecology*, 31(4):571–593.

[24] Jim Daschuk and Greg Marchildon, April 15, 2005, IACC Project Working Paper No. 7. "Climate and Aboriginal Adaptation in the South Saskatchewan River Basin, A.D. 800–1700"; see also Jim Daschuk (2009), "A Dry Oasis: The Canadian Plains in Late Prehistory," *Prairie Forum*, 34(1):1–29; on beaver bundles, see Gerald T. Conaty (May 1995), "Economic Models and Blackfoot Ideology," *American Ethnologist*, 22(2):403–412.

Bison flesh framed Northern Plains diets – not discounting the sizeable contribution of herbals, starchy roots and bulbs, imported salmon (salmon pemmican, specifically from the Dales on the Columbia, was held as a great delicacy on the plains), traded blue camus, and, of course, corn that came through trading networks. But bison meat predominated. One Métis remembered it comprising at least 90 percent of plains diets in buffalo days.[25] Its dietary primacy prompted a physiological as well as cultural accommodation among buffalo hunters. Many truly plains bison cultures, for instance, strictly observed taboos against fish eating. Despite the relative abundance of fish in plains streams, bison hunting specialists did not eat fish except in times of dire need, likely because of the digestive discomfort arising after mixing high-fat fish with lower-fat bison flesh. By contrast, where diets were not so completely given over to year-round bison hunting, in prairie and parkland territories, Cree hunters and gatherers could not be so strict. But, they moved between bison and other ungulates only with the greatest care and ate fish only in season. These groups made a critical dietary transition in late winter. Having eaten by spring dried bison meats, they made the jump to very oily fish flesh only by first consuming fattier bison fetuses and calves that they selectively culled from herds.[26] Those who did not regretted it. Fish-induced diarrhea awaited them. So did "mal de boeuf" striking those gorging themselves on the rich flesh of bulls that usually reached their prime later in spring. Almost inevitably a greenhorn trader on the plains, after passing a late winter season eating dried meat, could not stop himself from feasting on fattened bulls only to wind up bedridden for a week, with all the

---

[25] Marie Rose Smith, "I Remember," unpublished manuscript, ca. 1930–1940, Glenbow Archives and Library, 5. On the Columbian trade networks into the plains, and Dalles salmon pemmican, see Theodore Stern, Theodore Stern, Chapter one, "The Fort" and Chapter Two "The Columbian Trading Network," in *Chiefs and Chief Traders: Indian Relations at Fort Nez Perces, 1818–1855* (University of Oregon Press, 1993), 18–27. On the larger element of exchange in the Indian world, see Neil Salisbury, "The Indians' Old World: Native Americans and the Coming of Europeans," *The William and Mary Quarterly*, 3rd ser. 53(3), July 1996, 435–568.

[26] M. E. Malainey, R. Przybylski, and B. L. Sherriff (2001), "One Person's Food: How and Why Fish Avoidance May Affect the Settlement and Subsistence Patterns of Hunter-Gatherers," *American Antiquity*, 66(1):141–161; there is a countervailing view offered in Brian J. Smith, "The Historical and Archaeological Evidence for the Use of Fish as an Alternate Subsistence Resource among Northern Plains Bison Hunters," in Kerry Abel and Jean Friesen, eds., *Aboriginal Resource use in Canada: Historical and Legal Aspects* (Winnipeg: University of Manitoba Press, 1991), 35–49.

discomfort it entailed. To "accustom" themselves to bull meat, hunters usually ate tongues first.[27]

Plenty and Penury in the Parkland

At least initially, Europeans poised their trading posts above the abundance of the great bison herds and located themselves in more northerly parkland and prairie regions. The first meat trading did not typically occur on parched plains stretched to the horizon, but within copse valley areas, in prairie grasslands dotted by islands of deciduous parkland forests, and prairie hill outliers where enough orographic precipitation provided sufficient moisture for fescue bunch grass and more dense forest cover. Most Cree, Ojibwa, and some of the Assiniboine passed a good portion of winter seasons in the groves and copse islands of prairie. There, episodic, even stochastic, seasonal winter bison abundance made life easier. But, unlike true "buffalo" people who followed bison year round, these "wood adapted" parkland and prairie hunters divided their year between forest areas and winter bison convergence points strategically, for the most part intercepting rather than following herds. This did not mean that these hunters did not figure on bison as a source of significant caloric value, only that they very often had to generalize their hunting at other times of the year and, importantly, when buffalo hunting failed in winter in the areas they situated themselves.

Their hunting weapon of choice, a source of wonder to newcomers, was the communally constructed "pound" – a wooden killing pen into which hunters drove bands of bison in winter. Europeans setting up shop to trade soon described them. With the meat of a "fat cow" worth eight beaver skins in trade goods in 1793 (six for an "ordinary one") the

---

[27] "My people [many of them Ojibwa] are now all unwell, as usual every spring, from the sudden change of diet, from flesh to fat Sturgeon, they are troubled with a continual dysentery that reduces them very much and makes them weak and faint. Although they are most extraordinary gormandizers, the Sturgeon oil is too much for them." In Barry M. Gough, ed., *The Journal of Alexander Henry the Younger, 1799–1814*, Vol. 1 (Toronto: The Champlain Society, 1988), 158. Charles Larpenteur, *Forty Years a Fur Trader*, described "mal de vache" when his men ate too much fatty meat too early in the season, 20–21; Mais diande de tanreau n'est pas très agreeable au palais, ni très-facile à digérer: cependant on me servit le meilleur morceau, la langue; 'car, me dit-on, vous n'êtes pas accoutumé à manger de cette viande, et en goutant quelques autre piece vous prendriez le *mal de boeuf*." Lettre de M. Belcourt, November 25, 1845, *Letter from the Secretary of War: Report of Major Wood*, Ex. Doc. No. 51 (1st Sess., 31st Cong., Washington, DC, 1850), 45.

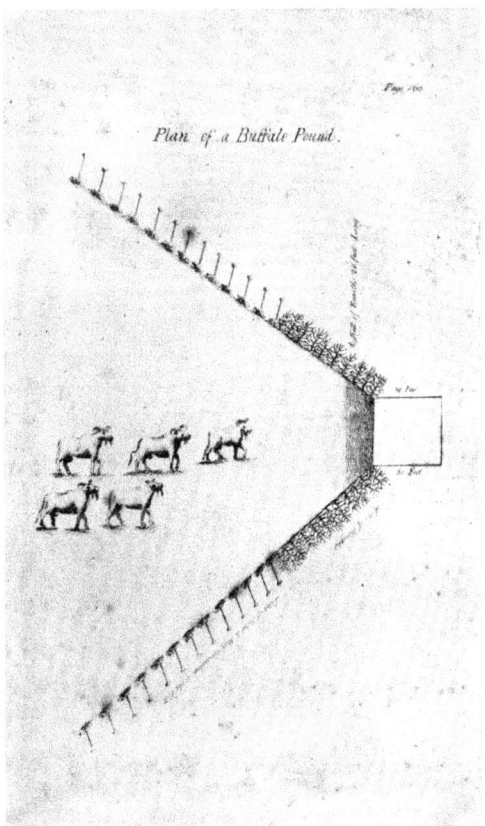

Figure 2.1. Edward Umfreville's 1790 sketch of a pound (Source: *The Present State of Hudson's Bay* (London: Charles Stalker, 1790, 160–161)).

incentives were good enough that these hunters often chose to make an incremental extra effort to create surpluses for trade using these communal works.[28]

One of the earliest descriptions of a bison pound appeared in the 1790s (Figure 2.1), just as the meat trade began in earnest. Edward Umfreville's memoir of the North Saskatchewan trade asserted that among the many ways of hunting bison, it was the pound, or "park," "by which the greatest numbers are taken."[29]

---

[28] HBCA. See agreement reached with Canadians to hunt, December 26, 1793, Brandon House Journals, B.22/a/1.

[29] Edward Umfreville, *The Present State of Hudson's Bay* (London: Charles Stalker, 1790), 160–161.

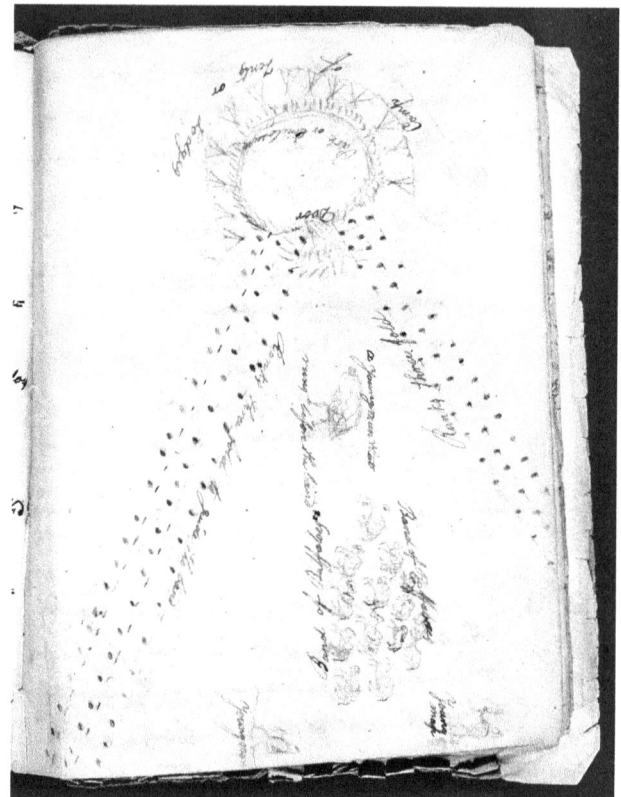

Figure 2.2. John Macdonell's manuscript sketch of an Assiniboine River pound, 1797 (Source: IMFTP # 0036, McGill Rare Books Collection).

John Macdonell of Garth left a faint pencil sketch of a pound in his own manuscript on the Assiniboine trade in 1797 (Figure 2.2).[30] The diagram shows a close-packed band of animals that would have been separated from a larger winter herd. Humans in front and back imitate distressed calves or threatening wolves to move the animals along, and people in ranks of three on both sides of the running lane drive animals into the "park" for their destruction.

These pounds usually astounded Europeans for their effectiveness. Duncan M'Gillivray at Fort George saw nearby pounds busy by December, 1796, in the poplar and aspen groves in the Battle River and Sand Hills complex of present-day Alberta. Similar to the pound later

[30] McGill Rare Books Library. John Macdonell, "Some Account of the Red River," Sketch, from manuscript, ca. 1797, MFTP #0036.

Figure 2.3. Paul Kane, "A Buffalo Pound" Plains Cree, Royal Ontario Museum 912.1.33.

romanticized by artist Paul Kane (Figure 2.3), Cree and "Strongwoods" and "Grand" or South Branch Assiniboine had a half dozen of these works organized in the fragmented parkland and in creek bottoms. M'Gillivray visited one pound orchestrated by the Cree camp of *Grandes Mains* to see running lanes extend far back into the forest-fescue grass patches. Thickets of brambles and felled small trees lined the lanes. Here and there, "deadman" sentinels were propped up like scarecrows to move wayward animals back into lanes. The killing area was invisible just over the brow of a hill where hunters rained arrows on the corralled animals. M'Gillivray commented that these poundmakers "have invented so many methods for the destruction of animals, that they stand no need of ammunition to provide a sufficiency for these purposes." [31]

Whatever the windfalls derived from these works in good times, the Cree and Assiniboine were never certain that winter conditions would favor poundmaking. Consequently, compared to plains "buffalo people" farther west and south, the Cree and some of the eastern Assiniboine bands were seasonal bison hunters. They were generalists who, should circumstances dictate, broke up pounding camps and hunted in smaller bands, or bandlets, over the winter. Moose, deer, bear, and other animals

---

[31] Arthur S. Morton, ed., *The Journal of Duncan M'Gillivray of the North West Company at Fort George on the Saskatchewan, 1794–5* (Toronto: Macmillan, 1929), 43–44.

awaited them in these "edge" ecological environments. Indeed, for these generalists, bison meat might have been "excellent eating" but was never regarded "so delicious and palatable as that of the Moose."[32] As Merle Massie has recently argued, such generalized subsistence and economic pursuits defined forest edge human adaptation. A chancier environment called for a broader repertoire of hunting techniques and varied subsistence rounds, unlike activities of hunters whose focus was on "core" hunting areas abounding in bison herds in the xeric grasses farther inland.[33]

For trading companies wanting food, however, this edge dynamic proved critical for their success. Trade benefited from the sheer uncertainty of the parkland, a proposition strongly at odds with a widely accepted "parkland convergence" model advanced in the 1970s. This posited that bison cycled regularly like clockwork out of summer plains territory to seek shelter in parkland ecotone in the winter. There, Assiniboine and Cree awaited their arrival to form large, well fed congregations. Ecologists such as Grace Morgan supported the idea. Morgan's plant ecology work emphasized the predictability of bison migration into arcs of plains, prairie, and parkland grasses that cured in different moments of the year. A type of creeping barrage of cool and warm season vegetation matured from spring, summer, and fall that moved bison herds on and off the plains every year. According to this view, winter grazers finally reached parkland. There they converged into large aggregations to munch on that king of grasses, bunch fescue. Late-curing and bulked up in nutrients far into winter, fescue belts within the aspen groves made for superb sheltered forage.[34] Assiniboine and Cree, meanwhile, hedged their bets on where winter grazers would migrate by burning. They set fire to some grasses in the fall (to encourage earlier and richer cool-season spring grass forage in one area) or in spring (to circumscribe a herd's movement away from a desired location) to increase the certainty of this cycling. The convergence model suggested that in cooperative camps, and facing declining opportunities as hunters and beaver traders elsewhere,

---

[32] January 15, 1801, *Harmon's Journal*, 32.
[33] Merle Massie, *Forest Prairie Edge: Place History in Saskatchewan* (Winnipeg: University of Manitoba Press, 2014), 26–67; see also Richard White, *Roots of Dependency: Subsistence, Environment, and Social Change among the Choctaws, Pawnees, and Navajos* (Lincoln: University of Nebraska Press, 1983), 167–171.
[34] R. Grace Morgan, "Beaver Ecology/ Beaver Mythology," PhD dissertation, Department of Anthropology, University of Alberta, 1991, 20–33, 37–45; Theordore Binnema describes the "annual cycle" of bison and hunters in *Common and Contested Ground: A Human and Environmental History of the Northwestern Plains* (Toronto: University of Toronto Press, 2001), 37–49.

Assiniboine and Cree rapidly reoriented themselves economically in the bison hunt and became specialist provisioners. "The increasing size of the provision requirement of the fur trade offered them new economic opportunities ... the primary focus of their trading activities [changed] from the exchange of furs to the bartering of dried meat and grease in a relatively short period of time," as Arthur Ray, one of the scholars advancing the parkland convergence theory, has written.[35]

Some of the convergence model holds true, in certain circumstances. Fur trade journals confirm that hunters waited for bison to "rise" with sharp, cold winter temperatures. "The bison are still a considerable distance farther out on the spacious Plains," Harmon wrote in early December from Fort Alexandria, "and nothing but severe Cold weather, will drive them into the more woody part of the Country."[36] The greater winter seasonality in the northern latitudes of the plains frequently provided this critical push into parkland. Zooarchaeologist Jonathan Driver

---

[35] Arthur J. Ray, *Indians in the Fur Trade: Their Role as Trappers, Hunters, and Middlemen in the Lands Southwest of Hudson Bay, 1660–1870* (Toronto: University of Toronto Press, 1998), 131. In one of the more important studies of the provisions market, Ray affirmed this thesis that "Indians were quick to appreciate the opportunities the new provision market offered to them.... The expanded market for buffalo meat products after 1789 had significant implications for the native suppliers." Arthur J. Ray (1984), "The Northern Great Plains: Pantry of the Northwestern Fur Trade, 1774–1885," *Prairie Forum*, 9(2):264–265. "The Assiniboine adapted themselves to the role of provisioners very quickly ... They had been suppliers of pemmican by 1780.... By 1790, the former interest in trapping and freighting was replaced by an ongoing quest for buffalo." Gerald Friesen, *The Canadian Prairies: A History* (Toronto: University of Toronto Press, 1987), 40. John S. Milloy carefully detailed the progression of "Saskatchewan Cree" adopting a "plains-associated way of life" before European direct trade. By the 1790s, he writes, "the transition from beaver hunts to buffalo, from forest to plain, was completed." *The Plains Cree*, 27. The same economic motive explains the opening up, later, of the provisions trade to Fort Union and the Upper Missouri Outfit under the direction of the American Fur Company, whereby Assiniboine seeking trade extended their provisions hunting ever southward to find American markets. The economic 'reorientation' of the Assiniboine is affirmed William A. Dobak (Spring 1996), "Killing the Canadian Buffalo, 1821–1881," *Western Historical Quarterly*, 27(1):39–48. On Assiniboine reorientation to Fort Union markets, see Nicolas Barbour, *Fort Union and the Upper Missouri Fur Trade*, 7. This materialist explanation was, understandably, popular among world systems anthropologists: see Eric Wolf *Europe and the People without a History* (Berkeley: University of California Press, 1997), 178–181. On economic specialization and market reorientation in other contexts of the Great Plains, see Dan Flores (September 1991), "Dan Flores, "Bison Ecology and Bison Diplomacy," *History*, 78(2):465–485; Andrew Isenberg, *The Destruction of the Bison: An Environmental History, 1750–1920* (Cambridge: Cambridge University Press, 2000); James E. Sherow (Summer 1992), "Workings of the Geodialectic: High Plains Indians and Their Horses in the Region of the Arkansas River, 1800–1870," *Environmental History Review*, 16:81.

[36] December 2, 1800, *Harmon's Journal*, 29.

has argued that the greater winter seasonality of the Northern Plains made for larger communal hunts in fall and early winter when animals – notably cows – were their fattest. He identified a zone 40 to 49°N latitude and beyond ideally providing for such group winter hunts. The incidence for such large events declined in more southerly latitudes, between 30° and 39° and 20° to 29°. These most southerly latitudes coincided with the territories of the Santa Clara, Jemez Pueblo, Navaho, and Paiute and Southeastern Indians.[37] Communal hunting, it would seem, was effective because it did not pay according to an equal ratio of effort. Rather, in pounding locations even an incrementally smaller effort translated into quantitatively larger returns – a minimum investment of human work could direct more animals into the same killing area, for instance. The payoff was in prized, life-saving fat, the food most sought in the low-carbohydrate worlds of Northern Plains and subarctic people. It was fortuitous, too, that bitterly cold winters in these northern latitudes even affected the physiology of bison. The animal, particularly cows in gestation, tended to become larger and fatter north of the Yellowstone.[38]

But although hunters waited for bison to "rise," the reality was that throughout the steppe and the parkland belt long periods could pass when the bison simply did not cooperate (Figure 2.4). The people of the Winnipeg Steppe frequently met with early deep falls of snow, unexpectedly mild temperatures, or devastating fires that disrupted bison migration into parkland areas. Archaeology since the 1970s has undermined the "parkland convergence" model by suggesting that likely larger herds – perhaps on the order of 4:1 in terms of numbers – remained on the plains year round, summer and winter.[39] Bison were admirably adapted to the high winds and bitter temperatures of the open plains;

[37] Jonathan C. Driver, "Meat in Due Season: the timing of Communal Hunts," Leslie B. Davis and Brian O.K. Reeves, eds., *Hunters of the Recent Past* (London: Unwin Hyman, 1990), 15–16.

[38] One Métis remembered the difference between bison north and south of the Missouri: "There were a lot buffalo living south of the Missouri. They were different from our northern type and smaller and more compact than ours…" Marie Rose Smith, "I Remember," unpublished manuscript, Glenbow Archives, Calgary, M1184. Henry Lewis Morgan was told at Pembina by an experienced trader that "the buffalo which come from the south of the Missouri are smaller than those north of it, and that the hunters can tell them at once." Lewis Henry Morgan, *The Indian Journals*, 142. The more recent physiology and anatomical examination confirms this. See Alice Marie Emerson, "Archaeological Implications of Variability in the Economic Anatomy of *Bison bison*," PhD thesis, Washington State University, 1990, 69–70.

[39] Henry Epp and Ian Dyck (2002), "Early Human-Bison Population Interdependence in the Plains Ecosystem," *Great Plains Research: A Journal of Natural and Social Sciences*, 325–326; Eleanor Verbicky-Todd, "Communal Buffalo Hunting among the Plains Tribes," 5–7. J. Rod Vickers and Trevor R. Peck, "Islands in a Sea of Grass: The Significance of Wood

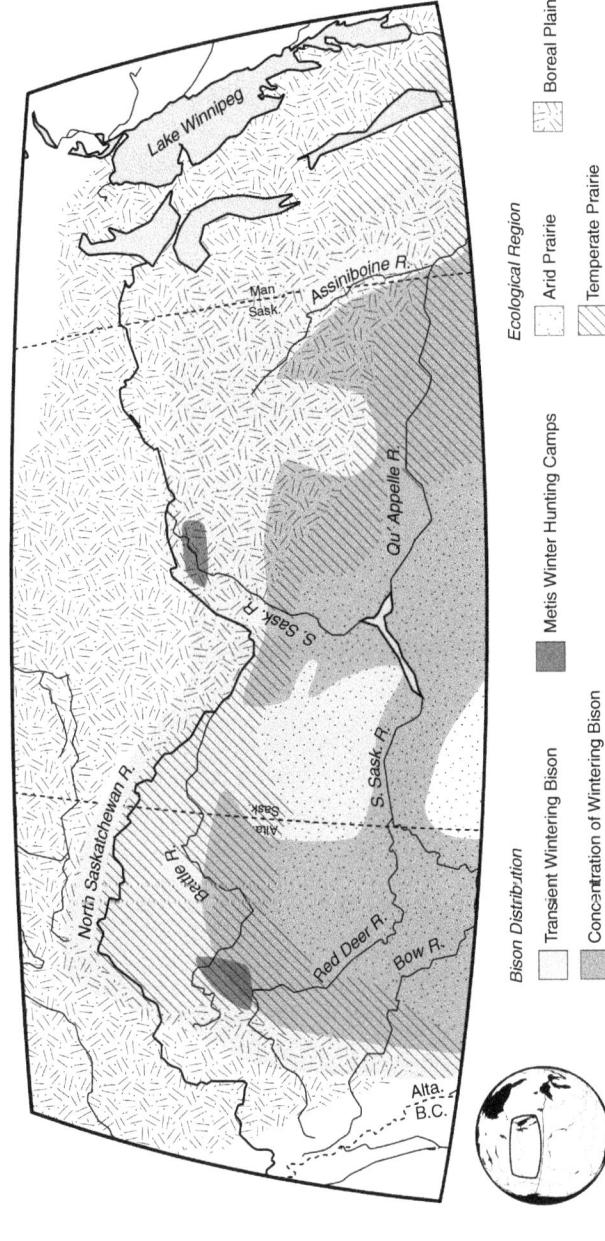

Figure 2.4. Likely winter bison distribution, 19th century (map by Shawn Mueller, 2013).

more importantly, high plains winds tended to sweep snow from the terrain exposing shorter grasses supercharged with C_4 energy that would have more than supported these grazers.[40] By contrast, deeper snow tended to accumulate in the moister climate of parkland, making it difficult for bison to reach grasses buried below. Massive winter kills followed freak snow dumps in forested valleys and outlier hill country – such early season and heavy snowfall likely sealed the fate for some of the last Utah herds in the 1870s. At the very least, mild or snowy weather could halt altogether the comparatively smaller migratory elements of large plains herds into the parkland areas.[41] It was likely the perennial difficulties met with early arrivals to places such as Red River, where hunting was uncertain from the start, that gave the erroneous impression that there was a "progressive 'retreat' or shrinking of the buffalo frontier," as F. G. Roe made clear.[42] In the Central Plains region, Richard White, in the case of Pawnee hunting territories, also suggests that these "peripheral" areas of tall grass were never attractive to true bison hunting specialists. They organized their seasonal rounds to bypass them directly to access the shorter grass areas of the plains, accordingly.[43]

The greater uncertainty of winter hunting, all the same, made parkland people hunting generalists. It also made them consummate traders, alert to the possibilities and benefits of food trading for their long-term survival. It is of some irony, then, that European traders, so often notable

in Winter Campsite Selection on the Northwestern Plains," in Brian Kooyman and Jane H. Kelley, *Archaeology on the Edge: New Perspectives from the Northern Plains* (Calgary: University of Calgary Press, 2004), 95–124.

[40] Merle Massie, "At the Edge," 46–48; Mary E. Malainey and Barbara L. Sherriff (1996), "Adjusting Our Perceptions: Historical and Archaeological Evidence of Winter on the Plains of Western Canada," *Plains Anthropologist*, 41(158):333–357; David Meyer and Henry T. Epp (1995), "North-South Interaction in the Late Prehistory of Central Saskatchewan," *Plains Anthropologist*, 35(132):321–340.

[41] Richmond Clow (Fall 1995), "Bison Ecology, Brulé and Yankton Winter Hunting, and the Starving Winter of 1832–33," *Great Plains Quarterly*, 15:259–270. On destructive effects of heavy snow falls, particularly the famous Laramie Plains killing, see Frank Gilbert Roe, Chapter 8, *The North American Buffalo: A Critical Study of the Species in Its Wild State* (Toronto: University of Toronto Press, 1951), 180–203; see Roe's article on this topic, "Buffalo and Snow," *Canadian Historical Review*, 17:125–146 (1936).

[42] F. G. Roe, *The North American Buffalo: A Critical Study of the Species in Its Wild State* (Toronto: University of Toronto Press, 1970), 369. Binnema suggests the parkland convergence model needs "only minor modification," and it likely does in the eastern slopes region and among the truly "buffalo people" who hunted bison year round. Binnema, *Common and Contested Ground*, 39. The model, however, has considerably less power in the eastern areas of the plains.

[43] Richard White, *Roots of Dependency: Subsistence, Environment, and Social Change among the Choctaws, Pawnees, and Navajos* (Lincoln: University of Nebraska Press, 1983), 167–169.

for the vast quantities they amassed and shipped out of the prairie and parkland, were in fact supported by food-sharing traditions reinforced by the frequently penurious conditions of the region. Indeed, it became common in the environs of Fort Alexandria, on the upper Assiniboine in 1800 and 1801,[44] or, at Fort Edmonton, in the middle sections of the North Saskatchewan, for post hunters and traders to offer a mix of alternatives to bison – notably elk and moose provisions – and for years in succession arrive with nary a mouthful of bison meat, suggesting how frequently these plains animals did not reach these areas.[45]

Parkland Food Sharing

Frequent periods of penury, not plenty, then, shaped human occupation of parkland areas. Certainly, the proposition that Cree and Assiniboine immediately specialized as fur trade provisioners and did so because they benefited from the predictable winter abundance of converging herds needs to be reconsidered.[46] People enjoying plenty are often not very quick to specialize and expend labor for a market of any kind. The sheer

---

[44] Archibald McLeod's experience at Fort Alexandria, in the catchments of the Assiniboine and well within the parkland belt, recorded the typical food trades of the steppe. In 1800 and 1801 he saw almost an entire winter pass in mild temperatures. The Assiniboine and Cree nearby had pounds ready for bison, such as those organized by the Vent du Nord, and by the beginnings of February, the post made sure to send gifts of tobacco to the Great Ones' pound, this to begin a trading relationship based on kin understandings. Archibald McLeod Journal, in Charles M. Gates, ed., *Five Fur Traders of the Northwest* (St. Paul: University of Minnesota Press, 1933), 159–160. One of the post's hunters, the Batard Anglois, arrived, "seem to have a good deal of Grease." However, with almost all pounding failing, Petit Bled and Petit Sonnan (probably the smaller Sonant, or Rattle, whose people long provided the Red River post with provisions) arrived with meat from bull hunting. Some eight sledges or large sleds returned with cuts selected for the trade, in this case, heavily balanced in fat: "40 Bladders grease a little pounded meat & the rest of their loads were made up with Bosses & Depouille [hump and backfat]" *Five Fur Traders of the Northwest*, 155, 191.

[45] It was a very accurate description of the post that a good trade in provisions was made there "*when* buffalo are within reach." HBCA. Edmonton Report on District, 1862, B.60/e/9; Fort Edmonton Journals, February 21, 1827 B.60/a/25. See the reports of deer, elk and moose, all parkland animals, being the primary provision at Fort Edmonton in the winter of 1833: on January 33, 1833, there were 225 thighs and 206 shoulders "all moose and Red Deers [elk] meat," at post. Fort Edmonton Journals, B.60/a/25.

[46] See, for instance, Whelan's use of relativist models, especially the work of Stephen Gudeman, to interpret Dakota trading to the American Fur Company, Mary K. Whelan (Spring 1993), "Dakota Indian Economics and the Nineteenth-Century Fur Trade," *Ethnohistory*, 40(2):256–273; on an overview of relativist and rationalist models, or formalist and substantivist, see Stuart Plattner, ed., and introduction, *Economic Anthropology* (Stanford: Stanford University Press, 1989), 1–17.

abundance in plains environments certainly slowed the market's inroads among Blackfoot and other "buffalo people" who had very few needs for European goods. Even in parkland areas, the logic of market trading was often blunted when times were good. Alexander Henry the Elder, seeing the abundance enjoyed by the Assiniboine in present-day Manitoba, was certain that these people simply did not need anything Europeans offered. At best, they separated out meats that they did not want to trade, while making demands for only luxury items, tobacco being one, alcohol another.[47]

In parkland, it was not really the market but traditions of food sharing that enlivened exchange among newcomers and Cree and Assiniboine. The latter shared in light of their comparatively more precarious existence. They heaped obligations on newcomers whom they expected would provide relief in the future, should conditions demand it. By the 1790s, these traditions enabled Europeans to amass dried meats, hard fats, and – perhaps most indicative of the welcome of strangers – bone greases from visiting bands. There was something of a summer hunt by this point, propelled by horse power, among the Assiniboine. They had joined horses also with guns to hunt during the summer months – Brandon House by 1799 recorded at least one Ojibwa, who seem to have specialized in summer hunting. He threatened to take his summer provisions, as scanty as they were, to the Canadians if the post's supply of powder, again, failed.[48] In 1800, Assiniboine about to begin their fall hunt, likely at pounds, were complaining "very bitterly" that Brandon House had so few 3½ foot guns, because "they answer so well to hunt cattle on horseback...."[49]

But this was not a close integration of the market, or even horse power, among plains hunters who, for the most part, brought surplus generated

---

[47] Such demands for luxury assortments on the plains was in fact well demonstrated by Arthur J. Ray when he compared fur trade goods sold typically to boreal forest hunters, who truly needed utilitarian wares to help them survive, and the plains trade where Indian demand extended to luxury cloth, consumables and trinkets. See Table 6: Goods Traded at Brandon, Carlton and Cumberland House, *Indians in the Fur Trade*, 149–153; Alexander Henry the Elder, *Travels and Adventures in Canada and the Indian Territories between the Years 1760 and 1776* (Edmonton: M. G. Hurtig, 1969), 275–276.

[48] It is telling that the complaint was made by Captain Jepormawish, an Ojibwa, March 27, 1799, HBCA, Brandon House Journals, B.22/a/6.

[49] HBCA. Brandon House Journals, September 21, 1800, B.22/a/8. By 1794, John Macdonell stated that horses "are spread all over as far as the plains extend – the natives use them in war and to [word illegible] down buffaloes," in John Macdonell, Gates, ed., *The Diary of Five Fur Traders*, 113.

at fall pounds to trade. During their first years at Brandon House on the Assiniboine, HBC traders hosted Assiniboine and Cree arriving from fall pounds in October. According to "the custom in these parts," they met these guests within the fort itself, these people bringing their trade almost indifferently to Montreal and English traders. The posts in turn made "captains" of chiefs with gifts of coats and hats, symbolically adopting these influential individuals through gifts of tobacco and other items. With this relationship established, bands arrived to trade "plenty of meat, fatt, and tongues."[50] As expected by their Indian initiators, trades like these mixed exchange with social expectations and onerous debt. Many of the exchanges were in consumable items – albeit often in notorious and sometimes lethal quantities of alcohol. So, the Ojibwa Captain Quinquehanea brought five cows (the equivalent of forty beaver skins) and "also fat," undoubtedly derived from a successful pound where such quantities did not constitute much effort on his band's part.[51] Locals not otherwise exerting themselves to trap furs brought excess flesh: they "brot few furs but plenty of beat meat" as Brandon's traders recorded.[52]

Women centrally figured in these exchange relations.[53] Hunters arriving with provisions brought women to help dry meats, prepare fats, and cut up bull skins for sacks and making pemmican. But they further

[50] HBCA. See Robert Goodwin's Brandon House Journals, October 22, November 161794, B.22/a/2.
[51] Ibid., February 21, 1795.
[52] Ibid., February 16, 1795.
[53] On women in the fur trade, see Sylvia Van Kirk, *Many Tender Ties: Women in Fur-Trade Society in Western Canada, 1670–1870* (Winnipeg: Watson & Dwyer, 1980), Jennifer Brown, *Strangers in Blood: Fur Trade Company Families in Indian Country* (Vancouver: UBC Press, 1980). Katherine Weist, "Beasts of Burden and Menial Slaves: Nineteenth Century Observations of Northern Plains Indian Women," in Patricia Albers and Beatrice Medicine, eds., *The Hidden Half: Studies of Plains Indian Women* (Washington, DC: University Press of America, 1983), 29–52. William R. Swagerty (April 1980), "Marriage and Settlement Patterns of Rocky Mountain Trappers and Traders," *Western Historical Quarterly*, 11:159–80; also, John Mack Faragher, "The Custom of the Country: Cross-Cultural Marriage in the Far Western Fur Trade, in Lillian Schlissel, Vicki L. Ruiz, and Janice Monk, eds., *Western Women: Their Land, Their Lives* (Albuquerque: University of New Mexico Press, 1988), 199–220. Susan Sleeper-Smith (Spring 2000), "Women, Kin and Catholicism: New Perspectives on the Fur Trade," *Ethnohistory*, 47(2):423–452. Michael Lansing (2000), "Plains Indian Women and Interracial Marriage in the Upper Missouri Trade, 1804–1868," *Western Historical Quarterly*, 31(4):413–433. Richard J. Perry (1979), "The Fur Trade and the Status of Women in the Western Subarctic," *Ethnohistory*, 26(4):363–375. Jennifer S. H. Brown, "Partial Truths: A Closer Look at Fur Trade Marriage," in Theodore Binnema, Gerhard J. Ens, and R. C. Macleod, eds., *From Rupert's Land to Canada: Essays in Honour of John E. Foster* (Edmonton: University of Alberta Press, 2001), 59–80.

cemented social relations at posts, when, for instance, war parties left women and children in the care of Europeans. The Cordoniers Ojibwa, going to the war against the Mandans, left their children and women with James Sutherland by 1798, now master at Brandon House, "a heavy burden," he fretted. The men, however, had already sent word to the larger Ojibwa kinship networks in the region to send provisions now and then to support the post's pensioners over the summer. By the end of the season, the band's men returned to join their women and children, Sutherland now finding them all "lying here still a lazy sett will not hunt and says we have a right to maintain them."[54]

John McKay, the brother of Mad Donald, helped open the bison trade and became a long-time Brandon House master (he eventually died in the summer of 1810, by an undisclosed and painful physical affliction, leaving an Ojibwa wife and eight children). He complained in 1803 of the Assiniboine invalids left at his house, which "creates a deal of expenses." Undoubtedly he was supporting them, and saw many others also arriving who, by custom, felt that they "must" treat these individuals and again when they left. "I have maintained since last Fall, a cripple man a blind woman and two other women, which lays heavy on the House particularly this poor year," he said of these drains on incoming food supplies.[55]

Fur traders understood that food exchanges were wrapped in implicit and at times explicit expectations of their reciprocation. They constituted gifts which, in the Indian sense, opened relations and usually obligated the receiver to return them either immediately or in the future. The Ojibwa helping some of James Sutherland's men survive on a poor hunting trip in 1796 knew that the men returning to the post with some 100 lbs. of fresh meat would be good for it. They expected it would "be paid for by and by."[56] There were also the Cree who saved the life of Jacob Henderson who had gotten lost hunting in the dead of winter outside of Brandon House and nearly froze to death. The Cree who discovered him brought him to their camp. The "natives was [sic] very kind to him," James Sutherland wrote, and "took great care of him," drying his clothes, giving him new moccasins, and restoring him back to health with food and water. When Henderson regained strength, he was returned to Brandon House. But after the chief trader gave gifts for their help, Henderson's

---

[54] HBCA. July 20–28, 1797, Brandon House Journals, B.22/a/4 1797–1798.
[55] HBCA. November 17, 1802, Brandon House Journals, B.22/a/11.
[56] HBCA. July 12, 1796, Brandon House Journals, B.22/a/3.

rescuers continued to return to demand more, "for the services rendered one of my men," Sutherland fumed.[57] What these bands practiced was not a form of tit-for-tat bartering of food, but a cycling of gift and counter gifts. Fundamental was to offer a share of the hunt, expecting as much from their own kin as their fictive kin relations. Hunting bands, much to the frustration of Brandon House employees, made it a custom of carrying indifferently a part of their trade "to the other houses."[58] Among Ojibwa, the rule of hospitality held, that they would "not suffer them to be in want among us," John Tanner in his own camp observed, and "if our own game was not sufficient, we were sure to be supplied by some of our friends, as long as any thing could be killed."[59]

The Nor'Wester, Charles Chaboillez, who traded nearby among the Ojibwa by 1797 (the HBC traders referred to this rival on the Assiniboine as the "diabolical rascal Chaboillez")[60] learned to account for the differences in food and fur trades. The fur trade typically necessitated credits and in his frequent meetings in September and October of 1797, Chaboillez noted advances to be paid in the future to the same amount. The food trade was another matter. Food in the form of fish, bales of dried meat, fresh meat, ducks, bags of fat, and bladders of grease arrived to the post, but they were often returned in different ways. Food exchanges rebounded between the parties in inflationary terms. In such circumstances, Chaboillez distinguished between three types of exchange: credit, related to the fur trade, and *sans dessein*, a type of native exchange usually in consumable product that led to onerous, often inflationary, reciprocation and implied a de facto forming of close kin or fictive kin relations. He also kept track of food "gifts," proper. However, to give food without its return was an embarrassment for everyone involved. To save face for one's partner, one took a reciprocal gift of food or some other consumable product, and, by doing so, participated in a sharing, quasi-kin relationship.

Chaboillez was encountering Ojibwa who had only recently moved into the plains region from shield territories to the east and whose food trading protocols proved important in these new circumstances. At the

---

[57] Ibid., December 28, 1796.
[58] HBCA. November 16, 1794, Brandon House Journals, B.22/a/2.
[59] Edward James, ed., *A Narrative of the Captivity and Adventures of John Tanner (US Interpreter at the Saut de Ste. Marie): During Thirty Years Among the Indians in the Interior of North America* (New York: G.&C.&H. Carvill, 1830 [1956]), 51.
[60] HBCA. Thomas Miller to Brandon House, November 15, 1797, Brandon House Journals, B.22/a/5.

forks of the Red and Assiniboine Rivers, Chaboillez met Old Erantes and sons. After the trader opened trade by showing his intentions in a standard gift of tobacco and a dram of brandy, Old Erantes "made a Present of Twenty Pieces [a *piece* was typically about 100 lbs.) Dryed Meat 8 Sturgeons – for which I paid Him Twenty Eight Pints Rum and gave them each Two Pints *sans Dessein*."[61]

Throughout his journal, Chaboillez made these distinctions. His visitors opened trade with a gift of food; Chaboillez paid for it, usually in consumable equivalents; he added a little more to show generosity and solidify trust upon which the fur trade could function. On the present-day Morris River, the French trader's exchanges often blurred completely into social exchanges that set up more substantial fur trading. The Ojibwa, in a party of at least eleven men and women with children, arrived in four tents. After his usual gift of introduction, the camp returned the gift and "made a present" of their own: fresh meat and grease to the value of a large keg of mixed rum that was duly paid back. The "boisson" then started, during which "more fresh meat" was given "to the amot of Ten Skins."[62] During the night, the exchanges thoroughly mixed up the parties involved. Chaboillez expended one-third of another keg *sans dessein*. Come morning, alcohol now made its ruinous mark. Fighting left two Ojibwa with stab wounds in the "Arms and Body." As the parties separated, fall credit attached to the fur trade was extended: some forty-nine skins worth of goods including tobacco, powder shot, balls, gunworms, and needles. These were understood to be returned with the skins in the spring.

Food exchanges made these posts social and political meeting places. In the case of the Ojibwa Gavion Bouche, who arrived with a good quantity of provisions, Chaboillez gave lavish presents: twenty phiols mixed rum and four pints of rum *sans dessein*. So persuasive was this gift that Bouche retrieved his "medicine bag" from Sutherland's HBC post, presumably to leave it at Charles' house instead. In the native world, the medicine bag was believed key to an individual's hunting or war success, linking him to animal gamekeepers who protected the hunter and gave up animals for human subsistence. Leaving it in the care of either trader implied complete trust.[63] Chaboillez, of course, was practically

---

[61] Harold Hickerson, ed. (September 1797), "The Journal of Charles Jean Baptiste Chaboillez, 1797–98," *Ethnohistory*, 14:278.
[62] September 18, 1797, "The Journal of Charles Jean Baptiste Chaboillez," 278.
[63] Ibid., October 6, 1796, 282.

orienting himself to the local customs. He lavished attention and gifts to bandlet leaders such as Little Outard, who, Charles openly admitted, likely stopped his followers "from Pillaging our People" who were, at that point, wintering, trading, and hunting in Ojibwa territory nearby.[64]

As critical, but rarely given their due in journals, were women and their considerable labor in transforming food. Although men often gave food in its rawest form fresh off the stage, in the hump, or simply dried, it was often the higher processed and, by implication, more valuable commodities that women owned and traded. So, typically, "Arrived a Woman who brought 4obs Grease, 2 Beaver Skins, 1 wolf," Chaboillez recorded. There was also the prominent Old Coutre Oreille, with her two sons, who were credited thirty skins.[65] Another "old woman" "brought four piece dryed meat, 3 Buffaloe sides [bull skins for pemmican bags], 2 packs cords & 2 Bladders Grease...."[66] As Bruce White has demonstrated, matrilineal and matrilocal Ojibwan bands recognized women as the owners of the food and goods they processed. That meant fur traders often dealt more with women than men when they sought wild rice, meats, and other foodstuffs. Like the Ojibwa, Cree trades at Brandon House too, seem to have been orchestrated by women, who in the 1790s exchanged their meats for ammunition.[67]

The value they added to food helps explain the large number of women at posts and the disproportionately high incidence of "country marriage" and sexual relations at these posts compared to elsewhere in the fur and skin trade. Posts enlarging production by necessity recruited or found access to the labor of more women. Alexander Henry the Younger noted at Pembina Post – a provisions post on the Red River – only three men, a lone Assiniboine interpreter, and some forty women and children.[68] Any real mass production at posts ultimately depended on large numbers of women. Only women offered butchery skills to slice meat thin enough to dry well on stages; in forts, they cut down *dépouilles* to be ready to melt when the weather warmed at the end of the winter.

---

[64] Ibid., December 1, 1797, 288.
[65] Ibid., August 26, 1797, 275.
[66] Ibid., February 21, 1798, 374.
[67] HBCA. See Robert Goodwin's note, October 5, 1795, Brandon House Journals, B.22/a/3. See also Bruce M. White (Winter 1999), "The Woman Who Married a Beaver: Trade Patterns and Gender Roles in the Ojibwa Fur Trade," 46(1):109–147.
[68] Noted by Alexander Henry the Younger, cited in Trevor Richard Peck, "Bison Ethology and native Settlement Patterns During the Old Women's Phase on the Northwestern Plains," PhD thesis, University of Calgary, 2001, 95.

At Fort Augustus (near present-day Edmonton), where twenty-eight men were posted, thirty-five women were on hand to cut down about three tonnes of back fat in two days in March of 1810.[69] Fort Edmonton itself had forty-six men, twenty-five women, and eighty-six children in 1833, the entirety of the post given over to pemmican making in due season.[70] Women also flensed *taureaux*, bags made from bulls' skins and representing a sizeable labor component in pemmican-making. Fort Pitt journals noted that traders "gave out to the women of the fort" hundreds of "pair of shears [the equivalent of scalping knives or scissors] to cut skins" for pemmican bagging.[71] The women at Fort Vermillion in 1809 used horses to leave for days at a stretch to collect choke, Saskatoon, and other berries in season (these becoming important to add to pemmican and preserve its shelf life); some thirty-three at the post switched to making bales of *wattapee* from bison sinew that year, among many, many other critical steps in provisioning.

The considerable work at provisioning posts provided by women is suggested in Alexander Henry the Younger's census of North West Company (NWC) posts in boreal compared to prairie areas. These indicate that on average there was double the proportion of women in conjugal relations with the post men in prairie postings (a woman for every 0.62 man) compared to subarctic, boreal posts (where there was only 0.36). The census, made in 1805, also estimates aboriginal populations. If "Indian" populations alone are considered, the proportional number of women to men is significant in the prairie post areas, where there were an average of 1.67 women per man; in the woodland areas, 1.24 women per man.[72]

It is difficult to know how many advantages actually passed to women doing such heavy labor. At Brandon House, Jollycoeur, a Canadian in

---

[69] The women started March 20 and ended March 21. *Journal of Alexander Henry the Younger*, II, 435. Henry recorded that they bagged 293 bags of pemmican and 84 kegs of grease by the end of the season, 438.
[70] HBCA. March 31, 1833, Fort Edmonton Journals, B.60/a/27.
[71] HBCA. March 15, 1832, Fort Pitt Journals, B.165/a/2.
[72] For the census, see *Journal of Alexander Henry the Younger* I 188; I have averaged Upper Red River, Lower Red River and Fort des Prairies as a representative of prairie posts: for "Whites," there were 1 woman for every 0.92 man; 1 for every 0.53 and 1 for every 0.43 men, respectively; and for the "Boreal": Athabasca, Athabasca River and English River Posts, where there was one "white" woman for every 0.23 man; and 0.32 and 0.53 for every man, respectively. The "Indian" populations for the same posts show 1.02 women for every man; 1.18 and 2.82 women for every man, respectively in prairie posts; and 0.69 women for every man in Athabasca River; and 1.80 women for every man in English River (the Athabasca Post numbers are unavailable).

employ at the post in 1798, "wanted an old woman to keep he having had one before this year only some of ye Canadians took her away last winter.... He says every Frenchman has a woman and why should we stop him."[73] The shift to larger scales of production most likely alienated some of a woman's means of production, and very likely exploited her labor. The "freemen" near Fort la Souris, during a particularly bad summer of hunting in 1806, had "actually disposed of their women and Clothing to the H.B.Co. people in Barter for beat Meat," according to Alexander Henry the Younger.[74]

Given their joining in food-sharing traditions, it is perhaps not surprising that provisions trading posts, so well stocked with food almost year round, became refuges. The Ojibwa, Cree, and Assiniboine often returned with their dead to be buried in European fashion at the post, or staged in Indian tradition, but almost always within a coffin supplied by the post's carpenters. The Cree Jepowmannish was one of many captains who provided "much provisions, fat, tongues" and "piece meat" to Brandon House. He also brought the corpse of one of his wives for staging at the post within a European coffin.[75] Many of the offspring of a post's major food suppliers did the same. Round Hill, an Ojibwa whose "crews" came and went from the post at Red River, had a daughter buried there in 1810,[76] as did Weetassaooiny, who buried a child at the post that year.[77]

Post storehouses benefited from the frequent buffalo abundance of the steppe prairie and parkland; but their trade depended above all on food-sharing traditions of people adapted to the comparative uncertainty of the edge environment. Posts generally dealt exclusively with generalist forest-adapted hunters who seasonally hunted winter herds when the sharp, cold temperatures drove them into shelter areas. Beyond the material benefits of the market for bison flesh, these food traders entered exchanges and heaped obligations on European newcomers that in the future might guard against want. Within two seasons of his own post's establishment in the prairie, Robert Goodwin recognized that

---

[73] HBCA. November 13, 1798, Robert Goodwin's Journal at Brandon House, B.22/a/6.
[74] August 10, 1806, *Journal of Alexander Henry the Younger*, Vol. I, 291.
[75] HBCA. Such as the case of Captain Grant and his wife, bringing the body of his child to the post. July 28, 1805, Brandon House Journals, 1805–1806, B.22/a/13.
[76] Library and Archives Canada [hereafter "LAC"]Old Blindy with the Round Hills Daughter to be buried," September 30, 1810, Red River Journals, *Selkirk Papers, Series A*, 16501–16524.
[77] LAC. December 8, 1810, ibid.

Brandon House "can supply the other settlements [in the subarctic] with Pemetcon in ye same manner as ye Canadians does." He frequently saw, as he did in the fall of 1797, the arrival of 300 men, women, and children with 400 to 500 dogs. A group of this size took an entire day to shuttle over the river to Brandon in the post's bateaux. Goodwin's post, however, was situated well within an ecotone region that encouraged food exchange and the obligations such relations implied. With seven chiefs representing the whole, the clerk finally gave up trying to describe the foods that arrived with them. He wrote, simply, "These savages have brot vast quantity."[78]

A Fat Frontier

The market eventually found fertile ground in this region for another reason. Alcohol, gifts, and ever larger disbursements of European wares, even luxuries, saw pound makers invest more effort into provisioning Europeans. The market began at some point to creep into existing modes of production, but only to a certain degree. This was likely occurring as early as 1795, when "vast numerous bands" visited Brandon House, the nearby XY Company post, and the NWC post, in such procession that a single Cree band arriving to the former numbering some 300 (with 400 to 500 dogs), and brought with them some 1,350 lbs. of dried meat, 400 lbs. of half dried, 600 lbs. of "green" (fresh), 400 lbs. of fat, and 168 lbs. of pounded meat, as well as 30 tongues to trade.[79] Surpluses grew and factory organization began to apply to stockpiles of meat and fat.

Initially, Bandon House's harried employees coped by making a "large lodge" from two tents to manufacture pemmican, undoubtedly with fires keeping vats of water boiling to separate fats.[80] Imposing log-walled cellars, meat sheds, and ice houses became center points in a post's economy. Meat sheds ranged in size between fourteen and twenty feet, as was the "hangard" at Fort George, to smaller affairs. In its first year, Brandon

---

[78] HBCA. See Robert Goodwin's Journal, Brandon House, on "custom in these parts," November 16, on Ojibwa sending corpse to post, December 17 on Captain Jepoumannish's tent, with dead child, February 6, Captain Pepea, tu, ca sending a son with meat and fat, February 10 "with much provision," on five lodges of Indians coming in, February 16; on Quinquehanea, February 21, 1795, B.22/a/2; and *John Linklater's Journal*, Brandon House, October 4, 1795, B.22/a/3.
[79] HBCA. October 6, 1795, Brandon House Journals, B.22/a/3.
[80] HBCA. May 9, 1796, John Linklater's Journal, Brandon House, B.22/a/3.

House stored meats "in the loft" of the main building, but by spring its staff scrambled to build something more protective. When warm temperatures in March caught employees off guard the post lost about a ton of beat meat. Without ice the "warm weather will soon spoilt the whole which is a great loss."[81] Brandon House's ice houses kept meat frozen only until August 1, when the summer heat finally got them, "the ice so bad" about 1,000 lbs. of "stinking meat" needed to be tossed.[82] Summer temperatures finally ruined ice houses, necessitating their burning to the ground at the end of a season before their rebuilding the next winter, with, one suspects, the rancid fats sizzling in their timbers.

Ice houses were a critical innovation in the Winnipeg Steppe, especially as the trade grew in size and effectiveness. The NWC's Pembina Post had an ice house of such size that, when bison were so close in December and January that animals were literally shot from the fort's walls, the ice house filled rapidly with ice and meat, "sufficient to last until July next."[83] Six months of fresh meat, much of it in the form of thighs and shoulders, would have comprised at least 63,000 lbs., if not more.[84] After meat sheds were constructed in mid-January 1814 and the chief trader gave staff orders to increase the provisions trade, the HBC's Carlton House saw days when 135 bison thighs (6,353 lbs.) were put away on a single day, similarly as on February 9 when another 69 thighs (3,217 lbs.) were put on ice. During the two months from December 9 to February 9, the post took in the meat of no less than 107 bison. The postmaster, John Pruden, fastidiously recorded weights when fresh meat arrived. They totaled 44,412 lbs.[85] So flush was the meat trade in these years that Carlton House in 1815 completely filled its meat sheds in a single month with some 200 bison, and by November 25, the staff scrambled to build extra staging in the courtyard for the meat still continuing to come in.[86]

---

[81] HBCA. April 1, 12, 1794, Brandon House Journals, B.22/a/1; Robert Goodwin, at Brandon House had to increase meat purchases in the autumn 1795 because his staff had been "obliged to throw away vast Quantitys of piece meat in Summer it could keep no longer and the dogs would scarcely eat it." October 3, 1795, Brandon House Journals, B.22/a/3.

[82] HBCA. July 31 and August 1, 1805, Brandon House Journals, B.22/a/13.

[83] January 1, 1808, *Journal of Alexander Henry the Younger*, Vol. I, 300.

[84] This is the weight Henry listed as meat consumed when he was postmaster there September 1 and June 1 that year, ibid., 317.

[85] HBCA. February 9, 1815, Carlton House Journals, B.27/a/4. These meat trade totals are derived from December 9 through February 9, 1815.

[86] HBCA. See November 25, 1815, Carlton House Journals, B.27/a/5.

When Europeans competed, eventually violently, for the supplies in the steppe, a point to be discussed in the next chapter, they enlarged ice houses in a bid to corner the market. When the HBC trader Peter Fidler took over command at Brandon in the lead up to what eventually became known as the Pemmican Wars, he refitted the ice houses to stock them with nothing less than twenty-nine tonnes of ice – the employees likely grumbling quite a bit hauling it. He boasted that he had so much snow and ice in the sheds that meats would store not only into the summer but "till snow again cover the ground."[87]

Meats were stored with the frost on. They more than served the post's needs for fresh frozen meat. A portion in spring was hurriedly transformed and sent down river in the form of pemmican. Bony meats like thighs were packed on the outside of meat piles for immediate consumption, as they tended not to store as long as roasts. The thigh bone was stored until spring, when it could be smashed down for its marrows and greases. Men regularly rotated the stock to avoid spoilage. At Fort Vermillion, the meat hanger was so well stocked that even after an entire winter's feeding at the post and 293 bags of pemmican were produced in spring (representing about 58,000 lbs. of fresh meat), the staff abandoning the fort for the season saw their icehouse containing some 400 unused limbs of buffalo, "still frozen as hard as ice."[88]

Icehouses allowed for unprecedented surpluses to accrue at European posts. They also permitted Europeans to apply mass production to traditional food making traditions, particularly pemmican making. In ideal conditions, Native tradition was to butcher bison intensively to create "traditional" and "fine" pemmican made from all elements of a carcass – its interior and exterior fats, and a variety of its meats. Mobility in the seasonal round and changing weather meant, however, that Native makers contended with less than ideal pemmican-making conditions. This was certainly the case in subarctic areas, where they frequently took recourse in varieties of "winter" pemmican production. The difficulty of drying meats (without smoke) inside Indian shelters, variable temperatures, and seasonal precipitation often forced their hands. The meat was often, properly speaking, "half dried" as it could not be beaten well to a powder and therefore could not be infused completely with fat in an airtight bag. Half-dried meat, then, was bagged together and fat was carried separately

---

[87] HBCA. March 23, 1816, Peter Fidler's Journal at Brandon House, 1815–1816, B.22/a/19.

[88] *Journal of Alexander Henry the Younger*, II, 447.

in bladders. Portions of this would be cut off to be boiled or fried with the meat when it was consumed, a type of "pemmican-on-the-go." Many references to "Ruchagan" were likely along this line – semidried bison meat mixed on the spot with grease or fat cut from bags carried along with. Because it could not be properly mixed, this pemmican also had a relatively short shelf life. Native winter pemmican was likely expected to go "bad" by early summer, if not before, but it sustained those producing it beyond the very difficult early months of the warmer season.[89]

A greater challenge was not really in drying meats as in handling fats effectively. Alexander Henry the Younger, before his pemmican-making went "in house," traveled with Ojibwa in the Park River areas of present-day Minnesota. His camps of women were cutting down *dépouille* and bear fats (the latter likely chosen as an alternative to marrow, as these bone fats required greater labor and easily went rancid). They created so much that they could not bag it in time. The weather suddenly turning "sultry" in late September, "great quantities spoil which was thrown into the river."[90] Two days later, the weather continued "fine and warm" much to the camp's misfortune: "we were under the necessity of throwing away great quantities of Bear, Biche [deer] and Buffalo meat, the hot weather comes it soon begins to spoil." A visitor to the women's work tents found "the Beach is covered with Bears Fat...."[91]

Variable fall temperatures were another hurdle. Later in the year, fats were difficult to handle as temperatures dropped in winter and interfered with the proper mixing of fats. The "Grease instantly gets cold and does not penetrate nor mix properly with the Beat Meat," Henry complained when he tried to begin pemmican production too early, in the winter. The ideal moment was in spring, when fats could be carefully warmed to just beyond their melt and, thus rendered, kept viscous long enough to mix well with – and preserve – meats in the skin bags.

Sedentary posts offered storage until ideal conditions prevailed. A meat shed kept an entire winter's trade in fat and meat frozen. In the best period, usually spring, a post then pooled its labor for factory production. Alexander Henry the Younger found conditions ideal on May 10 in 1808, when "clear and strong wind" prevailed and "clear and calm" skies began to stretch over the course of the week. Midday temperatures stayed around 13°C. Good weather lasted until the 19th, when Henry

---

[89] Vilhjalmur Stefansson, *The Fat of the Land* (New York: Macmillan, 1957), 193–194.
[90] September 17, 1800, *Journal of Alexander Henry the Younger*, I.
[91] September 17–19 and 21, 1800, *Journal of Alexander Henry the Younger*, I, 54–56.

was heading downriver with tons of provisions, towards Bas de la Rivière, itself a massive depot for Montreal canoe brigades.[92]

Ice houses safeguarded the post's bison fats, in these territories relished for their lifesaving values. Traders in the northern latitudes were too far from corn-producing centers and had few or no other plants, vegetable, or fruit matter for long periods of time. These fats balanced diets that would otherwise be dangerously heavy in protein.[93] In the switch toward factory production, there was a bias, however, toward harder over softer fats. As food sharing veered toward market exchange and native customs around food distribution now created surpluses at posts, subtle, but in the end, a significant new human use of bison emerged. Market trading encouraged the trade in interior fats rather than the more "distal" or exterior softer and more delectable humps and bone marrow. This would not have been lost on Native hunting bands, who, to supply the market, tended to provide harder and less attractive fare, and the more easily transported cuts of meat. In the switch to market hunting, local hands provided dried and pounded meat, *dépouille* (which transported easily), and bags of hard interior fat; but Native hunters rarely provided grease. In this, there was a turn away from trading the best and most prized fats, those "from the hip and shoulder joints down." Fat from the humerus and femur often achieved buttery consistency at room temperature, the rule of thumb being that fats "closer to the hoof"– toward the lower ends of bone matter – became softer and creamier, and in the most distal regions of bone, marrows sometimes had an oozy, wet firmness.[94]

This shift implied a different butchery for the market, and in the end, a different understanding of the animal itself. Less intensively harvested for its variety of fats, the bison joined humans in different exchange relations – those based less on the exquisitely tasting and harder-to-

---

[92] See May 10, 1808, *Journal of Alexander Henry the Younger*, I, 301; and Meteorological Observations for May 10–19, 1809.

[93] M. E. Malainey, R. Przybylski, and B. L. Sherrif (January 2001), "One Person's Food: How and Why Fish Avoidance May Affect the Settlement and Subsistence Patterns of Hunter-Gatherers," *American Antiquity*, 66(1):144; Vilhjalmur Stefansson, *Not by Bread Alone* (New York: Macmillan, 1946), 30–31.

[94] Meat consumption and meat sharing was likely a critical evolutionary moment in the human past. See, for instance, the archaeological work linking the centralized butchery, the common transport of meaty animal parts, and surplus meat production that likely encouraged redistribution between modern foragers and early *Homo* in Henry T. Bunn, "Hunting, Power Scavenging, and Butchering by Hadza Foragers and by Peleo-Pleistocene *Homo*," in Craig B. Stanford and Henry T. Bunn, eds., *Meat-Eating and Human Evolution* (Oxford: Oxford University Press, 2001), 211.

produce marrows and greases. In addition, these fats also had shorter preservation, as traditional and "fine" pemmican had higher quantities of lower melting point unsaturated fat, prone to rancidity. The kind of fare Native hands began moving to the market was harvested more easily. Sent to post were thighs; *dépouille*; dried meat by the bale (taken from the animal's more indifferently tasting quarters); and a great deal of waxy, yellowy, interior fat. Generally speaking, fats in an animal's body were hard and most stable at the center (its "axial" areas), where core "kidney" and organ fats were solid and unsaturated. [95]

As the market attracted more hunters to trade fats, their choice of what they brought to the market was also informed by climate. In the fall, there was a decided preference to trade *dépouille*, harvested relatively easily from carcasses. Given its mixed polyunsaturated and saturated fat content it transported well even during spikes of "sultry" weather that, as Henry understood well, spoiled more unstable oils. In winter, when bison were more easily butchered to the core, abundant quantities of organ fats could be bagged and sold to the posts.

As the market incited greater hunting efforts and the first summer harvesting among Native people, first Ojibwa, and then Métis and Freemen, the northern latitudes provided ideal climate in another critical respect: moderate extreme high temperatures in summer (Figure 2.5). These cooler summer regions in the northern latitudes gave hunters a distinctive geographic advantage for mass production of fat and dried meat, and it allowed them, when they began to respond to the market, to harvest meats and fat in enormous quantities even in the hottest months of the year.

Prime fat handling territories are indicated in Figure 2.5. Favorable July isotherms extended south into the territories of the Teton in present-day Minnesota, the Missouri west of the Yellowstone, and, in general, south into the sprawling Crow regions. This geographic advantage gave northern Assiniboine and Cree, in particular, the means to procure and trade meats and bags of fats in much greater quantity than the Mandan and other corn-growing people could. This climatic dynamic had long established the basis of exchange between northern fat and meat producers with Mandan/Hidatsa Missourians. Corn, hides, and other goods

---

[95] According to Steffanson, a northern hunter knew fat from the very bone it originated in, "so that if one is given a small piece in the dark he can tell, by the feel when he crushes it with his tongue against his palate, and by the taste, from which bone it is and from which end of that bone." Vilhjalmyur Stefansson, *Not by Bread Alone* (New York: Macmillan, 1946), 27.

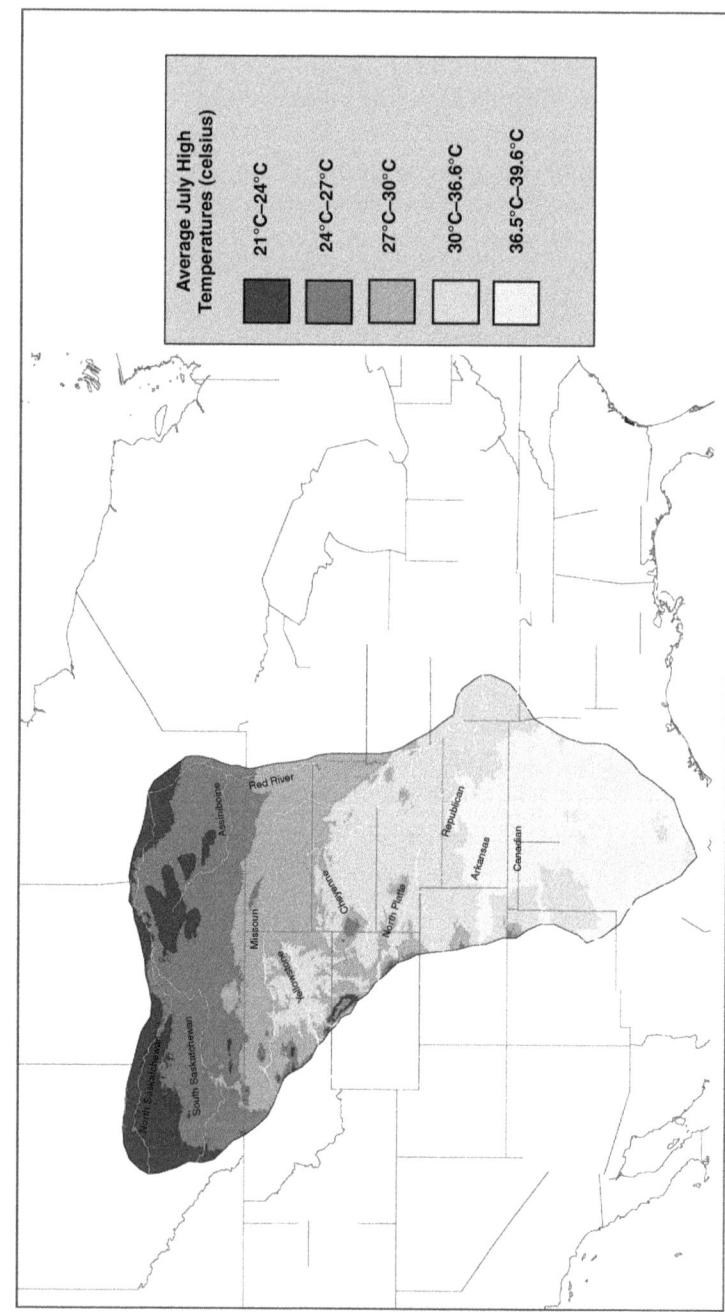

Figure 2.5. The Fat Frontier in the Great Plains. GIS mapping by Susan Mckee, University of Calgary Spatial and Numeric Data Services, 2012.

usually returned from these Missourians to Assiniboine fat and meat exporters in the north for this very reason.[96] Le Sieur de La Verennes et de La Vérendrye, one of the earliest Europeans to visit the Saskatchewan and Missouri watersheds, witnessed this trade in his first journey from present-day Manitoba to the Mandan villages in October 1739. His Assiniboine guides began hunting bison en route to procure meats and fats with which to trade among the Mandan/Hidatsa, and "to eat with the grain [corn] of which they always eat much, having seldom either meat or fat."[97] Milloy points out that La Vérendrye purchased Assiniboine fat before his party continued, likely with this fat scarcity on the Missouri in mind.[98] In their own diet, the Mandan were light fat-eaters. An important staple consisted of ground corn mixed with smaller quantities of the bison fat. This was *hominy* (grits), later praised by American explorers and travelers on the Missouri.[99]

The summer dynamic was simple. From the forks of the Red and Assiniboine to the Mandan villages there was a 4°C difference in average July temperatures. Probably more significant were higher average extreme temperatures: 32°C in the corn-growing agricultural areas as opposed to 26°C at the Forks. Since the Second Maunder Minimum, the climatic reality of northern cool growing seasons limited the extent of corn-growing on the plains, generally to the middle sections of the Missouri and west to the Yellowstone. But there, the same conditions made it difficult to handle and process fats in large quantities; an advantage in turn exploited by more northerly Assiniboine.[100] High ambient summer heat wreaked havoc in fat production, when marrow, grease, and even core fats went rancid before they could be rendered and bagged properly. Rancidity occurs when oxygen in the air combines with heat

---

[96] On the Cree-Assiniboine-Mandan trade and the venting of meat and fat to the latter, see John S. Milloy, *The Plains Cree* (Winnipeg: University of Manitoba, 1990), 50–51; and G. Hubert Smith and W. Raymond Wood, eds., *The Explorations of the La Vérendryes in the Northern Plains, 1738–43* (Norman: University of Nebraska Press, 1980), 39, 53.

[97] Quoted in Milloy, *Plains Cree*, 48.

[98] Ibid.

[99] "C'était cependant une précaution utile, vu que les Mandanes mangent leur grain cuit à l'eau et ne consomment que peu de viande." In this case, "viande" likely referred to meat and fat. Antoine Champagne, *Les La Vérendryes et les Postes de l'Ouest*, Vol. 12, *Les Chaiers de L'institut d'histoire* (Québec: Les Presses de l'Université Laval, 1968), 221. Grace Flandreau, in Lavérendrye's Overland Quest, translates the word in this way, cited in Milloy, 139.

[100] Joseph Jablow, *The Cheyenne in Plains Indian Trade Relations 1795–1840*, Monographs of the American Ethnological Society No. 19. (Seattle: University of Washington Press, 1966), 40.

and degrades fatty acids, most vulnerable to which were polyunsaturated fats. The fat emitted the destructive free radicals and "off flavors" that made the fat, simply put, go "bad." If the Missouri is used as an "ecological fault line," as it so often is in respect to climate, fats were more difficult to procure even in spring and fall not far south of it when ambient temperatures could still be so high as to thwart efforts in great stockpiling.[101] High ambient summer temperatures could always pose a threat to large quantities of provisions.[102] Certainly, bison hunting farther south of the Upper Missouri were affected more frequently by this phenomenon. The great hunts beyond the Platte might have supplied the needs of their plains participants, even in fats. But producing surplus quantities for a commercial trade was often out of the question for hunters like the Pawnee where, in present-day eastern Colorado, oral history remembers hunting in ambient spring temperatures high enough that fats had to be manufactured at night.[103] The Métis specializing in summer hunting gambled on these warmer conditions in a transitional climate territory to the south. The closer they came to the Mandan villages, the higher the odds that scorching summer temperatures would ruin their market-oriented hunt. Even

---

[101] See Gordon's remarks on the comparative importance of gathering in Colorado and the Canadian Plains, in Bryan H. C. Gordon, "Of Men and Herds in Canadian Plains Prehistory," Archaeological Survey of Canada, Paper No. 84, National Museum of Man Mercury Series (Ottawa: National Museums of Canada, 1979), 2. The Missouri as an "ecological fault line" is highlighted by Pekka Hämämälinen (December 2003), "The Rise and Fall of Plains Indian Horse Cultures," *Journal of American History*, 834.

[102] HBCA. "Mr. Linklater was obliged to throw away vast Quantitys of piece meat in summer it could keep no longer...." October 3, 1795, Brandon House Journals, B.22/a/3.

[103] Pawnee oral tradition holds that fats had to be made at night in the spring (and very hot) temperatures of the bison hunt beyond the Platte River in classically arid high plains country. Gene Weltfish, *The Lost Universe* (New York: Basic Books, 1965), 219–220. Pemmican, "so favourite a dish among the northern Indians," he said, was "not much in use among the Mandans." Maximilian, Prince of Wied, *Travels in the Interior of North America, 1833–34* in *Early Western Travels, 1746–1846*, Vol. 22, Reuben Gold Thwaites, ed. (New York: AMS Press, 1966), 391. The Assiniboine, La Verendrye reported, made him aware of the fact that among the Mandan, "most of the time they have neither meat nor fat"; they hunted buffalo on the way in order to have sufficient "sufficient fat to eat with the corn they would get there." Joseph Jablow, *The Cheyenne in Plains Indian trade Relations 1795–1840*, Monographs of the American Ethnological Society No. 19. (Seattle: University of Washington Press, 1966), 40. Interestingly, Charles Larpenteur, who dealt with component parts of pemmican at Fort Union, actually tasted it only in the upper reaches of the Missouri, among Assiniboine on the Poplar River: "I was invited into the lodges of the chiefs and leading men, to partake of a dish of pounded buffalo meat and marrow grease, as is their custom." In Elliott Coues, ed., *The Personal Narrative of Charles Larpenteur, 1833–1872*, Part I (Minneapolis: Ross & Haines, 1962), 230.

fall hunts, aimed to avail fresh meat for the winter, could be ruined by unusually warm weather in these territories.[104]

American explorers largely unwittingly traversed this fat frontier in the early nineteenth century. In their 1812 journey, Lewis and Clark noted St. Louis Company boats returning down river heavily laden with dried meats and fat from the northerly Teton Sioux. These boatsmen had traded the product beyond the great bend of the Missouri. The Siouan Dakota would soon make links with the St. Louis companies, such as Manuel Lisa's, following in Lewis and Clarks' steps. As the American expedition noted with concern, the Assiniboine–Nakota were trading tons of fat to the British companies in the Souris–Assiniboine region of present-day Manitoba in the form of pemmican – the kettles left at their camps near the Mandan villages indicated so. Later, Maximilian, the Prince of Wied, encountered pemmican – signaling fat surpluses – in his western journey about where Lewis and Clark had, near the Cannonball River and among the Yanktonai Sioux who had traveled from the Devils Lake area of Minnesota. He would be struck by the quantities of pemmican among the Assiniboine near Fort Union, who killed on occasion 700 to 800 bison from which "the women prepare the well-known pemmican... an important article of food for these people in their wanderings."[105] Pemmican, "so favourite a dish among the northern Indians," he said, was "not much in use among the Mandans."[106] Yanktonnai Sioux, meanwhile, extended the incidence of pemmican farther along the Missouri through trade. Fort Tecumseh, later Pierre, saw Yanktonnai traders travel sometimes great distances from their northern fat foothold to supply the post during its frequent periods of scarcity in late fall.[107]

[104] For instance, the Red River brigade travelling close to the Grand Coteau, "Those in quest of fresh meat were a good deal disconcerted by the extremely fine, warm weather." "Returned from the Buffalo Hunt," *Nor'Wester*, October 29, 1860, 2.

[105] Maximilian, Prince of Wied, *Travels in the Interior of North America, 1833–34* in *Early Western Travels, 1746–1846*, Reuben Gold Thwaites, ed. (New York: AMS Press, 1966), 22: 391. Osbourn Russell seems not to have encountered pemmican at all during his entire journey to and from the Rockies along the Missouri, and tried his first among the Sioux around the Black Hills. *Travels in the Interior of North America*, 23, 277.

[106] In 1837, "After an hour[']s dumb conversation a dish of roasted Buffaloe tongues was set before me accompanied by a large cake made of dried meat and fruit pounded together mixed up with Buffaloe marrow." Osborne Russell, *Journal of a Trapper: Or Nine Years Residence among the Rocky Mountains between the years of 1834 and 1843*, L. A. York, ed. (Boise, ID: Syms-York, 1914). Edited from the original manuscript by L. A. York.; see Larpenteur's encounter with pemmican, *Personal Narrative*, 230, and with the brother of the Assiniboine Iron-eyed Dog, 257.

[107] Fort Pierre had developed this trade with the Yanktonnais by the 1830s, and was building a post in haste among these hunters, "in order to collect provision as they could now be got

This did not mean that the factories forming on the plains functioned without incident. Here, too, hot spells could ruin fat harvesting. The infrastructure of these posts was often not sufficient, at least initially, to obtain real economies of scale for mass production. Red River's potato cellar, merely 9 × 16 feet, served in summer months as a meat shed. When its roof collapsed in 1814, some 2,000 lbs. of fat were buried inside.[108] Poorly stocked ice houses, or extraordinarily hot summers, could make a hanger ooze with decomposing meats, fill with blood flies, and exude unsupportable stench. A post handling large quantities of oils and fats in makeshift tents, with cauldrons of flammable tallow warming on fires, became veritable fatty acid chain powder kegs. In April 1794, at Brandon House, one Peter Houston "was drying some meat in the tent as usual," and by some accident the logs took fire "and burnt all the meat before it could be quenched."[109] But these were minor incidents in a region where on average cooler summer and colder winter temperatures allowed for the steady expansion of market-oriented hunting and fat rendering.

Commercial Pemmican

European posts, supported by vast amounts of female labor, benefited from ideal climate and an ecology favoring food sharing. They eventually imposed a sedentary factory system in a region where food had circulated in commensal exchange to create obligations between recipients and providers. Now, a far different, market-oriented economy emerged, effectively squirreling surpluses away in ice and meat sheds, shuttling quantities in season to depots and finally exporting it from the region altogether. Critical to its success, a standardized form of pemmican emerged more appropriate for the market. Factory production favored the use of harder, rather than softer, fats. Although initially hunters provided a wide range of fat, including bladders of marrow grease, with time, posts handled more back fat as a substitute, and then almost exclusively interior core fat.

---

easily and cheap" among the "Yanctonnais." Minnesota State Historical Society, Laidlaw to Pierre Chouteau, Jr., October 14, 1831. See Emillion Primeau's provisions trade with the Yanctonnais at White River, mentioned December 1, 1830. Reel 17, Letterbook of the Upper Missouri Outfit, Tecumseh, Papers of the St. Louis Fur Trade, Part 1, the Chouteau Collection, 1752–1925, Minnesota State Historical Society Archives.

[108] HBCA. August 13, 1814, Winnipeg Post Journals, B.235/a/3 1814–1815.
[109] HBCA. April 18, 1794, Brandon House Journals, B.22/a/1. The same accident occurred the next year when James Work, "in a large lodge of two tentings" unfortunately started a fire "and burnt the whole to atoms." HBCA, May 9, 1795, Brandon House Journals, B.22/a/2.

The Pemmican Bioregion, 1790–1810

Figure 2.6. A pemmican bag (Source: Glenbow Archives, NA-2360–1). Weighing approximately 90 lbs., this "Toro" of pemmican, sewn from a bull's hide, comprised almost half its weight in fat. In the fur trade era, commercialized pemmican was packed with higher proportions of the bison's saturated core body fats. These had lower melting points and if the sinew sewing shown here was well sealed with tallow to keep air out, the pemmican could store indefinitely.

There was some experiment in developing a recipe most suitable for commerce. Some mixtures had little shelf life, being poorly made, mixed, or sealed. Some pemmican was, simply put, uneatable: "the Pemitigan Mr. Sutherland brot down with him" to Brandon House in 1798, was rated by the chief trader, "no good the refuse of what he made use of...."[110] Alexander Henry the Younger experimented according to the conditions imposed on him, varying hard and soft fats, or fats of different sorts. At one point his Ojibwa crews of men and women made pemmican with bison meats mixed with bear oil, the latter available in copious quantities in the Pembina region. Such oils were more easily harvested from the upwards of twenty to thirty bears shot a day for the camp, than the more labor-intensive bison marrow and bone greases. Eventually, though, Henry tended to bag bear oil (always a delicate fat) separately and export it to depots. He settled, as most traders did, on bison *dépouille* and body fats to make his pemmican. Not all were having success. Portage La Prairie pemmican often turned "rotten" – either poorly mixed or poorly sealed. By 1803, Henry seems to have adopted an

[110] HBCA. August 13, 1798, Brandon House Journal by James Sutherland, B.22/a/4.

emerging standard and bagged dimension (Figure 2.6) and he was "fully confident my method of mixing and preparing it is good."[111]

Henry's pemmican, like most at these posts, was harder in saturated fats than sweeter in marrow and grease fats. Without getting wet, pemmican made from harder fats could store for years. By 1810, David Thompson described Montreal companies at Cumberland House using a mixture of 50 lbs. of pounded meat and 40 lbs. of fat. According to Thompson, Cumberland pemmican fats were made in a hard to soft ratio of 50:50, a combination "best made for keeping."[112] These were derived exclusively from core organ fats, traded in sewn bags, and softer fats from "back" *dépouille*, the "large flakes of fat that lie on both sides of the backbone." There was conspicuously little or no marrow fats and grease in this concoction. Posts that handled ever larger volumes of product were rarely in the position to trade enough truly soft fat greases and marrows (though they did get some in bladders) to make anything resembling traditional Native pemmican. John Pruden at Carlton house in 1816 seems to have been proud that year to pack pemmican with a soft–hard fat ratio of 1:5, the soft derived from bison thigh – but that resulted from an extraordinarily plentiful year in the trade.[113]

The shift to larger production also necessitated choices in butchery. Traders knew that thighs were best for drying and beating, but "shoulders are seldom made use of for this purpose (pemmican making) owing to the quantity of sinews therein."[114] After the 1820s, with need for this food ballooning, trade pemmican was manufactured almost exclusively with core body fats – tallow – and often without softer fats at all. This waxy, very unpalatable, product came to represent the standard.[115]

An emerging factory system along the Saskatchewan and the Red River Valleys, then, began supplying brigades going northward in full pace, "where nothing of the kind can be procured."[116] In 1796 at Brandon House, Robert Goodwin, finding that food caching was "the better half

---

[111] December 1, 1803, *Journal of Alexander Henry the Younger*, I, 151.
[112] J. B. Tyrell, ed., *David Thompson's Narrative of his Explorations in Western America, 1784–1812* (Toronto: Champlain Society, 1916), 434.
[113] HBCA. March 19, 1816, Carlton House Journals, B.27/a/5.
[114] HBCA. April 14, 1827, Fort Edmonton Journals, B.60-a-24.
[115] In the higher subarctic, it became harder to derive enough fats for pemmican production. The ratio was 35 lbs. grease to 55 lbs. of pounded meat, but at times the company had to make it leaner, to 33 lbs. of grease and 57 lbs. of meat. The tariff in the barren grounds areas encouraged the trade in fats, too, for that reason. See Innis, *The Fur Trade in Canada*, 300.
[116] John McDonald of Garth, Autobiographical Notes, in Masson, Vol. II, 18.

rotten or useless" or stolen by passers-by,[117] offered to "supply the other settlements with Pimectun in ye same manner as ye Canadians," that is, by bulk manufacture delivered to key depots to feed north-bound crews. By 1799, the HBC devoted more personnel to move Red River provisions down to "Pointe au Foutre" on the Winnipeg River, to supply the Lake Winnipeg posts in general.[118] The next year, the London Committee recognized the Red River as a post "of the first importance" and approved of Goodwin's system of procuring provisions and depoting them at Point au Foutre "with an abundance."[119] With the Napoleonic Wars tightening food stores everywhere, especially in England where wheat was at a premium, any saving on barreled flour would make a big difference. So extensive were the HBC's storehouses of Saskatchewan and Red River pemmican that Alexander Henry the Younger in 1808 made note of these massive warehouses serving the companies, "not kept up by us so much for the purpose of trade as for the convenience of a depot." At Cumberland House his own company brought some 300 to 500 bags of pemmican and "upwards of 200 kegs of [bone] grease." Henry saw much the same occurring at the HBC Cumberland depot, the post enjoying "superabundant" stock from the Saskatchewan. The HBC traders enjoyed so much quantity that it "affords them every means of supplying the wants of the [nearby woodland Cree and Ojibwa] Natives throughout the year, as the country around is most wretched, and destitute of [big game] animals."[120]

Conclusion

In 1822, Edward Ermatinger began the accounting book at Fort Ellice on the Assiniboine River with an oddly written aphorism. It held that when a man was "content to follow Nature he is just what nature made him." But, "the moment he presumes to improve him ... he becomes what he would make himself." Ermatinger then accounted for how he had apparently "improved" himself and the Nature of the post around him, summing the totals of that year's provisions trade. He filled 20 kegs of

---

[117] HBCA. September 4, 1796, Brandon House Journals, with James Sutherland's account of the inland journey, B.22/a/4.
[118] HBCA. Letter to John McNabb, May 31, 1799, London Correspondence Book Outwards, 1796–1803, A.6/16.
[119] HBCA. To John Hodgins, May 28, 1800, London Correspondence Book Outwards, 1796–1803, A.6/16.
[120] August 26, 1808, *The Journal of Alexander Henry the Younger*, II, 345.

grease, 80 kegs pounded meat, 10 casks salt meat, 10 bags dried tongues, and no fewer than 700 bags pemmican, the latter weighing 63,000 lbs.[121] Ermatinger's stock had become a thing changed from nature. But nature itself, the environment of the Winnipeg steppe, was as critical in providing the abundant stores this trader created. He might have had confidence in his own abilities as a trader but the region's winter seasonality, the relationships cultivated in parkland ecotone, and, by this time, the more moderate summer temperatures for hunters to handle copious quantities of fat, even in the hottest months of the year, were as important as Ermatinger's own efforts.

All the same, Ermatinger was correct in one respect. Not content in "following" nature, the provisions trader was in many respects creating a "second nature" that transformed the labor of Native people within the new, sedentary post system of companies.[122] These hoarded and did not redistribute, at least locally, food surpluses. Indeed, fur posts were inverting the logic of native food systems and the outcomes of their labor and gifts. There is no question that the individuals involved – Native hunters, servants, masters, women, and children – joined freely for the most part the work of these posts. Many of these traders lived long lives and contributed to complex cross cultural relationships established in the provisions trade. Their in-laws were often other post hunters, or even rival fur company employees. A quite massive, interrelated blood and fictive kin network radiated far from the ramshackle posts that dotted the riverways.[123] All the same, the food that they handled and processed was altered and its nature changed. The focus of trade was to create a product very different than the fare traditionally made in the region. Sweet or traditional pemmican dissembled a bison completely, drawing especially its inner core, subcutaneous back, and distal marrow fats. Trade pemmican was made of meats and fats selected for a factory process. It was not just the people in the steppe who were being enveloped in the market. So was the bison itself. Bison being killed at pounds were likely less intensively butchered. Hunters offered different cuts of meat and far less delicate, more unsaturated, fats to establish far different exchange relations. The greatest irony is that traditional native pemmican tasted better but had a shorter shelf life. The market emerging produced the infamously

---

[121] HBCA. Opening page of Fort Ellice Accounts, 1822–1823, B.63/d/1.

[122] The idea of a "second nature" is developed by William Cronan in *Nature's Metropolis: Chicago and the Great West* (New York: W.W. Norton, 1992), 93, 198.

[123] See Margaret L. Clarke, "Reconstructing the Fur Trade Community of the Assiniboine Basin, 1793–1812," MA thesis, University of Winnipeg, 1997, 4:70–75.

waxy and unpalatable "trade pemmican" so loaded with unsaturated fats that it had an almost indefinite shelf life. The bison's carcass, then, took a different form in the process – its meats often hurriedly beaten, mixed with all manner of dirt, twigs, and matted with bison hair in its quick production.[124] With much of the product destined for export from the region, and the herds being exploited differently with the market's expansion, the "trade pemmican" now moving in larger quantities represented an overall loss to the region, both in terms of the less intensively butchered animal and the interrelationships of people who might otherwise have consumed it. It was, however, a remarkable food system developing, one that now supplied a massive fur trade network beyond it, starved for calories. As Duncan M'Gillivray observed, the fur trade's very success now hinged on the uninterrupted supply of plains foods, and within them, critical bioenergy for work. If the bison hunt was stopped, it "would prevent progress & stop the Trade," he said. "It is wisely ordered by Providence that this should be so."[125]

But the very system in which M'Gillivray and, later, Ermatinger were implicated was already imperiling the resource it was based on. As surpluses were achieved, companies increased their use of the foodstuff to expand their operations elsewhere. By the end of the eighteenth century, "peak" production was met in parkland pounds. In turn, the market expanded as competition for bison foodstuffs increased. Traders now sought to corner their share of the supply. In a region by most counts still "superabundant" in food resources, food factory processes were tilting groups into competition and unbalancing power between them. River valleys broiled with violence and the region itself, soon enveloped in the "pemmican wars," was exposed to the reality of a more specialized market hunt and the society now relying on it.

---

[124] To save effort on flensing bull skins, Fort Edmonton employees were apparently packing pemmican with their hair inside, see William Tomison's instruction to the post "to pack the pelt side of the skins outward...." Letter to George Sutherland April 25, 1798, Alice M. Johnson, ed., *Saskatchewan Journals*, 133.

[125] Morton, *The Journal of Duncan M'Gillivray*, xlviii.

3

FOOD FIGHTS AND PEMMICAN WARS, 1790–1816

> *If permitted to read this proclamation [we shall] go on to shew [sic] that without this food called pemmican trade cannot in that country be carried on [and the parties in trade] if they did not receive it must starve.*
>
> – Defense Council remarks to Chief Justice Powell, Trial of those accused of the Seven Oaks Massacre, 1818[1]

British commerce depended on parkland people, their response to the market expanding around them, ideal climate, and, above all, the availability of winter fragments of bison herds moving within purview of pounding locations. With demand for pemmican jettisoning in the late 1790s, however, it was clear that Native traditions of food distribution could not cope with demand. It is possible that the communal basis of poundmaking with its onus on group reward-sharing skewed market exchanges or blunted the maximizing decisions of Cree and Assiniboine, to the great disappointment of traders who would have preferred to see them bring everything they could for sale. A problematic market interregnum, then, confronted fur companies organizing desperately needed supply. A critical breakthrough in production occurred as prices rose and first Ojibwa and, then, in the first decade of the century, Métis and freemen contingents began more concerted and intensive market hunting.

With greater plenty tapped for their use, fur trade companies still entered one of the most violent and bloody periods of rivalry, especially between 1814 and 1816, when the Selkirk Settlement, established in these years, was thoroughly routed by plains provisioners. Manitoba historian George Bryce once suggested that the Seven Oaks Battle of June 1816 constituted "the most notable event that ever occurred on the prairies of Rupert's Land or in the limits of the fur country." In just

---

[1] LAC Mr. Sherwood's Remarks, Monday October 26, 1818, Grand Jury Indictment, *Selkirk Papers*, Series A, 10524.

what way Seven Oaks was noteworthy, however, has becomes a question of historical debate.[2] Although it seems certain that Metis buffalo hunters waving as a flag the lemniscate, or infinity sign, over Brandon Fort that spring, or title attributed to them by Peter Fidler as a "New Nation" would indicate a formidable political moment in Metis people, the event was ultimately related to pemmican emerging as a plains market product, and Metis economic strategies around it.[3]

Seven Oaks was a culminating moment in the food warfare growing in the period, whereby participants in the fur trade rejected any sort of cooperative food sharing, and turned to rivalry and violence by 1814 to launch the "pemigan wars," as one trader termed them.[4] Ironically, part of the turn to violence is attributable to the greater energy supply now available to companies, especially after ideal provisioning conditions opened up pemmican supply in 1815.[5] Competing companies organized themselves around bison food while escaping some of the ruinous costs of importing European foodstuffs. With pemmican power, they tried to bully their way farther into fur territories, used discounted prices to strong-arm Native hunters trading furs and food, and, in fragile subarctic environments, paid hunters to create buffer zones between themselves and competitors. Game and fur "deserts" stretched across portions of the subarctic in this commercial expansion, and once denuding territories of furbearers and animal life, traders moved farther westward or northward in a continual zero-sum game of commercial expansion. Food supply in such leaps of expansion lurched between plenty and poverty. In the boreal and shield forest regions, too, still ineffective redistribution of prairie foods meant that in some places depots with enough supply could underwrite the needs of an entire district, including native hunters; in others, choking points formed where Europeans starved. Companies

---

[2] Quoted in Lyle Dick (1991), "The Seven Oaks Incident and the Construction of a Historical Tradition, 1816–1970," *Journal of the Canadian Historical Association*, 2(1):102. An overview of Red River historiography is usefully provided by Fritz Pannekoek (1981), "The Historiography of the Red River Settlement, 1830–1868," *Prairie Forum*, 6(1):75–85.

[3] On the oral history, and especially the Pierre Falcon song, "Chanson de la Grenouillere" see Margaret Complin's careful reconstruction in Section II, 1939, *Proceedings and Transactions of the Royal Society of Canada*, 49–58.

[4] LAC. The term "pemigan war" was used by A. Kennedy to J. D. Cameron March 28, 1814, *Selkirk Papers, Series A*, 8828.

[5] See Gerhard Ens, "The Battle of Seven Oaks and the Articulation of a Metis National Tradition, 1811–1849," Nicole St.-Onge, Carolyn Podruchny, and Brenda Macdougall, eds., *Counters of a People: Metis Family, Mobility, and History* (Norman: University of Oklahoma Press, 2012), 95–101.

exporting food resources, using them to maximize returns or cornering them to beggar their neighboring capitalized rivals, eventually turned to violence to gain advantage.

This chapter examines how, in the midst of plains and prairie plenty, commercial entities so quickly turned to violence and, in some irony, confronting an open access resource made decisions to control, not share, its bounty. Food fights and pemmican wars grew in this commons not from the actual scarcity of the resource, but from the way commercial entities sought to control its access. Although it is true that important historical events occurred in the era, most notably the Métis emerging as a commercial and, possibly, ethnic identity in the context of the rising prices around food, the issue explored here is the decision making of companies. Those using the buffalo commons to support their commercial expansion tended to seek its exclusive access. Short of succeeding in that respect, the same players turned to actions, as prisoners face in their classical "dilemmas," to undermine their rivals even to the point of their own peril.[6]

Toward "Peak" Pemmican Production

At least by 1800, growing demands on poundmakers took pemmican production to its "peak" in the steppe areas. Until this point, some of the most significant technological and transportation innovations were struck by companies making efforts to raise the efficiency of their operations. In the lead-up to a period of true food rivalry, the Hudson's Bay Company (HBC) consolidated its transport from Hudson Bay, adopting the Hays and Nelson Rivers as a prime entryway to Manitoba, and once there, getting to the plains and the larger northwest via the inner passage of Lake Winnipeg. After 1810, York Factory (as well as Albany and Churchill) was fully stocked annually with tons of pemmican to support incoming crews. The tributary food hanger Cumberland House was restocked in spring with Red River and Assiniboine bison products and in fall with foodstuffs coming from the Saskatchewan. It served as an important food depot. The company's awkward transport lines to James Bay, then, were cut. And, by 1798, after the London committee began agreeing to their feasibility, staff increasingly adopted the more efficient

---

[6] As per the classic game theory dilemma facing prisoners choosing independently their own interests. See Steven J. Brams, *Game Theory and Politics* (Mineola, NY: Dover, 2004 [1975]), 30–34.

York boat, which now drove inland with fewer hands and offered much larger cargo space. These boats also ran in a longer season and, compared to the birch bark canoe, were far more durable.[7]

The North West Company (NWC), emerging as the primary Montreal-based concern in the period, consolidated its own operations and made its own reforms. The Nor'Westers drew bison fat in the Red River/Assiniboine Valleys, sending traders as far west as the South Branch to trade increasing quantities. The need to send employees overland into the steppe, and, soon, animate a summer hunt led the company by the late 1790s to regularly dispatch traders to the Mandan/Hidatsa on the Missouri to purchase goods and furs. One of their more important purchases, however, was horse stock. The Mandan were linked to distant Indian trade networks to the Gulf of Mexico, including the great Comanche horse marts. The Nor'Westers made use of their gains in horse power to expand overland transport in the steppe or to sell as steeds or work animals to "freemen" growing in numbers and working on commission hunting bison in the Assiniboine and Qu'Appelle Valleys.[8]

The actual quantity of trade pemmican moving through the steppe in these years is difficult to ascertain with any precision. A commonly cited figure for the NWC is 644 bags annually by 1812 produced in the Red River and Saskatchewan districts.[9] Of that, perhaps 430 bags would be produced in the Red River area. But this was a wartime transport ration and likely, too, reflected the poor buffalo hunting at the time.[10]

---

[7] A large York boat had an efficiency of eleven pieces per man (a small seven to ten) compared to a Montreal canoe of six and North Canoe of four to five. See Dennis F. Johnson, *York Boats of the Hudson's Bay Company: Canada's Inland Armada* (Saskatoon: Fifth House, 2006), 183. Harold Innis, *The Fur Trade in Canada* (Toronto: University of Toronto Press [1930] 1999), 158–159; the contemporary debate on canoes versus York boats is highlighted by Alice M. Johnson, *Saskatchewan Journals and Correspondence: Edmonton House 1795–1800; Chesterfield House, 1800–1802* (London: The Hudson's Bay Record Society, 1967), xli–xliii.

[8] See W. Raymond Wood and Thomas D. Thiessen, *Early Fur Trade on the Northern Plains: Canadian Traders among the Mandan and Hidatsa Indians, 1738–1818* (Norman: University of Oklahoma Press, 1985); and John Milloy, *The Plains Cree: Trade, Diplomacy and War, 1790 to 1870* (Winnipeg: University of Manitoba Press, 1988), 50–56; on Brandon House's own horse purchases through alcohol sales see HBCA, February 8, 10, 1797, Brandon House Journals, B.22/a/4. On the designation and role of freemen in the trade, particularly after the 1805 coalition of the NWC and the XY companies, see Heather Devine, *The People Who Own Themselves: Aboriginal Ethnogenesis in a Canadian Family, 1660–1900* (Calgary: University of Calgary Press, 2004), 82–83.

[9] Arthur J. Ray, *Indians in the Fur Trade*, 130–133.

[10] Ens, "The Battle of Seven Oaks," 95.

Montreal partners had ordered the number to rein in expenses and included other cost-cutting measures such as staff cutbacks and accounting reforms at the Bas de la Riviere pemmican depot.[11] Poor recordkeeping by companies, especially the Nor'westers, makes it difficult to know for sure what was typical by that point. Actually, "normal" production in the Winnipeg Steppe likely exceeded this, certainly after 1812. In 1814, when Red River's governor famously seized the Nor'Wester's pemmican under order of the Pemmican Proclamation, the returns from the lower Qu'Appelle and Qu'Appelle Post, alone, numbered 575 bags. The fat seized at the same time was sufficient to produce another 235, meaning that the lower ends of the Assiniboine alone had the capacity to produce about 800 bags annually.[12] By 1816, when ideal climatic conditions returned, Qu'Appelle post regularly generated 500 bags a year.[13] Beyond the lower Assiniboine, the Nor'westers were producing other quantities. Lower Red River posts (Pembina, Hair Hills, and Grand Fourche near the Turtle River), could supply between 235 to 334 bags annually.[14] There were also the bags produced officially outside Assiniboia and therefore not seized under the Pemmican Proclamation. These included the considerable quantities, perhaps even exceeding Qu'Appelle's production, at Swan River and Dauphin in 1814.[15] Besides NWC returns were those of the HBC posts in the area. That company voluntarily gave more than 190 bags under the proclamation in 1814,

---

[11] In 1813, the company inaugurated radical wartime cutbacks to 250 bags from the Saskatchewan and 430 from the Red River for a total of 680; on top of this, Red River would produce 254 kegs of grease (pp. 277–279). Staff layoffs, by post, are found on page 273. The partners were concerned that "great inattention here prevailed in Keeping & forwarding the Accounts of the Provision ... & too great a waste of Pemican & Grease at that Depot in general" now "requires a radical reform...." W. Stewart Wallace, ed. *Documents relating to the North West Company* (Toronto: Champlain Society, 1934), 276.

[12] See Lord Selkirk's Notes on the Pemmican Affair, 1814, *Selkirk Papers, Series B* manuscript 207, viii.

[13] A. Macdonell at Qu'Appelle, October 20, 1815 to D. Cameron, reported having grease for 400 bags of pemmican and "upwards of 1000 dispoulles – say beat meat for near 100 bags...." *Selkirk Papers, Series A*, 9050.

[14] Alexander Henry the Younger provides the returns from that district in 1805 to 1808 (Vol. I, 303; 187). Macdonell estimated the "Red River" pemmican, likely Pembina, running in 1813 between 300 and 400 bags, with fat besides. See July 17, 1813, Miles Macdonell to Lord Selkirk, *Selkirk Papers, Series B*, 129.

[15] See A.S. Morton's important discussion of the proclamation's limited authority in the steppe. A. S. Morton, *A History of the Canadian West to 1870–71*, 561–563. Swan River posts, certainly, were making sizeable returns; and they seemed to have even doubled their production in 1814. John McDonald to Dougal Cameron 14 February 1815, *Selkirk Papers, Series A*, 9010.

but it seems to have been producing as many as 1,000 bags nearby in 1814, according to Selkirk.[16] The Red River area, then, was already producing considerable quantities of pemmican, particularly after ideal poundmaking conditions occurred after 1815.

But it seems certain that European traders had already reached "peak" supply from Assiniboine and Cree poundmakers. The inelastic response of plains hunters to the European market is perhaps best explained in reference to anthropological studies of food exchange, and, ultimately, the various meanings of food in transactions.[17] Just how far back humans shared meat and why they did so is a matter of great debate among scholars. In anthropology, a "home base" strategy likely developed early in hominid evolution that made more intensive hunting, meat preparation, and strategies in surplus meat distribution a critical beginning point to human societal development. Larger scales of butchering, gendered divisions of work in meat preservation, and the development of sharing protocols grew as human hunting groups organized cooperative kills and invested the requisite and considerable labor to preserve and redistribute the meat from their ventures, when they succeeded.[18]

Although anthropologists have not agreed whether modern examples of hunting and gathering can be applied to the historical period, many suggest that characteristics of human sharing and trading strategies have gone back a long time. The use of game theory has proven useful in explaining sharing behavior and choices made when hunters and gatherers, especially in the boreal environment, have given hunted meat to others.[19] Food exchange, or perhaps better said, "distribution," likely occurred quite naturally given the way that meat needed a great deal of effort for its preservation, and giving it away fresh was relatively easy. Food gifts also accrued esteem and status to their givers and obligations among their receivers. In many cases, the gift of hunted meat was

---

[16] The quantities are recounted in Lord Selkirk's Notes on the Pemmican Affair, 1814, 190–206.
[17] Sidney W. Mintz and Christine M. Du Bois (2002), "The Anthropology of Food and Eating," *Annual Review of Anthropology*, 31:99–119.
[18] Craig B. Stanford and Henry T. Bunn, eds., *Meat-Eating & Human Evolution* (Oxford: Oxford University Press, 2001).
[19] Bruce Winterhalder, "Intragroup Resource Transfers: Comparative Evidence, Models and Implications for Human Evolution, in Craig B. Stanford and Henry T. Bunn eds., *Meat-Eating and Human Evolution* (Oxford: Oxford University Press, 2001), 279–301. For the "home-base" argument, see G. Isaac (1978), "Food-Sharing and Human Evolution: Archaeological Evidence from the Plio-Pleistocene of East Africa," *Journal of Anthropological Research*, 34:311–325.

not truly "tit for tat," where one gave food that matched earlier gifts, and so on. Food exchange was remarkable for how asymmetric it could become in hunting and gathering traditions. The anthropological idea of a "good hunter" often identifies individuals sharing large portions of their game, sometimes even larger than the portions they kept themselves. This might have had to do with cost considerations, should a potential cooperative partner be lost in the future if food was withheld. Good hunters, too, might simply have been making a calculated gamble on the fitness of a particularly good potential trading partner, a strategy they hoped would pay off down the road.[20] In another way, in what is called "tolerated theft" or "tolerated scrounging," hunters might be willing to allow scavenging interlopers a portion of game given that the costs of defending territories, or the cost of repelling outsiders from a particular sized resource or food "package," were always high.[21] Human evolutionary theory suggests tolerated theft served to reinforce peaceful coexistence between erstwhile competing parties who, over time, eventually brokered accords with each other to share game and food. At the same time, food anthropology continues to suggest that unequal exchanges, rather than tit-for-tat, tend to be the norm rather than the exception, and shaped relations between hunting bands.[22] Asymmetric exchanges, or calculated altruism, can also be explained in light of modern-day hunter and gatherer cultures where good hunters often share large portions of their food because they tend to be given *greater* amounts of food when they find themselves in need of charity later.[23]

These perspectives help explain why food exchanges occurring in the steppe in the late eighteenth century were generous, circumscribed in their extent, and in their packaging compounded interest among their recipients. They also help explain the many intangible social

---

[20] Raymon Hames, "Reciprocal Altruism in Yanömamo Food Exchange," in Lee Cronk, Napoleon Chagnon, and William Irons, eds., *Adaptation and Human Behavior: An Anthropological Perspective* (New York: Aldine de Gruyter, 2000), 397–416.

[21] See, Michael Alvard (August 2004), "Good Hunters Keep Smaller Shares of Larger Pies," *Behavioral & Brain Sciences*, 27(4):560–561; Rebecca L. Bliege Bird and Douglas W. Bird (1997), "Delayed Reciprocity and Tolerated Theft: The Behavioral Ecology of Food Sharing Strategies," *Current Anthropology*, 38:297–321; and N. G. Blurton Jones (1984), "A Selfish Origin for Human Food Sharing: Tolerated Theft," *Ethology and Sociobiology*, 5(1):1–3.

[22] Michael Gurven (February 2006), "The Evolution of Contingent Cooperation," *Current Anthropology*, 47(1):185–192.

[23] Michael Gurven, Weley Allen-Arave, Kim Hill, and Magdalena Hurtado (2000), "'It's a Wonderful Life': Signaling Generosity among the Ache of Paraguay," *Evolution and Human Behavior*, 21:263–282.

ends Assiniboine and Cree sought in the opening up food trading at the time, guided not necessarily according to rules and expectations of the new market economy. Indeed, it can be questioned how much Native poundmakers moved far from their own economic strategies at the time and the gambles they were making on the fitness, future rewards, or help Europeans might provide down the road for their food distributions. Assiniboine and Cree are often glimpsed in the record arriving to European posts burdened by excess meats and more than willing to vent them to Europeans, always with a view of their future rewards for such trades.[24] They brought quantities by the ton, leaving them explicitly as credits given to Europeans who could only pay for portions "and the remainder they gave me in credit," as one trader stated.[25] These Europeans were apt to "get more meat and fatt from the Indians on trust"[26] when they found themselves short of trade goods. There is also the intriguing strategy manifested by bands of Assiniboine who arrived with furs and provisions, the former going to Montreal traders who had advanced credits for them; the latter being divided between the English and Montreal traders nearby.[27] The Assiniboine strategy of dividing and sharing their food between companies, likely as a means of hedging bets between potential future supporters, infuriated traders who wanted exclusive access to Indian foods to the detriment of their rivals.[28]

Europeans scrambled to take as much as possible from hunting camps. Offers increased. Prices rose. Throughout pounding territories from the Manitoba Steppe, to the Battle River catchments of the North Saskatchewan, inelastic supply began to drive up offers on Assiniboine and Cree provisions in the 1790s. Charles Isham's house at Swan River

---

[24] HBCA. So, from the Cree who only offered 15 skins in fur, Brandon House received 1,350 lbs. of dried meat, 400 lbs. of half dried, 600 lbs. of grease, 400 lbs. of fat, and 30 tongues, with 168 lbs. of pounded meat. October 6, 1795, Brandon House Journals, B.22/a/3.

[25] HBCA. October 20, 1795, ibid. See 29 July 1796. On the latter occasion, the Cree and Assiniboine "a great many" left the meats with Brandon House, but took their furs to the rival Montreal traders nearby. More credit was left by Indians on August 18, of some 200 lbs. of meat.

[26] HBCA. See September 2, 1796, Brandon House Journals, B.22/a/3.

[27] See "The Diary of Archibald N. McLeod," in Charles M. Gates, ed., Five Fur Traders of the Northwest: Being the Narrative of Peter Pond, and the Diaries of John Macdonell, Archibald N. McLeod, Hugh Fairies, and Thomas Connor (St. Paul: Minnesota Historical Society, 1965), 140–141.

[28] Quinquhanea "a Captn belonging to the NW Company for many years" nevertheless traded with Brandon House employees, HBCA, February 21, 1794, Brandon House Journals, B.22/a/2.

by 1794 had no fewer than eight competing Montreal houses almost at its very door, each making its bids for foods.[29] Given that they vied for the same, limited, product meant that posts with time paid more in gifts, honorifics, or social designators to trading bands.

Limited supply raised serious logistic issues for European posts and their personnel. Just feeding the men, women, children – and dogs – at posts, each fixed unnaturally in the landscape, proved a mindboggling problem. Given that post inhabitants had little else to consume than meat and fat, they ate a lot. As early as 1794, Duncan M'Gillivray at Fort George, which devoted its business to food trading with Assiniboine and Cree poundmakers nearby, found that despite good hunting and fine meat in the "hangard," managers felt fortunate to keep up with the post's own food requirements, which included about eighty men and as many women.[30] A post of this size easily went through 700 to 1000 lbs. of buffalo meat daily, if each person was given his daily ration of eight pounds.[31] (This, however, was still a bit of a "short" ration, as a reduction to six pounds daily could spark near-riots at posts).[32] A typical ration throughout Rupert's Land was 8 to 12 lbs. daily.[33]

Per diem servings like these added up to staggering costs. In 1795, Robert Goodwin estimated that the seasonal meat consumption at Brandon House amounted to around 12,365 lbs. of piece (fresh) meat, more than a ton of pounded meat, and a ton and a half of fat.[34] Alexander Henry the Younger's often-cited tabulation of food consumed at Pembina Post alone staggers the imagination. For only seventeen men, ten women, and fourteen children (with forty-five dogs), the post served

[29] Isham letter to Goodwin, February 5, 1795, Brandon House Journals, B.22/a/2.
[30] *The Journal of Duncan M'Gillivray of the North West Company at Fort George on the Saskatchewan, 1794–5* (Toronto: Macmillan, 1929) 41.
[31] This was John Franklin's remark at a nearby post where there were seventy men and sixty women and children. Ibid., footnote 2, 41.
[32] HBCA. See John Pruden's labour problems at Carlton House when he reduced rations to six pounds a day. The men stopped work early and refused to go "with one voice complaining of having not enough to eat," December 1, 1818, Carlton House Journals, B.27/a/8.
[33] George Colpitts, *Game in the Garden: A Human History of Wildlife in Western Canada* (Vancouver: UBC Press, 2001), 25. Duncan M'Gillivary, *The Journal of Duncan M'Gillivray of the North West Company at Fort George on the Saskatchewan, 1794–5*, ed. A. S. Morton (Toronto: Macmillan, 1924), lvii, 41; HBCA, Cumberland House Journals, September 2, 1784, B.49/a/15; and rations mentioned in Shepard Krech III, *The Ecological Indian: Myth and History* (New York: W. W. Norton, 1999), 132.
[34] HBCA. Expenditure of Provisions at Brandon House, 1795, Brandon House Journals, B.22/a/2.

up 45,000 lbs. of cow flesh (from 112 animals); 18,600 lbs. of bull flesh (thirty-five animals); plus three elk; three black bears; and the meat of four beavers, three swans, and one white crane. Although not accounting for them, Henry's post undoubtedly played host to a great number of visitors, what anthropologists in food sharing theory would call "free riders." Henry's post would have broken up, according to commensal food sharing traditions, portions of the post's food for groups residing there and, just as likely, parting ways. All the same, Henry's statistics suggest the enormous quantities consumed in a single winter. Henry also reported that Pembina Post residents ate some 48 water fowl, and 1,150 fish, and no fewer than 775 of the region's massive sturgeon (Henry said these weighed from 50 to 150 lbs. each!).[35] Given that the post had very few other carbohydrates in the form of corn, wild rice, or fruit (albeit the supplies from the garden he kept), the men and women were almost exclusively fat and meat eaters. Arthur Ray, calculating supply for just the twenty-one houses on the Assiniboine River in 1795, taking Pembina as typical, reckoned that they "would have produced a demand of the order of at least 1,323,000 pounds per year."[36]

As early as 1795 food needs among these sedentary posts along the Saskatchewan and the Red River Valleys grew so quickly that all was bought only "dearly" from the winter pounds. Some of the great cost was intentionally raised: Duncan M'Gillivray noted *Gens du large*, in this case the Blackfoot near Fort George, burning grasses near the post to capitalize on demand and throw prices even further upwards: "The Indians often make use of this method to frighten away the animals in order to enhance the value of their own provisions."[37] Strategic Cree burning around the HBC's Hudson House had similarly raised prices on pounded meats.[38] It is possible that the aim of such strategies was to weaken other Assiniboine and Cree pounds, better drive bison into specific directions, or divert trade. Despite the fact that M'Gillivray's post cleared 10,000 lbs. of meat by the end of the season it was an expensive trade. The post's hunters who brought in 200 of 413 animals by year-end demanded

---

[35] HBCA. Recapitulation, 1807 in *Journal of Alexander Henry the Younger*, I, 317.
[36] Arthur J. Ray, *Indians in the Fur Trade: Their Role as Trappers, Hunters, and Middlemen in the Lands Southwest of Hudson Bay, 1660–1870* (Toronto: University of Toronto Press, 1998), 130.
[37] *The Journal of Duncan M'Gillivray*, 33.
[38] "On purpose that they might get a great price for provisions" Robert Longmoore complained at Hudson House, January 17, 1781, in *Cumberland House Journals*, II, 175.

between 700 and 800 beavers' worth of goods in return; M'Gillivray estimated that the price of producing only three bags of pemmican was a pack of furs. The quantities and sheer cost of food purchases, coupled with their utmost importance for the fur trade outside the region, meant that provisions, "therefore [had] to be considered as constituting [a] very considerable part of our returns."[39]

Prices were likely higher in the Red River district comprising the Red, Assiniboine, and Qu'Appelle River posts. John Sutherland, at Shell River in 1795, gathered some two to three thousand pounds of dry meat and fat, enough to send word to Brandon House to go "easy" on its own provisions trade. But none of the stock had come cheaply, as all was paid for in great quantities of brandy, tobacco, powder, ball and knives, and "[w]e must pay a very heavy price for it," he peeved.[40] Brandon House's Robert Goodwin lamented even higher prices by 1798, that "It is a great hurt to the [company] for every piece of meat [likely the standard 90-lb allotment] is converted equal to a wolf skin and paid for as such," he said that fall.[41] By spring he had purchased "upwards of 3000lb now exclusive of what the men have eat during ye fall and winter which have cost a great deal of expense to what was last year."[42] By December 1799, winter provisions at Winnipeg Post tripled in price from the previous year.[43]

Poundmakers raised prices in many ways, often to exact social benefits rather than simply more goods in return. When they traded at Brandon in 1798, the Assiniboine refused drinking in the tent provided for them "and insisted on drinking in ye House as they do at other places or else would not come any more." A band of ten men and eight women who arrived in early December demanded the same: "I wanted to make a tent out for them but they absolutely refused as they always drink in at ye other houses...."[44] In 1800, Assiniboine and Cree at Brandon House established unheard of prices from the HBC fort and the two NWC posts and an XY house nearby. John McKay complained that all was "spoil'd in every respect the natives will now ask for their meat clothes

---

[39] *The Journal of Duncan M'Gillivray*, 55.
[40] HBCA. Letter from John Sutherland to Goodwin, February 18, 1795, Brandon House Journals, B.22/a/2.
[41] HBCA. November 3, 1798, Brandon House Journals, B.22/a/6.
[42] Ibid., April 27, 1799.
[43] HBCA. Miller paid "the Indian that hunted with Easter [a post servant and hunter] 3 gallons of brandy for 2 cattle and he thought that he was not well paid I would get 6 for it last year...." Thomas Miller's Winnipeg Post Journal 1799–1800, B.235/a/2.
[44] HBCA. Robert Goodwin's Journal, Brandon House, November 4 and December 3, 1798, B.22/a/6.

and blankets a thing in R[ed] R[iver] never heard of before." They even demanded brandy and ammunition as gifts, not traded commodities;[45] and the free alcohol flowing had at least one Assiniboine party leaving Brandon House "as drunk as possible," John McKay stated, and "I really believe their horses and dogs were drunk also." Adding further cost were trade formalities elaborated upon by Native provisioners who would have more than just muskets fired on their arrival, the usual courtesy. A fort cannon now was to be discharged in their honor: McKay estimated that, combined, the three houses nearby blasted "above five pints of powder" saluting these demanding traders this way.[46]

Spiraling provision prices placed premiums on nearby pounding locations. The dozens of European posts in the Assiniboine Valley were sending out horses throughout the fall and winter in a bid to buy up whatever they could from pounds, "breaking their necks and cutting each others throats" in the bargains they were offering.[47] It was likely in these years that customs of winter market provisioning were further refined. "Hunter camps" hired by posts not only raised prices, but also stopped short of processing in any way the food they hunted. Europeans had to send employees to join in their camps' labor and provide all of the transport. The standing agreement at Fort Carlton was that hunting tents, hired by the post, killed animals; they usually staged the meat (to save it and protect it from wolves) but the fat was the post's responsibility, and if the hunters bagged it, they traded it, even though the animals might have already been purchased by the post.[48] Apparently they were not offering to do much more. Posts hustled to send sleds to these pounds to claim at least some of the good meat. Otherwise, if they weren't offering their own labor, living within the camps themselves, or being on hand to at least offer gifts of alcohol or tobacco, they risked getting the throwaway cuts, lower value fats, and, even, the poorest fare usually designated as dogs' meat.[49]

---

[45] HBCA. September 26, 1801, Brandon House Journals, B.22/a/9.
[46] Ibid., October 25, 1801.
[47] Ibid., November 2, 1801.
[48] HBCA. For instance, at Carlton House, where "the 3 hunters and another Indian who was hunting with them came to the house to trade rum with fat they have made out of the inside of the animals they had killed and which belonging to me if the men had collected but the hunters informed me they wont be at the trouble to bring it out of the place." January 14, 1819, Carlton House Journals, B.27/a/9.
[49] HBCA. Fort Edmonton made sure to send three employees to a Buffalo Lake pound "and should there be plenty at the pound to load their sledges with the best; as we want it to salt for headquarters," February 8, 1829, Fort Edmonton Journals, B.60/a/26.

The competition for the trade forced Europeans to give away, rather than trade, gunpowder. The limited gauge of HBC trade guns initially discouraged firearm use against bison. Certainly the commonly used "fouling pieces" were too small to hunt buffalo, and the ball had to be loaded so heavily that it cost a "many a waste shot and is very expensive on the powder which is so precious in this country," Brandon House employees stated, requesting that large-bore muskets with suitable ball be sent "to kill buffalo."[50] Assiniboine seem to have overcome the problems of fowling pieces by using 2.5-foot guns at close range, on horseback; these were in great demand by them for such purposes at Red River by 1800. The Ojibwa hunting for Alexander Henry the Younger in 1800 seemed to have adopted that gun, and enjoying free supplies of gunpowder, in idle moments fired their muskets as amusement at worthless bulls near their camp.[51] It was likely these gratuities, and other encouragements given to Ojibwa to hunt in the Lower Red River, a large war zone with the Sioux, that led Henry to rate pemmican he made at Pembina at an astronomical sterling value of a shilling a pound in 1801.[52]

With their gaining value for trade product, pounding locations also became contested spaces. Rannie has noted that the provisions trade likely spurred increased incidences of deliberately sparked fires by the turn of the century.[53] Anthropogenic fire raged over more territories as Indian pounders attempted to drive animals toward their winter works.[54] They likely fired areas to keep animals within their own territory, away from their enemies, and, likely, from other pounds, too. Of course, many fires simply got out of control and burned everything. Infernos drove up and down the Assiniboine River, sparked in the dry seasons in the first years of the century. They were something John McKay had never witnessed

---

[50] HBCA. January 5, 1797. Brandon House Journals, B.22/a/4.
[51] *The Journal of Alexander Henry the Younger*, I, 35.
[52] He rated 102 bags produced there weighing 8,772 at 1 shilling per pound or £432.12. *The Journal of Alexander Henry the Younger*, I, 132.
[53] W. F. Rannie (Spring 2001), "'Awful Splendour': Historical Accounts of Prairie Fire in Southern Manitoba Prior to 1870," *Prairie Forum*, 26(1):17–46.
[54] See Arthur's discussion of native use of fire and smoke, and effective herd management and diversion in George W. Arthur, "An Introduction to the Ecology of Early Historic Communal Bison Hunting Among the Northern Plains Indians," Archaeological Survey of Canada Paper No. 37 (Ottawa: National Museums of Canada, 1975), 23–24; and Stephen J. Pyne, *Awful Splendour: A Fire History of Canada* (Vancouver: UBC Press, 2007), 31–40; William M. Denevan (1992), "The Pristine Myth: The Landscape of the Americas in 1492," *Annals of the Association of American Geographers*, 82(3):369–385; and " Shepard Krech III, "Fire," from *Ecological Indian: Myth and History* (New York: W. W. Norton, 1999), 101–122.

in such size and power. The flames nearly burnt Brandon House to the ground in 1801, and after his men fought them off, the trader noted in wonder how "the fire rolled along the plain like the waves of the sea." He summed up a poor provisions season on the Assiniboine River in May 1802 in which warfare, fires, and competition had cut the quantities sent on to Red River, and "The whole of the provision that we have expended this winter has been purchased at a very high rate as no Cattle being near we could not hunt a single mouthful for ourselves...."[55]

Blackfoot and the Provisions Market

The pemmican trade developing in the eastern sections of the British plains helped drive the fur trade's own spectacular spatial and capitalized expansion into the western tracts. Despite Cree misgivings downriver in eastern sections of the prairie on the Saskatchewan, fur traders moved posts progressively westward to gain them direct access to the trade in the North Saskatchewan upper basin. They took trade directly to Siksika and other Blackfoot-speaking people who frequented the constantly changing spots where Fort Augustus and its sister HBC post, Fort Edmonton, stood; Kainai of the Red Deer River basin now directly traded with Europeans and, without middleman costs attached to their goods, found prices falling in their favor. By the 1780s, European traders had established contacts in the foothills of the Rocky Mountains, now among the comparatively horse-rich Piikani. Their direct trade, especially in cheap firearms, allowed the Blackfoot people to enjoy both larger horse herds through trade and far greater firepower. Both were used to gain for the Blackfoot a formidable reputation by the turn of the century as some of the most powerful and feared warriors of the Northern Plains.

The market's expansion touched off serious regional disequilibrium, however.[56] Cree lower on the Saskatchewan felt new pressure as they lost coveted middlemen status with the western tribes; they saw brazen Montrealers and English heading up the Saskatchewan in well-gooded

[55] HBCA. May 2–20, 1802, Brandon House Journals, B.22/a/8.
[56] Binnema, *Common and Contested Ground: A Human and Environomental History of the Northwestern Plains* (Toronto: University of Toronto Press, 2001), 178–179; Milloy, *The Plains Cree*, 32–37; the other possibility is that the 1806 breakdown was simply part of an ongoing contentious relationship between Cree and Blackfoot; David Smyth, "The Niititapi Trade: Euroamericans and the Blackfoot Speaking Peoples to the Mid-1830s," PhD dissertation, Department of History, Carleton University, 2001), 174–189; 250–253.

canoes and even in the first bateaux (the prototypes of the later York boat) that could withstand the shorter ice-free seasons, the rapids, and the speedy tempo of that river's wild sections. As Cree influence declined in the eastern areas of the Winnipeg Steppe, their prairie divisions also found access to Blackfoot horses narrowing, and with the Mandan markets closed to them, the "downriver" and eastern plains Cree either raided their trade allies or traded with their allies' enemies to gain access to horses.

As the Cree trade with Europeans soured in the first decade of the century, bands increasingly resented the market's westward push. Most vulnerable to both Cree theft and plunder, however, were Gros Ventres, sandwiched between their shaky Blackfoot alliances on the west and the South Branch people to the east. These former Missourians who had moved northwest into the xeric plains to hunt the great bison herds found in what is now south-central Saskatchewan, felt themselves targets for Assiniboine and Cree horse raiding. These latter tribes also made direct forays to the Missouri in these years; they raided with greater daring, themselves increasingly threatened by the growing horse power of the Dakota and Lakota who, too, were gaining access to firearms. By 1793, the Dakota, likely using horses, raided and massacred an Assiniboine camp on the Red River. Assiniboine and Cree counter raids and plunder parties sparked the regional "Horse Wars," as they are termed, some of the most bloody and costly spates of violence stretching after the turn of the century to the 1840s.[57]

Europeans making bulk food purchases did not help stabilize the plains. A growing, almost inexorable rush to arm animated the nations in the environs of the Battle River. Warfare was growing almost everywhere – the Cree against alienated Gros Ventres; and, now, the Blackfoot against the Crow, the Flathead, Kootenay, and soon "Snake" or Shoshone; to the east, the arming Ojibwa/Saulteaux against Yankton Sioux in the upper reaches of the Red River; and finally, the expanding market made Cree and Blackfoot competitors rather than trading partners, and their great rupture by the turn of the century provided reasons enough for pounds to sell excess bison meat to Europeans, this to procure arms for defensive or offensive military purposes.[58]

---

[57] Milloy distinguishes between the "Horse wars" and the "Buffalo Wars"; see *The Plains Cree*, 83–88.

[58] LAC. And so, the Premier, a Saulteaux chief sent pounded and dried meat to Miles Macdonell as well as the Nor'west traders just before prevailing on them for ammunition,

Typically these tribes used horsepower to make war and occasionally hunt in summer, but they continued to integrate horses into the traditions – and very large returns – of communal hunting, especially at winter pounds. Until the end of the bison era, Northern Plains people tended to append their developing market hunting within their own subsistence activities, especially at winter pounds where excesses were more easily created (see Figures 5.1, 5.2, and 6.1).

Rising regional tensions help explain the beginnings, still only that, of a more stable trade developing between Europeans and Blackfoot. Unlike most of the prairie tribes Europeans were accustomed to trading with, these and other "buffalo people" of the foothills and xeric plains were fully dependent on the seasonal rounds of bison; from the beginnings of contact with the "hairy faced people," the Blackfoot needed the least from these newcomers' trade, and, in turn, they offered the most shaky and instable commerce relations. While Blackfoot benefited from European expansion into their territories, their exchanges were still more political than economic, and clearly on Blackfoot, not European, terms. The commodities of Blackfoot exchange were in wolf skins and other lower-value furbearers, which, after the 1780s, steadily lost market favor in Europe. As seen earlier, plains tribes of Blackfoot-speakers usually had strict taboos against killing beaver to conserve beaver-dammed water and therefore better manage bison herds on the arid semi-desert expanses of what is now southeastern Alberta and northeastern Montana.[59] Given the limits of market integration among Blackfoot speakers, it is telling that Fort George, located near the Battle River, relied almost exclusively on Cree and Assiniboine poundmakers to make its returns; the many Blood, Blackfoot, and Piikani, as well as Gros Ventres nearby, visited merely to negotiate and renegotiate places for these newcomers on the peripheries of their territories, on their own terms.

"I have seen one of this tribe employ a ½ hour in bartering a Dozen Wolves and twice as many *Dépouilles*," Duncan M'Gillivray complained of the Siksika, "and so unreasonable as to demand a Gun, Pistol, or any other article that attracted his attention... and yet seem but little

---

as his Saulteaux, the Crees and Assiniboine were "going to war against the Sioux" July 13 and 14, 1813, Miles Macdonnel's Journal, *Selkirk Papers, Series A*, 16843.

[59] See Smyth, "The Niitsitapi Trade," 200–210; and "Man/Beaver Relationships" in R. Grace Morgan, "Beaver Ecology/ Beaver Mythology," PhD thesis, University of Alberta, 1991, 63–80.

disappointed on being offered 2 feet Tobacco for it."[60] With these plains tribes, provisions, and political relations, were highly priced and only conditionally offered. The Blackfoot certainly had no reason to rush into the arms of these newcomers. Having them nearby offered benefits in metal, guns, powder, and knives for war, but posed threats: the guns being carried to Blackfoot could be diverted into the hands of the Kootenay and Crow either by opportunistic Europeans, Cree, or Blackfoot sell-outs. By the late 1790s, keeping mountain tribe Kootenay embassies from Fort George parlays and creating a *cordon sanitaire* between mountain tribes and Europeans required careful vigilance on the part of Blackfoot. Senior chiefs had managed in the 1780s to do so through diplomacy in the belief that trade could be monopolized with these outsiders. But younger chiefs occasionally thought the safer alternative was to rid the territory of traders who might easily unbalance Blackfoot supreme power in favor of mountain tribes. By the time Duncan M'Gillivray was at Fort George, younger chiefs moved between the two options.[61]

European traders found the people of the foothills and xeric plains a formidable force, enriched and empowered by their bison food surpluses. Elaborate protocol framed their diplomatic overtures. By the turn of the century, Alexander Henry the Younger would open talks with the Blackfoot by sending tobacco, wrapped in paper and tied with vermillion ribbon, to headmen via young runners; chiefs consenting to meet would have their camps sometimes numbering in the thousands settle in nearby. Trade would begin only with the procession of chiefs and esteemed war chiefs to a council in the post. These numbered twenty to thirty at a time. Just how respected the head of the processional was determined how far the chief trader went out from the fort to greet him. During their stay, fur traders had nothing to do with the rest of the tribe camped in his post's environs. The power of these diplomats was considerable.

---

[60] Arthur S. Morton, ed. *The Journal of Duncan M'Gillivray of the North West Company at Fort George on the Saskatchewan, 1794–5* (Toronto: Macmillan, 1929), 46–47.

[61] The Blackfoot *Gros Blanc*, once taking part in the Gros Ventres sacking of the Pine Island posts and the South Branch houses in 1793 – both to avenge Cree killings in the South Branch area and gut the fort of guns and other tradable plunder – now arrived to Fort George on apologetic terms. M'Gillivray saw the marked change in the chief's demeanor. Gros Blanc took the trader's tongue lashing, and then had his juniors open bales of wolves and 800 lbs. of pounded meat and "with a sufficient quantity of Fat to employ twice as much." *The Journal of Duncan M'Gillivray*, 46–47. On the changing diplomacy of Blackfoot and the shift from older to younger chiefs' strategies, see Theodore Binnema (March 1996), "Old Swan, Big Man, and the Siksika Bands, 1794–1815," *Canadian Historical Review*, 77(1):1–32.

Chiefs could, with a nod, arrange for the feeding of an entire fur trading establishment such as Henry's Fort Augustus – with upwards of seventy-two men, thirty-seven women, and sixty-five children –with fresh bison meat daily during their entire stay. By 1808, a year of particularly tumultuous Cree–Blackfoot–European relations, Blackfoot, Piikani, and Kanai visited alternatively, sometimes together. Vast quantities of provisions were offered almost gratis from these great bison hunters who used horses, surrounds, and fall pounds most effectively.

It was without coincidence that year when Painted Feather, a regular trading chief perhaps wanting to display just how impressive Blackfoot pounds could be, repeatedly invited both Alexander Henry the Younger and his HBC neighbor nearby to visit his pound – one of many in the upper reaches of the Athabasca Valley. Once Henry was on the ground, he and his traders were set up in a special tent. The camp's principal men visited there. Painted Feather himself did. And from its lofty vantage, the chiefs, war chiefs, and traders could view the spectacle from afar. This was undoubtedly to clinch relations, to impress fur traders with a show of sheer Blackfoot power in the chase, especially with their massive horse herds now making pounds unbelievably effective, "the young men driving up whole herds, and coming from different directions with them." Likely to Painted Feather's embarrassment, the wind was not in his camp's favor and smoke from their fires drove animals away before they entered the enclosure. The entire exercise, however, had the potent symbolism of a Soviet May Day missile parade. It was meant to impress Henry as "their principal object was to get what they could from us..."[62] Fort Augustus men, meanwhile, visited the sprawling Blackfoot camp in ease and were "in their glory," as the Blackfoot were "giving plenty to eat, and offering their Wives to sleep with them, upon easy terms," as wife-exchange and the offering of sexual favors to esteemed or valuable trading partners was not an uncommon diplomatic overture among people on the Missouri and the foothills region.[63] A few days later, young

---

[62] Barry M. Gough, ed., *The Journal of Alexander Henry the Younger, 1799–1814*. (Toronto: The Champlain Society, 1988), II, 421–422; on Painted Feather's generosity and cheap provisions, 397–98.

[63] *The Journal of Alexander Henry the Younger*, II, 422. Henry later spoke of the Piikani and their wife barter; "In their visits to our Establishments, their women consists of one of their articles of temporary Barter with our men, a few inches of Twist Tobacco their demands. A Gros Ventres will barter the person of his wives or daughters with as much sang froid, as he would make a bargain for a horse." Ibid., 545. On women figuring in trade relations and diplomacy, see Michael Landsing (Winter 2000), "Plains Indian Women and Interracial Marriage in the Upper Missouri Trade, 1804–1868," *The Western Historical Quarterly*, 31(4):413–433. Alice B. Kehoe (1970), "The Function of Ceremonial Sexual

men from other Blackfoot camps, including that of Black Bear's, arrived with similar invitations, "to go and see the Buffalo enter the pounds," but Henry was tired of the spectacle by that time.

The Blackfoot were likely renegotiating the place of Nor'Westers and HBC men by this juncture. The Napoleonic Wars had closed down all but the luxury fur markets, including now wolf pelts, and the costs of the trade had jettisoned. The Nor'Westers had already stopped buying now worthless skins or offered next to nothing for them, and the HBC was following suit. Along with mountain rivals, Cree and interloping Assiniboine having no scruples in hunting beaver in Blackfoot territories, and soon even some Piikani starting to trap for the sake of buying guns, the Blackfoot, indeed, were in a precarious position. By 1809, Blackfoot parties led by Painted Feather were making new terms with Nor'Westers, bringing vast quantities of "dried berries, pounded meat and Grease, Backfat," skins, robes, and horses, "all which [we] get very cheap," Henry said.

But the true Blackfoot provisions trade was only nascent, steeped in political meaning. The Blackfoot offered food as gifts to enter into exchange. It would only be with their fresh standoffs with the Crow in the late 1820s and early 1830s and the gathering threat of now well-armed Kootenay and Flathead, when a true buffalo market hunt developed and even Piikani pemmican was offered for sale. Only by that point did Fort Edmonton become besieged by Tsuu-Tsina (at the same time as Cree did) to demand "guns and kettles," the one for self-preservation in bloody warfare, the latter to make easier the preparation of greases and fats to sell to the market; such posts as Fort Peigan, opening briefly in 1831–1832, became superabundantly stocked with traded bison fat and meats and even ready-made pemmican (albeit still in small quantities) at that point.[64]

For the time being, traders like Alexander Henry the Younger perceived that the Blackfoot, whatever their open-handed generosity, were bringing only what they did not want themselves – fats and meat of a lower quality than those offered by the Assiniboine.[65] By 1810, the

---

Intercourse among the Northern Plains Indians," *Plains Anthropologist*, 15(48):99–103. Albert Hurtado (1996), "When Strangers Met: Sex and Gender on Three Frontiers," *Frontiers: A Journal of Women Studies*, 17(3), 52–75.

[64] HBCA. See Bow Fort Accounts, 1832–1833, where returns of the Blackfoot, Blood and Sarcee are enumerated. B.21/d/1.

[65] Henry noted that Assiniboine brought beat meat and grease "of a much superior quality to that of the Slave Indians" in 1809. *Journal of Alexander Henry the Younger*, II, 423.

Piikani received traders with deep suspicion now that David Thompson had enlarged trade, as feared, to the Kootenay, and the Piikani had experienced some of its first losses from now armed mountain tribes. The Athabasca River route over the mountains was blockaded in 1810 by parties led by Black Bear and other Piikani. These war chiefs were welcoming enough to Nor-Westers like Henry, provided that they were trading on the East Slope and not with the beaver-producing Kootenay.[66] Still powerful, but now facing American expansion on the Missouri in the wake of Louis and Clark's explorations, the awful position of the Blackfoot-speaking people was perhaps best personified in the person of L'Homme à Calumet. He was an "old offender" of attacks made by Piikani and Gros Ventres against the South Branch and Island Forts in 1793. His name had changed by 1811 from L'Homme à Calumet to Day Light, and then to The Horns. Now he went by Iron Shirt. Having left his own country for a time, he had joined with Gros Ventres/ Aitsina for a journey to the south, probably as far as the Spanish settlements in California. There he had gotten hold of an iron mail garment, "Made of small links of iron or steel close connected together, it reaches down below the Hip, and below the Elbow, is close around the Neck...."[67] He wore the iron mail shirt on his visits to posts and while donning it "imagines himself Ball proof." But, Henry knew that a musket ball from any of the Blackfoot's newly armed enemies, or even "a good Broad Sword," would certainly "demolish it." Like the Western Plains tribes, in general, the onrush of commerce raised opportunities but problematic questions. The Blackfoot found themselves ensconced in a "dark storm" now swirling at the very foot of the Rocky Mountains.[68]

When they were in the market, venting products from the winter pounds, Blackfoot at least had the market in their favor. At Cumberland House, the HBC's largest food depot, pemmican, dried meat, and fat prices, pegged in sterling as of 1810,[69] revealed the trend that had seen Blackfoot food products rise in price on the market. Local hunting failures, so common in the Upper Saskatchewan Valley, aggravated the

---

[66] Ibid., II, 482.
[67] Ibid., II, 559.
[68] The expression is Belyea's and references Peter Fidler's 1792 descriptions of the west slope, see Barbara Bellyea, *Dark Storm Moving West* (Calgary: University of Calgary Press, 2007), xi.
[69] It was Andrew Colville's reform of the HBC's trade in 1810 which moved the company from accounting in "made beaver" to sterling. See E. E. Rich, ed., *Robertson's Letters*, xxxii.

regional trend and could, on an annual basis, send prices jettisoning at Fort Edmonton. In 1812, a mild winter and the effects of widespread fires left plains hunters around Fort Edmonton near starvation, and, between September and the following April, 1813, not more than 20 lbs. of pemmican had been produced.[70] Prices escalated by the following fall when Fort Edmonton instructed its traders to make "extraordinary payment" to encourage hunters to make provisions beyond their own needs.[71] With Edmonton unable to match its earlier contributions to Cumberland's northern brigades its factor soon offered hunting camps "a greater price than they have been accustomed to receive" for any provisions they produced, although it was uncertain whether the same hunters would offer much.[72]

Inelastic Supply from Pounds

Like the Blackfoot, Cree and Assiniboine poundmakers in the Red and Assiniboine Valleys were in no hurry to increase production in these years. In the case of the latter, purchasing power doubled and sometimes tripled from 1796 to 1801. Having relatively few needs to begin with, the only commodity Assiniboine might have taken was in luxury consumables. But native demands for even these products were already being met. Donald McKay was quite amazed by the quantities of brandy in the Red River as early as 1794. Canadians up and down the Red and Assiniboine Rivers were pouring rum "like water,"[73] and, there were few reasons for Cree and Assiniboine to hunt "as they get Plenty now between so many houses as there is now on this River at Present," he said. That year, there were at least nine settlements near Brandon House, alone, and "brandy is the cry now of every one."[74] By 1796, so much competition thrived around pounds that, at least at Shell River, draining into the northern arm of the Assiniboine, "All the traders gives that the Indians do not hunt there the buffalo and traders is too many this year."[75]

---

[70] HBCA. April 20, 1813, Fort Edmonton Journals, B.60/a/11.
[71] Ibid., December 29, 1813.
[72] Ibid., November 24, 1813.
[73] HBCA. March 27, 1794, Brandon House Journals, B.22/a/1.
[74] Ibid., March 7, 1794.
[75] HBCA. Letter from John Sutherland, February 26, 1796, in Brandon House Journals, B.22/a/1. The relatively small, in not insignificant, amounts of alcohol in the HBC trade with Cree and Assiniboine in the early eighteenth century is well analyzed by Ann M. Carlos and Frank D. Lewis, *Commerce by a Frozen Sea: Native Americans and the European Fur Trade* (Philadelphia: University of Pennsylvania Press, 2010), 90–95. The

Posts pressed their own hunters to continue forays in the summer to make up for crews staying on for the season or to make supplies for the fall brigades. But this was not a traditional time for intensive hunting. By summer Cree preferred making spiritual journeys to Moose Head and other prairie outliers "to conjure," this usually in May and June; their summer culminated in traditional ceremonials, Sun Dance gatherings, or, more simply, amusements. Hunters rested at Brandon House and categorically refused to exert themselves in the hot summer days; "starving," the Brandon House master complained. He blamed it "through more laziness [than inability] to hunt. They do nothing but smoke and play at the platter," the latter a dice game popular throughout Native North America. But he must have been conscious that these hunters' winter contributions to the post's commissary entitled these hunters to a portion of summer pemmican. And, if the ice in the sheds did not melt they could claim some of the fresh piece meat still frozen, too.

The Assiniboine arriving in the last days of May 1795 in Brandon House, then, expected alcohol, gifts, food, and other returns for their previous food trades. They brought a scant 32 lbs. of beat meat, 24 lbs. of fat, and a little fresh meat. Their camp undoubtedly drew on the post's stored supplies and some of its brandy stores while camped nearby. Another very large Assiniboine party arrived the next day with nary 16 lbs. of fat, but "very troublesome in asking for brandy, cloth and blankets," and, when it left the following evening, the party – probably a bit hung-over – made off with the post's watch dog "before they set off," likely to eat it.[76] The implied social obligations rarely impressed these traders, who found the "meadow" people always a troublesome lot. It is interesting that Alexander Henry the Younger, who made some of the most extensive trades in the Winnipeg Steppe for food, and had to turn to Ojibwa to do most of his hunting, never seems to have forgiven Cree who likely snubbed his greatest outlays of gifts, goods, and credits: "a useless set of lazy, indolent fellows, a mere nuisance ... found in large Camps Winter and Summer, where they remain Idle through out the year."[77]

---

ways competition raised the scale of alcohol trading is discussed by Arthur J. Ray, *Indians in the Fur Trade: Their Role as Trappers, Hunters, and Middlemen in the Lands Southwest of Hudson Bay, 1660–1870* (Toronto: University of Toronto Press, 1998), 85.

[76] HBCA. May 23–26, and July 6, 1796, Summer journal kept by Thomas Miller, Brandon House Journals, B.22/a/4.

[77] *Journal of Alexander Henry the Younger*, II, 368.

Raising Stakes, Inciting a Summer Hunt

The need to increase production grew in the late eighteenth and early nineteenth centuries. Accordingly, posts dispatched their own employees to meet the elusive and largely untapped summer herds far inland. Horses proved critical. However, even when the HBC could send out employees on horseback, they found Assiniboine and Cree farther inland defensive of these inland refuges and activities there that might imperil their own winter pounding locations. In August 1798, Brandon House's "hunters returned with flesh, plenty of cattle, but the Indians are drawing them away." The meat they did get went rancid easily in any case; it didn't store well, and special drying stages in the field, not at the post, had to be built.[78]

These summer hunters traveled, conspicuously, in summer temperatures. Although dry and hot summer weather favored meat drying, it could seriously imperil meats if they were not staged quickly enough, and fats, without care, went rancid before being properly rendered. This was no pastime for amateurs. The Brandon House employees who went with dogs to the plains on July 28, 1798, returned with only a little buffalo flesh, "the weather being so hot they could not bring more as two of the best dogs died for want of water in the plains the rest narrowly sav'd the life till they came to the river."[79] This mostly bulls' meat was easily ruined in hot weather, or hot spells, such as in 1800 when on June 23, Brandon House hunters returned with one bull "almost spoild" by the "sultry" weather in the field, and a week later, another bull "entirely spoil" by the same conditions.[80]

HBC and Montreal traders had little luck animating a market-oriented summer hunt among Assiniboine and Cree but they did, however, encourage more individualist winter forays and finally a summer hunt among Ojibwa. These people were well positioned to exploit the growing demand by Europeans, having proven to be capable beaver hunters and already familiar with the workings of the eastern fur trade. As newcomers to the region, they also saw great advantages in political and economic ties to the HBC posts, and especially the Red River Colony, which joined the scramble for local food resources in 1812. From the very beginnings such chiefs as the Premier, Passongab (the

---

[78] HBCA. August 21, 1798, Brandon House Journals, B.22/a/4.
[79] Ibid., July 28, 1798.
[80] HBCA.June 23 and July 8, 1801, Thomas Bunn's Journal, Brandon House Journals, B.22/a/9.

Murderer), and Murderer's Son, established long-standing food and fur trades with these newcomers and were quite happy to see the colonists' Fort Daer at the Pembina in 1813 constructed and hoped "that the fire of it will not be extinguished," as one of the Ojibwa chiefs told the colonists.[81]

The Ojibwa, however, were not poundmakers in the usual sense. They certainly had less experience than Cree and Assiniboine farther inland with the large summer herds or even the smaller migratory fragments that moved into winter shelter belts. The Ojibwa with whom John Tanner hunted on the Assiniboine River seemed to have never resorted to a pound, and likely did not have the numbers or historic tenure in the area to construct one in any case.[82] It was among Ojibwa, nevertheless, that Alexander Henry the Younger drew hunters and meat and fat handlers to work at Pembina and the Hair Hills, and it was among them he organized the first recorded market hunts in summer, furnishing them with gunpowder cheaply, if not gratis. In 1804, Henry had a summer post at Hair Hills produce much of his returns of pemmican. He made captain, with a suit of clothing and other gifts, the "fine hunter" and Ojibwa provisioner, Naubunoitouog, or Man with One Ear. By the end of April presents of alcohol were given to squads of Ojibwa who agreed to Henry's proposition and "decamped" to the plains for a summer hunt. This band, however, was relatively horse poor, as Henry noted that when one group headed for the Horse Hills by May 7 they "formed a long string in the plains above a mile long, 65 men and women, 10 horse and 60 dogs."[83] The limits to Ojibwa horsepower in the early nineteenth century were captured in Henry's description of one of his ablest hunters, Le Boeuf, reputed to have run herds of bison in winter *on foot*, when there was little snow on the ground. Le Boeuf had the knack– not to mention courage – to run among stampeding animals, firing and reloading his musket on the fly, and killing as "many animals as he wished, and always keeping himself in the thickets of the herd."[84] Tanner saw such individualism in the techniques employed by Ojibwa with whom

---

[81] LAC. March 12, 1813, Miles Macdonell's Journal, *Selkirk Papers, Series A,* 16804.

[82] The Ojibwa in Tanner's company hunted bison in winter on foot, with guns, using stealth and hiding places in wooded areas to their advantage. Edward James, ed., *A Narrative of the Captivity and Adventures of John Tanner (US Interpreter at the Saut de Ste. Marie): During Thirty Years Among the Indians in the Interior of North America* (New York: G.&C.&H. Carvill 1830 [1956]), 62.

[83] May 7, 1804, *Journal of Alexander Henry the Younger,* I, 159.

[84] Ibid., November 2, 1802, 137.

he hunted on the Assiniboine, about the same time as Le Beouf was sprinting around fall herds. It was likely a correct assessment made by Miles Macdonell, the appointed governor of the Red River Colony arriving in 1812, that at least among the Ojibwa (Saulteaux) in the Red River Valley, "No dependence could be put on supplies from the [Ojibwa] natives" for provisions. "The Salteaux or Bungee Indian never make pounds to catch buffaloe. The Crees, Assinbioine, and other natives to the westward hunt with great success in that way, but these were at a great distance from us."[85]

The Ojibwa were probably some of the first to truly shift into summer market hunting. But they were being joined for the economic payoffs at hand by other groups who, in their joining of new technology and horses, were in the throes of "ethnogenesis." Large-scale summer market hunting organized in the struggling, largely mixed blood community emerging in the Red River area, at least by the first decade of the nineteenth century, when the potent combination of better-maintained horse herds, and the technical know-how to use them for summer market hunting (Figure 3.1), joined with the heavyweight Red River cart. These technologies first gained use within mixed Cree, Assiniboine, Ojibwa, and French-descendent freemen in the northeastern plains of present day Manitoba, Minnesota, North Dakota, and likely farther to the west. This emerging, polyethnic mixing was based on an inclusive adoption of outsiders and the technologies they offered, which likely provided advantages for an emerging plains culture based on joined "worldviews, lifeways, mentalities and materialities to form a new and original society of Native Americans," as Vrooman has argued.[86] Described as part of a larger multicultural tradition, and competing with European market economies on their own terms, the *nêhiyaw-pwât* "Iron Alliance" of Northern Plains people in the end constituted a highly mobile and independent entity on the plains. At least by the 1790s, it was this market-oriented aboriginal group soon gaining an identity as Métis within the Red River region that better organized, with horsepower, mounted hunts with short-length trade muskets, to

---

[85] LAC. Macdonell to Selkirk, July 17, 1813, *Selkirk Papers*, Vol. I, 111. This does not preclude the adaption of woodland pounds for plains bison herds. For a description of a Plains Ojibwa pound see Eleanor Verbicky-Todd, *Communal Buffalo Hunting among the Plains Indians*. Archaeological Survey of Alberta Occasional Paper No. 24, 1984, 104–106.

[86] Nicholas C. P. Vrooman, *"The Whole Country was ... 'One Robe,'": The Little Shell Tribe's America* (Helena: Drummlon Institute, 2012), 5, 21.

Food Fights and Pemmican Wars, 1790–1816   125

Figure 3.1. "Buffalo Hunting" (Rebellion of 1837–1838) c. 1839 Coke Smyth; (Source: (Lithographed by A. Ducote, London HBCA P-39) HBCA N5251).

run bison en masse and return with marketable product for fur trade companies.[87]

The amalgamation of the NWC and the XY Company in 1805 – both heavily capitalized by London financiers and using Montreal as their base – led to large-scale layoffs of personnel, portions of which continued to hunt, provide labor, or carry goods on a contractual basis for the company emerging. Many in turn joined camps of Ojibwa, Cree, or Ojibwa in the steppe, a roster of petty traders and employees who followed the

---

[87] The term "iron alliance" is used by Innes to describe the multiethnic basis of the Cowesses Band in Southeastern Saskatchewan, being Plains Cree, Assiniboine, Ojibwa and Métis. See Robert Alexander Innes, "The Importance of Family Ties to members of Cowessess First nation," PhD dissertation, University of Arizona, 2007), 46; Jacqueline Peterson suggests the importance of Red River technology in the emergence of a distinctive Métis culture, "Rocking the Cradle of the Plains: The Emergence of a New Aboriginal People in Northern North America," unpublished paper, May 2009, provided to author. By 1800, Robert Goodman, at Brandon House, found Assiniboine demanding more 2½ foot guns than he could supply as "they answer so well to hunt cattle on horseback." HBCA. Robert Goodman, September 21, 1800, Brandon House Journals, B.22/a/8 1800–1801.

profits of the time and ended formal affiliation with Montreal or English companies. They became independent hunters, cashing in on the rising value of hunted product at the turn of the nineteenth century. Brandon House employees in the fall of 1805 were helped by freemen "hunting for themselves" who sold at least 200 lbs. of fresh meat to the crews – at what price not mentioned.[88] Much to the embarrassment of the HBC's Red River Post, which condemned such things, mixed blood freemen were stealing Assiniboine horses in June 1805, apparently in time for the summer hunt.[89] Their camps were hardly cohesive, although undoubtedly freemen camps tended to attract similarly minded male fraternities. The predominant planning and organization of John Tanner's adoptive Ojibwa mother, who decided where and how her sons would hunt in their journey from present-day Ontario to the Qu'Appelle Valley, suggests some of the ways these male-dominated, but female organized and planned, hunting parties worked.[90]

Freemen-Métis were very much the "people who owned themselves" as natives began terming these groups.[91] Alexander Henry lamented "peddlars" pestering him to sell dried meats, fats, and pemmican to the hungry crews going to wintering posts. One J. M. Bouch[é] at the Portage la Prairie worked from a hut that even offered an oven to bake bread for the voyageurs going to wintering quarters, with "a great stock of Provisions and other articles for sale." Henry complained that "Those petty traders are really a nuisance on the route."[92]

Competition and Conflict

It was in the context of new entries into the steppe hunt and rising prices on food that the "pemigan wars," as Alexander Macdonald called them,[93]

---

[88] HBCA. August 26, 1805, Brandon House Journals, B.22/a/13 1805–1806.

[89] HBCA. "Twenty five Canadians went down the [Assiniboine] River before they went off they stole five Indians horses, that is a pretty example to set the natives," June 6, 1805, Brandon House Journals, B.22/a/13.

[90] John Foster, "Wintering, the Outsider Adult Male and the Ethnogenesis of the Western Plains Métis," in Patrick C. Douaud, ed., *The Western Métis: Profile of a People* (Regina: Canadian Plains Research Centre, 2007 [1994]), 94–95; Jennifer Brown, "Fur Trade as Centrifuge: Familial Dispersal and Offspring Identity in Two Company Contexts," in Raymond J. Demallie and Alfonso Ortiz, eds., *North American Anthropology: Essays on Society and Culture* (Norman and London: University of Oklahoma Press, 1994), 119–217.

[91] Heather Devine, *The People Who Own Themselves: Aboriginal Ethnogenesis in a Canadian Family* (Calgary: University of Calgary Press, 2004).

[92] *Journal of Alexander Henry the Younger*, I, 143.

[93] LAC. Alexander Macdonald to Archibald McLellan, December 7, 1816, *Selkirk Papers*, Series B, 121.

began between 1810 and 1816. Existing historiography of the warfare emphasizes the commercial rivalry that finally turned violent in these years, truly a sort of "fur trade wars," as J. M. Bumstead described them.[94] Central to the story is the Métis growing as a people around the provisions trading occurring at such places as Qu'Appelle Fort, by then a groaning, bloody pemmican factory. This idea of a cultural birth in the trade has held favor with the work of A. S. Morton and, later, Marcel Giraud. According to the latter, the Métis, who originally worked without opposing the Selkirk settlers, became increasingly radicalized by the prohibitive measures of the appointed governor of the colony, Miles Macdonell, especially as he increasingly closed down their opportunities to export bison outside the Assiniboia Colony.[95] By offering this, Giraud sought to identify an emergent Métis identity and even a nascent nationalism among these hunters and provisions makers.[96] Gerhard Ens, recently, has situated the pemmican wars in an ecological and environmental perspective. Overturning Tim Ball's attribution of some of the conflict to supposedly straightened circumstances following the Tambora Volcanic eruption in 1815, Ens emphasized first the difficulty facing many of the provisioning posts in the region by 1812, and then under changing climatic conditions, observed a flush of provisions throughout the post system the following years. He argued that there were more provisions than ever in 1815 through 1816. The violence in the same years amounted to a strategy concerted by Montreal partners that led to an unexpected and bloody confrontation at Seven Oaks and the killings of sixteen colonists in June of that year.[97]

---

[94] W. L. Morton, *Manitoba: A History* (Toronto: University of Toronto Press, 1967), 42; see J. M. Bumsted, *Fur Trade Wars: The Founding of Western Canada* (Winnipeg: Great Plains Publications, 1999); an overview of Red River historiography is usefully provided by Fritz Pannekoek (1981), "The Historiography of the Red River Settlement, 1830–1868," *Prairie Forum*, 6(1):75–85; on the oral history of Seven Oaks, especially the tracing of the Pierre Falcon song, "Chanson de la Grenouillère" see Margaret Complin's careful reconstruction in Section II, 1939, *Proceedings and Transactions of the Royal Society of Canada*, 49–58; on Métis nationalism at the time of Seven Oaks, see A. S. Morton, *A History of the Canadian West to 1870–71* 568–569; one of the more engaging accounts of the personalities of the pemmican wars was written by Margaret MacLeod and W. L. Morton, *Cuthbert Grant of Grantown* (Toronto: McClelland Stewart, 1974), 24–47.

[95] Marcel Giraud, "The Transformation of the Metis," in George Woodcock, trans., *The Metis in the Canadian West*, Vol. I (Edmonton: University of Alberta Press, 1986), 394–396.

[96] Lyle Dick (1991), "The Seven Oaks Incident and the Construction of a Historical Tradition, 1816 to 1970," *Journal of the Canadian Historical Association*, 2(1):91–113.

[97] Gerhard Ens, "The Climatic and Ecological Background to the Battle of Seven Oaks, 1816." Paper Presented to the 43rd Northern Great Plains History Conference, Brandon, Manitoba September 24–27, 2008; Ens was responding to previous assertions

However, one needs also to consider the irony of the situation where the first food wars occurred in the midst of new plenty, not scarcity. Commercial rivals were gaining access to much needed food supplies by the time they came to blows. Indeed, it would seem that violence grew as companies opted to corner the market to meet their open-ended bids for commercial expansion elsewhere. In that respect, instead of rationally sharing supplies among themselves and ensuring their own access to a requisite quantity at a reasonable price for their immediate needs, they chose the more perilous course of eliminating rivals in the market to free their hands for both commercial survival and an imagined unlimited dividend profit. This latter course almost inevitably led to violence, as many participants at the time fully understood.

The degeneration into violence certainly coincided with a critical juncture in the provisions trade by 1810. At that point, fur trade companies wanted unlimited supply for what might be termed "imaginary" wants (rather than needs), for their commercial operations. By that date, the HBC, facing some of its worst years in terms of financing (having for only the second time in its history held back its yearly dividend to shareholders) adopted "retrenchment" policies to return to profit. The HBC sent orders to plains posts to spare no effort to increase their provision purchases to free up supply for traders to better compete in the Lake Winnipeg area, and, eventually, to use pemmican as a fuel to expand into the Athabasca district, by then a preserve of the Montreal companies.[98] The more aggressive approach was embodied in the case of William Hillier who, with tough Irish recruits, was to face Montreal bully boys by then harassing HBC men trying to move northward. The contingent traveled from York Factory and wound up at Red River to winter, and instead of fighting toe-to-toe with their rivals, settled in with other Irish settlers now arriving at the new colony, ate existing food supplies, and then mutinied in protest, likely realizing just what an awful place

---

made by historical climatologist Timothy Ball, "Climatic Change, Droughts and the Social Impact: Central Canada, 1811–20, a Classic Example;" and "The Year without Summer: Its Impact on the Fur Trade and History of Western Canada," C. R. Harington, ed. *The Year Without Summer: World Climate in 1816* (Ottawa: Canadian Museum of Nature, 1992). See Ens, "The Battle of Seven Oaks," 101.

[98] See Alex Colville and the London Committee's order to William Auld, May 31, 1810 to Winnipeg and Saskatchewan Factories, now designated to "supply the others with pemmican & dried meat which they may require." Quoted, footnote 86, in Margaret L. Clarke, "Reconstituting the Fur Trade Community," MA thesis, University of Winnipeg, 1997, 4–92; E. E. Rich describes the 1810 retrenchment, E. E. Rich, *A History of the Hudson's Bay Company 1670–1870*, Vol. II (London: Hudson Bay Record Society, 1959), 292–293.

they had found themselves.[99] The 1810 debacle underlined the importance of greater food supply and its efficient distribution.

HBC directors also ordered massive purchases to reduce European food imports. Pemmican in unprecedented amounts would stock Albany House on James Bay, and York and Churchill, on Hudson Bay. Red River was to send this stock rated as low as 4 pence per pound (d/lb) in the first two cases, and 5 d/lb in the case of York.[100]

The Nor'westers themselves were in a bind to collect more pemmican, now in their drive to exploit the Pacific coastal trade and expand to Canton, China. Although the War of 1812 undermined the company's fortunes, it had committed intermediary posts in the Upper Saskatchewan to provide pemmican to supply Pacific-bound brigades en route.[101] Red River pemmican, then, had to be supplied for the company's extensive transport into the north. If the HBC was imagining the wealth to be tapped in Athabasca furs, the Montreal companies already there now saw the tantalizing chimeras of massive profits in furs traded to Chinese princes.

The other fantastic leap was made in 1811, when Thomas Dugald, the Earl of Selkirk, dispatched colonists to begin the ill-fated settlement at Red River. Lord Selkirk's settlers arrived by 1812 in rag-tag contingents aboard bateaux from York Factory. Their voyage to Red River is well recounted elsewhere. So, also, is the almost immediate antipathy the colonists raised among the Montreal traders represented by the NWC, and, eventually, after spring of 1814, a good number of the "freemen" hunters already in the Winnipeg Steppe who generally did business with the Nor'westers. The agricultural settlement, launched in a bid to find new lands for displaced highland crofters and Irish cotters, and also support with farmed surpluses the company's Athabasca expansion, was a calculated, but controversial, gamble.[102] Its most contentious aspect was raised with the HBC's grant of "Assiniboia" to Selkirk, the land base from which his colony would be carved. It sprawled in size from modern-day

---

[99] E. E. Rich, ed., *Colin Robertson's Correspondence Book, September 1817 to September 1822* (Toronto: Champlain Society, 1939), xl.
[100] HBCA. William Auld letter from the London Committee, May 31, 1810, London Correspondence Book Outward, 1810–1816, A.6/18.
[101] E. E. Rich, *A History of the Hudson's Bay Company 1670–1870*, Vol. II (London: Hudson's Bay Record Society, 1950), 275.
[102] W. L. Morton, *Manitoba: A History* (Toronto: University of Toronto Press, 1967), 42; on the Métis "transformation" in the midst of the Selkirk Colonization, see Marcel Giraud, *The Metis in the Canadian West*, Vol. I, trans. George Woodcock (Edmonton: University of Alberta Press, 1981), 389–409.

Minnesota and North Dakota, to the old point of Carlton House on the Assiniboine, to Lake Winnipeg and the entirety of the Red River Valley – falling almost completely across the prime provisioning territories of the rival NWC.

Experienced fur traders seconded to the Red River Settlement's service in 1812 saw the colony for what it was: a massive food problem in the making.[103] The first, albeit reduced number of settlers arrived as an awfully "useless" lot in that respect. Given that most of them were in no position to hunt, gather, or trade food, and their low-yielding crops, it turned out, did not fare well, it was fortunate that only eighteen of the thirty-six leaving Scotland for the valley actually arrived that year. But another 120 were en route that fall, and by 1813 the Kildonan contingents, near-refugees from the Sutherland clearances, would number some eighty-three.

Peter Fidler, an experienced trader and fretting planner, took these numbers seriously in 1812. Assigned as the community's victualler from the company's Red River post, he knew winter would bring want, especially among settlers who arrived to the Forks to find that the post's previous manager had not stored even a bag of pemmican for their use. Fidler scrimped on what stock was available. During the hot, dry months at the Forks, he ordered as much meat set aside for winter pemmican. He forced the resentful newcomers onto short rations and a diet of the insipid flesh of mid-summer catfish. The enormous apatite of these highlanders horrified Fidler; they could out-eat fur traders, given a chance or the charity of the colony's cooks, who, contrary to his orders, continued to apportion oatmeal too generously to the work crews busily building quarters. Rife with internal divisions between Gaelic speaking Highlanders and cursing Irishmen, the colony had none of the cohesion and hardly any of the subordination of the fur trade establishments in which Fidler had worked. He saw his planter colony eating nothing short of 30,000 lbs. of dried meat that summer.[104] No wonder that the next year, after being reassigned into fur trade duties and coordinating the settlement's supply from Brandon House, Fidler became one of the most aggressive – and resented – meat buyers in the steppe, offering any price to buy what was coming from the pounds.

---

[103] Rich, *A History of the Hudson's Bay Company*, Vol. II, 320.
[104] HBCA. On fish, the "extravagant" appetites of men, women and children, and the cook's liberality, August 9, 1814, Red River Journals, B.235/a/3.

Fidler had more reason to be concerned by 1815 when he was taking time out of his duties to plan the Jack River depot to launch HBC crews formally into the Athabasca district. The HBC's entry to the Portage La Loche's doorway had been thwarted in 1791 and 1802, given the NWC's superior food organization system.[105] The HBC was now resolved to undertake the Athabasca enterprise on a "large scale" and dispatched Fidler and a team to Jack River, an outsource of Lake Winnipeg, to build up the Athabasca Country depot, eventually located at Knee Lake in 1815. It would grow, eventually, transform and move into the Norway House depot. That summer, men from the Swan River, the Saskatchewan River, and the "low country" posts shuttled goods and provisions northwards for the "Athabasca Expedition." Fidler laid out the two small buildings to house men and masters who would, over three years, construct three buildings for the depot: each ninety feet long, twenty-five feet wide, and two stories high. Jack River would constitute one of the largest and imposing pemmican hangers to that date in the history of the fur trade.[106]

But although there were significantly larger demands for food, greater supply was in the making. Regional changes facilitated it. In 1810 the farthest western segments of the Blackfoot-speaking people, the Piikani, suffered sixteen dead after Rocky Mountains Kootenay attacked them with muskets recently supplied by Cree gun-runners. Expecting Blackfoot and Piikani retribution, sections of the "Southward" (Plains Cree) nations who had formerly used pounds in the Battle River and Neutral Hills region, sharing a lot of space with Kainai, Siksika, and Piikani, shifted eastward toward territories south of Carlton House.

The climate in these years favored their pounds there. The regions these newcomers were trammeling, meanwhile, were prized locations among Assiniboine. Their value in the winter season is suggested in the case of a single Assiniboine pound on the Qu'Appelle River in 1814 where hunters killed no fewer than 400 cows on a single occasion.[107] If not overrun by competitors pounds could be reused even in the same

---

[105] On the first of these occasions, Philip Turnor had tried to undertake the "ill-provided" explorations beyond Île-à-la-Crosse; the second occasion was the failure of Peter Pond, having established Nottingham House on Lake Athabasca, abandoned by 1806. Both are recounted by E. E. Rich, *A History of the Hudson's Bay Company* Vol. II, 139–140; 276–277; there was also the hesitancy of the company to act decisively in the area, despite pleas from traders in the field. See E. E. Rich, ed., *Robertson's Letters*, xxxii–xxxv.

[106] HBCA. July 16 and August 12, 1815, Brandon House Journals, B.22/a/19.

[107] LAC. March 7, 1814, Miles Macdonell's Journal, *Selkirk Papers, Series A*, 16850–59.

season. The Eagle Hill Creek Assiniboine, one of many groups pounding near Fort Carlton in 1813, drove portions of the same herd into their pound no fewer than four times by early December in 1813.[108] The Assiniboine just above the elbow of the Saskatchewan killed 700 animals on one occasion a few weeks later, and these hunters' return to Fort Carlton exactly a month afterwards with yet more meats for sale suggested that they had reused their pound. They likely did throughout that particularly good pounding season.[109]

How many Cree had relocated by the summer of 1815, when Cree planned "war proceedings"[110] from these quarters is not certain, but many were no longer tarrying even in the northern rim of parkland. By fall 1816, "Slave" (likely Piikani, Blood, and Blackfoot combined) "intended to make this part of the country the seat of war upon the Stone [Assiniboine] and Cree Indians," John Pruden, at Carlton House, said.[111] Cree killings of Blood women and children just south of the South Saskatchewan Elbow ruined any hopes of reconciliation in the short term. Indeed, the Blackfoot–Cree war would extend through half a century, one of the most bitterly contested in the bison territories. Now, Cree camps relocated even farther east to the lower areas of the Qu'Appelle. Both at the old Carlton House on the upper Assiniboine and Fort Qu'Appelle, near the present-day Manitoba border, traders saw "Great number of [Cree and Assiniboine] Indians" arrive to trade "on account of wars amongst the Slave indians and they have fled this way for safety."[112] It was the convergence of these pounders that explains some of the upward turn in pemmican production by 1815. The opportunities they presented even gave York Factory superintendent William Auld the idea of trying to divert some of the camps to the elbow of the South Saskatchewan where he hoped to monopolize Assiniboine returns for the HBC's now larger needs.[113] The NWC attempted something similar

---

[108] HBCA. December 11, 1814, Fort Carlton Journals, B.23/a/4.
[109] HBCA. On December 28 they arrived with 1,383 lbs. of pounded meat and 987 lbs. of fat; on January 28, the "Stone Indians from Sandy Ground north of elbow" traded again 699 lbs. of fat and 890 lbs. of pounded meat, Fort Carlton Journals, B.23/a/4.
[110] HBCA. See December 12, 1814, Carlton House Journals, B.23/a/4, "2 Southward Indians arrived – came from Touchwood Hills with messages to Other Indians concerning war proceedings next summer."
[111] HBCA. October 28, 1816, Carlton House (Saskatchewan) Journals, B.27/1/5.
[112] HBCA. See December 23–26, 1815, Peter Fidler's Journal at Brandon House, B.22/a/19.
[113] LAC. "Mr. A[uld] disapproves the arrangement [the pemmican treaty] made with NW Co and thinks had he been here, it would have been different. Talks about R[iver] Qui

by 1816, building the South Branch house on the river, likely in the area of present-day Diefenbaker Lake. But fires drove up almost the entire length of the South Saskatchewan to hurry hunters away; it might be that these were strategic burnings laying the basis of what John Palliser later described as a massive neutral or war zone developing between Cree- and Blackfoot-speaking people in this great hunting area.[114]

With that dividing line established, more camps moved into larger, better protected assemblies in the lower river areas of the Saskatchewan or southeast on the Assiniboine itself. The region now on a war footing, Carlton traders by 1816 grew accustomed to seeing quite massive spring gatherings. For instance, traders at Carlton saw over a hundred tents of Assiniboine and Cree resting at the post before heading south and east some forty miles away to form war councils that spring.[115]

The Cree and Assiniboine shift brought mixed blessings to the traders. While Edmonton House's provisions trade fell off with the withdrawal of some of its most assiduous poundmakers (by 1817, only 400 of the 500 bags on the Saskatchewan River were made as a result),[116] Carlton House enjoyed windfalls from the shift of these hunting and warring people. As early as 1814/1815, refugees of the Blackfoot war were providing greater quantities to Carlton, aided, too, by ideal winter conditions. Many of the camps successfully pounded twice and even three times that season. So confident were the Cree in the great conditions that nine tents nearby on the Saskatchewan that had built a pound sent word that they "got nothing yet, but buffalo are numerous around them." There was every indication of a bumper year at Carlton: the January dressed weight of cows averaged between a low of 295 lbs. to a high of 344 lbs. each.[117] The meat sheds filled by early fall and come spring the post produced without much effort almost seventy-six bags of pemmican before the post's

---

Appelle when there he spoke to the Indians to leave that place and drawn near to the Elbow. He when last here wishes me to send people there to procure provisions as the NWC would not send men there...." July 1, 1814, Miles Macdonell's Journal, *Selkirk Papers*, Series A, 16912.

[114] HBCA. December 25, 1816, Carlton House Journals, B.27/a/6.

[115] HBCA. March 3, 1817, Carlton House Journals, B.27/a/5.

[116] HBCA. May 27, 1817, James Bird's Journal at Carlton House, B.27/a/6: "no mare than 363 bags of 80 each of pemmican and about 1200 lb of loose fat which is about 100 bags less than were procured last year."

[117] HBCA. The master, John Pruden, weighed the meat per cow arriving to post: eleven January, three buffalos weighed 1,004 lbs. (averaging 334 lbs.); January 13, two cows weighed 780 lbs. (averaging 390 lbs.), and the January 25 weight of six buffalo was 2,065 lbs. (averaging 344 lbs.). See January entries for 1815 Carlton House Journals, B.27/a/4.

real production began.[118] More telling of the season's success was not only the primed condition of the animals, but John Pruden, the master at Carlton, also had enough marrow fats to mix his pemmican with fats one-fifth soft, a delectable departure from the harder subcutaneous fare most posts were producing at the time.[119]

The general order in the company throughout the Red River and Saskatchewan was to buy as much food as possible of this new supply. Although this order was intended to be "secret" from the HBC's rivals,[120] few believed that it could be kept under wraps. Fidler knew what the outcome would be. When the Nor'Westers began to comprehend the massive scale of both the colony's food needs and those of the HBC's Athabasca campaign, their reprisals could be expected.[121]

A Settlement in Need of Food

In the Red River, Miles Macdonell, the new governor of the colony, was either too inexperienced or uninformed to perceive the dangerous turn in competition. He certainly was not gifted enough as a leader to bring companies and his settlement to share a limited but bountiful enough resource. Petulant and soon resented by his own colonists, Macdonell vacillated in his treatment of Montreal traders competing with him for food and the steppe hunters with whom he entered into a variety of agreements. His greatest shortcoming was his woeful negligence in managing the colony's own food needs and the reality of the pemmican trade around him.

By the end of summer 1813, with few agricultural returns, the settlers at the Forks were hastily removed from their few, built structures and planted crops. Men, women, and children relocated to the south to what Peter Fidler would call the "land of Plenty" in winter, the forks with the Pembina. Fort Daer, built by the end of the fall, sheltered many of the women, children, invalids, and anyone not able to go to hunting tents scattered among the wintering herds in its western hinterlands.[122]

---

[118] HBCA. January 30 and May 27, 1815, Carlton House Journals, B.23/a/4.
[119] HBCA. March 19, 1816, Carlton House Journals, B.27/a/5.
[120] HBCA. See Letters to William Auld, March 4, 1812 and James Sutherland, March 4, 1812, London Correspondence Book Outward, 1810–1816, A.6/18.
[121] Peter Fidler, November 6, 1815, Brandon House Journals, B.22/a/19.
[122] Fidler described the later evacuation of settlers reluctant to go to Pembina, "but they are too lazy to benefit by the ... advice. They would seemingly remain here and half starve than give themselves a little trouble ... which would put them to the Land of Plenty...." November 11, 1815, Brandon House Journals, B.22/a/19.

There Métis were on hand – there might have been 200 families in Red River, the White Horse Plains Colony, and the Pembina Fork. These included families well equipped with what Henry called the ingenious Red River cart and horses to pull them. Many already formed commercial ties to the Montreal companies in the steppe. The main camps, such as those led by Lagodimière, hunted in family organizations; some fifteen from the colony aided Lagodimière; eight helped another leading family, the Tranchemontagne.[123] They were likely hampered by mild winter conditions stopping bison from finding winter shelter in the direct environs of Fort Daer its first winter. From January to March, conditions were so poor that the colony and its Pembina outpost nearly starved. It moved to short rations when dry meat was available and then completely to a six-pint daily allotment of oatmeal. The Fort Daer rationing book, surviving from that winter, makes plain the enormous dependency on oatmeal: some 14,642 lbs. were served out.[124]

The poor prospects immediately nearby forced Miles Macdonell to make frequent purchases of dried and fresh meat from the nearby NWC post, whose master benefited from ties with a more extensive network of hunters dispersed across the plains to the south who were, fortuitously, well supplied in horses and carts to make up distances to his fort. But, both the Red River Colony and the NWC posts at Red River and Pembina went hungry at various points in the winter of 1812–1813. For the "settlers" it was an abrupt and harsh lesson of the difficulty of farming in present-day Manitoba. They were immediately dependent on winter hunting, imposing a steep learning curve. It is hard to know how many Highlander Scots even knew how to wield a flintlock, much less fire effectively at the snorting animals that burst from their forest shelter.

Macdonell rushed letters for help to the larger HBC network. Swan River posts and those in the Qu'Appelle, and even the Carlton House kept by John Pruden received his pleas. Despite an uncertain spring and unfounded fears that Carlton House's trade was failing, the HBC shifted into a food purchasing program on the colony's behalf. In 1813, Fort Edmonton promised (unrealistically) to collect nothing short of 10,000 lbs. of pemmican (about 1,200 bags) for the colony above and beyond its usual production for the HBC service.[125]

---

[123] Giraud, *The Metis in the Canadian West*, I, 390.
[124] HBCA. Red River [Fort Daer] Settlement Account Book 1811–1812, E.7/1, fol. 14.
[125] LAC. March 18, 1813, Miles Macdonell's Journal, *Selkirk Papers, Series A*, 16808.

For Miles Macdonell, a priority formed to control food supply and, relatedly, prices. In January 1814 after his first difficult fall at Pembina, he penned his "Pemmican Proclamation" as part of a larger imposition of the HBC's presumed jurisdictional authority and Lord Selkirk's proprietarial claim to "Assiniboia." The proclamation prohibited the export of provisions of any sort from the grant area, not really the region itself, and certainly not all of the pemmican-producing areas, especially those now found on the upper reaches of the Assiniboine and west on the Qu'Appelle.[126] But the need to control the export of food to safeguard colonists' needs became more urgent again before summer, and in June, an explicit proclamation against the running of bison was announced, apparently to control the practice that dispersed herds for the following winter.

In issuing the proclamations, Macdonell was directly challenging the labor supply in the region. By 1814, new ranks of market hunters, both freemen and Metis, were hiring onto the employ of the Montreal and HBC forts on extravagant terms; many were not even entering into contracts on an annual basis but guarding free status in order to move between the buyers to demand whatever they wanted for their foodstuffs. Those who entered contracts did so only for handsome annual salaries. For instance, the mixed blood, Isham, interpreter and laborer for the Red River Settlement had a son sign on at a salary of £15 a year as its hunter.[127] It is unclear whether his obligations extended to much more than shooting animals at his camp. Times were too good for these hunters to commit much more of their labor. The colony hired Lagimodière, one of the more faithful and productive hunters in the steppe – who remains a popular figure in the history of the colony – but he did so only at the sum of £30 a year[128] (this when a clerk who would deal with all the Ojibwa at Red River earned only £10/ year[129]). Even by the end of the near-disastrous winter of 1812–1813, Miles Macdonell was dismayed to find his settlement's accountants settle up with Lagimodière to credit him at the same rate as the company's servants. This "rather officious"

---

[126] The most complete analysis of the proclamation is offered in A. S. Morton, *History of the Canadian West to 1870–71*, 2nd ed. (Toronto: University of Toronto Press, 1973), 560–562.
[127] Giraud, *The Metis in the Canadian West*, I, 391.
[128] Giraud, *The Metis in the Canadian West*, I, 390.
[129] LAC. December 28, 1814, Miles Macdonell engaged Cadotte for twelve months as clerk in charge of "all the Indians that should come here" for £10 in salary. Miles Macdonell's Journal, *Selkirk Papers, Series B*, 16870.

decision had been made "without my being consulted," he peeved, but his hands were tied. Macdonell, his accountants, and Lagimodière, himself, knew how valuable his services were.[130]

There was also François Enos (et Hémault) *dit* Delorme, who bargained his labor to the Red River Settlement, serving first as interpreter and then high-paid hunter. Resisting any servitude by contract, he and Miles Macdonell finally fell out in 1814 over the very issue of wages. He served with the NWC before returning to the colony's employ under Governor Colin Robertson.[131] In his disposition to the Coltman commission looking into the eventual Seven Oaks killings, Delorme made clear that at no time did he work under contract or a fixed wage, but that at one point he nevertheless earned the salary of a company clerk.[132]

Hunting wages were never better for these camps that supplied HBC, NWC or the colony (a separate food buyer) between 1814 and 1815. In spring 1815, the NWC was forced to pay outlier camps on the Turtle River around thirty ballots of merchandise for sixty animals, including clothing, extra food for families, and whatever horses were needed to replace the freemen's own stock. Delorme cited some of the most prominent heads of family now enjoying such wages: Beaulieu, Tranchemontagne, Dauphine, Calluss, and Ducharme.[133] The latter was likely from the Ducharme family, whose senior male member, Pierre, had in 1776, taken an Ojibwa wife. By 1801, at least two Ducharmes were sent out to bison hunt by A. M. McLeod, a NWC trader in the area. They were said that year to have been killing some twenty-one cows near the White Mud, in a separate hunting camp.[134] For his part, throughout 1814 and 1815, Macdonell was lucky to engage Joseph Bellegarde hunting with Assiniboine in large camps well supplied with horses and dogs. But many of the freemen liked to remain free agents, taking their excess foodstuffs to whoever was convenient or paying most. Sometimes that worked in the colony's favor, sometimes not. Poor road conditions on River Botino inconvenienced

---

[130] LAC. April 19, 1813, Miles Macdonell's Journal, *Selkirk Papers, Series A*, 16817.
[131] François Eno dit Delorme, *Selkirk Papers, Series A*, 16157. See also Heather Devine, *The People Who Own Themselves: Aboriginal Ethnogenesis in a Canadian Family, 1660–1900* (Calgary: University of Calgary Press, 2004), 292.
[132] Francois Eno dit Delorme deposition, *Selkirk Papers, Series A*, 16157.
[133] LAC. Deposition of François Eno dit Delorme, September 2, 1817, *Selkirk Papers, Series B*, 16157–16171.
[134] Clarke, "Reconstituting the Fur Trade Community of the Assiniboine Basin, 3–53.

freemen enough in early November to prompt their unloading of food from the hunt to the Red River Colony's Pembina outpost in 1814, a fortuitous windfall. Bonhomme, Ducharme, Beautino, Deschamps, Bonnard, Bercier, Desmart, and, the same week, Laverdure and Melanson arrived, some of the prominent names appearing in Miles Macdonell's journal.[135] They all brought in pounded meats and fats. Even freemen/Métis who later became avowed enemies of the colony, such as Peter Pangmen *dit* Bostonois, hired themselves as colonist hunters, when the pay was good.

These *gens libres* were defining themselves and much of their emergent ethnic identity as "Métis" in the context of the high prices in a commercializing provisions trade. Indeed, "being and becoming Metis," so often ascribed to kinship affiliation and self-identifying as a distinct aboriginal group, was very much being and becoming a market hunter. In a period when their foodstuffs were more dearly needed and larger Assiniboine and Cree camps were simply not increasing their efforts to produce them, these camps ramped up production, selling product when convenient or at the highest price. So, even François Deschamps Jr., after his family pushed off from the Red River Colony, found a reason to stay on as a seasonal hired hunter, for whatever price is not known.[136] Miles Macdonell had little to say when employees made the decision to quit the colony altogether in a bid to strike out for themselves as hunters, such as in 1815, when John McVicar and Hector McEachern headed out hunting. The latter, a now-free colonist, "wants to get his time to himself and engages to kill cattle for me at a certain rate per head."[137] The supreme freedom, usually from want, in these mobile hunting camps often using horses to get to very distant herds, attracted colonists, otherwise poorly paid voyageurs, and English servants. And even when an agreement was entered, one could still find escape, such as in the case of Deschamps, who had promised the colony his hunted food but, in the end, "he kept them for himself," Macdonell noted, evidently peeved.[138]

---

[135] LAC. November 6, 1813, *Selkirk Papers, Series B*, 16817–16870; See ibid., Macdonell's note on too many foods coming in during these good times. October 27, 1813, Laverdure and Melanson, "free Canadians" came in with meat, and on the 29th admitting that "We are much plagued" by these meats.
[136] Ibid., November 6, 1813.
[137] LAC. February 6, 1815 Miles Macdonell's Journal, *Selkirk Papers, Series B*, 16956.
[138] LAC. October 27–29; November 6, 8, 27, 30; December 2, 1813, Miles Macdonell's Journal, *Selkirk Papers, Series B*.

Pemmican Proclamations

The first winter was beset with provisioning problems. The colony frequently came close to starving. Macdonell was unable to purchase enough food from nearby freemen camps and hunters. News that Selkirk would be sending out between 90 and a 100 new colonists that year and possibly as many the next panicked the colony's governor. He wrote that "he found it indispensable to procure food for them in virtue of his authority."[139] The measure prohibited all manner of foodstuffs from being exported from the region, applying equally to the HBC as it did to the NWC. Macdonell justified his measure in light of the foodstuff's importance. Gathering up the pemmican of the land, the governor would provide commercial companies with enough provisions to run their canoe brigades to their merchandise depots, but reserve the rest for the colony's survival. The measure, whatever its justifications (and Macdonell believed it might even drive the NWC out of the area altogether), would take the Montreal partnership off guard.[140] The proclamation's legitimacy was immediately rejected, as was a further restriction made in the spring against the running of bison by horseback; in the first case, John Wills at Brandon House refused to post the proclamation at the NWC's fort gates; in the second, the forthright Nor-Wester, Duncan Cameron, is said to have pulled it from his post and shredded it, theatrically, in front of the *gens libres*. He posted his own permission to the hunters to run bison as their natural right.[141]

The proclamation, to take effect for a year's duration, deemed the provisions of the country insufficient "for the requisite supply" of the colony and prohibited those taking foodstuffs from exporting them. The exception was for "what may be judged necessary for the trading parties at this present time within the territory," who could export supplies only though an application for a license to do so. The proclamation also allowed that in order "that no loss may accrue to the parties concerned, they will be paid for by British bills at the customary rates" for any products reserved for colonial use.[142] The measure implicated but was not applied equally to both the HBC and the NWC.

---

[139] LAC. Macdonell to Selkirk, July 17, 1813, *Selkirk Papers*, Series B, 107–141; Miles Macdonell's Journal, *Selkirk Papers*, Series A, 15813–15814.

[140] A. S. Morton, 561. J. M. Bumsted, *Fur Trade Wars*, 102–103.

[141] See Macdonell's description of his proclamation and its fallout in Macdonell to Selkirk, July 25, 1814, *Selkirk Papers*, Series B, 186–189.

[142] January 8, 1814, Proclamation reproduced in *Report of the Proceedings connected with the disputes between the Earl of Selkirk and the North-West Company at the Assizes, held at*

A key matter in the pemmican "treaty," however, was how it rated pemmican in terms of price. In both the spring advances and those to be furnished the following winter, Macdonell would have all of it "paid for at a fair value by Bills on England agreeable to the original terms of the Proclamation as well understood by the said parties."[143] Negotiations over the "treaty" took place over some three days. But the key sticking point proved to be a "fair" price for what the NWC paid back in pemmican advanced by the colony. That was never agreed on. As Macdonell testified at the Coltman Commission, despite the general agreement established, "no particular reference was made thereto owing to their not having agreed upon a price for the said provisions."[144] Here, the NWC negotiators was likely dithering because it had purchased high and the treaty threatened to rate it low later in the season. Since 1810, the HBC had begun to rate pemmican, fats, and dried meats in sterling. Accounts at Cumberland House suggest how dramatic inflation was in these years. Pemmican prices had risen from 4 to 5 and then to 6 pence a pound in Cumberland House accounts between 1813 to 1816. Beyond this rampant inflation was amazing regional and local price volatility. Brandon House prices in 1813–1814 were 4 pence a pound, but Red River pemmican doubled that, at 8 pence/lb.[145] Most likely, what Macdonnel wanted to establish as "fair" was close to what the HBC had originally rated the pemmican Red River would supply to Albany and Churchill (4 pence a pound) and York (5 pence) in 1810.

The treaty, however, was signed by McDonald, Duncan Cameron, and another NWC partner, apparently John Stewart or John McLoughlin, and likely both. Whatever its restrictions, and despite incompetent management on the part of Macdonell, the pemmican treaty did create a single food buyer that could disburse supply to companies at what it purported to be a reasonable price. With runaway inflation now evident as a problem to all parties (and by 1821, regional prices would spike to 9 pence a pound) this was, indeed, an important consideration for those entering, even under duress, the Pemmican Peace. It was this attempt to hold provisions to a "customary price," however, that proved the more important aspect of the affair. Delorme in his deposition remembered

---

York in Upper Canada, October, 1818 (Montreal: James Lane & Nahum Mower, 1819), 133–134.
[143] Selkirk Papers, Series A, 15815.
[144] Miles Macdonell Deposition, Coltman Commission, Selkirk Papers, Series A, 15815.
[145] Different Red River and Brandon House prices on pemmican and fat are recorded in HBCA, Brandon House Accounts, 1813–1814, B.22/d/4.

the agreement explicitly in these terms, that after the seizure of the Nor'Wester's pemmican from the Qu'Appelle district, Macdonell had agreed to supply enough to the companies for their brigades' transport to merchandise depots, and then reserving the rest for the colony's use, "pour un prix raisonable."[146]

However, at Lac La Pluie by the end of the summer 1814, the proclamation and the Pemmican "treaty" was "greatly attacked" by the great partners of the NWC. They likely felt it would tie the company's hands and limit their own commercial expansion. It would also give further life to their HBC rivals.[147] Instead of submitting to the large cooperative being created with the treaty, one that would see bison foodstuffs pooled between the three entities and prices controlled, the wintering bourgeois, notably Duncan Cameron, were instructed to mount a vigorous campaign against it. They were well informed of the Montreal partners' disapproval of any wintering man who went soft on the colony's incursions and any threat to its pemmican supplies.[148]

In the spring, Selkirk colonists were alerted at Fort Daer that Nor'Westers were manufacturing and caching in secret pemmican for export to Bas de la Rivière, contrary to the colonial proclamation. A free-fall to conflict ensued. The colony's newly appointed sheriff seized the Nor'Wester's Qu'Appelle river pemmican; later, the bags and fat coming from the upper Assiniboine at Swan River were also seized. These were just a portion of the massive supply now flowing from camps in these river basins. By June some 500 bags of the NWC's pemmican were in the colony's possession; about 190 of the HBC's bags were voluntarily passed over to Macdonell's shopkeepers by June.

From that point, traders competed to purchase supplies to meet their largely imaginary and unlimited needs elsewhere. There really was no upper maximum to what they would purchase in order to undermine their rivals or to create capacity to energize far-flung and commercial expansion whether in the north, the northwest coast, or beyond. Nor'Westers had little difficult rallying up freemen followers,

---

[146] LAC. Disposition of François Eno, dit Delorme, *Selkirk Papers, Series A*, 16174.

[147] See J. McLoughlin to J. D. Cameron, August 16, 1814, "Our Pemigan Peace has been greatly attacked," McLoughlin reported, "when I first gave the particulars as slightly as possible I was attacked on all sides" over this "famous treaty." *Selkirk Papers, Series A*, 8621.

[148] The partners of the NWC meeting in July 1814 condemned the pemmican seizure and the settlement "not much to the credit of the concern"; and its "men of Red River ... who had ill-behaved on the seizure of the Provisions were pointed out to the others and disgraced." Wallace, W. Stewart, ed., *Documents Relating to the North West Company*, 291.

most mounted and armed with muskets in far-flung areas. Although the proclamation legally lost its relevance by January 1815, its imposition and the Qu'Appelle seizures mobilized Metis, freemen, and some aboriginal hostilities against the settlement. Macdonell's efforts, after all, signaled an attempt to eliminate competitive buying in the steppe areas. Nor'Westers continued to spread messages to camps, such as those at Turtle River, that Macdonell would "take their provisions by force" under his pretended authority.[149]

By spring of 1816, with the pemmican treaty long lapsed, parties simply worked against each other. Fort Edmonton aggressively purchased pemmican to support not only the colony, but the company's Athabasca expedition, at all cost. Fort Carlton was given the order to purchase as many provisions as possible from nearby pounds, "for feeling the urgent necessity there is for our procuring a large quantity of provisions at this place, I desired Mr. [John] Pruden to pay them better for their provisions than he has been accustomed to do, although he has always paid them a high price."[150] Brandon House refitted its icehouses and Peter Fidler was purchasing whatever he could at whatever price. Fidler was right, then, to be alert to the reprisals likely to be taken by Nor'Westers looking on as the HBC and its colony now purchased the lion's share of this food. By 1815, he stated that "we naturally imagine the NWC would wish to destroy to defeat that [Athabasca] Expedition besides it makes them pay much dearer as well as getting much less from the Natives than they would otherwise."[151] At Qu'Appelle, the HBC was monopolizing purchases through John McKay's buying: by February 1815, he had collected an astounding quantity of 20,000 lbs. of fat and 10,000 lbs. of beat meat – the equivalent of 5,000 bags of pemmican.[152]

Nor'Westers were contending at Swan River with HBC men going in by the droves outbidding NWC men; whatever the NWC was getting was only at "a dear rate," the Nor'Wester, John Macdonell complained to Dougal Cameron.[153] Many of their own Assiniboine pounders, meanwhile, were "starving" that winter, and the NWC was relying almost

---

[149] LAC. Delorme's deposition described the unwarranted fears spread in part by Alexander Macdonell. Delorme deposition, *Selkirk Papers*, 16171–16173; and Miles Macdonell, "Narrative of the History of the Red River Settlement from September 14, 1814 to June 1815, *Selkirk Papers, Series B*, 207, xxiii.

[150] HBCA. December 27, 1816, James Bird's Journal, Fort Carlton Journals, B.27/a/6.

[151] HBCA. April 7, 1816, Brandon House Journals, B.22/a/19.

[152] LAC February 16, 1815, Miles Macdonell's Journal, *Selkirk Papers, Series A*, 16961.

[153] LAC. A. Macdonell to J. D. Camaron, March 1, 1815, *Selkirk Papers, Series A*, 319.

exclusively on the tributary farther to the south of the Assiniboine, the Souris, where the la Souris Post collected much of its product from Montagne à la Bosse nearby.[154] The NWC, strapped financially, however, could not match the HBC's purchasing power or its determined cornering of the food market. And, to make matters worse, the Montreal traders were saddled with a particularly unpopular form of tobacco. The Cree and Assiniboine universally reviled it.

It is ironic, then, in a moment when posts were producing significantly larger quantities (in these years, Qu'Appelle post was regularly producing 500 bags from its facility, alone) that each of their attempts to corner the market resulted only in upward moving prices. In 1812, 1813, and 1814, pemmican overall rose in price from 4 to 5 to 6 d/lb.[155] In 1814, when Brandon House prices in 1813–1814 were running at 4 d/lb, Red River prices were already double that at 8 d/lb. By the time of the amalgamation of the companies in 1821, prices had soared to 8.5 and 9 d/lb.[156]

In the now more desperate gambit to purchase from Native hunters, Métis and freemen, the Nor'Westers seem to have contemplated simply bursting upon Cumberland House to seize its stock and stop the HBC's Athabasca expansion altogether.[157] The Montreal traders' ire was raised further by the incoming governor replacing Macdonell, Robert Semple, whose primary concern for supplying the settlement with provisions led him to destroy the NWC post at Red River, Fort Gibraltar. With such provocation, in spring 1816, the Nor'Westers directed employees, hunters, and traders usually moving down river together in the spring, and incited them to sack Brandon House. The fifty or so Métis, "Canadian," freemen and Native people that charged as a "New Nation" under a flag given by their Montreal employers, carried off everything of value in the fort. But the Nor'Westers would see that the greatest antipathy was

---

[154] LAC. John McDonald to J. D. [Dougal] Cameron, February 1814, *Selkirk Papers*, Series A, 328.
[155] HBCA. Prices are assembled here and in the charts in Chapter 4 from annual accounts kept at Cumberland House 1811–1882, available in the B.49 series of the D (accounts) records of the HBC archives, Winnipeg, Manitoba. Cumberland House accounts are found in files 1 through 119 (B.49/d/1–119) on microfilm reels 1M459–463 and 1M1360–61.
[156] HBCA. Different Red River and Brandon House prices on pemmican and fat are recorded in HBCA, Brandon House Accounts, 1813–1814, B.22/d/4.
[157] Gerhard Ens, "The Climatic and Ecological Background to the Battle of Seven Oaks, 1816," suggests this was a possibility, citing James Bird at Edmonton House who feared by spring 1816 that the NWC would seize Cumberland. Ens cites Edmonton House Journal, May 30, 1816, HBCA, B.60/a/15, fo. 40d.

directed toward the Selkirk Settlement itself. That spring its promptings to freemen throughout the parkland belts had already seen them converge toward the Qu'Appelle. At Fort Carlton, horse-riding freemen ominously rode past the bastions vowing to attack the Selkirk Settlers. They painted themselves, sang war songs, and promised to find dogs' meat from the bodies of the Red River newcomers. And by June, freemen on horseback were now at the Selkirk Settlement.

At first, their intentions vividly played out in a comic stunt: Metis horsemen reined up to the few domestic cattle the settlers had and drove them into the Frog Plains, chasing them as bison in mock hunts, picking them with spears and crying war whoops at the dumb, docile beasts. It was a highly meaningful act, inverting the governor's restriction on bison running and using their force as the region's hunters against the few domesticated animals in the colony. By the time the governor was able to get out there to put a stop to the spectacle, a camp had killed his lone bull and were "roasting its steaks" on the fire. [158]

This was only a few days before a larger contingent of Métis, led by Cuthbert Grant Jr., made its way with carts and provisions to Fort Gibraltar and cut through the Frog Plains to skirt the Selkirk Colony. The new colonial governor Robert Semple, intent on provisioning his settlement and seize the Nor'Wester's supplies, saw ill intent in the contingent's movements and sent his own contingent of men out to meet the Métis in the Frog Plains. An argument sparked a fight most had long expected, and sixteen of the colonists were killed, including the settlement's governor.

The Coltman Commission later investigating the seven oaks routing at Frog Plains, and then dispersal of the Selkirk Colony, helped put to rest most of the rumours that the freemen and Canadians had scalped and "butchered" the bodies. The era of competition and violence at a time when pemmican supplies were increasing, however, was not addressed. If given a choice, most of the participants led by the needs imposed by unlimited commercial expansion, had elected to compete, rather than cooperate, in this seemingly unlimited bison commons.

Conclusion

From the mid-1790s to 1816, company purchases of bison meats and fat clearly began to exceed that which poundmaking Assiniboine and Cree

---

[158] LAC See entry, June 7, 1815, Miles Macdonell Journal, *Selkirk Papers, Series A*, 17022–17023.

could or would provide. The wider scramble for food supply began. New ranks of summer hunters including Ojibwa and, especially, freemen/Métis, moved into the market. As a bioregion, the pemmican-making territories were not limited to the Red River valley or the outlines of Selkirk's colony of Assiniboia. The Cree and Assiniboine shift from the west into the Carlton hunting grounds in the 1810s, the likely beginnings of a war zone to the east of the south branch, the greater numbers of hunters converging on Qu'Appelle and Upper Assiniboine Valleys and the sheer rising number of new entities in pound territories in winter, all raised production of pemmican in the greater plains and parkland. For English and Canadian fur trade companies depending on the food supply in these areas, even larger supply could not, however, dampen prices on provisions with the consequence of ruining profits and imperiling the very fur trade itself. Many of the very attractions for freemen, leaving NWC or HBC service in these years, were the profits to be had in prices that continued to climb as demand for food stuffs escalated. Never was it better to be a bison hunter when camp leaders could be paid higher than company clerks, camps receive a ballot of goods for every pair of animals killed, and not one but three markets existed for products. The Métis moving in and out of this type of market were in the midst of ethnogenesis, one of the most important cultural developments in Rupert's Land. In the buffalo commons, freemen and Métis joined to pursue their interests and strategize in the emerging pemmican market.

Amidst the plenty at hand, however, companies and players sought to control and corner the food supplies for their unlimited use in commercial expansion. No better example existed than the case of 1816, when Montreal traders in the Fort Vermillion area deliberately starved to death sixteen HBC employees.[159] That year, John Clarke was sent to move the HBC into the Athabasca district, but, without enough provisions, he made the fateful decision of relocating his fifty men, in eight canoes, up the Peace River to present-day northwestern Alberta, thinking that game populations there would be more plentiful to support his wintering camps of men. Instead, his Montreal Nor'Wester rival, William MacKintosh, learned their plans and sent his own men ahead of the contingent to fire guns along the river to chase away game and pay off local aboriginal hunters who might otherwise feed the HBC contingent. When the "poor devils" fighting the Peace's current finally arrived in late

---

[159] LAC. The incident is recounted in Charles Grant to Frederick Grant July 26, 1816, *Selkirk Papers*, Series A, 8717.

fall and the main body took up at a place called Loon River "where the ice stopped them," they were already out of food. They were subsisting on squirrels, partridges, wild rose buds, and moose browse.[160] Over the course of the winter, the group in desperation broke up in search of any support. The Nor'westers located one party led by George McDougall, with three of their canoes spilled across a riverway, barely alive: "indeed some of them could not walk already." The HBC men hurriedly broke open their bales of goods to buy whatever food they could from these competitors, or enough to get to them to their trading house. They were not treated generously. Given the scantiest aid, one of the men died of hunger making the trip to Clarke's post. Once the contingent was back together, Clarke lost three more men before selling his entire trading supply to the Nor'Westers for 700 lbs. of dried meat and pemmican, enough, it was hoped, for an ill fated evacuation to Fort Chipewyan. Tramping to that center, all but three of the twelve perished.[161] Ferdinand Wentzel, who had already starved out rival traders from the environs of his own subarctic post in 1800,[162] wrote in "exultation" of the event. "No less than 15 men, 1 clerk with a woman and child died of starvation going up Peace River," he wrote with barely concealed satisfaction. Colin Robertson, looking back on "the starving of Mr. Clarke's Men in Athapascow," cited it as "the most deliberate and wanton acts of cruelty towards the Company's servants" ever occurring.[163]

The grim ends of zero-sum food wars in the end served no one well. Montreal and British companies were, after all, still competing for the same supply, whether tapped in the winter pounds of Assiniboine, Cree, or Blackfoot still marginal to the market but enjoying fantastic prices when they entered it, or hard bargaining with specialized truly market Metis hunters beginning, in fact, a summer market hunt in these years. The provisions prices that rose to 8 and 9 d/lb. regionally (pegged at

[160] LAC. The report from Dunvegan of Colin Campbell to McRobb and Cowie, May 10, 1816, *Selkirk Papers, Series A*, 8760–8763.
[161] LAC. *Selkirk Papers, Series A*, 8760–8763.
[162] See Wentzel's own food fight against an XY Company opponent at Grand River in 1800. By creating a game desert around his opponent and stopping Indians from trading with them, the XY post was reduced to eating the skins on the windows and the entire trade goods were swapped for 24 skins of goods, 72 lbs. pounded eat and grease and a little barley corn. George Colpitts, "Moose-Nose and Buffalo Hump: the Amerindian-European Food Exchange in the British North American Fur Trade to 1840," in Diane Kirkby and Tanja Luckins, eds., *Dining on Turtles: Food Feasts and Drinking in History* (Hounsdmills, Basingstoke, UK: Palgrave Macmillan, 2007), 64–81.
[163] See Philip Goldring, "MacKintosh, William," in Vol. VII, *Dictionary of Canadian Biography* (Toronto: University of Toronto Press, 1988), 567.

Cumberland House), and by 1820 could reach a staggering shilling/lb. near Red River, eventually broke the companies. They would, in 1821, join together in large measure to avoid the ruinous expenses of the provisions trade. Much of the subsequent history of the pemmican trade after Seven Oaks and the short years of competition that followed, unfolded very differently after 1821, when a single buyer purchased all provisions. The united concern that emerged that year, bringing together all companies into formidable monopoly based in London under the old name of the Hudson's Bay Company would now control commerce across the immense fur trade in Rupert's Land. Native people, freemen and Metis stood the most to lose from the terms of this market. Moreover, the single buyer now dealing with them quickly lowering prices, established quotas from territories, and gave hunters very few options than to hunt more to buy goods dearer to them. Monopoly, emerging in 1821, would in fact seal the fate of the bison herds, already being intensively hunted for the food, to a very bloody and uncertain end.

4

SELLING BISON FLESH IN THE BRITISH MARKET AFTER 1821

> I had first to learn the difference between tallow fat or suet and market fat or lard, between tender meat and hard meat, packed in bladders in which Indians bring it to us, and whether the dried strips of flesh were cut from a cow or an ox.[1]
> – Rudolph Friederich Kurtz, at Fort Union, 1833

Runaway operating costs and ever larger amounts of debt began ruining profits in the fur trade even by the turn of the nineteenth century. By 1810, most of the companies were on the ropes. Companies talked of joining together that year, when Montreal firms under the banner of the North West Company (NWC) made opening offers to Hudson's Bay Company (HBC) investors, but the deal was eventually scuttled. In the end, a biotic entity proved to be one of the most decisive factors, one bringing about the largest structural change in the history of the British fur trade. In 1819 and 1820, measles and whooping cough spread across Rupert's Land. As Paul Hackett observed, the epidemics left "large numbers of dead and the fur trade teetering on the brink of financial ruin."[2] It was not the first time that crowd infectious diseases wrecked havoc in the trade;[3] however, from a commercial perspective and given the difficult financial straits of the companies, the mourning rituals that grieving Indian bands observed could not have come at a worst moment. To

---

[1] *Journal of Rudolph Friederich Kurz*, ed. J. N. B. Hewitt, Bureau of American Ethnology Bulletin 115 (Smithsonian Institution, 1937), 240–241.

[2] Paul Hackett (Summer 2005), "Historical Mourning Practices Observed among the Cree and Ojibwa Indians of the Central Subarctic," *Ethnohistory* 52(3):514, 503–532. On the histories of crowd infectious diseases in the trade, see Paul Hackett, *A Very Remarkable Sickness: Epidemics in the Petit Nord 1670 to 1846* (Winnipeg: University of Manitoba Press, 2002).

[3] A superb analysis of disease and impacts on aboriginal populations in the context of the fur trade is offered by James Dashuk, *Clearing the Plains: Disease, Politics of Starvation, and the Loss of Aboriginal Life* (Regina: University of Regina Press, 2013), 11–77.

mourn deaths in families, Native bands often abstained from trapping over a period of time, abandoned or destroyed their own possessions, or burnt furs otherwise destined for the market. English and Montreal traders scrambled to devastated camps to claim furs already paid for by fall credits or attempted to incite hunters to continue to trap. Many arrived only in time to see swirling black clouds rising from campfires, their fur returns ablaze. The financial losses were colossal. The Union of Concerns, already in the works, now became reality in a covenant signed by the NWC and the HBC in 1821.[4] From that date, a single monopolized concern extended its reach across the vast British territories north of the 49th parallel.

Monopolization breathed new life to commercial enterprise and invigorated both the reach of capital and the pace of colonization in its train. The new HBC redefined its priorities and grew to be one of the most powerful capitalized trading companies on the continent. Key was the Columbia River and control over the Pacific coastal trade, both to that point being lost to American entrepreneurs, sailor traders, and settlers. In 1821, the HBC's Governor George Simpson began drawing from the company's sources of London capital to wage a trade war against smaller American companies on the river mouths and in the fjords along the coast. His traders undervalued their goods; purchased up furs at a loss; built up large coastal depots at Forts Vancouver, McPherson, and Simpson; and finally employed steamships to arrive earlier in the season than their sail-dependent rivals could. Its sacrifices paid off, giving the HBC monopoly of the North Pacific coast by 1833 when American traders made some of their last visits along its coastline.[5]

From the Columbia, the HBC turned a scorched earth policy against its American rivals. HBC managers at Fort Vancouver sent Peter Skene Ogden and bully boys in canoe brigades up the Columbia, the Snake, and the Green Rivers, eventually as far as the Gulf of California in wide-arcing circuits of destruction. Along the way shield Saulteaux, St. Laurence Iroquois, Plains Cree, Métis, and Salish-speakers from the

---

[4] A good overview of the amalgamation of the companies is provided in R. Harvey Fleming, ed., *Minutes of Council: Northern Department of Rupert Land* (Toronto: The Champlain Society, 1940), xvii–xxii; also Heather Devine, " 'Oeconomy must now be the order of the day': George Simpson and the Reorganization of the Fur Trade to 1826," in Michael Payne, Donald Wetherell, and Catherine Cavanaugh, eds., *Alberta Formed: Alberta Transformed*, Vol. I (Edmonton: University of Alberta Press, 2006), 161–178.
[5] Richard Mackie, *Trading Beyond the Mountains: The British Fur Trade on the Pacific, 1793–1843* (Vancouver: UBC Press, 1997), 44–68.

cordillera filled out the ranks of "Snake River" brigades. They effectively laid waste to game and furbearer populations, this to discourage mountain men and Spanish traders from firming up their presence in such territories.[6] Concurrently, on the Green River, HBC men hauled goods in such quantity that they undermined the mountain man rendezvous at its very source, helping drive it out of business by the mid-1840s; with their costs rising and beaver pelts devaluing, American companies such as Pierre Chouteau's, turned with new interest to the larger profits of a plains bison robe trade in the Upper Missouri.[7]

As Lorne Hammond has pointed out, the HBC's Pacific campaigns had continent-wide scope and implications. The company sought markets for all manner of wildlife, birds, and marine life. Where there was no metropolitan market for products, it sought to create one. Those commodities that encouraged American, Russian, or Spanish rivalry, the company manipulated in the metropolitan market, Simpson's famous beaver conservation on the prairie being a case in point. Launching a policy to "nurse" back the prairie country devastated by earlier competition, the company closed posts, provided incentives to hunters to trap other animals, and discouraged traders from buying pelts. A chief goal of this conservation program, which enjoyed only limited success in its implementation among Native hunters, was to bolster beaver populations in seven years so that the HBC could dump on the international market to devalue the fur and drive Americans, facing slimmer profit margins, out of business on the Missouri and Columbia. Put on foot in the 1820s and again in the 1840s across its web of prairie posts, these constituted, as Arthur Ray has pointed out, some of the first coordinated and region-wide wildlife conservation programs in North America.[8]

---

[6] Mackie 104–110; on the gunboat frontier, see Barry Gough, *Gunboat Frontier: British Maritime Authority and Northwest Coast Indians, 1846–1890* (Vancouver: UBC Press, 1984); and on the changing nature of the land versus coastal trade, see Robin Fisher, *Contact and Conflict* (Vancouver: UBC Press, 1992); see K. G. Davies, ed., *Peter Skene Ogden's Snake Country Journal 1826–27* (London: The Hudson's Bay Record Society, 1961).

[7] John E. Sunder, *The Fur Trade in the Upper Missouri, 1840–1865* (Norman: University of Oklahoma Press, 1965), 14–15.

[8] See Lorne Hammond, "Marketing Wildlife: the Hudson's Bay Company and the Pacific Northwest, 1821–1849," in David Freeland Duke, ed., *Canadian Environmental History: Essential Readings* (Toronto: Canadian Scholars' Press, 2006), 203–222. On the policies, see Arthur J. Ray (1978), "Competition and Conservation in the Early Subarctic Fur Trade," *Ethnohistory*, 25(4):347-357. Arthur J. Ray, "Some Conservation Schemes of the Hudson's Bay Company, 1821–1850: An Examination of the Problems of Resource Management in the Fur Trade," in Lary M. Dilsaver and Craig E. Colten, eds., *The American Environment: Interpretations of Past Geographies* (Lanham, MD: Rowman & Littlefield, 1992), 33–49.

Bison conservation, too, initially concerned even the HBC after its consolidation. Simpson attempted to engross the pemmican trade and "regularize" its returns, the policy meant to "shake off the prodigious expenses of our Plain Establishments and give those exhausted countries an opportunity of recruiting."[9] Such a pursuit would, it was hoped, free up cheaper provisions for the company's fur trade elsewhere. To pursue that end, the company inaugurated region-wide purchasing where "Standing Orders" passed annually by a Northern Council effectively pegged prices and established quotas for each of the company's three prairie and plains districts. District ordering had a remarkable effect on price. It effectively pitted Saskatchewan Cree hunters against Red River Métis, the latter now growing as important provisions hunters in the prairie, especially in summer. The same market soon expanded to include the Blackfoot. Unlike the period of competition where market forces, bad winter hunting, destructive fires, or the local collusion of hunters could drive up prices, the HBC after 1821 enjoyed "monopsony" (or single-purchaser) buying advantages that drove down and stabilized prices. If conditions in one area of the prairie threatened to raise the value of foodstuffs, the company simply bought elsewhere in the buffalo commons.

It took until 1826 to gain full control over prices, but after that date the HBC had moved pemmican, dried meat, and fat to a quarter of their prices from two decades before. Prices remained suppressed until the end of the bison era. By the late 1820s and 1830s, Cree, Assiniboine and now the Blackfoot speaking people in the far western plains contended with the double edges of a fearsome sword: suppressed and unmoving provisions prices on the one side and a growing need for European goods, especially guns, ammunition, and other weaponry now that the plains country was thoroughly violent in warfare. Their only recourse was to hunt more.

The monopolized fur trade, then, changed the nature of the bison commons. It also presented choices for the HBC itself. Shortly after gaining its privileged position, and given the cheapness of pemmican now at its disposal, the company could not resist the temptation and progressively increased quotas. This food energy animated a growing workforce driving York boats, and divided it between well timed and regularly scheduled Athabasca and Red River brigades that delivered goods, military officers, missionaries, and naturalists effectively to the larger expanses of Rupert's Land.

[9] LAC. May 31, 1824, George Simpson to Colville, *Selkirk Papers, Series A*, 8251.

Beyond district quotas were the sizable discretionary funds of pemmican built up by posts and often disbursed each season. Because pemmican was rated so low in price, post managers could purchase it in bulk to encourage trade near their posts, give as gifts, or feed hunters continuing to trap on lands becoming exhausted of game and furbearers. It was such discretionary purchases, in fact, and not quotas, that arguably took the greatest toll on the Canadian herds. In present-day Manitoba, for instance, discretionary purchases at Fort Ellice eventually underwrote Ojibwa fur trapping in the largely devastated Riding Mountain area where Ojibwa consumed between 3,000 and 4,000 pounds of pemmican over a single winter in the 1870s.[10] Red River, not assigned a quota in the early 1830s but typically providing about 300 bags annually to Norway House transport, had massive discretionary food funds. These were bought cheaply mostly from Métis. By 1838, surpluses amounted to some 73,000 lbs. In 1842, Red River supplied 435 bags, mostly to Norway House for brigade travel, but discretionary funds remaining "on hand" that season ran to some 795 bags. In total, these 1,230 bags weighed 100 lbs. each, and so their collective weight reached some 123,000 lbs.[11]

The monopolization of the British fur trade, then, not only created a new type of trade, but also reshaped the nature of the buffalo commons. Suppressed prices presented hunters with fewer options than to increase effort to gain trade goods or search out alternative markets for their hunting. Métis hunters, in particular, organized the first large-scale and highly destructive summer hunting in this period. But from the company's perspective, the same market also offered a choice between tending to its long term interests and a food resource's conservation, and another that, in the end, proved more attractive. That was for the company to increase consumption of a cheapened resource and use it to support the rapid expansion of its business in the region, and leverage power in adjacent, ecologically vulnerable areas of the parkland and boreal forests beyond. Cheap pemmican prices drove early western Canadian history from that point.

1821 and Monopoly

The new position of the HBC after it amalgamated with its competitors in 1821 was immediately felt in the once expensive North

---

[10] Peers, citing Traill, *The Ojibwa of Western Canada*, 194.
[11] HBCA. I have reconstructed the "transfers" to other districts and the "on hand" figure that year from 1842–43 Red River Account, B.235/d/87.

Saskatchewan trade. There, provisions prices were cut in half almost immediately.[12] Throughout the plains and prairie, the company cut costs, closed unnecessary posts, reassessed its buying policies, retracted credit from Native customers, and searched for markets for anything of value from its domains, from whale bone to isinglass, to bales upon bales of swan, goose, and bird feathers. To reduce expense the company slashed its workforce and furloughed hundreds of fur traders. Many with Native wives and families had few options of returning home and gravitated toward Red River. The settlement, routed in 1816, had struggled on with a population slowly but steadily growing and now heavily composed of former fur traders and mixed blood French and English families. At Red River, the population grew from "about 600" in 1823, to 2,300 in 1831, to 4,073 in 1840, and 6,523 in 1856. By 1871, the census counted about 11,000 residents.[13] The HBC, in the meanwhile, took special concern for the colony's agricultural and moral progress. Despite its conditions immediately after the Selkirk Settlement's dispersal, the company had reasons for optimism. After 1817, Roman Catholic priests served the residents, particularly the majority population of Métis, and extended priestly services to the bustling Pembina Post.[14] Anglican ministers soon followed, given the company's full support.

But, economically, the settlement struggled. The labor surplus at Red River was evident as early as July 1823, when hundreds of traders and their families who took up plots of land found immediate wage employment wanting, especially in public works. In the slow summer months, they became "completely dependent" on Fort Douglas, the company post, for cash work. Worse prospects awaited in winter. Throughout the decade, the bison herds were distanced from Red River. George Simpson believed fires and drought discouraged herds from moving northward from the Minnesota territories. The colony's meat buyers were only intermittently successful accessing herds even from Pembina. Freemen hunters and proto-Métis bands were also distant, but likely better established, and from these circumstances

---

[12] R. Harvey Flembing, ed., *Minutes of Council: Northern Department of Rupert Land* (Toronto: The Champlain Society, 1940), xxxvi.
[13] William A. Dobak (Spring 1996), "Killing the Canadian Buffalo, 1821–1881," *Western Historical Quarterly*, 27:40–43.
[14] See Heather Devine, *The People Who Own Themselves*, 115–117; Gerhard Ens, *Homeland to Hinterland: The Changing Worlds of the Red River Métis in the Nineteenth Century* (Toronto: University of Toronto Press, 1996), 19–25.

they returned to the settlement only occasionally to sell meats at extraordinarily high prices.

The generally poor winter hunt favored them in this respect. The Métis had the largest numbers of horses and therefore the best access to distant prey. These meat-hunting opportunists often did not even deliver it dressed to Red River but sold it in the field to the company's buyers. In the first years of the monopoly, the hunt was so poor that, generally, bouts of winter privation, if not near starvation, plagued the colony. This scarcity was not restricted to Red River. Fort Ellice had so little bison fat in the winter of 1823 that it packaged barley with salted meat as a substitute for pemmican.[15] In Red River by spring most of the "poorer class" were often reduced to eating a lean variant of *hominy*, that is, boiled corn in water (the Mandan ate this with bison fat). French Canadian settlers at Red River, especially, were "wretchedly ill off for want of food" at that point. But, as the HBC clerk at Fort Douglas noted in his journal, the problem was that wealthy individuals purchased any foods that did arrive – there were, after all, quite a number of pensioned fur traders still having savings – who propped up prices to high, at times astronomical, levels.[16]

Typically a few hunters struck agreements with the company for orders of cows delivered throughout the winter. But the truly enterprising freemen found better prices selling meat to settlers (who could afford it) for double the prices offered by the HBC (a full £3 a cow carcass, rather than 30 shillings). The settlement's governing body, the Council of Assiniboia, itself dominated by the company's dictates, made the first move to control local prices. In November 1823, it ordered a cap on fresh bison meat to 3.5 d/lb.[17] But, that was still an extravagant price, when typically fresh cow meat sold at 2 and bull meat at 1.5 d/lb.

The Red River Colony's prospects and provisions trade concerned George Simpson, serving as the London Committee's inland governor. The "Little Emperor" was a scurrying, feared manager, acerbically appraising individuals and usually not forgiving their shortcomings. Post staff nervously awaited his arrival to audit books, which he did personally – often, as he did at Fort Chipewyan, with a bagpiper wailing at the front of his rapidly approaching canoe. From the start, Simpson

---

[15] HBCA. See April to June 1823, Fort Ellice Journals, B.63/a/3.
[16] HBCA. July 15, 1824, February 23, March 17–18, 23, 1825 Winnipeg Post Journals, B.235/a/6.
[17] R. Harvey Fleming, ed., *Minutes of Council: Northern Department of Rupert Land* (Toronto: The Champlain Society, 1940), xxviii.

was keenly interested in reforming the provisions trade, one of the most costly expenses in the fur trade before the amalgamation. He provided lengthy reports on Red River and its food problems, initially confident that the issue would take care of itself. Agriculture would prevail, he believed. Indeed, he thought that crops of wheat, barley, and oats would eventually more than meet the colony's needs and much of the fur trade, too. One of the newly appointed governors of the colony, nephew of a company director, A. E. Pelly in 1823, seemed to Simpson the right sort to lead this movement onto an agricultural footing. The arrival of Church of England clergy, too, boded well for civilizing Red River in the clutches of rabble and troublemakers.

In the meanwhile, the company began to lay the basis for monopsony buying advantages in order to lower prices on provisions trade. Initially, company officials enjoyed only marginal success in doing so. The colony constituted a separate purchaser from the company, complicating matters. In addition, the enlarging local population itself created a competition for provisions that hampered the company's abilities to drive down prices.

In an effort to at least corner some of the market to its advantage, the company attempted to prohibit settlers from using their own goods to purchase food from native hunters – however much it struck colonists as patently unfair, if not an interference with their natural rights.[18] What became a long-term strategy was for the company to single out hunters it felt were reliable and industrious, heaping upon them preferential treatment and generous credit. It likely did so to discourage mass participation in the hunt over agricultural activities. One of its first longstanding arrangements was with Augustin Nolin in 1822. A tripman in the carrying trade from York Factory, a hunter with influence, and fur trader, Nolan in May of that year entered into a provisions contract. At the end of the summer, he made good on his promise, resisting "the temptations" to sell to the many settlers offering better prices, and delivering 4 to 5,000 lbs. of bison meats. The company got its pemmican at 6 d/lb., dried meat 5 d, beat meat 5 d, and grease at 6 d.[19] This was a bargain. Given that the company's pemmican from only a year before was still rated at a shilling a pound, the price effectively cut purchasing costs to the company by half. Nolan himself resisted the urge to sell at

---

[18] LAC, Donald Livingston to Alex McDonell, October 9, 1822, *Selkirk Papers, Series A*, 7773.

[19] HBCA, May 15, 1823, Winnipeg Post Journals, B.235/a/5.

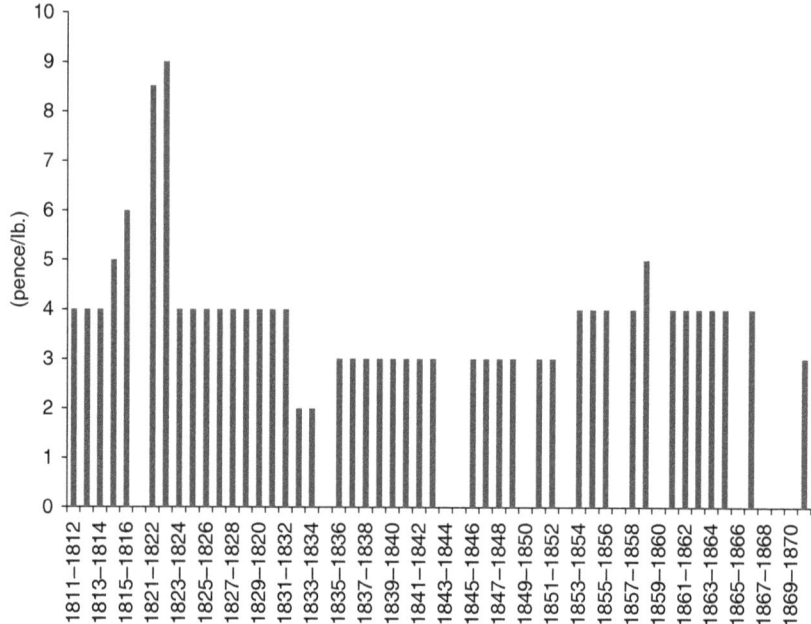

Figure 4.1. Pemmican book prices, 1811–1871, Cumberland House (compiled from HBCA B.49/d/1–119).

the soaring prices nearby likely because he was paid in sterling, in a bill drawn by the company's agent in Montreal.[20]

The company's purchasing clout and coveted sterling payments meant that it could shield itself from the turmoil on food prices unfolding in the frequently starving settlement. Within two or three years, it cut its offer to hunters to a regional standard of 4 and, then, by the early 1830s, 2 d/lb (Figures 4.1–4.3). These regional prices, as seen in Cumberland House accounts, represented the very most the company would pay.

At Red River, the company brokered similar deals with a succession of hunters. One of them was Cuthbert Grant, Jr., the young but influential trader from the NWC – and former insurgent among the Métis at the Battle of Seven Oaks. In the early 1820s, Grant's personal qualities, decisiveness, and leadership potential impressed Simpson. Although his provisioning hunt was initially quite miniscule, and Grant diverted most

---

[20] HBCA. See Accounts, Stock in Hand [from 1821] in Red River Accounts 1821–1822, B.235/d/3.

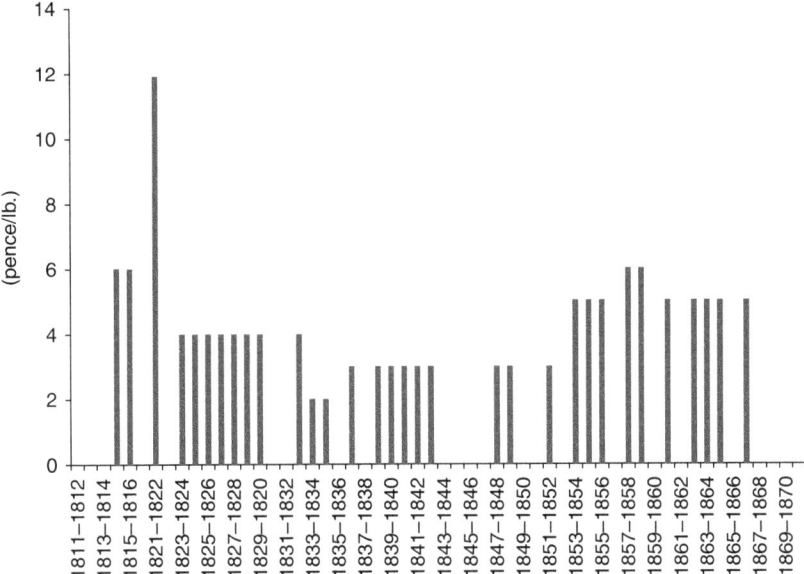

Figure 4.2. Fat book prices, 1811–1871, Cumberland House (compiled from HBCA: B.49/d/1–119).

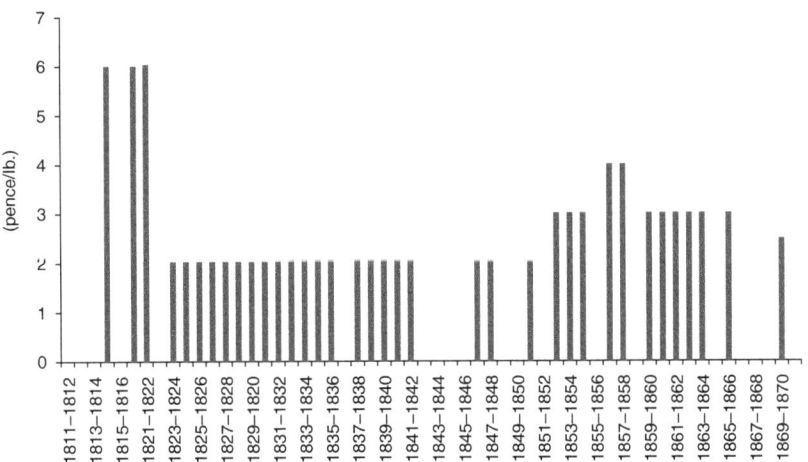

Figure 4.3. Dried meat prices, 1811–1871, Cumberland House (compiled from HBCA, B.49/d/1–119).

of his energy into a leased fur trade with Assiniboine,[21] he was destined to lead larger numbers of bison hunters in the 1830s. Apportioned seigneurial lands at White Horse Plain, divided among prominent buffalo hunters – "all married steady men"[22] – Grant and the White Horse Plain contingent constituted a coterie of preferentially treated hunters who provided, in turn, a safe supply as the company's chief food hunters. Simpson's sympathies clearly lay with such freemen as Augustin Nolin, Grant, and those with whom James Pritchard and Alexander Ross, two company buyers, dealt directly. Even accepting the lower company prices, these hunters could do quite well for themselves with the assured market and sterling payments. John Corcoran, a company hunter in 1826, sold to Fort Douglas some 16,591 lbs. of pemmican in November that year, fetching some £27 sterling. This was not a bad return considering that most of the Red River settlers could fulfill most of their needs in trade goods with £9 or 10 a year.[23] John Bourke, Pierre Berland, and Cuthbert Grant all did quite well providing many of the foodstuffs for the transport service in these years.

From the beginning, the HBC made it a policy, however, not to rely only on one individual but to purchase from a group of select hunters. Alexander Ross remembered this well, that "when the expedition [from the plains] arrived the Hudson's Bay Company, according to usual custom, issued a notice that it would take a certain specified quantity of provisions, not from each fellow that had been on the plains, but from each old and recognized hunter...."[24] At least by fall, 1823, just before hunters departed, local Fort Garry managers had awarded the provisions trade exclusively to a small group of respectable Métis. Now with an unexpected inrush of retired fur traders and their families arriving, and needing to safeguard its stock at Fort Garry from these hungry newcomers,

---

[21] HBCA. His accounts at the HBC shop in 1826/27 totalled £198, selling only about 1,100 lbs. of pemmican that year from the summer hunt and making most of his returns on fur. By contrast, John Corcoran sold 1,659 lbs. of pemmican in November that year. See Retired Servants Accounts Colony Shop, Fort Garry, 1827–1828, B.235/d/30. In 1827 Grant provided only 1,184 lbs. of pemmican. See Cuthbert Grant Entry, Fort Garry Colony Shop Accounts 1827–28, B.235/d/34.

[22] LAC. Simpson understood Cuthbert Grant Jr.'s importance, and, at White Horse Plains and his being joined by McGilles, Poltro, Bolinot, Inkster, "all married steady men and about 80 to 100 families of half breeds." May 31, 1824 George Simpson to A. Colville, *Selkirk Papers, Series A*, 8244.

[23] HBCA. John Corcoran's account and transaction for November 3, 1826. Retired Servants Accounts, Colony Shop, Fort Garry, 1826–1827, B.235/d/30.

[24] Alexander Ross, quoted in Roe, *The North American Buffalo: A Critical Study of the Species in Its Wild State* (Toronto: University of Toronto Press, 1951), 372.

Simpson saw the benefits of cornering the market: "in order that we may have the entire command of the market and hunters, it is agreed that we (the Coy) furnish any supplies they may require," and that year he singled out, "respectable freemen such as Botinot and Beauchemin for that purpose."[25]

"Provisions," Simpson said with some overconfidence, "say Green Meat, and Pemican have hitherto been kept up at a most extravagant price in consequence of the Competition." The company would "take that part of the business entirely into our hands," he said, "and supply him [Governor Pelly in charge of the colony] at fair and moderate prices." To that end, he instructed Donald McKenzie, running Fort Garry, to "engage the best hunters at Pembina to whom we can dictate our own terms, so that this branch of the business I expect there will be a very considerable saving."[26]

As the colony leaned heavier on paid, credited hunters, most of them freemen or settlement employees, it turned decisively from Native provisioners. At least in the Red River valley, the Assiniboine and Cree were effectively squeezed out of the market as a management strategy. Repeated references in the record to troublesome "Plains Indians" in these years make clear that poundmakers like Assiniboine and Cree resented the monopoly and set upon making "mischief" by driving herds far away from the colony to "render them pitiful" in the new situation.[27] More likely, they were already seeing Métis incursions into their winter pound areas, many of them using horses in far greater number than they had themselves and, in summer, disrupting the hunt that they relied on in fall. By 1824, Simpson closed the entire upper Red River (the lower Assiniboine and Qu'Appelle posts), the Swan River and Red Deer River posts, likely to end the trade with Native provisioners, confident that Métis contract hunters could do the job. "The provisions of Upper Red River we do not require," he said, "nor can we find a market for the robes and leather it produces."[28] He even felt that "The colony now produces more grain than its inhabitants can consume, the surplus must be taken by the Coy, it therefore becomes necessary that we abandon our provision posts and make Grain our staple article of living

---

[25] LAC. George Simpson Letter to Donald McKenzie, August 20, 1823, *Selkirk Papers, Series A*, 7921.
[26] LAC. George Simpson Letter to A. Colvile, September 8, 1823, *Selkirk Papers, Series A*, 8025–8026.
[27] LAC. George Simpson's assessment, in *Selkirk Papers, Series A*, 7591.
[28] *Minutes of Council*, xxix.

by so doing we encourage the colony..."[29] Only by 1828 when Cuthbert Grant, relocated from his farms at Whitehorse Plains to supervise the trade near Brandon House, were the "troublesome" Assiniboine reintegrated into the provisions trade, but on largely the terms dictated by the company.[30]

The Meat Trap

Whatever his strengths as a manager, Simpson had been overly optimistic about the colony's potential for agricultural improvement. Rather than conforming to the agricultural ideal of a Little Britain, Red River proved to be a "Lybian tyger," he finally fulminated, "The more we try to tame it the more savage it becomes."[31] The colony showed no signs of great agricultural success, or, more importantly, of making a decisive move from its large wild meat dependency. The continuing agricultural busts in Red River made it doubtful that there were sufficient wheat surpluses to support a population that continued to recruit from retiring fur traders, mixed marriages, and a heavy-drinking hodgepodge of adventurers who always find their way to frontier settlements. As an American newspaper commented, the settlement "isolated... in the high latitude of the north" had become something of a "community of Robinson Crusoes. Their crops having failed the last two seasons, they have been forced to break out of the wilds again, and seek food in the markets of the Great brawling world."[32]

Poor yielding crops, frequent flooding in bottom lands along the Red and Assiniboine, grasshoppers and other scourges, early frosts, and late springs all conspired against the colony's improvement. Red River stubbornly resisted any imported agricultural or even pastoral model. The sorry state of the Swiss colonists arriving in 1822 made that, perhaps, evident. During their first winter, they were ignobly dispatched to hunting tents in Pembina. Their very survival depended on it. The thirty-two settlers with their families consumed nothing short of 17,789 lbs. of

---

[29] LAC. George Simpson to Colville, May 31, 1824, *Selkirk Papers*, Series A, 8251.

[30] HBCA. December 31, 1827, Winnipeg Post Journals, B.235/a/9; later in spring, "Mr. Grant, it was reported to us this morning, has succeeded in pacifying the Stone Indians about his trading post near Brandon House," the journal stated, "and is making an excellent trade. By May 5, he had traded, apparently from the Assiniboine some 50,000 muskrats and other furs, besides "a considerable quantity of provisions, robes and leather." March 15, 1828, Winnipeg Post Journals, B.235/a/9.

[31] Quoted in Mackie, *Trading Beyond the Mountains*, 92.

[32] Ibid.

fresh buffalo meat, 5,300 lbs. of dried meat, and a comparatively meager amount of barley, wheat, and salt pork they got their hands on. One family was apportioned "about 2 ½ lbs [fresh meat] per day per head old and young!" the provisioning accountant at Pembina stated, evidently aghast at the high consumption.[33]

There was not much of a choice in the matter. As Herman has suggested, buffalo hunting continued to be the most viable subsistence pursuit, especially among Métis, in a settlement chronically beset by agricultural disappointments. He listed no fewer than thirty reported crop failures between 1812 and 1870, and those constituted only the officially reported ones.[34] The ongoing demand for caloric safeguards meant that town merchants, and the company's own storekeeper, continued to sell goods to Native hunters for meat, rather than furs, and "From the head of the colony to the lowest settler encouragement is held out to all Indians to devote their time and attention to large animal hunting, the consequence is that the leather and provision trade is totally ruined and the Red River opposition attracts Indians from very distant parts of the country," Simpson soon lamented.[35]

For the most part, the company used its supply of goods, not to mention its sterling bills, to try to bring its own suppliers down to lower prices.[36] But the local market was out of control, given the growing size of the population and the sheer precariousness of agricultural success. Although the company was able to strike piecemeal deals with individuals, its hands were tied with current prices among private buyers so high. James Hargrave was alarmed to find settlers, such as one Couc[h]on, worrying for his family's own food supply, paying 25 to 30 shillings to a local native hunter for half a side of a moose, with its skin, "a most

---

[33] LAC. "A Copy of a paper found in the office at Red River Colony purporting to an account of provisions issued by Mr. Fletcher at Pembina to the Swiss Settlers During the Winter 1821/22. *Selkirk Papers, Series A,* 7571.

[34] Herman G. Sprenger, "The Métis Nation: Buffalo Hunting vs. Agriculture in the Red River Settlement (Circa 1810–1870)," in Antoine S. Lussier and D. Bruce Sealey, eds., *The Other Natives: the Métis,* Vol. I – 1700–1885 (Winnipeg, Manitoba: Manitoba Métis Federation, 1978), 124.

[35] LAC. George Simpson Report, May 20, 1822, *Selkirk Papers, Series A,* 7600.

[36] In September 1822, freemen were leaving the settlement well supplied with the company's credited goods, "which will be paid in provisions during the course of the winter...."HBCA September 18, 1822, James Hargrave's Journal, Winnipeg Post Journals, 1822–1823, B.235/a/5. In these years, the company provided fall credits much as it had in the longer fur trade, with the Red River company store giving generous powder, ball, and no end of camp materials, in October, November, and December. HBCA See Red River Store Accounts, B.235/d/24.

enormous price," he said. He suggested the high prices in the settlement revealed the "foolish spirit of competition" that still ruled the colony.[37]

Indeed, it was likely the sizable local market that, by the later 1820s, finally sparked one of the largest and arguably most distinctive hunting phenomena in northern plains native history – the coordination of the mass Métis summer hunt. By then, poor winter hunting in the district continued to affect prices, and given the steadily growing settler population and its heavy reliance on meat in its diet, summer hunting emerged as a distinct strategy to cash in on the slightly higher prices offered on "seasoned" rather than fresh fall meats.

It happened, suddenly, in summer 1826. During the preceding summer and winter of 1825/26 the Red River Colony's crops and fall winter hunting failed. This was not expected at all. In the summer of 1825, settler crops fared well from plenty of spring rain. Good prospects for the harvest, in turn, encouraged Métis hunters returning from a summer hunt in July to sell their surpluses rather than save them, having the habit "of not thinking for the future," the relatively newly arrived Roman Catholic bishop, Joseph Norbert Provencher, wrote. Given the confidence in the wheat, barley, and other crops now maturing well in the Manitoba sunlight, the Métis indeed sold their provisions "to the last mouthful" to local merchants and individuals buyers.[38] The Métis also sold them for another reason not mentioned by the Bishop, that they could not get the price they wanted for these "seasoned" meats from the HBC, which by now had cut prices to around 4–6 d/lb. and rejected the Métis demands, simply, as "unreasonable."[39] In fact, the company, as the largest buyer, simply beat down the overburdened freemen over the week of the hunters' return, and like commercial vultures, bought only when the Métis "at length lowered their prices, and now get a ready sale for their provisions, among the settlers."[40]

Still confident in a good crop and now with less to show for their earlier hunt "a great number of settlers set out from the settlement with horses and carts, for the plains beyond Pambina on a hunting excursion"

---

[37] HBCA. He said it was "the more unaccountable when it is considered that they can purchase the same provisions in the company store at 2 d/lb." September 21, 1822, James Hargrave's Journal, Winnipeg Post Journals, 1822–1823, B.235/a/5.

[38] Centre du Patrimoine, St. Boniface. Letter, Joseph Norbert Provencher to Amable Dionne, July 17, 1826, Provencher Papers, P-0227.

[39] HBCA. "Several freemen also arrived from Pambian, with a considerable quantity of seasondd provisions, which they propose selling, but their prices are unreasonable." July 23, 1825, Winnipeg Post Journals, B.235/a/7.

[40] HBCA. July 30, 1825, Winnipeg Post Journals, B.235/a/7.

in mid August.[41] Within a week of their departure, however, the wheat and barley crops, thought to have been blessed by early rains, were showing unexpected damage. Their pummeling by heavy winds earlier in the season had reduced grain on the stem; and now the entire crop showed unmistakable evidence of smut. Once cut by the 24th, an alarming "very great drawback" was evident, especially in wheat yields. The other scourge squeaked. The colony was plagued with ravenously hungry mice that ate up the threshed wheat as quickly as settlers could store it. They now had to choose what to do with far less: set aside their grains for winter consumption or sell it for still needed goods. Most chose the latter: the clerk now purchasing up grain for the HBC found colonists were, again, selling him everything. "Many of them sell nearly the whole of their grain now so as to purchase clothing for themselves and families, and trust to labour in the settlement or hunting in the plains for their winter subsistence." Indeed, "it is vain to dissuade them from trusting soley to chance." Their reply to him was that "it is bad in either case and that it is just as well for them to starve to death, as to be frozen to death in the winter."[42]

The first hunting contingents returned by October 1 with a large supply of meats.[43] This proving insufficient for the colony's needs, winter hunters then organized and set out on November 17, with the intention to capitalize on the quickly cooling temperatures to find the herds and send back product when it was procured.[44] On December 1, the last of the farmers who had sold virtually all of their grain set off "in pursuit of Buffaloe, on which they now place their sole dependence for the winter subsistence."[45] But here luck failed them. By December 25, the first reports filtered back to the colony that the hunters had no success locating bison. And, by then, the season changed for the worst.

Alexander Ross wrote three decades later that the winter of 1826 was "one of the most fatal ... that ever befell Red River."[46] Having followed the herds beyond Pembina 150 to 200 miles, the hunters and families were caught in a sudden and bitter cold snap stopping them in their

---

[41] Ibid., August 16, 1825.
[42] Ibid., November 29, 1825.
[43] Ibid., October 1, 1825.
[44] Ibid., November 17, 1826.
[45] Ibid., December 1, 1835.
[46] Alexander Ross, *The Red River Settlement: Its Rise, Progress, and Present State* (London: Smith, Elder & Co., 1856), 98.

tracks. Horses froze. Families huddled together, far distances from the next. The cold weather caught Métis and plains native bands all unprepared. Those managing to get off the plains settled in at the settlement gates, vowing not to return for fear of what awaited them. It "exceeds in extent any thing of the kind, ever, experienced, at any former period in this quarter," the HBC clerk wrote.[47] Those getting back reported families eating their horses, dogs, and even the leather on their clothing. In total fifteen perished on the plains.[48] Indian corn warehoused at Pembina was quickly distributed to the families arriving to that post, and runners were sent out to the plains to try to provide sustenance to the sufferers.[49] The HBC's grain stores were now opened to sales and for relief, as well as Indian corn, dried peas, and barley – the latter now given to the livestock dying without winter fodder.

Throughout February refugees crowded into the settlement. They descended on family and friends but found little food to support them. The HBC offered some relief by providing scraps of cloth, some pemmican, hardware, and other items from its general store – of fifty-four families and individuals, the company extended some £160 of relief trade goods.[50] But by the beginning of March, the HBC clerk at Fort Garry counted no fewer than three discernible groups organizing "insurrections" to seize the food locked up in the company's store awaiting its spring brigades' use. The clerk had good reason to fear the starving colonists: It had both driven down in price and purchased up in bulk a good portion of the Métis' small summer hunt, and then purchased up the entire settlement's agricultural produce, offered, again, on the most advantageous terms for the company. That unhappy colonists did not just burn Fort Douglas to the ground is a matter of wonder.

Meanwhile, whatever food was available was being purchased up by the few who could: the wealthy, "such as have money offer an extravagant price on any kind of provisions," and those without money were offering the clothes off their backs to get at least a few morsels.[51] In Red River, the few provisions that were available on the market immediately rose in value: to 8 pence per pound by the end of the winter.[52]

[47] HBCA. January 2, 1826, Winnipeg Post Journals, B.235/a/17.
[48] See the event described J. Hargrave to Rev. W. Rattray, September 5, 1826, in Helen E. Ross, ed., *Letters from Rupert's Land, 1826–1840: James Hargrave of the Hudson's Bay Company* (Montreal and Kingston: McGill-Queen's University Press, 2009), 57–58.
[49] HBCA. February 20–25, 1826, Winnipeg Post Journals 1825–1826, B.235/a/7.
[50] HBCA. See Charity Fund, 1826–27 Winnipeg Post Accounts B.235/d/31.
[51] HBCA. March 2, 1826, Winnipeg Post Journals 1825–1826, B.235/a/7.
[52] Alexander Ross, *Red River Settlement*, 104–106.

By spring, more hardship awaited. The Assiniboine went into an awful flood, taking out most of the settlement's houses. On a single day during half an hour, some forty-seven houses were swept away from the cresting river, bloated with melting and charging ice. With spring crops likely imperiled and the horrors of the hungry winter fresh in their minds, at least one group had had enough. The Swiss de Meurons, a military unit dispatched with families to settle at the colony early in the decade, vacated when the opportunity presented itself. On July 11, about 130 of the settlers – about 50 men and 80 women and children – left for the United States.[53]

The HBC accounts at Red River make plain a new hunting strategy emerging in the immediate aftermath of the famine of 1825/27. By 1827, the Métis hunters produced and sold some 16,000 lbs. of pemmican in summer. By 1831, they raised that to almost 26,000 lbs.; and by 1837, almost 90,000 lbs. In the same period, traded winter meats (apparently fresh) ranged in weight from 8,000 to 11,000 lbs. in some years, to almost 14,000 lbs., as was the case in 1834.[54] A particularly revealing sale occurred In 1842/43, when the summer hunt produced some 417 bags of pemmican (sent immediately on to Norway House to await the brigades in the spring), while another 795 bags were left "on hand" at the Red River post, representing more than 100,000 lbs. in pemmican.[55]

A number of factors had apparently spurred the Métis to undertake larger summer hunts from Red River. The ongoing uncertainty of the colony's agriculture was one, as Métis settlers and townsfolk hunted for their own diets and responded to the generally high price within the settlement for "seasoned" meats. Prudent settlers made purchases from hunters returning from "summer" hunts, paying summer prices that were higher than fall ones and indeed far higher than the controlled price of the HBC.[56] The larger summer hunt seems to have become a

[53] HBCA. July 11, 1826, Winnipeg Post Journals 1825–1826, B.235/a/7.
[54] These weights have been derived by adding together the incoming product of brigades and hunting captains in summer and winter months, as indicated in Red River Accounts, B.235/d/87.
[55] Red River Accounts for the year 1842/43, B.235/d/87.
[56] Alexander Ross, *Red River Settlement*, 98, 104–106. The event is also described by J. Hargrave to Rev. W. Rattray, September 5, 1826, in Helen E. Ross, ed., *Letters from Rupert's Land, 1826–1840: James Hargrave of the Hudson's Bay Company* (Montreal and Kingston: McGill-Queen's University Press, 2009), 57–58. Higher summer prices constituted a problem for the HBC purchasers in Red River, who cut deals with particular hunters and offered sterling bills, in order to gain them cheaper. The company's journals make this clear. For instance: "Several freemen also arrived from Pambian, with a considerable quantity of seasoned provisions, which they propose selling, but their prices are unreasonable." July 23, 1825, Winnipeg Post Journals, B.235/a/7.

fact afterwards, as early Red River historian George Bryce and Red River pioneer John McLean both suggested in their narratives.[57]

Given that the HBC preferred to purchase summer provisions to lay up in time for spring brigades and was using now preferred and credited individuals as the most reliable provisioners,[58] it was only natural that they began to serve after 1827 as emerging "captains" of ever larger contingents of hunters, drawing from mixed-blood bands in the district. Still completely autonomous as a mass – and thereby distinctive economically from tribal hunting contingents – the leaders and adherents constituted jointly connected but economically atomic entities moving into the summer territories.

Out of the calamitous 1825/26 winter, the structures of the Red River provisions economy were struck. The clerk at the HBC, then, believing that "now reduced to the last extremity of want," the experience – "if experience ever can teach them prudence" – would probably "have the effect of causing them hereafter to devote more of their time and attention to agriculture," proved simply to be wrong.[59] If anything, the equal uncertainties of agriculture and the poor parkland winter hunt fostered new strategies around the market. The Métis now hunted in summer. The HBC's own purchases at Red River alone jumped from a mere 4,880 lbs. in 1826 to 16,127 lbs. in 1827.[60]

In such times, the HBC, as one of the largest buyers in the area, purchased only to its advantage in the summer market. It could, after all, depend on other districts to purchase the bulk of its needs if Métis hunters demanded more than the regional price. The company's staple supplies were, besides, usually met by its appointed, individual hunters. By August, when it was clearer whether crops would survive, the company

[57] George Bryce, *The Remarkable History of the Hudson's Bay Company* (London: Sampson Low, Marston & Co., 1910), 356; McLean refers generally to the period after the amalgamation in 1821; however, it was after the great flood after the starving winter of 1826, that he remembered "The Buffaloes, however, proved abundant, and afforded a supply of provisions enough to prevent starvation," suggesting that the avails of the summer hunt were great that year (372–373). John McLean, *Notes of a Twenty-Five Year's Service in the Hudson's Bay Territories* (Toronto: Champlain Society, 1932), 372–373
[58] The strategy appears in HBCA. See Accounts, Stock in Hand [from 1821] in Red River Accounts 1821–22, B.235/d/3HBCA May 15, 1823, Winnipeg Post Journals, B.235/a/5.
[59] HBCA. January 25, 1826, Winnipeg Post Journals 1825–1826, B.235/a/17.
[60] HBCA. These figures are derived from servant accounts in the Red River Post's Accounts for the years 1826 through 1828. In these years almost all of this product was obtained from Augustin Nolan, minimally from Cuthbert Grant and from Andrew McDermot, Red River Accounts, B.235/d/29-30-31.

bought up the stock of freemen hunters at a moment when it was often devaluing. The company clerks then squirreled large portions of what they got from the settlement altogether and – always remembering the near insurrections during the winter of 1826 – safely stored them at Norway House, which now grew as a large warehouse. This kept a requisite quantity on hand for the spring brigades, and left it far away from hungry mouths should, God forbid, famine fall again on the settlement in the winter months.

When, by 1827, the company was in the position of buying in bulk at cheap prices, its traders then built up discretionary funds of pemmican. They came in with dried meat, fat, and the surplus barley, wheat, pork, and "hams," appearing in its accounts as "Red River produce" in summer and fall. The sterling value of Red River "produce" that included surplus pemmican was impressive: in 1826 summer and winter purchases totaled £70 and £112, respectively. Summer product values thereafter jettisoned to £96, £336, £2143, and £1,094 in the summers of 1832, 1833, 1836 and 1837. Winter purchases grew only to £861 by 1838. In all three years of 1839, 1840, and 1841, the company increased its bison product purchases to £1,600/ year – more valuable than the entire agricultural sector combined.[61] Once 300 or so bags of pemmican were collected and sent off to Norway House, the rest of the surplus could be kept on hand to help in the still-important fur hunt to the east and north of Red River. A manager drew on his discretionary funds to give food as gifts or, more often the case, provide food as credit with the understanding that most Ojibwa trappers who accepted them would pay back in furs. Cheap pemmican, in the end, allowed the company to pay for Native trappers specializing in fur hunting, a matter of great importance in the quickly exhausting interlake areas of the Ojibwa. Already in the fall of 1826, for instance, the company purchased up so much cheap pemmican from summer hunters that a good portion of it was provided to Ojibwa muskrat hunters who could now devote themselves to trapping rather than provisions hunting.[62]

---

[61] Alexander Ross gives £5,000 being paid in total over these three years and specifies that in 1841, hunters got £1,200, "rather more than all the agricultural class," *Red River Settlement*, 273.

[62] HBCA. See entry for January 31, 1828, where the post was selling pemmican to Ojibwa for their muskrat harvests, when they had no other goods to trade. The trader noted that he had such surplus pemmican because of it had been "plentiful in the fall, [when] we fortunately laid in a good stock." Winnipeg Post Journals 1827–28, B.235/a/9.

Summer Market Hunting in the Late 1820s

Métis developing organized summer hunts in the 1820s were completely overthrowing native traditions in the area to hunt in fall and winter, and, despite the fantastic risks involved, were expanding in the heat of the summer deep into the "heart of buffalo country," as Captain John Palliser described the summer territories.[63] The obvious change was not just in the new horse power being used, but where it was employed for the market, and how it contended with the difficulties of prairie climate.[64] Brenda Macdougall and Nicole St.-Onge argue that the summer "brigades" that formed thereafter, pursuing ever-larger circuits into the prairie based on kin affiliation to specific male heads, made mobility a distinctive marker of Métis identity in the post-1820s era.[65]

Whatever the cultural impact of such an emergent hunting tradition, the summer hunt grew considerably. Alexander Ross suggested that some 540 carts left the colony to meet the herds in the 1820s, and used that number to demonstrate the "rapidly increasing" plains hunters in the settlement by the 1840s. He listed 680 in 1825, 820 in 1830, 970 in 1835, and 1,210 in 1840.[66] But it was only in the late

---

[63] On C_4 grass structure, see Don Gayton, *The Wheatgrass Mechanism: Science and Imagination in the Western Canadian Landscape* (Saskatoon: Fifth House, 1990), 71–78.

[64] On the impact of the horse and the bison hunt, Pekka Hämäläinen, *The Commanche Empire* (New Haven: Yale University Press, 2008), 244–247; the environmental impact is explored in Pekka Hämäläinen (December 2003), "The Rise and Fall of Plains Indian Horse Cultures," *Journal of American History*, 834; and Pekka Hämäläinen (Spring 2001), "The First Phase of Destruction: Killing the Southern Plains Buffalo, 1790–1840," *Great Plains Quarterly*, 21(2):101–104; The disequilibrium of horse plains cultures is offered in Dan Flores (September 1991), "Bison Ecology and Bison Diplomacy: The Southern Plains from 1800–1850," *Journal of American History*, 78(2):465–485; and Andrew Isenberg, *The Destruction of the Bison: An Environmental History, 1750–1920* (Cambridge: Cambridge University Press, 2000). The overall understanding of horse and Indian hunting is offered by Frank Gilbert Roe, *The Indian and the Horse* (Norman: University of Oklahoma Press, 1955); Alison Landals, "Horse Heaven: Change in Late Precontact to Contact Period Landscape Use in Southern Alberta," in Brian Kooyman and Jane H. Kelley, eds., *Archaeology on the Edge: New Perspectives from the Northern Plains* (Calgary: University of Calgary Press, 2004), 231–262; Harold P. Danz, *Of Bison and Man* (Niwot: University Press of Colorado, 1997), 54; See chapter, "Effect of the Horse on Trade Relations," in Joseph Jablow, *The Cheyenne in Plains Indian Trade Relations 1795–1840* (Seattle: University of Washington Press, 1950), 12–24. Gerhard Ens suggests the proto and historical ethnogenesis of Métis around commercial opportunities in *Homeland to Hinterland*. I am benefiting from Jacqueline Peterson, "Rocking the Cradle of the Plains: The Emergence of a New Aboriginal People in Northern North America," unpublished paper, May 2009, provided to author.

[65] See Brenda Macdougall and Nicole St-Onge (Winter 2013), "Rooted in Mobility: Métis Buffalo-Hunting Brigades," *Manitoba History*, 71:21–32.

[66] Ross, *Red River Settlement*, 246.

1820s when returns of "seasoned meat" or "dry meat" became relevant in the market.[67]

Summer market hunting became a preserve and in many respects a specialty of the Métis. Their impact on the herds has been open to controversial debate. F. G. Roe defended the Métis from the "lofty and needlessly severe reflections" of both Hornaday and Allen who charged the Métis with the very extermination of the bison.[68] Indeed, Hornaday, in his classic, *Extermination of the American Bison,* pointed squarely at the Red River settlers who "aided, of course, by the Indians of that region... [were] responsible for the extermination of the bison throughout northeastern Dakota as far as the Cheyenne River, northern Minnesota, and the whole of what is now the province of Manitoba."[69] Roe defended the Métis from such a charge, claiming that they controlled the hunt so that it would not be a free for all slaughter, and naturally sought cows for meat, or robes, according to the basic human logic that all hunters seek females. In this respect, however, Roe seems to have missed some of the glaring characteristics of a market-oriented summer hunt that need to be taken into account.

There is no doubt that summer hunting, perfected by Métis, was terrifically wasteful. But it was really the pressures they were under in the market, and the effects of more individualist market orientation among Métis hunters, that made their summer hunting so consequential to the bison's long range sustainability. The market was, in effect, pushing the Métis to develop a hunt that killed cows, generally, at a time when they were sometimes half their prime, in summer. They were also killing males that, though fatty just before the rut, quickly became skinny and completely worthless for their meat. The very illogic of hunting bison in summer was well respected traditionally by Native hunters. Within the two seasons of the Native calendar, bison biology tended to encourage greater "winter moon" hunting. In early summer, it was usually only males that gained any real weight. Alexander Henry the Younger found that bulls by July 1 could weigh, with offal, some 1,800 lbs. These behemoths were the only animals worth hunting. On one sortie on July 16, near the Souris River and en route to the Mandan villages in 1806,

---

[67] LAC. Letter from Pembina, August 3, 1823, Andrew McDermot to J. P. Bourke, "The Freemen are not yet arrived. They say how they will not be back till the middle of this month." *Selkirk Papers, Series A,* 7966.

[68] Roe, *North American Buffalo,* 373.

[69] William Temple Hornaday, *The Extermination of the American Bison* [1889] (Washington, DC: Smithsonian Institution, 2002), 489, 504–507; an example of Allan's condemnation

Henry described traveling on the pan-flat level plain where "we soon fell in with great numbers of Buffalo all in motion passing from East to West, bellowing and tearing up the ground as they went on. We chased them and killed a Bull, the flesh of which is more palatable at this season of the Year than the Cow Buffalo."[70] Two days later, his party took an extraordinarily fat bull with a considerable quantity of *dépouille*, or back fat. "A Bull seldom has any extraordinary back fat. Their fat is principally to be found in the inside of the animal. I make no manner of doubt but this Bull we killed here would have produced near one hundred weight of tallow from his inside only."[71]

A bull's back fat quickly thinned, however, and the body lost its attractiveness to hunters. It became too lean soon after the rut later in the summer. Older bulls remained year round notoriously unpalatable, butchered very selectively and even at that, the "part of an old bull" that arrived at Brandon House by the end of July probably well represented many males, "the flesh as tough as a horse's hide."[72] Certainly, by December, traders usually saw bulls having little if any inside, tallow or backfat, most important to subsistence hunters needing large amounts of fat energy.

Cows mobilized fat in almost an exactly opposite way than bulls. Pembina-country cows at the turn of the nineteenth century (perhaps benefiting from extraordinarily good forage) weighed 600 to 700 lbs. after dressing in fall. Pregnant cows weighed a mere 300 lbs. in summer (barren cows, by contrast remained fat). It was only after the rut in late summer and during gestation that cows quickly gained fat.[73] Although plains hunters organized surround hunts in summer, the comparatively lean cows and, later in the summer, the ferocity of the rut meant that, traditionally, far more native organization and plain common sense diverted much of the hunters' energies to the fatty pregnant cow hunt in fall.[74] The relatively small contingent of hunters Father Bellcourt accompanied in the fall of 1840 hunt, then, took

---

is found in 529; Joel Asaph Allan, *A History of the American Bison* (Washington: Government Printing Office, 1877), 537.

[70] *Journal of Alexander Henry the Younger*, I, 206–207.

[71] Ibid., 210.

[72] HBCA. July 20, 1796, Summer Journal by Thomas Miller, copied in Brandon House Journals, 1797–98, B.22/a/4.

[73] A fat cow killed in autumn weighed some 600 to 700 lbs. (butchered), while a lean did not exceed 300. The average weight of 150 butchered cows in September to February was 400 lbs. each. In the same period, winter bulls weighed as little as 550 lbs. each. "Recapitulation, 1808," Gough, ed., *The Journal of Alexander Henry the Younger*, I, 317.

[74] Dale F. Lott, *American Bison: A Natural History* (Berkeley: University of California Press, 2002).

1,776 animals – mostly cows – and after they made pemmican had more than 33,000 lbs. of tallow left in store.[75] More than 18 lbs. of tallow fat per animal was derived and stored, then, beyond that which was used for pemmican production. By stark comparison, one summer hunt well described in the Red River newspaper, the *Nor'Wester*, shows the mixed male and female animals availing as little as 2 lbs. in surplus tallow per animal.[76] Summer hunting often availed little if any surplus tallow, suggesting that bags of pemmican were being created with the fat of not one but two or more cows. Ross's classic description of the large Métis summer hunt he joined in the 1840s, with 2,500 animals killed, listed only pemmican having been made, with the surplus tallow, if any, being not worthy of mention.[77]

Summer herds were also spread out into bands, and by mid-summer moving together toward the rut. The mixed quality of the animals meant that in summer hunting, Métis might have killed bands on their first sighting, and, if better animals were found later, would abandon the skinnier animals in preference for fatter ones more worth the effort. [78] Closer to the rut – although not during it – summer hunting contended with herds mixed with males and females. How much males protected females in such circumstances is open to debate among bison biologists[79]; however, the frequent observation at the time was that summer hunters contended with males that protected females, leaving hunters with the task of killing unwanted males to access the prized cows inside stampeding flanges. Indeed, much of the greatly admired Métis horsemanship, tack, and musketry skills, with horses trained to gallop alongside a cow while a hunter spit a ball down the barrel of his musket on the

---

[75] So, after 1,776 fall animals were killed and slaughtered the Métis had 228 bags of pemmican, 33,200 lbs. of tallow fat (in bags), which equaled 18 lbs. of tallow per animal *after* pemmican was made. See "Lettre de M. Belcourt," 51.

[76] The recourse was to take tallow bulls. See, for instance, the returns from a June hunt where 3,270 buffalo were taken, with 1,151 bulls, 1,893 cows, and 226 calves. The carcasses produced 1,964 bags of pemmican 2,429 bales of dried meat, 15,120 lbs. of marrow fat, and 9,600 lbs. of tallow. The tallow was likely derived exclusively from the male animals. "Account of the White Horse Plains Hunters," August 28, 1860, *Nor'Wester*.

[77] He says "out of that number only 375 bags of pemmican and 240 bags of dried meat were made!" Ross, *Red River Settlement*, 264.

[78] See, for instance, the case in 1861, when "Six hundred fine cows were killed, whereupon the bull's meat with which they had previously loaded up, was thrown away to the wolves," in "The Fall Hunt," November 15, 1861 *Nor'Wester*, 2.

[79] George W. Arthur "An Introduction to the Ecology of Early Historic Communal Bison Hunting Among the Northern Plains Indians," Archaeological Survey of Canada Paper No. 37 (Ottawa: National Museums of Canada, 1975), 45-47.

fly, were honed around the need to access cows within wild and stampeding flanges of bulls.[80]

Métis specializing as summer hunters certainly took advantage of relatively cooler northern maximum temperatures. It was only because the northern latitudes generally favored fat handling in summer months that tradable surpluses could be generated at all. Their fats were nevertheless vulnerable to the effects of extraordinary hot spells. Some of the subcutaneous and core body fats of a bison likely had melting points as low as 37–39°C and would have started turning well below that. Rancidity could set in quickly on a good hot summer day much below that, the factor of heat increasing the oxidation and rancidity of fat.[81] Marrow fats were far more unstable. The Métis, then, ranged far, but within northern territories with ideal summer temperatures. They made pemmican in spaces peripheral to the truly hot and dry expanses of the American Great Plains proper and the great heat of the Missouri Plateau to the south in present day Bismarck and Pierre. Initially within the Missouri Coteau, and then, later, in areas north of the Missouri hotspots, and finally, within the upper Missouri basin with comparatively cooler summer temperatures, they chose prairie spots with cooler temperatures, with a minimum of 12 and maximum of 27 °C.[82]

This, of course, could sometimes not work in the favor of summer hunters. One Métis hunt that left Red River in 1862, then, easily locating "immense herds" just north of the Missouri in the Grand Couteau. In the first runs where about 1,000 animals were killed, "The weather was so excessively hot most of this time," a newspaper account reported, "that although great numbers of buffalo were slaughtered, much of the meat was spoiled before it was used." With insufficient supplies created, parties continued farther south to try to fill their carts while others gave up and returned from the Missouri.[83]

The perilous nature of summer fat and meat handling certainly explains the emergence of a well-timed, outdoor butchery perfected by the Métis. Their efforts went to preserve as quickly as possible meats and fats of value to the market, but often left the rest. The butchery

---

[80] Alison Mercer, "Half-Hitches, Dressed Leather, and Nice Easy Long Strides: Métis Horsemanship in the Mounted Buffalo Hunt," Honours thesis, Department of History, University of Calgary, 2007.
[81] Al Shaefer, Agriculture Canada, Lacombe Laboratory, to author, December 16, 2009 offers this melting point.
[82] 42d. Northern Missouri Coteau," See "Ecoregions of North Dakota and South Dakota," of the Northern Prairie Wildlife Research Centre, February 19, 2013.
[83] "Running the Buffalo," *Nor'Wester*, September 11, 1862.

undoubtedly innovated on Native precedents (the Ojibwa used a variant of this in their own market hunting), but the Métis themselves designated it as *éparer* (likely derived from the word *parer*, meaning cutting and tooling leather, and, in other designations, cutting meat for cooking). *Éparer* became a signature Métis technique that harvested as quickly as possible the most easily accessible meats and fats.[84] Pemmican was often manufactured strictly with hard tallow. Under the best conditions bladders of grease were filled for sale separately. An animal was laid on its belly, cut down the spine, and then its robe peeled off, usually discarded. (These summer skins were often hairless and valued only as cheap leather.) More commonly, bull skins were cut in half and sewn together as "taureaux" or pemmican bags. The large hump (*bosse*) was then extracted as a meat overlain with a larger layer of fat; this came from both sides of the enormous dorsal spines of the back. To the back was the *petite bosse* (the sirloin cap easily scooped with a blade from the rump area); the two *dépouilles* were then taken. These were literally the back fats of the animal located easily on either side of the backbone under the skin. Nicked with a knife, it was hard and sufficiently unsaturated that it detached quite easily with a peeling motion. The shoulders gave two sides of flat iron or chuck meats on the outside of the bone, again, cut along the bone and pulled. Two shoulder pieces followed, two fillets likely taken from the front leg, two thighs could be cut off with or without the bone – the large knuckle could be later used for marrow, and what would be large inside rounds taken from there. Two sides with ribs could be hacked free, and the belly availing a brisket.[85]

Field butchery undertaken in hot temperatures left Métis discriminating between animals found simply too skinny to be left on the ground unused, with perhaps only their hump and tongue taken. Indeed, it was likely in respect to summer hunting that the Métis earned their unenviable reputation as some of the most efficient hunters for the market, but also the greatest wasters of meat. By 1845, Father Belcourt provided one of the more careful overviews of factory processes by then adopted by the Métis. He listed sixteen components of the cow taken by hunters

---

[84] See the term "éparer" defined in Fur Trade Food Glossary." Father Belcourt describes the technique in "Letter de M. Belcourt," November 25, 1845," in *Letter from the Secretary of War Transmitting Report of Major Wood*, Ex. Doc. No. 51 (1st. Sess., 31st Cong. Washington, DC, 1850), 47–48.

[85] *Journal of Alexander Henry the Younger*, I, on how buffalo are butchered for the market by Ojibwa I 318. Belcourt lists 16 pieces of the bison butchered for the market, "Lettre de M. Belcourt," 48.

that, even in a fall hunt represented only the most succulent and fatty parts – "the rest stays on the field, the wolves' inheritance." Belcourt reported that these hunters were making pemmican mostly from fat from the interior of the animal, "cut up and melted in large kettles." They were making some "fine pemmican," too, but, only from about six liters of marrow fat per cow. The streamlined production was impressive, the camps slaughtering "with a truly surprising ease and rapidity." Of the 1,776 animals slaughtered, the fall camp produced some 228 bags of pemmican, 1,213 bales of dried meat, 166 *boskoyn* bags of grease (each 200 lbs.), and 556 bladders of soft grease (each 12 lbs. in weight).[86]

The terrific waste of summer hunting struck Alexander Ross. He said of the 2,500 animals killed "only 375 bags of pemmican and 240 bales of dried meat were made!" He believed the meat of only 750 of the animals were preserved (375 bags of pemmican and 240 bales of dried meat): "the food, in short, was wasted.... Scarcely one-third in number of the animals killed is turned to account."[87] The oblate priest Léon Doucet also remarked on the waste. Having lived among the Plains Cree and seen both them and Métis hunt, he noted that the latter "are better hunters than the Indians; they are better armed. But they kill as much as they can and take only a portion. A great waste."[88] This selectivity at the cost of the larger carcass struck a *Nor'Wester* correspondent accompanying the fall hunt in 1860: "Capital butchers these men of the plains are, not very dainty dissectors, nor quite in the style of an English market, but just in the quickest and simplest way for themselves and they do it well.... the meat is thrown in [the cart] and off they go to cut up another and perhaps a third, or more if the hunter has been fortunate.[89] Of course, these contingents ate prodigious amounts en route and on return, a matter that became more consequential as herds withdrew farther west and south. There were, too, other matters of these hunts. When he counted 1,630 people on his own hunt, Ross also found no fewer than 542 dogs.[90]

---

[86] "Lettre de M. Belcourt," November 25, 1845, *Letter from the Secretary of War*, 51.
[87] Ross, 264.
[88] Provincial Archives of Alberta, o.m.i. My translation of "Les Métis sont meilleurs chasseurs que les Indiens; ils sont mieux armés. Mais ils tuent autant qu'ils peuvent, et n'en prennent qu'une partie. Un vrai gaspillage.' Léon Doucet's Journal, 1868–1890, 71.220 Item 6382, Box 151, 25.
[89] *Nor'Wester*, November 15, 1860.
[90] Ross, *The Red River Settlement*, 246.

But beyond these considerations was the more fundamental issue of financing Métis summer hunting. Large hunts were embarking on a comparatively more expensive, long-distance journey that by necessity placed its participants in debt before they even left for the plains. When Alexander Ross viewed large hunts forming from Red River they were driven by "the evils of long credit" ("One wants a horse, another an axe, a third a cart; they want ammunition, they want clothing, they want provisions..."). So extensive had lending been to hunters that this credit practice "is now deeply rooted, and infused into all the affairs and transactions of the place."[91]

In these communities, debt extended down to the Métis household and the individual hunter, reminiscent of other sites of the buffalo skin hunt, where it prompted the bison's large-scale killing on the American frontier.[92] Ross pointed out the expenses to the community that took diverted resources, time, and materials to mobilize by then some 1,200 carts. Behind it all was debt. The 1,630 "souls" participating (men, women, and children) carried all description of goods and equipment, the most expensive being buffalo runners and horses, as well as carts. Much had been procured in credit, at higher the cost for that reason, a state of affairs that necessitated greater returns to make a hunting contingent meet its initial outlay.

Peter Garrioch in 1842 faced the same costs. First hired by the American Fur Company to trade buffalo robes on the Souris River, he set up a post and then headed to Red River for credit. In these years, Fort Union now had steamship service and there were numerous Métis parties illegally evading the HBC monopoly (which held until 1849) to hunt robes, or return from hunting provisions to sell back to the company. He initially got goods from Red River merchants Sinclair and McDermot, to the tune of £110 to £120 in advance at 25 percent above their usual selling price. Eventually, the merchants backed out of the arrangements to send their own trader to the Souris River.[93] The close profit margins with such expenses prompted Garrioch to be a selective trader and hunter. His fall run to Devils Lake in 1845, for instance, returned to Red River with a conspicuously small quantity of pemmican and a much larger quantity of high-priced cuts, especially pickled tongues, which ran at 7

---

[91] Ibid., 243.
[92] See Andrew Isenberg, *The Destruction of the Bison: An Environmental History, 1750–1920* (Cambridge: Cambridge University Press, 2000), 156–158.
[93] Manitoba Provincial Archives, Peter Garrioch Journal 1843–1847, MG2 C38, 7–11.

pence each. That year, he carried 500 tongues, 130 cured bosses, 2 bulls of green meat, 5 bags of pemmican, 2 bags of hard fat, 9 bladders of marrow, 100 bales sinew, 5 ridge bones, 17 skins, and 15 bundles of dried meat.[94]

The Métis were beholden to town merchants and creditors in important ways, and similar, but smaller credit lines extended with contingents from the North Saskatchewan. But the financial underpinnings of the hunt created very different group dynamics, certainly very unlike Native hunting contingents of the time. The Métis, developing large well defended brigades, organized and divided surpluses more individualistically, rather than within the community. The debts of particular households required them to do so. In Native tradition, communal hunts tended to profit the whole, not individuals. This likely placed certain curbs at winter pounds and summer hunts on maximizing activities. Native hunters, for instance, usually laid claim to their kills and had their wives process and organize the redistribution of meats. It was often remarked that Native hunters shared all meat, but more precisely, individual hunters garnered the honor of successful hunting, and then gained esteem when their wives gave away surpluses to the less fortunate. Wealth attained from robe or pemmican sales, too, was redistributed to the larger group. These redistributive systems impressed Europeans unfamiliar with such generosity at home. Indeed, sometimes, successful hunters ended up having less for themselves than the unsuccessful. The ethic that "we must not suffer them to be in want among us" held true in camps when game failed for one party, and the successful made it up in food gifts.[95]

---

[94] Ibid., 59.
[95] "In a hunt, the meat belongs entirely to the man who has brought down the animal, but when an Osage has killed two bison he generally gives half of the second one to a less lucky hunter. When he is back in camp, he makes presents of meat; besides he always sends a piece of beef to every one of the war lodges," in John Francis McDermott, ed., *Tixier's Travels on the Osage Prairies*, translated from the French by Albert J. Salvan [1844] (Norman: University of Oklahoma Press, 1940), 195; "...[F]or if our own game was not sufficient, we were sure to be supplied by some of our friends, as long as any thing could be killed," Edward James, ed., *A Narrative of the Captivity and Adventures of John Tanner (US Interpreter at the Saut de Ste. Marie): During Thirty Years Among the Indians in the Interior of North America* (New York: G.&C.&H. Carvill, 1830 [1956]), 51 "...an extraordinary custom prevailed among them... the meat taken into their Huts, where it was spread out upon the ground... Soon after it is arrived the women whose husbands nor sons have been hunting on this occasion, enters the huts of those who have meat, when the Mistress instantly gives them a share... it often happens that there remains not a mouthful for her own family. Those who had not been hunting there was more meat than in those who had been out...." *Journals of Alexander Henry the Younger*, I (Toronto: Champlain Society, 1988), 228.

The closer market integration and heavier credit obligations among Métis organizing their large hunts meant that the product of the hunt was divided differently. Ross estimated that a captain had the command of ten lieutenants. These served like warrior societies by policing the hunt, stopping individuals from starting early and dispersing animals.[96] However, the Métis hunt was grounded in the fortunes of the individual hunter who, once given the signal from the hunt captain, entered the foray as a separate entity within the whole. Ross emphasized this individualism, that during summer expeditions, there might be ten or twelve general races, but when the bison were found only in small bands, "only a few horses run in turn these should be left for the poorer party, who have but indifferent horses; but this is not the case.... their vanity is greater than their generosity." He explained that "a feeling for the poor of their own people is often overlooked; hence they not infrequently return back as empty as they went."[97] Moreover, those with the best horses were given the first runs, and the less fortunate, with slower horses, were given runs only afterwards. The kills, then, were organized, butchered, and processed by wives and families, but rather than being redistributed to the poorer, were designated for the market. Ross, who never missed out on the opportunity to do so, criticized the Métis on this count, suggesting a lack of charity where those with the best horses ended up taking the most profits. The successful often carried away much and the unsuccessful nothing from the same hunt.

This type of market hunt, it would seem, formed around the massive surpluses offered at the time. It is important to point out that in times of overall poor hunting or when animals were scarce, the Métis seemingly shifted back into Native tradition. Later in the buffalo era, when scarcity was widespread, the Métis staged hunts in which food was shared equally among everyone.[98] But in times of surplus, and in much of the buffalo era, market oriented hunting created surpluses that went back to lines of credit. They accrued to individuals, not the community.

The resulting dynamic can be perceived in an intriguing legal case between two Métis in Red River, a hunter and his hired woman. In 1861, the Red River court heard the case of Angélique Bourassa, a woman who contracted her services to a Métis hunter, Jollibois. Bourassa was to use

---

[96] Ross, *The Red River Settlement*, 250–251.
[97] Ibid., 265.
[98] See "Minis-a-wak" in Fur Trade Food Glossary. The tradition of sharing the hunt in times of scarcity is recorded in Marie Rose Smith, "I Remember," Unpublished manuscript [ca. 1940] Marie Rose Smith Fonds, Glenbow Archives, M1184).

her own carts and oxen to go out to the hunt, and Jollibois "agreed to kill four animals for me and every fourth animal he killed was to be mine till I had my quantity." Bourassa was to butcher, pound the meat, and make the pemmican, as well as dress the skins.[99] Jollibois, however, claimed that the hired woman had neglected in her duty, lost one of his axes en route, and wasted meat from the cows (by then, the herds were scarce enough that this was a concern). He retaliated by not delivering up to her the proportion of cows agreed upon. The court eventually found in favor of the woman. However, both, it would seem, were likely in debt to Red River merchants in some way, and both brought their separate, not corporate interests, to the summer buffalo hunt now forming in the commons.

The Quota System

At Red River, the Métis summer hunt quickly availed more than what the company would purchase. In Red River these hunters contended with a strict pricing policy, as established by the Northern Department almost annually. Its council pegged prices to be paid for pemmican, dried meat, and fats. The Métis, for that reason, became field butchers and pemmican makers, as opposed to providing bales of dried meat and bags of fat, because of the comparatively higher value of this value-added commodity on the market. A bag of pemmican fetched 25 shillings of goods, after all. But the company also established a quota system in which Métis at Red River quickly exceeded what the company demanded, finding themselves at a certain point, usually in early fall, with far much more product on hand than the market would bear. Over-supply, in general, undoubtedly affected the regional price series, especially in the early 1830s, when the company's surplus stock and reduced demands for the northern brigades allowed the Northern Council to order a rock-bottom pricing on pemmican, fat, and dried meat.[100] Indeed, in general, between 1827 and 1835, when the Red River summer hunt organized, the HBC demands were more than met. According to Gluek, the saturation point was reached in 1832, when the HBC could not purchase all the pemmican the Métis made for the market since it "had no occa-

---

[99] Manitoba Provincial Archives Angélique Bourassa vs. Jollibois, March 21, 1861, MG 2 B4, District of Assiniboia, General Quarterly Courts. My thanks to Jean Friesen for alerting me to this document.

[100] HBCA. York Factory Minutes of Council, 1821–31, July 9, 1832.

sion for it," George Simpson reported, mentioning that the hunters were "rather clamorous & dissatisfied" for that reason.[101]

As early as 1835, Fort Garry Métis demanded that "the prices of provisions to be raised; and an export demand for tallow, robes and other articles of the chase."[102] The company however, raised pemmican prices only from 2 to 2.5 d/lb. and made this concession not because of the power of the Métis as a collective hunting force – now otherwise impressive in size – but because of a more worrisome Red River petition from agriculturalists and farmers for higher wheat prices. The company did not want to grant it because of the higher quality and cheaper prices on wheat available from Canada and the United States at the time. A wheat concession, it was feared, would have encouraged an import trade to the detriment of the struggling agricultural sector, and so the company lessened pressure off meat traders by raising the price on their product.

By the 1830s, as it was doing elsewhere, the HBC used its quota system to effectively offset the increasing size and collective strength of Métis hunters (see Figure 4.4). Initially after the amalgamation, the Northern Council established quotas for the Saskatchewan district, mostly to provide a minimum amount of pemmican to Cumberland House or Norway House to be sure that spring brigades could be fed. It alternated between the Saskatchewan and the Red River district in these years, one year taking almost a thousand bags from one district, the next taking it from the other (see Figure 4.3). Poor hunting in Red River in the 1820s meant that there were no limits placed on purchases in that district. It would seem, in reconstructing purchases entered into the Red River accounts, however, that the company's favorite hunters produced more than enough so that about 200 to 300 bags of pemmican were commonly procured and sent on to Norway House. By then, the rebounding fortunes of the hunt, low prices, and set quotas, meant that Métis likely parted with their foodstuffs at low prices, too. Fort Douglas, by 1837, for instance, built up its discretionary purchases in these years. Indeed, the post amassed some 73,000 lbs. beyond what it sent off to the transport in 1837 to total some 90,000 lbs. that year. It could do so only with provisions prices so low.[103]

---

[101] Alvin C. Gluek, Jr. (Winter 1958), "Industrial Experiments in the Wilderness: A Sidelight in the Business History of the Hudson's Bay Company," *The Business History Review*, 32:426.
[102] Donald Gunn, *History of Manitoba: From Its earliest Settlement to 1835* (Ottawa: Maclean, Roper and Co., 1880), 284.
[103] HBCA. See 1837/38 Accounts of Red River b.235/d/54–60.

180 Pemmican Empire

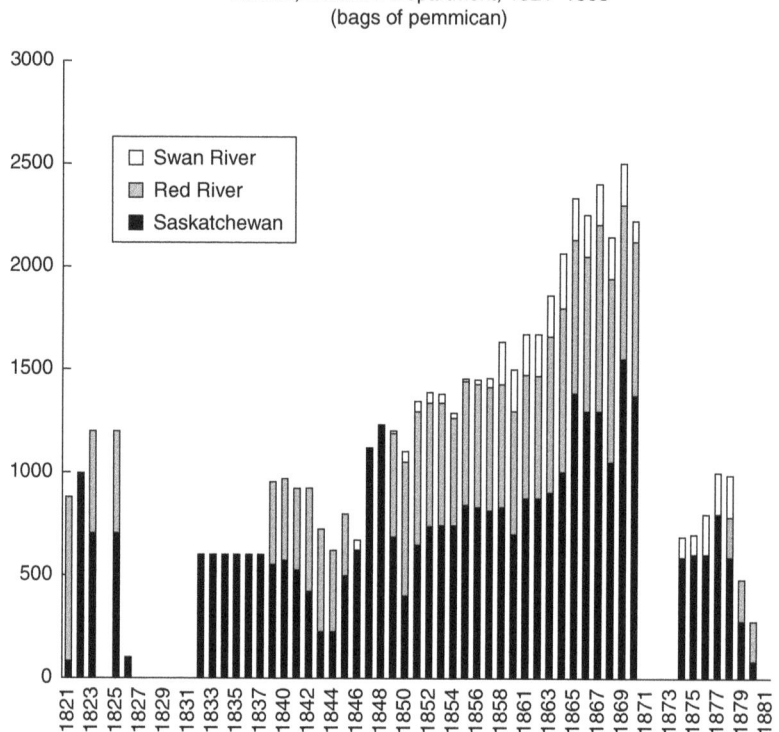

Figure 4.4. Quotas, Northern Department for Swan, Red River, and Saskatchewan districts (compiled from B.39/k/1-3).

By the mid-1830s, quotas placed on Red River effectively placed the Métis and all plains hunters in the bind of low prices and upward limits to what was purchased from them. Between Red River, Swan River, and Saskatchewan, the company raised or lowered quotas annually. If hunting failed, or prices threatened to rise in any of the areas, the company redirected its purchases elsewhere. The starving winter of 1826, then, might have affected local prices paid by Red River citizenry, but the HBC's cap on prices still held there– and Cumberland House still rated pemmican overall at 4 d/lb. and by the early 1830s, 2 d/lb.

The company was even able to surmount significant regional winter hunting failures with this system, as seen in the events unfolding in 1829 to 1833. Beginning in 1829 and becoming most pronounced in 1830–1832 a regional winter mild spell wrought disaster to many hunting bands. In the winter of 1832–1833, the Teton and Bois-Brulé of the Missouri and Upper Red River area were caught by the extraordinary mildness of the winter, which kept bison on the plains. "Starving winter" conditions in 1832–1833 were recorded from Fort Ticumseh to Fort Union along the Missouri. Maximilian, the Prince of Wied noted the mildness of the 1832–1833 winter when he made his journey to Fort Union.[104] Clow, examining the event, demonstrated how an uncharacteristically mild winter could throw into disarray hunting strategies, and even the trade in areas of the Upper Missouri when herds ended up not finding winter shelter in predictable ranges.[105] But mild winters were not restricted to the lands of the Bois-Brulé and Teton Sioux. They also affected winter hunting in 1829 at the briefly opened Fort Peigan (near present-day Calgary), then Rocky Mountain House and Edmonton. In response, Blackfoot, Piikani, Tsu-Tsina, and upriver, wood and mountain Cree converged into the environs of Fort Pitt and Carlton where winter pounding remained viable and bison herds relatively plentiful. They took up pounds in the Neutral Hills complex to the southwest of Fort Pitt, and south and southeast of the forks where Fort Carlton was in operation. Interestingly, despite being at war with one another, the crisis in winter hunting led these parties to a series of winter peace accords whereby Blackfoot, Sarcee, Assiniboine, and Cree often joined each other's pounds. Peace worked in such circumstances because any warfare would have dispersed the herds, to everyone's detriment.[106]

[104] "The winter of 1831–1832 had been remarkably mild in these parts. The Missouri had scarcely been frozen for three days together," Maximilian, Prince of Wied, in Reuben Gold Thwaites, ed., *Travels in the Interior of North America, 1833–34* in *Early Western Travels, 1746–1846* (New York: AMS Press, 1966), 22, 386.

[105] Richmond Clow (Fall 1995), "Bison Ecology, Brulé and Yankton Winter Hunting, and the Starving Winter of 1832–33," *Great Plains Quarterly*, 15:259–270.

[106] HBCA. H. H. Fisher, at Rocky Mountain House in 1829 described the mild winter around him, predated by fires nearby in the North Saskatchewan River Valley. January, normally one of the coldest months of the year in the Alberta foothills, was unseasonably warm: Fisher recorded "very fine day," no less than fifteen times in its journal of daily occurrences that month, "not very cold" once and "very cold," only 10 times. More typically, Fisher highlighted unseasonably moderate temperatures, as on January 12, when "weather continues clear and warm." See, for instance, February 22, 23, and 24, 1832 Rocky Mountain House Journal B.184/a/4. Piegan Post, or Bow Fort, saw remarkably consistent late season rains and gale force winds – no less that 25 days of almost continuous blowing and "hard gale" winds were recorded there in the two fall months of 1833; For the rest of the winter, the post journal writer recorded almost in wonder of the "weather very mild, snow melting" and by February 6 "many patches of ground clear of snow." February 4 and 6, 1833. By the end of February "little or no snow to be seen," remained on the ground. The winter ended officially on April 11 when the river broke earlier and faster than anticipated; ibid., February 25 and April 11, 1833. J. E. Hardisty's Journal, Bow Fort 1833–1834, B.21/a/1. Fort Edmonton's hinterlands were similarly mild and consequently bereft of game, bison herds not "rising" as they should have in winter but remaining dispersed to the south and downriver as far as Fort Carlton. Coupled with the effects of ruinous fall fires that extended to the

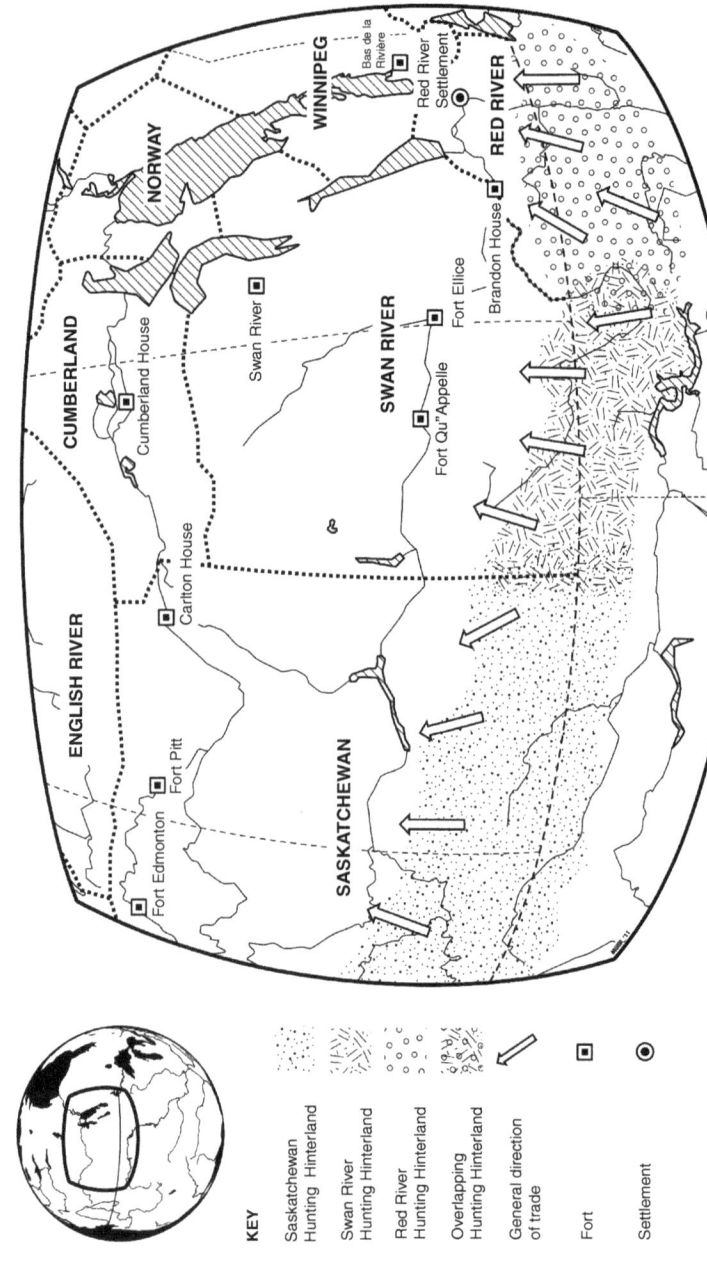

Figure 4.5. Fur trade districts, with Hunting Hinterlands after 1821 (map by Shawn Mueller, 2010).

Despite the widespread nature of its provisioning problems, the company's regional quota system allowed traders to buy only at low price, taking food alternatively and at its cheapest from any of its three plains districts (see Figure 4.4). Cumberland's pemmican prices in fact dropped to as low as 2 pence per pound in these years. The hunt failed in these winters, then, but, unlike earlier periods of difficulty, the fort turned to Fort Carlton and Fort Pitt "to make the quantity required" for the supplies at Île-à-la-Crosse and the northern brigades.[107] And so, despite difficulties at Fort Edmonton getting provisions from starving Cree and Blackfoot, C. J. Pruden, heading Fort Carlton, reported that "as the buffalo are now coming in towards the woods I have hope in being able to procure the quantity of dried provisions required."[108] Even if Pruden failed, Red River's Alexander Christie had also received Fort Edmonton's message reporting a failing hunt and reported that, given the previous summer's wet conditions and the bolstered herd populations in his own environs, "the plains hunters were more than ordinarily successful, which collectively, will afford a much larger quantity of pemmican and flour to be brought to Norway House next season, than will be sufficient for every purpose connected with the general business for the next outfit."[109] These effective communications provided the company crucial leverage to overcome local and sometimes chronic provisioning difficulties, purchase cheaply where hunting was good, and overcome native demands for higher prices.

The stability of prices in Rupert's Land is remarkable considering the apparently higher prices on the Missouri during the same hunting crisis. Americans contending with the failures in the early 1830s purchased fat dearly, so much so that Charles Larpenteur at Fort Union in 1834 had to partner up with another trader to buy bags of fat from

Battle River, Fort Edmonton's provisioning activities dropped by 1832. By the end of December, the fort had, since the previous spring collected "so inconsiderable" that the staff had not bothered adding provisions to the fort's returns, except for some grease and back fat. Fort Edmonton Journals, December 30, 1832. I have described the "Peace and War in Changing Climate: The Case of the Neutral Hills and Mild Winters in Alberta's Fur Trade Era: 1832–34," in a paper at the Under Western Skies: Climate, Culture, and Change in Western North America Conference, Calgary Alberta October 13–17, 2009.

[107] HBCA. Letter from Fort Edmonton January 7, 1835, George Simpson Correspondence inward, 1828–37, fol. 99, D.5/4.

[108] HBCA. January 31, 1835, George Simpson Correspondence inward, 1828–1837, fol. 101, D.5/4.

[109] HBCA. W. Christie's Letter from Red River December 14, 1835, George Simpson Correspondence inward, 1828–1837, fol. 137, D.5/4.

Assiniboine at 50 cents each, which was about 2.5 times the British price for the same commodity.[110] In British territories, the district quota system effectively pitted Native hunters against each other in the market and surmounted, it would seem, the very uncertainties of the northern plains climate.

Cheap Prices, Growing Consumption

Ironically the company, having driven down price, ended up consuming more, not less, pemmican. Its overall quotas to each district, with time, increased. At Norway House, the rising consumption was evident in ever larger amounts given over to the York boat crews. Even though adopting after 1821 the York boat over the canoe and gaining about 1/3 greater space with less manpower needs, the company steadily increased its pemmican consumption to support what became ever larger Red River and Athabasca brigades. Carefully timed to the short hydrological cycle of the boreal and shield areas, Red River Métis, hired as York boat men, and eating pemmican, began in the spring driving boats north on Lake Winnipeg. They delivered goods first to Norway House and then took furs from there downriver to York Factory. After arriving, they hurried bales of goods for the next season to Norway House and left a portion there for Red River while it went on with the rest to the Methye portage. After they intersected with the Athabasca brigades at the portage, the Red River crews returned to Norway House, collected goods again, and got back to Red River by fall. When crews finally returned, exhausted, to the colony, they had traveled at least 5,000 miles in a single summer season. Concurrently, the Athabasca York boat men timed their own season to coincide with the Red River brigades' arrival at the Methye Portage, making sure to get goods to Lake Athabasca, Slave River, the Peace, and the upper Mackenzie. By the 1830s, they were linking with crews arriving from the first posts being established on the Yukon River, competing now with Russian traders for the Tlinget and Han trade.[111]

At Norway House, where York boat crews got some of their traveling rations, supplies disbursed to crews grew in size from 7,180 lbs. in 1822 to 8,840 lbs. in 1827, to almost 30,000 lbs. in 1831, to 36,720 lbs. in 1835. Beyond this upward trend were the even larger shipments in 1832

---

[110] Elliott Coues, ed., *Forty Years a Fur Trader on the Upper Missouri: The Personal Narrative of Charles Larpenteur, 1833–1872*, Vol. 1 (New York: F. P. Harper, 1898), 60.

[111] Dennis F. Johnson, *York Boats of the Hudson's Bay Company: Canada's Inland Armada* (Saskatoon: Fifth House, 2006), 49–57.

and 1833: 47,520 lbs. and 62,509 lbs., respectively.[112] Arthur Ray points out that though the 1821 amalgamation of companies "temporarily reduced the overall labour force of the fur trade by as much as one-third, thereby temporarily diminishing the size of the provision market, this market rebounded a short while later." He was right: demand continued to expand in the now more efficiently run, but more extensive company operations. Ray estimated that fresh meat equivalents of bison meat being purchased exclusively by the HBC for its transport rose from 482,000 lbs. in the 1840s, to 579,870 in the 1850s, to 615,625 in the 1860s, to 864,053 lbs. in the 1870s, on the eve of the collapse of the bison herds.[113]

Not accounted in district quotas and transport uses was a probably more significant expansion of stocked surpluses at practically every post. With prices so low, traders purchased supplies well beyond their district quotas. Indeed, it became the norm to make discretionary buys that allowed traders to give gifts to trappers, support those finding their territories overtrapped or hunted, or disburse in times of cyclical and increasingly frequent periods of poor hunting. At Red River, discretionary purchases far exceeded their assigned quotas: in 1842, of 123,000 lbs. of pemmican purchased from Métis, only about 43,000 lbs. was actually sent on to Norway House for the York boat crews. The rest was left "on hand," where it found likely numerous purposes in the colony and Ojibwa lands nearby.[114] Pemmican surpluses also accrued at the periphery of the plains trade posts, especially in carryover places to Athabasca country. At Île-à-la-Cross, an informal depot of pemmican formed that supported an ingathering of Métis, Cree, and Athapaskans from Dene territories including in 1822, a post of about sixty-one women and children.[115] One factor, undoubtedly enjoying the cheap prices on bison foods, seems to have gifted so much pemmican to local Cree and Athapaskans that he was sanctioned and heavily fined by the Northern Council for the "waste" of pemmican at his post. Voyageur crews were some of the worst offenders.

[112] HBCA. Totals reconstructed from Norway House Accounts as follows 1821–1822 (7,180 lbs.); 1826–1827 (8,840 lbs.); 1828–1929 (10,260 lbs.); 1830–1831 (29,880 lbs.); 1831–1832 (47,520 lbs.); 1832–1833 (62,509 lbs.); 1833–1834 (28,395 lbs.); and 1834–1835 (36,720 lbs.), Norway House Account Books, 1821–1835, B.154/d/14–15, 26, 28, 29, 31, 39.

[113] Ray, "Fur Trade Pantry," 269, and see table at 271.

[114] These amounts are assembled from quantities recorded being sent on to mostly Norway House, but also left "on hand" See Red River Accounts, 1847, B.235/d/87.

[115] HBCA The post's personnel and numbers are listed in the introduction to Isle a la Cross (English River) Post Journals, B.89/a/5.

These informal pemmican purveyors packed so much pemmican that they could sell it en route to subarctic Ojibwa and Dene, the latter happy to trade fresh meats for this supercaloric energy source. Ojibwa on Lake Winnipeg made a point of hunting fresh meat and seeking out voyageur crews with whom to make trades for pemmican. The practice became so widespread that the Northern Council took pains to outlaw the practice altogether, likely unsuccessfully. [116]

With time, as will be seen in Chapter 6, discretionary pemmican purchases subsidized fur trading efforts in territories already overtrapped and exhausted of game life. Both a staple of life, it also became a means of underwriting the territory's environmental denuding for the market.

Conclusion

When he visited Red River in 1861, Henry Lewis Morgan was struck by the low prices on buffalo products. To make a single sack of pemmican, he was informed, required the meat of three buffaloes and the fat of six. The Company's officers "pay them [the Métis] for it delivered at their posts, but 3 d sterling per pound, or 6 cents of our money." At the same time, the company paid only $2.50 for the robe of a fall hunt, $1.25 for one from the summer (used only as leather). With the tongue worth a shilling, he estimated that hunters and their wives fetched about $5 for every animal they killed and processed – "rather a poor return" he said, in evident understatement.[117]

The amalgamation of companies in British territories in 1821 changed the history of the bison "commons" there. A centralized London company applied strikingly sophisticated conservation measures. Beaver and buffalo were both conserved in the 1820s, indeed earlier than elsewhere in North America. However, the ends of that conservation reflected the priorities of financial capital. The company's inland governor, George Simpson, wanted bison in the Winnipeg Steppe to "recruit"

---

[116] The 1824 Northern Department resolution 102 noted that "the practice of allowing servants to trade provisions, leather or other articles be discontinued and that no traffic or barter of any kind be permitted with either Freemen or Indians...." HBCA. York Factory Minutes of Council, B.239/k/1; Joseph James Hargrave, *Red River Settlement* (Montreal: John Lovell, 1871), 360–361; the Northern Council's concerns for provisions expended at Lac La Ronge, HBCA. June 6, 1826, York Factory Minutes of Council, 1821–1831, fol. 104 B.239/k/1.

[117] Henry Lewis Morgan, *The Indian Journals 1859–62*, 141.

so that his company could undermine the power of provisioners and suppress what he believed were their unreasonably high prices. The company monopolized the commons to disadvantage individuals and regional groups. The amalgamation certainly halted the rising trend on food prices that would have certainly dampened this resource's exploitation. The most significant element of the new regime in 1821 was that, in the end, it had the effect of artificially suppressing prices on aboriginal products so that more could be purchased. This cheap fuel could underwrite commercial expansion elsewhere. The Métis at Red River, meanwhile, sought to exploit the slightly higher summer prices and the overall agricultural uncertainty of the region to launch a highly destructive summer hunt, aided by horses. Cheap pemmican, in this respect, led to the destruction of animals often at half their prime weight and harvesting practices that left waste in the field. Although the zenith of the plains provisions hunt was yet to be achieved by the 1850s, the seeds of the herds' destruction were planted in 1821, when a distant, capitalized company monopolized the British bison commons for the profits of investors and made certain choices in its power over its hunting producers.

American traders at St. Louis and the Missouri, then, had every reason to resent the sound, as they called it, of the "iron footsteps" of the HBC nearby in the 1840s.[118] The united concern north the 49th parallel expanded the power and influence of the HBC, especially its ability to coherently organize a food supply system that provided pemmican cheaply and in ever larger quantities for all manner of transport and supply. The differences between the British and American West, in that respect, could not have been starker. Even the large and often criticized American Fur Company supplied goods to independent agents and traders in the field who, in turn, continued to compete, often viciously, with each other for the Indian trade, and used credit, high prices, and large varieties of goods to meet the demands of plains Indian bison hunters.[119] In British territories, a different commons developed, offering different choices to participants. For Cree and Assiniboine poundmakers, monopoly narrowed options. Many were excluded completely in the Red River trade, which was redirected to more "respectable" Métis hunters. Those

---

[118] Isaac Lippincott (April 1916), "A Century and a Half of Fur Trade at St. Louis," *Washington University Studies*, 3, part II(2):224.

[119] On the differences between HBC and AFC operations and the competition in the American west, see Lippencott, 234; and "Fur-Trade and the Hudson's Bay Company," 24.

who supplied Qu'Appelle, Carlton, or Edmonton, some of the major buyers in their region, were then significantly impacted by regional quotas and low prices. When Canadian naturalist Henry Youle Hind visited a Qu'Appelle Lakes Cree chief in 1859, he heard about the effects of monopoly now into its third decade. Mis-tick-oos (or Short Stick) reminisced about better days when Cree got "good pay" for their provisions, but after fur trade companies monopolized in 1821, his people "had not fared half so well," he said. The Cree "received bad pay for their provisions, and were growing poorer, weaker, and more miserable year by year."[120] By then, indeed, Mis-tick-oos was seeing his poundmaking territories over-run and over-exploited by competing pemmican makers. The effects of a monopolized market now extended over the whole of Rupert's Land. It soon did the unimaginable: it undermined the extent and massive size of the bison herds themselves.

---

[120] Henry Youle Hind, *Narrative of the Canadian Red River Exploring Expedition of 1857 and of the Assiniboine and Saskatchewan Exploring Expedition of 1858*, Vol. II (London, 1860), 357–359.

5

COMMERCIAL WAR ZONES IN THE BISON COMMONS, 1835–1850

The British enjoyed cheap and, until the end of the bison era, a seemingly inexhaustible food source to underwrite commercial expansion, improved transportation, and the beginnings of colonization. Between the 1830s and 1850, their pemmican supplies served as an amalgam of empire. Bison foods and fats could even energize "the cause of discovery and science," as George Simpson, the governor of the Hudson's Bay Company (HBC) liked to call it, including the work of British naturalists and naval explorers who laid sinews of imperial authority to the north and northwest. The failure and then success of Captain John Franklin's 1819–1822 and 1825–1827 overland expeditions to chart much of the Arctic coast turned ultimately on the quantities of pemmican they carried. In his first expedition, Cumberland House had little in stock owing to ongoing fur trade rivalries. Franklin's parties starved in the Coppermine largely as a result. Between 1825 and 1827, Franklin's crews made a priority of better supplying themselves and Franklin's contingents mapped the Arctic coast to Beechey Point on the west and the Coppermine's mouth on the east.[1] The Arctic explorer Vilhjalmur Stefansson pointed out the successful mapping, surveying, and exploring work availed with pemmican supplies in these years: to 1840, British Arctic and Yukon reconnaissance was made with HBC foodstuffs derived for the most part from the plains bison herds. Its stunning achievements included those of Thomas Simpson's, who mapped the Alaskan coast to Point Barrow.[2] George Simpson himself boasted of his company's capacity to supply Arctic science and discovery in these years. In 1833, his company provided much of the food for the Lt. George Back expedition

---

[1] Vilhjalmur Stefansson, *The Fat of the Land* (New York: Macmillan, 1957), 240.
[2] Stefansson, *The Fat of the Land*, 240. Stefansson's "second pemmican war" against US military food scientists is well explored by Robert E. Feeney, *Polar Journeys: The Role of Food and Nutrition in Early Exploration* (University of Alaska Press and American Chemical Society, 1997), 101–109.

to the Arctic. When the officer's camps faced starvation by spring in the wind-battered barrens of what is now Nunavut, traders at Piegan or Bow Fort near present-day Calgary dispatched some 2.5 tons of pemmican by rapid York boat to his Arctic camp, some 1,500 miles away.[3] By then, proliferating boat brigades, a relatively uninterrupted supply of foodstuffs, and low regional prices made George Simpson confident to characterize his near-continental trade empire, a "whole machine ... working smoothly and to the entire satisfaction of the classes and descriptions of people in this country."[4]

But by the late 1840s, the machine faltered. In spring 1847, George Simpson had to inform the British navy that "through the failure of the buffalo hunt on the Saskatchewan," it could not supply an upcoming spate of Arctic explorations. The British, already beginning to make a home variant of pemmican for its expeditions, shifted into large-scale manufacture at its Clarence Victualing Yard, using round beef steak and cow suet. Instead of skin bags, the navy tinned pemmican in 85-lb. cubes, which in the long term proved inadequate to preserve the fare.[5] Franklin's failed third expedition had sailed carrying tins of this home manufactured alternative. Some of the tins were eventually found, with some of the rest of the expedition's wreckage, by Leopold McClintock on King William Island (Figure 5.1). Sir John Richardson, who had tasted Saskatchewan pemmican in his naturalist studies in western Canada, eventually oversaw the navy's pemmican manufacture in 1847. The Clarence Yards produced some 35,000 lbs. of this pricey stock for what turned out to be the navy's body searches for the lost Franklin expedition (this pemmican, however, was rated at 1s/7 ¼ d – about nine times the price of buffalo pemmican in Rupert's Land at the time).[6]

The 1847 supply problem was surmounted by the HBC in the now usual way. Saskatchewan's pemmican could be had elsewhere and regional pemmican prices remained largely unperturbed. But the British Navy's emergency switch to an alternative supply highlights some of effects of market hunting hemming in bison ranges north of the Missouri. Indeed, whatever Simpson thought of his "machine" running smoothly, the native world itself was feeling the turmoil of more intense

---

[3] See George Simpson, Report to the Governor and Committee in London, 1834, D.4/100.
[4] George Simpson, Report to the Governor and Committee in London, 1839, D.4/106.
[5] Feeney, *Polar Journeys*, 17–19.
[6] Stefasson reprints Richardson's reports, *Fat of the Land*, 241–243.

warfare around hunting horses and a scramble for guns and other trade goods within the more constrained buffalo commons.

By the late 1840s, bison infrequently returned to winter shelter in many of their former peripheral spaces. In the northwestern areas of the North Saskatchewan, after the starving winter of 1847–1848 – the worst in any memory – the band led by Cree Chief Maskepetoon made the difficult decision to move downriver on the Saskatchewan, to take up summer hunting in the remaining territories.[7] They were not alone. The migratory herds that frequented present-day Manitoba had clearly fallen away in steps toward the same territories, taking downriver Cree, Assiniboine, Ojibwa, and Métis hunters with them. It was soon impractical for bison hunters from Red River to return to the settlement and they began wintering near the herds in makeshift *hivernants* communities.[8]

The extent to which this massive resource had diminished would have been debated at the time. Large remnants remained in hill country. Bands of considerable size ranged in and out of shelter belts. Remarkable demographic booms and busts in winter ranges obscured the decline. They fell over large swaths of the peripheral plains, one year the dearth being "unexampled" and enveloping the entirety of parkland from Edmonton to the Red River Valley[9] and the next seeing "abundance of provisions" hunted in the Swan River district, seemingly in as large quantity as ever.[10] Walter Bown, a trader in the region, was not the only pioneer to have seen some remnant herds so large that he remained convinced that the animals' range collapsed only after 1870.[11]

Many of the traveler and published fur trade records of this time have been meticulously analyzed by Frank Gilbert Roe, in what remains a classic of the buffalo's history.[12] This chapter does not attempt to develop a comprehensive reconstruction of the bison herds' decline. It does,

---

[7] See Hugh Dempsey, *Maskepetoon: Leader, Warrior, Peacemaker* (Victoria: Heritage, 2010), 131.

[8] On the development of *hivernants* communities, see Gerhard Ens, *Homeland to Hinterland*, 78–79.

[9] HBCA. A.11/122 same, 1856–1862, Simpson letter, June 26, 1856 London inward, correspondence from HBC posts; fol. 67 reports: From George Simpson April 12, 1858 A.11/121.

[10] HBCA. Simpson Letter, in respect to Swan River, June 28, 1859, fol. 134.

[11] Walter Robert Bown Testimony, "Select Committee on Natural Food Products of the North-West Territories," 1887, Appendix 1 *Journals of the Senate of Canada* Session 1887, 21 (Ottawa: Maclean, Roger and Co., 1887), 111.

[12] F. G. Roe, *The North American Buffalo: A Critical Study of the Species in Its Wild State* ([1951] (Toronto: University of Toronto Press, 1972).

however, suggest as many scholars have, that by the 1850s bison numbers had considerably fallen. Isaac Cowie likely drew from contemporaries, one of them undoubtedly his Fort Ellice boss, William McKay, to argue that the Red River herd's most easterly ranges had fallen back to Brandon House by 1830 and to the Touchwood Hills by 1850. By the late 1860s, Fort Ellice had to establish outposts to get anywhere near the herds.[13] Bands of bison, some very sizeable, could all the while reappear in the now raggedy buffalo frontier, but by 1859, Qu'Appelle Post only saw its summer territories repopulated by animals wintering to the southwest as far as Wood Mountain. Between Qu'Appelle's magnificent valley complex and Touchwood Hills, the Cree were, simply put, starving.

Although porosity of tribal boundaries and very blurred meanings of territoriality continued to shape the region's history, the contraction of herd ranges did much to change plains intertribal relations. Since the fur trade's beginnings in Western Canada, devastating crowd infectious diseases had depopulated areas and begun Native tribal and band movements and displacements in their wake. Especially after the smallpox epidemics of the early 1780s Assiniboine populations in the West collapsed and many woodland Cree in the lower Saskatchewan areas simply disappeared. Inflowing wood Cree and Shield Ojibwa joined remnant kin in the west, and mixing of Cree, Assiniboine, Saulteaux/Ojibwa and Metis created distinctive multi-ethnic bands and nations within a regional "Iron Alliance" fully emerging by the early nineteenth century.[14] The shrinking of the bison herds brought groups even further into contact and competition in smaller spaces. Tolerated theft was really no longer a viable alternative to warfare when animals were scarce enough that they were worth the fight. Irene Spry suggested that the plains and its "commons" were now transforming, from one of common property, to open access, with discernible groups limiting the entry of interlopers and monopolizing regions and resources.[15] By 1858, Cree and

---

[13] Isaac Cowie, *The Company of Adventurers: A Narrative of Seven Years in the Service of the Hudson's Bay Company* (Toronto: William Briggs, 1913), 187.

[14] See James Daschuk, *Clearing the Plains: Disease, Politics of Starvation and the Loss of Aboriginal Life* (Regina: University of Regina Press, 2013), 34–44; Robert Alexander Innis, *Elder Brother and the Law of the People: Contemporary Kinship and Cowessess First Nation* (Winnipeg: University of Manitoba Press, 2013), 43–69.

[15] Irene Spry, "The Great Transformation: The Disappearance of the Commons in Western Canada," in Richard Allen, ed., *Man and Nature on the Prairies* (Regina: University of Regina, 1976), 21–45. Terence O'Riordan (Spring 2003), "Straddling the 'Great Transformation': The Hudson's Bay Company in Edmonton during the Transition from the Commons to Private Property, 1854–1882," *Prairie Forum*, 28(1):1–26.

Assiniboine (many polyethnic bands) often staked claim to territories in the Carlton Hunting grounds to the south of that post. The Blackfoot stood off against Crow, Flathead, and Kootenay entries into their own regions in the east slopes. They remained vigilant against incursions of western wood Cree parties that now out of necessity built pounds regularly beyond the Battle and Red Deer Rivers. When John Palliser passed through the summer bison grounds east of the South Branch in 1859, he learned that most xeric grasslands (near present-day Moose Jaw), rolling gently with birds flitting about the bunch and buffalo grasses, constituted a war zone. Only Assiniboine and Cree, with Metis joining them, ventured there in large war parties to hunt. Isaac Cowie, too, noted that the eastern areas of the Cypress Hills had transformed into such a zone by the 1870s.[16]

Bison hunting now was given over to horse-powered contingents traveling in summer ranges. Given their numbers, they were, properly speaking, war parties that hunted buffalo and buffalo hunters traveling as armies. These groups now hunted for the market in a bid to arm themselves or gain new trade goods. Their market orientation transformed traditional "gift giving, generosity and reciprocity" now to blatant and unabashed commodity selling, the "market values and hard bargaining" now predominant, as Richard White has noted of a similar transformation having occurred among the Choctaw.[17] A hunting heyday was also spurred on as the HBC fixed prices at record low levels. Not only did the prices effectively allow the Company to purchase far more pemmican than it likely would have otherwise, but prices in British territory shaped aboriginal strategies in the market. The profit generated by the provisions market proving insufficient for the growing needs of hunters, these decades saw new hunts added – in particular, a notable one, the American robe hunt – attracting Blackfoot, Métis, and Assiniboine close enough to Missouri posts. The robe hunt adopted by Métis also raised the tenor of the fresh meat winter hunt, and, becoming common in these years, a third, fall hunt provisioned winter camps now diverting most of their work to dressing heavy buffalo robes. Warfare, increased hunting, and new levels of competition between hunters, then, remade

---

[16] John Palliser describes this war zone, September 19, 1857 and September 21, 1857, in Irene M. Spry, ed., *The Papers of the Palliser Expedition, 1857–1860* (Toronto: Champlain Society, 1968), 143–146; Issac Cowie, *The Company of Adventurers* (Toronto: William Briggs, 1913), 303–304.

[17] See Richard White, *Roots of Dependency: Subsistence, Environment and Social Change among the Choctaws, Pawnees, and Navajos* (Lincoln: University of Nebraska Press, 1983), 71.

Figure 5.1. Royal Navy pemmican tin. Sir John Franklin's doomed 1845 search for the North-West Passage was only partly supplied in Royal Navy pemmican. Navy pemmican by then modeled what the Hudson's Bay Company produced for its inland empire, using dried beef and beef tallow. The Clarence Victualing Yards mass produced pemmican to support the search for Franklin's lost crews. This pemmican tin, carried on Franklin's *Erebus*, was recovered by Francis McClintock's party on King William Island in 1859 and returned to England. (Source: Royal Museums Greenwich).

the native world. A market economy lay siege to a now much smaller bison bioregion.

The Widening Métis Hunting Footprint

In 1856, Alexander Ross penned the quintessential description of the great Métis summer hunt. Former HBC clerk at Red River, letter writer, and journalist, Ross was evidently struck by the size and organization of the hunt now figuring centrally in the lives of Red River Métis. Evidently he did not like what he saw. This odd agricultural outpost of empire had not shaken off its dependency on wild animal meat, but, quite the opposite, had organized an elaborate and distorted market economy around it. The Métis, central to it all, were clearly a distinct ethnic entity on the plains having in the 1830s and 1840s capitalized on market opportunities, a common land tenure and social structure synonymous with "being and becoming" Métis. Gerhard Ens has well described the "peasant"

Red River economy's orientation to the pemmican trade which, perhaps beginning in the 1820s, appended to it a mixed agricultural base.[18] By the 1830s, the poor returns of the difficult winter hunt behind them, the Métis developed large, equestrian group hunting techniques. These "movable armies," as Ross called them, became adept at brigade travel. Generally, there were two divisions, one from the Whitehorse Plains or Saint Francis Xavier parish, the other from Red River (St. Boniface) and the Pembina. In the 1830s, Cuthbert Grant emerged as the HBC's official warden of the plains and usually led expeditions as a captain. Other Métis contingents organized on the peripheries of the North Saskatchewan and Fort Carlton environs, although in terms of numbers of carts, they remained about a quarter of the size of the Red River Valley groups. A Fort Carlton summer hunt also took advantage of the comparatively cool climate island in the summer territories nearby, and steadily formed through its *hivernants* camps the riverine genesis of a buffalo hunting parish on the south branch of the Saskatchewan – the future mission of St. Laurent and Batoche. Concurrently at Red River, agriculture struggled in fits and starts. Indeed, cereal crops, pork, and even beef surpluses found their way into the fur trade from Métis, mixed blood, and European settlers.[19]

Ross's narrative recounted his accompanying a "spring" hunt into the breadbasket of the bison's summer ranges now near the Cheyenne River. The scarcity of animals now pulled hunters some 250 miles into the Grand Coteau. They followed the headwaters of rivers for easiest travel and ended up on July 3, nineteen days from Red River, via Pembina, in the summer ranges.[20] Significantly, their first runs were against a herd mixed with both bulls and cows, suggesting animals were moving together toward the rut. In their first run, at least 1,375 animals were killed in two hours, if the final count of tongues was correct. Eventually, some 5,000 animals were taken.

The Métis brigades were now trammeling Sioux territories and in 1851, their incursions sparked the great Battle of Grand Coteau, a rallying moment in Métis identity. That year from Red River, the St. Boniface and Pembina parties left with the smaller Saint Francois-Xavier or Whitehorse Plains brigade in tow. After organizing themselves outside of

---

[18] Gerhard Ens, *Homeland to Hinterland: The Changing Worlds of the Red River Metis in the Nineteenth Century* (Toronto: University of Toronto Press, 1996), 28–56.
[19] Cited in Hattie Listenfelt, "The Hudson's Bay Company and the Red River Trade," in *Collections of the State Historical Society of North Dakota*, Vol. IV, 1913, 263.
[20] Listenfelt, "The Hudson's Bay Company and the Red River Trade," 256.

Pembina, both groups traveled together and then split to move separately but parallel to the other, for their mutual aid but also not to disturb each other's hunting successes. The two went directly west and south west of Pembina. They tried to skirt as much as possible Sioux territories, but their hunting landed them between the headwaters of the Cheyenne and the big bend of the Souris. The larger party traveled near Dog Den Butte, on an outlying ridge of the Coteau de Missouri, or Grand Coteau.[21] The smaller Whitehorse Plain brigade ended up about 20 or 30 miles to the northwest where scouts soon encountered a sprawling, powerful, Sioux camp. After these plains warriors took a couple of the Métis reconnoiters hostage, made an overture to open talks and proposed a meeting, the Métis were on guard, knowing that the Sioux simply intended on sacking their comparatively small camp. In the rush to prepare against their far superior numbers (estimates ranged between 2,000 and 2,500 Sioux) the Métis circled their carts, tied oxen and horses within, and hid families as best as they could. Men and boys dug foxholes outside the circled carts – even a young preteen Gabriel Dumont, the later leader of the 1885 rebellion, shouldered a musket on the occasion. Fortunately for the Métis, the Sioux still raided as individuals instead of using their combined numbers for a coordinated assault. Over two days of raids, the Sioux lost heavily to Métis muskets before they retreated, the event permanently etched in Métis nationalist lore, and, more importantly, raising Métis confidence to strike even farther afield in well organized and large contingents. As W. L. Morton wrote, they "were masters of the plains wherever they might choose to march."[22]

Red River and Pembina Métis camps already threw a formidable hunting footprint across the prime fat-making summer territories. In 1851, a Red River camp was on the Missouri: "All were dressed in bright colors, semi-European, semi-Indian in style – tobacco pouches, girdles, knife cases, saddles, shoes and whips were elaborately decorated...."[23] Also in 1851, an artist in Minnesota noted Métis in large numbers congregating for the markets there. They "have found it greatly to their advantage to

---

[21] W. L. Morton, "The Battle at the Grand Coteau, July 13 and 14, 1851" [1859–60], reprinted in Antoine S. Lussier and D. Bruce Sealey, eds., *The Other Natives: The Métis*, 52–53. For an overall descriptions, see Garrett Wilson, *Frontier Farewell: the 1870s and the End of the Old West* (Regina: Canadian Plains Research Center, 2007), 123–132.

[22] Morton, "The Battle of the Grand Coteau," 61; on Sioux warfare, see Steven C. Haack (Winter 2010), "'This must have been a grand sight': George Bent and the Battle of Platte Bridge," *Great Plains Quarterly*, 30(1):3–20.

[23] T. J. Brasser, "Métis Artisans: Their Teachers and Their Pupils," in Lussier and Sealey, eds., *The Other Natives – The Métis*, 45–46.

do so, for their caravans or trains have annually increased in number, and now two hundred carts make up the yearly pilgrimage across the prairies... to St. Paul. They are laden with buffalo hides, pemmican...."[24] The HBC's own demand for pemmican so easily saturated, the Métis sought any alternative markets for their bison flesh. Métis were then openly carrying illegal furs in greater number to American traders across the line. In 1851, when they were noted in Minnesota, many were likely supplying pemmican to the parties now signing the Treaty of Traverse des Sioux that year. Métis were feeding the new and growing needs on Minnesota reservations in these and the troubled years to come. Already by 1847, Henry M. Rice, an Indian Agent in Minnesota, noted that "British half breeds" had large quantities of pemmican for sale at St. Peters and also the mouth of the Crow Wing River, and "I purchased several thousand pounds," he said, in respect to the needs on his own reservation.[25]

The problem for Métis hunters was that the economy at Red River was not expanding to match the growing population or the increasing returns from their brigade work. Annually, the HBC awarded its quota to Red River through Fort Garry, representing its share of the company's transport network. This grew considerably over time. Ray, making pemmican equivalents for the HBC's provisions demands, suggested that, through its quotas, it purchased 90,900 lbs. in 1840; 120,375 lbs. in 1850, 137,375 lbs. in 1860, and 202,680 lbs. in 1870.[26] Even with its posts' large discretionary purchases on top of this, the company's selective system on the whole frustrated the ambitions of individuals and the large family-based Métis hunting camps dependent on returns from the market for trade goods.

In 1850, the typical, often disappointing, purchasing pattern was well established. The company at Red River made its first buy that May from winter camps that had diverted some of their labor into pemmican making. Upward to a hundred bags were collected at this time, and sent off to the Lower Fort for the spring transport. In late May and early June, Métis families found credit from Red River merchants to put together traveling kits, carts, and horses. About two months later, the HBC got advance warning of the returning hunters and dispatched boats with traders to

---

[24] The artist was Rudolph Kurz, quoted by Brasser, "Métis Artisans," 46.
[25] Letter from the Secretary of War, Report of Major Wood, Relative to His Expedition to Pembina Settlement, March 19, 1850, Rice Letter from Long Prairie, November 30, 1848 (1st Sess., 31st Cong., House of Representatives, Washington, DC, Ex. Doc. No. 51, 9).
[26] Ray, "Pantry in the Northwest," 271.

Pembina. William Hardisty and an assistant, with some twenty-seven men, left to meet the first traders and purchase about 500 bags of pemmican on the spot. The main bodies of hunters then began arriving at Pembina and moving on to Red River. Over the next two weeks, other portions of hunters and their families began arriving at the settlement, clamoring to make their sales and pay back town merchants. The HBC, however, made sure to deal with both hunts separately and only after posting a notice of a set day for their purchases.[27] By that time, the company was well positioned to offer goods only for a "limited" quantity of their wares and, at that, on its own terms.

Though significant in overall sterling value, and, according to Ross, still surpassing the total value of the colony's agricultural sector in 1851, 1852, and 1853, the pemmican market was limited, at least in the environs of Red River. Immediately after the union of the companies in 1821, the HBC had hoped to see a manufacturing base develop to provide an alternative economic activity in the colony and produce saleable exports that, in their realization, could raise the civilized tenor of community life. But there was hardly enough wage employment to encourage local markets or an export trade to balance imports. Beyond agriculture, trials to introduce value added industries floundered. Most returned in some manner to the almost overshadowing bison presence to the west. A buffalo wool company was created immediately after the union, its manager John Pritchard overly optimistic that as the pemmican trade was replaced by the colony's agriculture, Assiniboine and Cree providing up to 3,000 cheap robes a year would bring windfalls of profit. The wool, however, proved of low value and robe wool could never be as cheaply combed from pelts and transported across the Atlantic as the wool sheared from sheep in England.[28]

More successfully, the company encouraged a bison tongue trade. Lord Selkirk had been the first to see its potential after samples were sent him "as a curiosity" and proved "so delicate a quality that I have no doubt they would bring a high price in London."[29] He cautioned his Red River governor to that care that the tongues were prepared for market well. No "tainted" tongues could be barreled in the brine water sent home. After the Union of 1821, tongues by the thousands were pickled in barrels selling, usually, at a handsome 7 d to 9 d each at home.

[27] HBCA. Winnipeg Post Journals, 1851–1852, B.235/a/15.
[28] LAC. See Letter from John Pritchard, July 4, 1821, to Selkirk Estate, *Selkirk Papers, Series A*, 7298.
[29] LAC. Selkirk to Macdonnell, April 12, 1814, *Selkirk Papers, Series B*, 141.

More substantial interest, however, would grow in the tallow trade. Tallow candles lit the dark "satanic mills" of Manchester and London. They flickered in dank and dark coal mines. Almost every household, even rich, burned tallow candles. In 1813, Selkirk alerted Miles Macdonnel of the market's potential, guessing, rightly, that bison had more tallow than domestic cattle, and "the quantity that may be obtained must be very considerable." The settlement could "safely" reckon on 40 shillings net profit at York Factory for every hundredweight quantity (115 lbs. in England).[30] After the Union of 1821, the London committee continued to send orders to buffalo country for tallow: "If you have an abundance of tallow in the provisions country, it may probably answer and send it home, as it will be of very little expense if any to bring it to York Factory." The company felt that the prices in London could now fetch between 57 and 60 shillings the hundredweight.[31]

An ill-fated tallow company at Red River also attempted to manufacture the stuff from the small domesticate cattle herds. Severe winter weather, however, forced its manager to keep animals stabled in debilitating conditions. In summer, wolves killed them in droves. Tallow from Rupert's Land, it would seem, was to come from bison. Posts were to "collect as much good tallow" as they could, deriving it usually from bison core fat or boiled down from back fat, rendered cleanly in 100- or 200-lb. barrels.[32]

Although almost all posts soon reported returns it was enterprising Métis hunters, desperate to find additional markets, who would supply most tallow to the HBC. James Sinclair, a Red River merchant, had sent some tallow to London aboard one of the company's ships, and finding the venture profitable, "a number of his countrymen determined to try the same thing."[33] A joint stock company in 1841 rallied hunting families to ship bison tallow directly to British markets and circumvent the HBC's absurdly low prices offered on fat.[34]

---

[30] Ibid.
[31] HBCA. Resolution 38, Instructions to Donald McKenzie, June 24, 1822, E. R. Harvey Fleming, ed., *Minutes of Council, Northern Department of Rupert's Land, 1821–31* (Toronto: The Champlain Society, 1940) 16, 25; HBCA. May 1820, fol. 188, London Correspondence Book Outwards, 1816–1826 A.6/19.
[32] HBCA. Standing Orders, 1821 and 1822, B.239/k/1.
[33] Listenfelt, "The Hudson's Bay Company and the Red River Trade," 284–287.
[34] James Edward Fitzgerald, *An Examination of the Charter and Proceedings of the Hudson's Bay Company, with Reference to the Grant of Vancouver Island* (London: Trelawney, 1849), 202–203.

200 Pemmican Empire

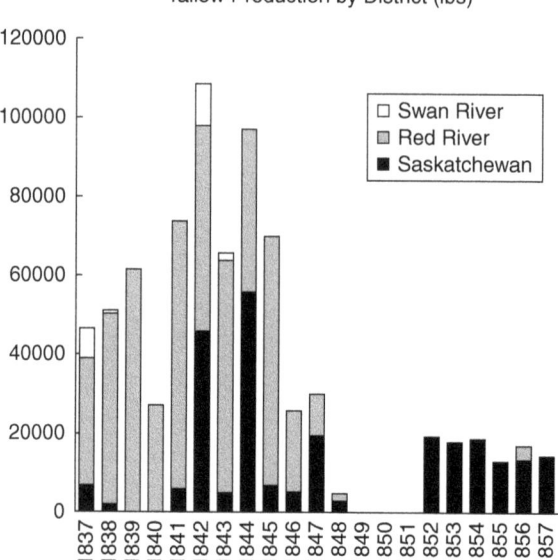

Figure 5.2. Bison tallow production, Northern Department, 1835–1857 (compiled from HBCA B.239/h/1–7).

But the HBC opposed this entrepreneurial initiative. The absolute peak year of production was achieved in 1843, when more than 143,000 lbs. of tallow were produced and shipped (see Figure 5.2).[35] Given that such fats could lose well over a fifth of their weight once rendered,[36] the 1843 tallow production was enormous, representing about 178,750 lbs. of fat. Much of the product from Red River was undoubtedly the tallow drawn from summer hunts. Spring and early summer bulls were particularly heavy in this fat. But, much of that year's return was actually confiscated two years earlier from the Métis joint stock concern. Sinclair had not only formed his company to circumvent the company's control (exploiting a loophole in the company's monopoly that allowed for value added manufacture), but he also demanded preferential carrying charges on company boats back to London. In 1843, the company refused to ship his product, making the dubious claim that there was not enough steerage in the outbound ships. The tallow was warehoused at York Factory instead. After it was left a second season, the company simply seized the tallow and purchased it at its standard, low rate (2 d/lb.).

[35] Tallow production in Figure 5.2 is derived from HBCA, York Factory District Fur Returns, 1821–1875, B.239/h/1–7.
[36] HBCA. James Bird calculated that the 527-lb. back fat traded on one occasion would render only 300 lbs. of fat. HBCA October 8, 1813, Fort Edmonton Journals, B.60/a/12.

The tallow scandal contributed sizably to the Métis free trade movement culminating in 1849.[37] It was likely the complete failure of tallow as a secondary source of revenue that spurred Métis towards another alternative. Red River hunters completely abandoned the trade, leaving it to North Saskatchewan Cree and other hunters, while they redirected their efforts toward the south, to the more attractive alternative market emerging: robes.

An American Robe Trade

Given the heavy weight of robes and difficulty getting them to European markets, the HBC had never encouraged robe trading in British territories. In 1827, however, former North West Company (NWC) trader Kenneth McKenzie, now an employee of the American Fur Company (AFC), oversaw the opening of a post on the White River in present-day North Dakota. In 1829, he managed the building of what would become the most important commercial centre in the upper Missouri, Fort Floyd, later Union, on the mouth of the Yellowstone. This began the AFC's quick expansion from the Mandan villages westward, toward the tantalizing headwaters of the Missouri. Fort Union's immediate market was forged among Assiniboine, but McKenzie's diplomacy with visiting Blackfoot formally opened trade opportunities upriver and at Fort McKenzie (later Benton). The river transport on the Missouri, at least to Fort Union, was via impressively large keel boats – some 75 feet long, 18 feet wide. These ponderously large barges drew some four feet of water and had to be hauled by *cordelle*, a line pulled by twenty or forty men along the bank.[38] However labor intensive, Missouri transport favored bulk. Fort Union soon entered into a burgeoning, soon exploding, trade in bison robes for the AFC.

American expansion on the Missouri was fueled by varying mixtures of corn and bison meats. Dried meat and corn dominated the diet at the Mandan villages where some of the first forts operated. Fort Tecumseh (later, Clark) heavily relied on bales of summer dried meat provided by both Mandan and Hidatsa. Yankton Sioux hunters provided some of the fats to balance that. In 1830, outlier camps traded robes and meat (likely including fat) at the Medicine Hills; Yanktonnais followed bison on and off the plains into the river valley, hunting sometimes within ten miles of

---

[37] George Bryce, *The Remarkable History of the Hudson's Bay Company* (London: Samson Low Marston, 1910), 438–440.
[38] See John Upton Terrell, *Furs by Astor* (New York: William Morrow, 1963), 391–392.

the post. At others times, traders followed them far into their camps to carry away product.[39] Trading parties returned from these camps heavily weighted, but their prime quarry was the heavy exterior of bison, not its inner fats. As early as spring 1830, Fort Union returns comprised some 50 or so horses loaded with 108 packs of robes (more than a thousand), a little beaver, corn, and some tallow.[40]

The limited needs for provisions beyond their Missourian posts' own requirements dampened the provisions trade. Indian labor was usually diverted into more lucrative robe production and, especially on the river's mid-sections, dried meats and far less fat. Conditions were not ideal for surpluses of fat to accrue on much of the river to Fort Tecumseh. The comparative dearness of fat among the Mandan had always meant that corn dominated, and pemmican production was almost nonexistent in the environs. Fort Tecemseh got hold of meats and robes from Big Bend camps, but its real surpluses were in corn, and, indeed, its men served to transship these carbohydrate surpluses by keel boat to Fort Union. This corn lifeline from lower on the Missouri saw keel boats and, when needed, mule trains "laden with maize" move to the upper Missouri.[41] Fats were minimally exchanged from these lower ends. From the Arikara in 1839, then, some 1,000 bushels of corn were procured in the spring and "a quantity of fresh meat."[42] The Sioux camps on the Cheyenne were not parting with much fat either, simply the dried meat made in the summer temperatures, likely produced with minimal effort.[43] Keel boats, and then steamboat service, meant that much of the post's needs were in fact balanced with pig fat. St. Louis piggeries delivered it surprisingly early and cheaply to Fort Tecumseh. By 1830, Fort Tecumseh rated hogs lard and tallow, carried in by keel boat, as low as 3 c/lb.[44]

The food history of the Missouri fur trade was significantly influenced by the size and capacity of keel boats, and then, the transformative effects of steamboats, reaching Fort Tecumseh in 1831 and Fort Union the next year.[45] These allowed for a massive spring flush of barreled and salted supplies from as far downriver as St. Louis, a mid-summer deluge

---

[39] Minnesota Historical Society, Fort Techumseh Journal, April 4 to May 15, 1830, Part I, Chouteau Collection, American Fur Company Papers, Reel 17.
[40] Ibid., May 21, 1830.
[41] See ibid., July 25 and August 6, 1830.
[42] Ibid., September 22, 1839, Reel 25.
[43] Ibid., September 24, 1830, Reel 17.
[44] Ibid., Invoice of Stock of P. D. Papin and Co. at Fort Tecumseh, October 16, 1830.
[45] Annalies Corbin and Bradley A. Rodgers, *The Steamboat* Montana *and the Opening of the West: History, Excavation and Architecture* (University Press of Florida, 2008), 32–33.

of corn from the middle sections, and then in fall, a sloshing back of upriver meats and fats produced in the comparatively cooler environs of the Upper Missouri once they became available. With the forming of the Upper Missouri Outfit, after the Columbia Fur company was purchased by the AFC, new sources of fat opened up in these territories higher in regions where it was procured much easier and it appeared more often in trade. Fort Union and its own outposts made these types of trade in Assiniboine territory; Fort McKenzie, too, now tapped Piikani and Blackfoot fat production. The Americans in these quarters were now poised above a new socioeconomic trade dynamic. Downriver among Hidatsa, Mandan, and Teton Sioux, robes figured as the real prize for the company and could be purchased in summer after their winter hunting with meats, and especially fats, sent from these upriver prime fat territories. Fort Union, on the Yellowstone in 1834 (after the particularly bad hunting season that year), for instance, was buying robes from groups at the old Mandan villages: "they eagerly give robes for meat," a correspondent stated, all the reason why its traders at camps on the Milk River, in present-day Montana, were to bring down "all the meat and grease you can spare" for these downriver, very lucrative, trades.[46]

As was the case generally in northern latitude posts, the upper Missouri trade opening a floodgate of fat to downriver corn eaters, were frequently diverted socially and economically into the protocol demands of meat reciprocity and food exchange. At Fort Sarpy near the Yellowstone in Crow territories, the post's journal writer, James H. Chambers, lamented the fort's complete giving-over to social interrelations implied with food exchanges. Given that in season Sarpy's primary purpose was to trade food from the Crow for use elsewhere in his company's fur trade, this is perhaps not surprising. However, it is quite striking how the post's senior trader, Robert Meldrum, a Kentucky born blacksmith who had joined the AFC as a very young man, seems to have "gone native" in this food trade. Edward Denig spoke of Meldrum in none too flattering terms, suggesting that his trader had gained esteem among the Crow "for his prodigal liberality, on account of which he has fallen into debt instead of accumulating money."[47]

---

[46] Minnesota Historical Society McKenzie's Letter to D. D. Mitchell, January 21, 1834 Fort Union Letter book 1833–1835, American Fur Company Papers, Reel 22.

[47] "The Fort Benton Journal, 1854," and "The Fort Sarpy Journal, 1855–1856," *Contributions to the Historical of Montana*, Vol. 10, 1940 (Boston: J. S. Canner and Company, 1966), 284.

Much of Medlrum's poor accounting, at least for the purposes of the fur trade, can be traced to strong, distorting effects of food reciprocation. The Crow moved enormous quantities of meat and fat to Meldrum's post; and he returned them at other times with generous counter gifts of food. As his clerk complained, the fort resembled less a bustling and profitable business as much as a profligate "hotel" catering to demanding Indian guests. At one feast in January, 1856, the "bill of fare" given to Crow was nothing less than "Fresh Meat Boiled to be eaten with dépouille [bison back fat] it makes no odds how fat the meat is the cold dépouille if not given is called for.... about 12 [P]M Supper Fat meat & coffee." The feasting continued until morning when visitors shifted to rice, sugar, berries, pancakes, and molasses: "the edibles that have been daily & nightly spread before the patrons of hotel & their name is Legion…"[48]

Concurrently, the food exchange encouraged social and sexual relations. Two Crow camps, Bear's Head and Gordon's, moved into the fort's social orbit through food gifts. With them, the extended kin groups performed scalp and "squaw" (likely war) dances, and then, fatefully in the eyes of the post's clerk, the proffering of women began with the daughter of a prominent Crow chief, "Princess May," her "Maid of Honor," and others. Princess May became the second of two marriage partners for Muldrum. Chambers' frank descriptions of sexual favors being given in return for fat were so "obscene" that the journal's editor for publication in the 1960s felt it necessary to delete many of the explicit words for the published version.[49] But even Chambers' more staid descriptions suggest how food blurred social distinctions and barriers. The clerk fumed over the Princess's soon dominant status in the fort, her ordering around post employees, and Muldrum's "not being satisfied with one whore house has converted the Store in to another" where sexual relations occurred "all night the goods all open, the Fort full of Indians the windows of the Stores haspe on the inside they can easily pass what goods they like out."[50]

Muldrum formalized relations with his "Princess" by giving lavish gifts to her family. She in turn marked the marriage with a "coronation

---

[48] Ibid., January 8, 1855, 106.
[49] Montana State Historical Archives. Such as the language found in the January 23 entry, "I find this morning that Murrell took to himself another wife last night A dirtly little lousy slut that was offer'd to me last fall," Fort Sarpy – Chambers Journal, 1855–1856, Folder 1–13 Pierre Chouteau, Jr. and Company Collection, MC 4 Box 1.
[50] "The Fort Sarpy Journal," 109.

feast ... well attended lots of Grubbers." With that sealed, Muldrum's new mother-in-law Wolf Skin erected a lodge within the Fort itself – one suspects pretty centrally – and the company "has another family to clothe and feed at their expense. Fort full of Indians filling their guts and receiving presents..."[51]

These food trades transformed Fort Sarpy into something far different than a European or American commercial outpost. When Bears Head camp "Brot a little meat & a few tongues Most of the meat after trading it goes to Old Wolf Skins Lodge her and her Brats must have good Fat Meat to Eat and the men poor dry meat without Fat..."[52] And, when Meldrum left camp at one point, telling his clerk that he was going for meat, his clerk noted, "yes it is meat but is squaw meat & Mag's [the Princess's] meat ...."

By the end of February the post's food supplies began to dwindle and marital relations weakened. Spring ended the need for social relations of this scale and intimacy. By March 2, the trade in furs was beginning and the post's Crow bands were readying to part. May, Muldrum's wife, was leaving with them. His verbal entreaties, gifts, and even a precious bail of *dépouille* could not change May's mind. She was soon gone with the rest of the Crow, but the clerk adding "there is not as much fat in the fort as she took with her...."[53]

Close relations struck between provisioners in these upper portions of the Missouri were, understandably, of concern to the HBC. Fort Union, in particular, had intimate ties to meat and fat providers. The Assiniboine were a large clientele of the post, which purchased their robes and so much meat and fat that it was frequently a place of great feasting for visitors and Assiniboine alike. The Gros Ventres and Mandans in the 1830s at war with Assiniboine could easily identify Fort Union, as the Crow did with Fort McKenzie, as a force allied with their enemies. In the latter case, the high proportion of men intermarrying or cohabitating with Assiniboine women, especially in the large tented village just outside Fort Union's bastion walls, necessitated their evacuation before Gros Ventres raids.[54]

---

[51] Ibid., January 24, 1855, 109.
[52] Ibid., 110–111.
[53] Ibid., March 2, 1855, 111–112.
[54] See Charles Larpenteur, who said that the Gros Ventres and Mandans even sent warning to the fort to clear its young men out of the Assiniboine tents before a raid, a warning not heeded by all the men. Charles Larpenteur, *Forty Years a Fur Trader*, 80–81.

Blackfoot in the Market

As early as 1828 and 1829, Blackfoot moved farther into the market. By then, Cree were beginning to regularly pound in winter on the Red Deer and Battle Rivers. Piikani were now fighting Crow and Snake, and their closer allies, the Sarcee, were facing combined threats of Cree and Assiniboine or Nakoda Stoney in their hunting territory. There was no coincidence with the timing of the Blackfoot entry into the market. In the course of the winter, Blackfoot arrived to Fort Edmonton now with bales of dried meat, and unlike earlier overtures that were typified by easily harvested back fat, these traders now offered the more labor-intensive bladders of grease. A Blackfoot party in March brought beat meat and grease in such quantity that it could create some sixty bags of pemmican. They had traveled "so far" for tobacco, but, most notably, ammunition. They "have had a battle with the Crow Indians and four or five of the Blackfoot and Blood [Kainai] Indians were killed."[55]

The Blackfoot, however, were fewer in number, having with the Piikani moved southwards toward the Missouri and its new American trade. The shift was most evident in the fall, now with Sarcee arriving to Fort Edmonton: "troublesome for the want of kettles and guns, which is their principal demand." The Fort could not supply the kettles and the Sarcee sent a word of reprimand to the post: "we must make provisions for you too and you would wish us to make the grease in our pipes and wooden dishes[!]" The Sarcee, apparently, had "stood with ready payment in hand" but the post had not the kettles they required.[56] The Cree were under similar pressure. Some twenty-three representatives of a larger band arrived to trade a few furs for blankets, cloth, files, ammunition, and tobacco. "Guns and kettles are also much in demand." Later, their pounds sent fifteen horse-drawn sledges loaded with meat to the post. Clearly the pounds were producing for the market, the Cree sending word that they had some twenty cows on the stages by February and they would have a good quantity of pounded meat and grease, "but the latter they cannot melt down for the want of kettles and say these have no more than three amongst them all 26 tents." The Fort complied and sent what it could: three large kettles "to enable the Crees to melt a little grease."[57] By 1829 Cree from Vermillion Creek sent word that

---

[55] HBCA. See October 3, and November 8, 1828, Fort Edmonton Journals, B.60/a/26.
[56] Ibid., October 22, 1828.
[57] HBCA. On Blackfoot trading bladders and dried meat, see October 14 through 20, Sarcee trading October 22, on Cree trading November 26; and on Cree pounding

"if we are inclined to send for 100 buffalo they would kill them," the journal stated.[58]

The opening of Fort McKenzie (later Benton) only a year earlier presented something of a respite for the pressured Blackfoot. In general the late eighteenth century push of companies westward had presented opportunities, but also problems to these people. The Siksika and Piikani, the latter after its violent encounter with Lewis and Clark's expedition in 1806, had traded with the "northern white man" on the Saskatchewan and chosen to continually harass American commerce and the inroads of trappers and mountain men afterwards.[59] Their trade and plundering had empowered them, and, with horses, they had grown to be a formidable warrior nation soon into the nineteenth century.

The Piikani once traded beaver to HBC posts, most of it plundered from enemies or American mountain men that they perceived as a threat in their western camps, given that they often intermarried among the Blackfoot's mountain enemies. George Simpson said that most of Peigan returns were plundered from their "less warlike neighbours" – the Piikani themselves did not trap. Fort Edmonton and, especially, Rocky Mountain House, occasionally benefited from the Peigan and Blackfoot plunder and frequent killing of American traders and trappers on the Missouri.[60]

By the early 1830s, Blackfoot, like Sarcee, needed to gain firmer entry in the market given the growing pressure on them from neighbors. In 1830, they arrived in an embassy to meet Kenneth McKenzie, entered into a treaty with the Assiniboine, and then invited McKenzie to open a fort directly in their lands on the Missouri. Fort McKenzie (later Fort Benton) would offer a new and far more lucrative trade to these western plains people. It drew many Blackfoot away from the congested pounding areas on the Saskatchewan toward the Missouri. The prime concern of Blackfoot speakers would be to forestall any more incursions into the summer territories and limit hunting rivals in mountain fescue belts and river valleys along the Missouri in winter.

The HBC tried to stop the shift. It opened Fort Piegan, or Bow Fort, near present day Calgary in 1831–1833 and traded large quantities of

---

production see January 12, February 13, and on shortages of kettles see February 26 and 27, 1828 and 1829. Fort Edmonton Journals, B.60/a/26.

[58] HBCA. February 16, 1829. Fort Edmonton Journals, B.60/a/26.

[59] Lesley Wischmann, *Frontier Diplomats: Alexander Culbertson and Natoyist-Siksina' Among the Blackfeet* (Norman: University of Oklahoma Press, 2004), 55–56.

[60] HBCA. On the state of trade, see Simpson's Report to London Committee for 1830 D.4/97.

provisions from Piikani, Blackfoot, and Kainai. But effective diplomacy on the part of Benton traders sealed their fate: the British chose to evacuate Bow Fort and abandon the territories south of the Red Deer River. In 1835, the HBC figured it was losing 3,000 beaver a year to the Missouri post and Piikani were getting the same goods there at a third of the HBC's prices.[61] Simpson claimed that Blackfoot prosperity now allowed these nations time to gamble and take part in "war and horse thieving excursions."[62]

The Blackfoot enjoyed an advantage given the attractive terms being offered at Fort McKenzie, Rocky Mountain House, and the massive, northern bastion of Fort Edmonton. At the latter fort, John Rowand, the roly-poly diplomat and generous glad-hander – one of the most influential traders in the west – tried anything he could to curry Blackfoot trade. "Rowand's Folly," as Fort Edmonton was called, was supplied with everything to impress its Indian clientele: the chief factor's table stretched below a gallery where a bagpiper wailed in front of glass-covered windows. Some of the only bread to be found east of the great divide was served at fine dinners for guests.[63] The Blackfoot, moving between the North Saskatchewan and the Missouri, benefited from the outlay of wealth proffered them. And though they found the greatest offers on the American side, Alexander Culbertson at Fort McKenzie could still be "disappointed" with these "northern Indians." Even his presents "which had grown in value, did not have much effect at this time," he complained, when his Blackfoot, Piikani, and Kainai customers picked and chose between British and American traders.[64]

All the same, the Blackfoot continued, like the Cree, to align the market itself with their own subsistence rounds. They did not veer their hunting efforts far from their usual practices, but instead captured greater profits in the exchange by adding value to the food they gathered. By the early 1830s, and certainly by the 1840s, Blackfoot traded ready-made pemmican. Fort Piegan, opening briefly, had captured in its accounts the tell tale appearance of more labor-intensive pemmican being offered at a time when guns were at a premium. Wissler all but identified a moment occurring when trade pemmican began to be made and sold

---

[61] HBCA. Simpson's Report to London Committee for 1835 D.4/102, fol. 39.
[62] Ibid.
[63] Garrett Wilson, *Frontier Farewell: The 1870s and the End of the Old West* (Regina: Canadian Plains Research Center, 2007), 13–14.
[64] Mckenzie to Culbertson, January 12, 1835, Fort Union Letterbooks, American Fur Company Papers, Reel 22.

by the Blackfoot. He said there was a difference between the pemmican in Blackfoot cuisine and the stuff made in large quantity in camps and sold to Europeans. He drew a distinction between what the Blackfoot produced to meet the "demand" of fur companies, in which "the Indians supplied a kind of pemmican, packed in large bags sealed with tallow. In buffalo days, the Blackfoot produced a great deal of this material." He went on to say, "For their own use, they often stored buffalo meat, cut into small pieces and mixed with dried and toasted back fat."[65]

The Blackfoot also aligned their own meat, fat, and pemmican trade to the soon flourishing robe market at Benton. At about the time of the devastating smallpox epidemic of 1837, said to have killed between 60,000 and 100,000 Missouri Native people, the robe trade sharply increased. Explaining the upsurge is not easy. It may have been due to a fatalistic outlook of Indian survivors in complete disarray in the aftermath of disease, or, more simply, robes that would have clothed larger populations were now available for the market.[66] That year, 10,000 robes were traded at Fort McKenzie; by 1841, 21,000. Estimates of up to 67,000 and more, annually, were made thereafter.[67]

The Benton post journal 1854 to 1856 suggests the ways and cultural context of the pattern developing. In October the fort began receiving its traders' wagons from camps full of meat and needing weighing. Alexander Culbertson, its head trader, now figured as a key to such protein and fat wealth. He established much of the fort's trade through his first marriage into Piikani bands. He entered a matrimonial agreement within three weeks of his arrival at Fort McKenzie, into the family of White Buffalo: there, in a very short time, his protection against a formidable Assiniboine raid helped seal the fort's place in the Piikani world.[68] By 1840, he remarried into a more prominent family, to take Natawista as wife from the family of Seen From Afar. The two have been termed "frontier diplomats," given the importance of Natawista's place within her tribe and the Piikani's own importance in the bison territories to the north. It was almost prescient that the family made sure to fill "new, brightly painted parfleches with pemmican, dried meats, and berries for the wedding feast."[69]

---

[65] Clark Wissler (March 1910), "Material Culture of the Blackfoot Indians," *Anthropological Papers of the American Museum of Natural History*, V, part I:24.
[66] Wischmann, *Frontier Diplomats*, 73–75.
[67] Ibid., 76.
[68] Ibid., 45.
[69] Ibid., 94.

Much of the posts' fall and winter meat purchases came from Piikani intermarried with men at the fort, notably the family of Culbertson himself. His brother-in-law, Little Dog, for instance, began some of the Piikani's trades in October and November 1855.[70] The "meat equipment" (carts led by post employees) went regularly out to familiar Blood and Piikani camps to trade food. The post stayed alert all the while to Crow reprisals now that the fort was firmly, through marriages, attached to the enemies of these downriver plains hunters.

Fall hunting availed huge surpluses. The post's men visited Marias camps, returning with meat "well packed with fat cow meat" as on September 25, 1855, but the Blackfoot who went out with them also returned just as well supplied: "They killed I learn one hundred and seventy six cows – if this aint Slughtering buffalo by the whole sale you can 'take my hat,'" the clerk wrote.[71] (He thought that the Blackfoot might as well hunt with such abandon since when "(you) 'get old' you will have no buffalo to kill as Gov. Stevens railroad hands will consume them all.")[72]

The Blackfoot clearly appended their meat trade to their emerging, ever-larger robe hunt. In winter chiefs arrived with fresh meats, despite the fact that it "now is becoming a very unacceptable article of trade, we want Robes," the clerk wrote. There is no indication, however, that the fort could reject meat (likely insulting to native provisioners), or that hunters stopped providing it (as it opened trading and social relations). Throughout January, Spotted Calf, Two Elks, Bad Head, and Tobacco Pants all arrived, "with any quantity of meat for trade" but only a few robes. The clerk, however, knew that "Plenty meat portends plenty Robes." Even though Gros Ventres, Blackfoot, Piikani, and Blood continued to arrive with "a lot of that now dispised [sic] article Buffo. meat for trade," the post bid its time. Though the clerk later admitted "getting heartily tired of this meat business," and "we do wish they would stop it but it seems they will come with it notwithstanding all we can say," and Big Feather (a Blood) and Culbertson's own brother-in-law again arrived with "meat, meat meat," the post finally saw the end – robes began to arrive by February and March. At that point large Blood and Gros Ventres camps, likely with women in requisite numbers to provide the labor, arrived with upward of a hundred robes a day.[73] By February,

---

[70] See November 4, 1854, "The Fort Benton Journal, 1854–1856," in *Contributions to the Historical Society of Montana* 10 (1940) (Boston: J. S. Canner and Co., 1966), 6.
[71] September 25, 1855, "The Fort Benton Journal," 48.
[72] Ibid., 48.
[73] Ibid., February 13 and 14, 1856, 63.

the "season really began" when 400 to 700 robes a day arrived, sometimes as many as 800. In March, the post cleared 1,400 packs of robes (ten per pack).[74]

Undoubtedly, these leading provisions trades were not a loss to tribes offering them. They sealed intentions. They likely reflected, too, the expectations and obligations arising in intermarriages occurring at Fort Benton itself. Culbertson's own place in that trade was difficult for that reason. He was stretched to make generous fall advances, and, as the HBC was well aware, make good on promises to lower prices to his own kith and kin. It is likely that Culbertson's own diplomatic missions, such as in July 1870, when he made a difficult forty-day overland journey from the Marias to Red Deer River (nearly dying of thirst doing so) in present-day central Alberta, culminated with meetings making clear terms of trade. Meeting the large delegations of Blackfoot speakers, Culbertson undoubtedly made his (very expensive) kin relations among the Piikani better known.[75] And, fall food advances to the robe trade also formed something of a cushion for local bands. By spring, when some groups such as the Gros Ventres faced food scarcities, "a considerable number of Gros Ventres chiefs and Soldiers" arrived to the post with 100 robes "entirely for provisions."[76]

The Assiniboine visits to Forts Benton and Union raised numerous fears for the HBC. The company understood that successful trading on the Missouri would encourage American entries into British domains. Fort Ellice, opening in 1831 on the old spot of Beaver House on the confluence of Beaver Creek with the Assiniboine (on the border of present-day Manitoba and Saskatchewan) was built for that very reason. The HBC, never a big robe purchaser given the difficulty of transport, now began purchasing robes at a loss to keep Assiniboine in its trading orbit. It also began purchasing any provisions the Assiniboine arrived with, needed or not.

For a time this worked. Many Assiniboine, at least those finding themselves in the direct vicinity of Fort Ellice, initially met their needs by more conveniently trading provisions to Fort Ellice. These, it would appear, still relied on bows and arrows, not firearms, for their hunt. This was why their chief demand was "guns, ammunition, tobacco and few

---

[74] The "unacceptable article of trade" was lamented from January 14, 1856, ibid., 59.
[75] Montana State Historical Archives. Journal of a journey written by Alexander Culbertson to Canada from Marias River, July 10, 1870; SC 586. Correspondence, diary, and journal of Alexander Culbertson,
[76] See April 11, 1856, "The Fort Benton Journal," 70.

trifles required more for ornamental than use."⁷⁷ But, like Blackfoot, Assiniboine needs were growing. Numerous divisions of the Assiniboine, the Gens de filles, the Canoe Assiniboine and others, and leading chiefs such as Iron Child, made direct overtures to the American post as early as 1834. Increasingly bitter warfare along the Missouri between Crow, Blackfoot, Assiniboine, and the Gros Ventres downriver made it difficult for any tribes to simply opt out of a market hunt, especially when it offered firearms.

Perhaps nothing better displays the Assiniboine's closer kin-ties to Americans and market hunting at Fort Union than an event taking place in November 1834 when the Assiniboine made their fall trades and then, in a large party of around eighty warriors led by L'Ours Noir and (the fatefully named) La Chance, went to attack the River Gros Ventres (Hidatsa) villages, in the middle sections of the river. The dire circumstances of the starving winters of 1833–1834 likely contributed to the conflict – the Hidatsa seemed to have been particularly badly hit for provisions. The AFC was hastening a trade upriver among Crow to ship meat and fat downriver to buy robes from starving Hidatsa and Mandan the next spring. Although Assiniboine had also suffered during the mild, killing winter of 1833–1834, they were at least in the position to trade provisions and apparently at a high price at Fort Union.

Unfortunately for the Assiniboine, the Gros Ventres caught wind of La Chance's party and thoroughly routed it before reaching its destination. Hearsay reports filtering back to Fort Union described some thirty Assiniboine killed, with ten wounded. But it was the fate of La Chance, one of those killed as captives, which spoke of the Assiniboine power derived from traded food. Charles Larpenteur, a clerk at Fort Union, wrote in his personal journal that he heard that La Chance was stripped naked before being put to death and underwent "the most cruel act that Indians ever invent:" the war chief's flesh was skinned from his body while "his bones were bruised and boiled in a pot, and a bladder was filled with the marrow extracted from them."⁷⁸ In the aftermath of the mild winters of 1833–1834, then, the Hidatsa symbolically transformed the Assiniboine into the very trade commodity that had strategic importance

---

[77] HBCA. Simpson Report to London Committee on 1835, D.4/102 ff 40–41.
[78] See footnote quoting the original journal, in *The Personal Narrative of Charles Larpenteur, 1833–1872*, Vol. I; J. Archibald Hamilton at Fort Union reported to McKenzie the incident. "La Lance and L'ours with 80 warriors had gone to fight the Gros Ventres "village," Hamilton to McKenzie, March 29, 1835, Fort Union Letterbooks, American Fur Company Papers, Reel 22.

in the market hunt. The upsurge of warfare in turn encouraged market hunting to purchase more armaments, hardware, and other goods, with the Gens de Filles, Rock, and Canoe Assiniboine now intent on exacting retribution. As Fort Union traders reported, "war, war, war is their constant cry."[79]

An Ascendant Market Hunt

Farther east, the robe market eventually raised the greatest attractions to Red River hunters after Norman Kittson built Pembina Post in 1844, just on American territory. Already taking contraband robes to the Missouri or meeting traders in Fort Union's hinterlands, the Métis began widening their winter hunting now to a larger scale. Métis were also running furs to Americans in the same manner. The HBC attempted through its chief factor, John Ballenden, to stop the nonsense once and for all. Ballenden was already having the wardens, Cutherbert Grant included, arrest fur and robe runners, and seize their carts heading toward the line. The matter came to a head in 1849, when four Métis traders were arrested for free trading. One of them, Pierre Guillaume Sayer, from the Whitehorse Plains, was tried at the Quarterly Court in May. The company successfully argued its case against the smuggler, but the jury brought a plea for leniency and because the verdict was not followed up by a punishment, given the indignation of a mob of Métis forming around the courthouse, the trade was, from that point essentially freed.[80] It also allowed American merchants, already in the colony providing goods to hunters, to purchase robes on the spot, and, as feared, use Red River as a jumping off point to send traders farther into the environs of the frontier. By the late 1850s, Americans were reintroducing competition, at least for robes and furs, in Cumberland House environs and the Fort Edmonton region.

During these years, the dry meat hunt continued in summer. There was, after all, little demand for pemmican among American traders and the HBC offered goods that the Americans could not, especially given the closer regulation of the trade on the Missouri (the AFC had officially assumed federal Indian Affairs duties). Liquor, and, farther from

---

[79] J. Archibald Hamilton at Fort Union to McKenzie, March 29, 1835, Fort Union Letterbooks, 1833–1835, American Fur Company Papers, Reel 22.
[80] See A. S. Morton, "The New Nation, the Métis," in Antoine S. Lussier and D. Bruce Sealey, eds., *The Other Natives: The Métis*, Vol. I, 33; and Heather Devine, *The People Who Own Themselves*, 134–135.

the posts, firearms were harder to get from the new American traders. The summer hunt, indeed, expanded considerably from Red River and new, subsidiary, Métis contingents formed and spread out from Fort Edmonton and Carlton.

At the same time, the winter robe trade encouraged an ever larger effort in the colder season. The smaller winter hunt had traditionally been used by Métis to supply themselves and some of the colony with fresh meat. As wintering camps extended farther to the west and, by the 1850s, figured in many of the hill complexes, these wintering *hivernants* settlements gained impressive size in their own right, requiring much more subsistence and far more hunting. It was directed at female animals, now in their prime and often carrying young. Both their fatty meats and heavy winter robe were targeted. In 1856, George Simpson described the "frontiers" of the Saskatchewan district now hiving with these camps. One "large body" taking up in the neighborhood of Forts Carlton and Pitt "congregate for convenience and safety in villages, consisting of huts roughly constructed, but sufficient to protect them from the weather and to afford them room for their goods and furs." At Grosse Butte, the previous winter, there had been a settlement of thirty or forty "houses or huts."[81]

These *hivernants* settlements shifted constantly. They developed around heads of families, extended relations, and by the 1850s, the visits of Oblate priests who moved between them with portable tent-chapels. The robe hunt undoubtedly competed with and in places overran traditional pounding areas of Cree, Assiniboine, and other plains hunters. But wintering robe settlements also needed more provisions and by the 1850s, when the Métis applied ever greater specialization to produce robes for market, it became more common for a third hunt in the fall to collect sufficient food to support these winter camps.[82]

Carts frequenting the St. Paul markets by the 1850s steadily increased in number, suggesting, as Gerhard Ens has argued, the ways that Métis at Red River were responding to changing market opportunities. Métis carried furs and robes to St. Paul directly in ever larger numbers, from 6 in 1844 (when it was considered a contraband trade) to more than 1,400 by 1865. There were between 500 and 800 in the last years of the

---

[81] Simpson quoted in Ens, *Homeland to Hinterland*, 78.
[82] Glenbow Archives, Calgary "Before we settled anywhere for the winter we generally roamed around the plains to kill buffaloe for our winter meat, then we could go to a suitable place to winter." Marie Rose Smith, The Adventures of the Wild West of 1870, 8, Unpublished manuscript, Marie Rose Smith Fonds, M1184.

1850s, when carts hauled by early spring heavy loads of robes to traders there. "It was common," Ens writes, "to have 1,000 to 1,500 Red River Metis carts encamped around Larpenteur's Lake in June in the western part of St. Paul loaded with buffalo robes, furs, pemmican and leather goods."[83] Still, with the herds now farther distanced, it was difficult for many in the colony even to maintain their agricultural lands. A portion of Red River's population devoted themselves to an ever more specialist pemmican and, especially lucrative, winter robe hunt, and abandoned the colony altogether. They were now taking up semipermanent *hivernant* camps in the far west.[84]

The numbers involved were enough to gain the attention of HBC factors on the Saskatchewan and observers in the United States. An army officer providing an intelligence report on the Pembina district by 1848 included a description of one hunt leaving Red River comprising no fewer than 1,200 carts and venturing deep into Minnesota territory and destroying bison "by the thousands." The slaughter was not for their hides at that time of the year, but "meat, tallow and tongues." Major Wood remarked on the "dried meat" and "pemmican" derived from such forays, "articles of subsistence which are almost the sole dependence of the people of that country."[85] Minnesota fur trader and Indian Agent Henry M. Rice, also commenting in Major Wood's report, pointed out how these products returned to Red River – some of them were purchased by the HBC, while a good quantity was soon *re-exported* to the United States.[86] US Indian Affairs itself had considerable support from the cheap imports from Red River. There is some irony that in 1860, the Grand Forks treaty talks with Ojibwa were fed with much Red River pemmican, "experience having proved that," as an observer to the treaty pointed out, "to reach an understanding you have to appeal to the stomach."[87]

As the commons narrowed, Métis robe hunters and summer pemmican makers added new pressures on herds. In the late 1850s, Métis contingents with goods credited from Americans were moving into the already congested areas of wood Cree and Assiniboine poundmakers. Almost everyone agreed by that point that the North Saskatchewan, the

---

[83] Ens, *Homeland to Hinterland*, 80–81.
[84] Ibid., 90.
[85] "Letter from the Secretary of War, Report of Major Wood, Relative to His Expedition to Pembina Settlement," March 19, 1850, 1st Sess., 31st Cong. House of Representatives, Washington, DC, Ex. Doc. No. 51, 8.
[86] See Henry M. Rice's Letter, included in "Letter from the Secretary of War," 27–28.
[87] "A Trip 'Up' South," *Nor'Wester* September 28, 1860, 3.

Swan River, and the Red River areas were in decline, especially in the winter. Generally, the hunting was still consistently good on the Carlton Hunting grounds southeast of the Saskatchewan forks. But, by 1856 the remaining good territories around Forts Pitt and Carlton were worrisomely "open at all seasons" and the previous winter Red River traders (American or Métis backed with American goods) had proceeded into the area: about 90 men with 300 carts, "well provided with goods by the Americans." They established their *hivernants* camps, with "roughly constructed huts and trade for [each] his separate interest." In these years, Americans supplied hunters tea, whiskey, printed cottons and other goods; the HBC still held a monopoly on guns and ammunition.[88]

In January 1859, buffalo were "driven out by so many Indians tenting beside our hunters, no less than 70 tents out there where the meat was staged," a Fort Edmonton journal lamented. The Fort was sending out, almost daily, sleds with horses. In February contingents of thirty horses with sleds were leaving for the congested hunting territories to the southeast. As a result, "Buffalo being very far out [on the plains]... the freemen are starving."[89] In the spring of 1858, the winter hunt had busted and Saskatchewan provisions were "smaller than usual," there was "great scarcity" in Swan River, and the inroads of "opposition" (now American traders on the spot, or Métis credited by American) had meant HBC traders only "with difficulty provisioned during the winter."[90]

Conclusion

The robe hunt was ultimately appended onto a still robust, always growing pemmican trade. Ironically in British territories the market ended up forcing hunters to search for alternatives or strategize around the suppressed food prices offered by the HBC. The ever larger hunting footprint of Métis brigades was only a small manifestation of a search for larger returns from the market, usually farther afield. The insufficiencies of wool, tongues, and tallow as supplements left Métis ready to expand, when given the opportunity, into the American robe market. Native hunters in the same position followed suit. By the 1830s, there were few tribes that could stand back from the comparatively higher returns,

---

[88] HBCA. George Simpson to London Committee, June 26, 1856, London inward, correspondence from HBC posts, A.11/122.

[89] HBCA. January 28, February 4 and 6, 1859, Fort Edmonton Journals, B.60/a/30.

[90] HBCA. George Simpson to London Committee, April 12, 1858, London Inward. Correspondence from HBC posts – Abstracts, 1856–1862 A.11/121.

especially in ammunition, that this form of hunting offered. Fort Union, Fort McKenzie/Benton, and finally, Pembina, all offered northern meat producers an attractive twin market to pemmican trading. After 1849, with the trade now freed, the robe hunt was unimpeded. If delivered to Pembina, a robe could fetch 15 shillings to 15 shillings, 4 pence. Even at Fort Garry, a robe sold at 12/6 to 13/6. The highest price paid in 1856 was 14 shillings per robe.[91] The HBC finally opening the trade to stop a complete reorientation of Native hunters toward American forts, found the means to deliver them to Montreal. Robes found ready sales there and surprising profits. Of 25,000 hauled back to Montreal, the HBC sold at 33 shillings/robe.[92] All the same, it was the American market that loomed large if not unlimited in scope. The Missouri, though a difficult stream to navigate, allowed transport that from the start favored bulk. St. Paul purchased robes directly at handsome prices. Fort Union and, now, Fort Benton were buying as many robes as hunters could supply.

The Métis were the most independently pursuing and exploiting the market opportunities in both British and American territories. Blackfoot, Assiniboine, Cree, and other plains people continued to integrate the market into traditional subsistence rounds. As Benton traders learned, the robe trade, at least before the hunt was given over the madness of the whiskey era in the late 1860s, always began with "meat, meat, meat," however detestable and burdensome the trade became to American forts that often had little use for it. Upper river posts, after the opening of the Upper Missouri Outfit, were well positioned to amass bison fats in quantities that could balance downriver surpluses of corn. However, heavy transport capacity on the Missouri allowed for a different dietary dynamic to mark the American trade. Pig fats from St. Louis could be had more cheaply than bison products in some cases. The upper river posts were nevertheless driven by the dictates of food exchange, especially when meat was concerned. Piikani, Blackfoot, and Blood, though entering a market trade and, to the north, providing more labor-intensive trade pemmican to the British, initially integrated these outsiders' market into the expectations of kin-based exchange.

But cumulatively, a larger summer, winter, and fall hunt made a grievous impact on the herds. By the late 1850s, the smaller confines of the buffalo hunt had, ironically, provided greater incentives for Native participants to hunt for the market. Choices narrowed as the bison commons

[91] June 26, 1856, ibid., fol. 59.
[92] Ibid., fol. 63.

did. Those not living semipermanently within purview of the herds, such as those seasonally squatting in *hiverant* outposts, faced challenges getting to and from these animals. Longer-distance hunts coming and going ended up, ironically, "destroying" the very provisions they were sent to procure. The other issue was their very capitalization. Those most closely attached to the market availed themselves of credit that changed the tenor of the hunt itself. Métis, for instance, traveling farther afield, had to turn to capital merchants and the HBC to advance goods and supplies in larger quantities, raising overall costs which drove hunters to try to increase their returns with larger hunts. As Métis, Blackfoot, Assiniboine, and Cree negotiated their ways into the smaller hunting territories, and began to take what amounted to the last of the buffalo for their food or trade, the commons presented them with both new, but narrower, options, and, finally, the most awful of choices.

6

ENDING THE PEMMICAN ERA

> What would become of the Great White Queen and her people if we did not send them our pemmican? Of course, they would all starve to death..."
>
> Pee-wa-kay-win-in near the Cypress Hills to Isaac Cowie, 1868

In the mid-1860s, Qu'Appelle River fur trader Isaac Cowie heard an incredible story. Recently posted to a region of present-day Saskatchewan, by then the jumping off point to the last bison hunts to the west, Cowie was visited by Cree relating to him the destruction of a "Prairie Sodom and Gomorrah" nearby. A friend and colleague of Cowie's, Willie Traill, by then trading at Fort Ellice, apparently heard the story, too. It was about the Young Dogs, a Cree and Assiniboine warrior society. The story went that the Young Dogs had begun following a course of "incest and bestiality, of robbery and murder" that had so offended their Cree and Assiniboine groups of origin that they were turned out of their camps, despite the vulnerability of everyone to enemy Blackfoot raids.[1]

The Cree reported that the Young Dogs moved alone to the Elbow of the South Saskatchewan (in the area of present-day Diefenbaker Lake) and had no sooner formed camp when from the heavens above a swirling, hot cloud descended upon them. Instead of much-needed rain the cloud wrought divine fury. Burning hot acid razed the camp's lodges and lean-tos, carts, and poles. The plains warriors and hunters were burnt to blackened carbonized forms, crumbling to dust with the slightest touch. Cowie had to wait until 1873 to visit the site where he heard the conflagration took place and check it out for himself. He discovered the ground apparently still bearing the mark of the apocalypse: "The circle in which the camp had stood could still be distinguished by the barren

---

[1] Isaac Cowie, *Company of Adventurers: A Narrative of Seven Years in the Service of the Hudson's Bay Company during 1867–1874* (Toronto: William Brigs, 1913), 308–309.

clay supporting scattered growths of weeds in a depression which was surrounded by an open and grass-grown prairie."[2]

The story can be dismissed as fanciful bunk on Cowie's part. But Cowie's reminiscences, though put to paper after the turn of the century, tended to stay pretty close to his journal notes. He certainly wasn't given to complete fabrication in his narration of events. If there was any fancy or error, it likely arose in how he interpreted the story, in this case literally, as might be expected of a newcomer to the West, when he might have considered Cree narrative traditions. These could weave multiple layers of meaning in their stories and touch, in their very telling, various identities, including *Nehiyawiwin* or "Creeness," as Cree scholar Neal Macleod has pointed out.[3]

Whatever its origin and meaning, the story probably had less to do with the biblical account of God having smote a sinful people, and more to do with the destruction and, presumably, rebirth of a tribal entity. Ethnohistorians have pointed out that groups such as the Young Dogs, by then converging upon more distant hunting territories, were forming new identities as they fused different cultural elements from their respective backgrounds and opened up lands from which they derived their sustenance.[4] In many respects, Cree *whakootowin*, which

---

[2] Cowie, *Company of Adventurers*, 309.

[3] On Cree story-telling, see Neal McLeod, *Cree Narrative Memory: From Treaties to Contemporary Times* (Saskatoon: Purich Publishing, 2007), 7. McLeod (2000) also discusses the fluidity of pre-treaty plains bands in "Plains Cree Identity: Borderlands, Ambiguous Genealogies, and Narrative Irony," *The Canadian Journal of Native Studies*, 20(2):441; for contact narratives, see John Sutton Lutz, *Makuk: A New History of Aboriginal-White Relations* (Vancouver: UBC Press, 2008), and the "spiritual performance" and humor interwoven into stories related to newcomers, see John Lutz's and Patrick Moore's contributions to John Sutton Lutz, ed., *Myth & Memory: Stories of Indigenous-European Contact* (Vancouver: UBC Press, 2007). For the important ways that Native cosmology and origin stories infused contact, see James (Sákéj) Youngblood Henderson, *The Míkmaw Concordat* (Halifax: Fernwood Publishing, 1997). Willie Traill would have heard this story only in his first bewildering years in the fur trade, a period when he admitted freely to having difficulty understanding and even being interested in Cree and Ojibwa ceremonialism and: "I went yesterday to see an Indian performance. I do not know what to call it but it was a ridiculous affair. It was a kind of religious festival." August 8, 1864, K. Douglas Munro, ed., *Fur Trade Letters of Willie Traill, 1864–1893* (Edmonton: University of Alberta Press, 2006), 30.

[4] Theodore Binnema, *Common & Contested Ground: A Human and Environmental History of the Northwestern Plains* (Toronto: University of Toronto Press, 2004), 11–13; Susan Sharrock (Spring 1974), "Cree, Cree-Assiniboines, and Assiniboines: Interethnic Social Organization on the Northern Plains," *Ethnohistory*, 21:95–122; Patricia C. Albers, "Changing Patterns of Ethnicity in the Northeastern Plains 1780–1870," in Jonathan D. Hill, ed., *History, Power, and Identity: Ethnogenesis in the Americas, 1492–1992* (Iowa City: University of Iowa Press, 1996), 1–110; David G. Mandelbaum, *The Plains Cree: An*

developed communal identify from kinship bonds and responsibilities attached to specific landscapes, had inflected into this story of the Young Dogs.[5] The story really speaks to the ending of tribal entities and the beginning of another in the South Branch bison territories. The destruction of the old was implicit in the independent action taken by this hunting cooperative. Tribes usually punished individuals or small parties who broke rules by striking out on their own hunting expeditions.[6] The Assiniboine, from whom the Young Dogs had split, punished lone hunters who went before a moitie's leader by shredding and burning his camp, his tent, lodge poles, and buffalo robes, and killed even his horses and dogs, a total destruction of the individual's property, and sometimes life.[7]

By the 1860s, the Young Dogs and many plains tribes were coping with the rapid retraction of the bison herds from traditional territories and doing more than just changing their usual hunting rounds. Competition intensified around more scarce resources, and westerners were moving away from open access property understandings to those of "common property,"[8] where groups made claim to "circumscribed or limited

---

Ethnographic, Historical, and Comparative Study (Regina: Canadian Plains Research Center, 1979), 9–10. American historians have begun to examine strategies emerging at the end of the buffalo era, see Jeffrey Ostler (Spring 2001), '"The Last Buffalo Hunt" and Beyond: Plains Sioux Economic Strategies in the Early Reservation Period,' *Great Plains Quarterly*, 21(2):115–130; also, William Farr, '"When we were first paid,': The Blackfoot Treaty, the Western Tribes, and the Creation of the Common Hunting Ground, 1855,' in the same volume, ibid., 131–154.

[5] On *wahkootowin's* definition and applicability to Métis identity, see Brenda Macdougall, *One of the Family: Métis Culture in Nineteenth-Century Northwestern Saskatchewan* (Vancouver: UBC Press, 2010), 3–4, 131–136, 242.

[6] "[F]or the first offense the offenders hunting apparatus are broken and destroyed for second his horses are killed his property destroyed and he beaten with rods," Osborne Russell, *Journal of a Trapper Or Nine Years Residence among the Rocky Mountains Between the Years of 1834 and 1843*. By contrast, Edward Denig believed that the Arikara's semi-agricultural lifestyles, with less dependency on the hunt, made such strict hunt regulation impossible among them, and "everyone hunts on their own account," in John C. Ewers, ed., *Five Indian Tribes of the Upper Missouri* (Norman: University of Oklahoma Press, 1961), 61.

[7] Robert H. Lowie (1910), "The Assiniboine," *Anthropological Papers of the American Museum of Natural History*, IV:35–36; the account seems to originate with Denig, see "The Assiniboine," in *Five Indian Tribes*, 445.

[8] Irene Spry (February 1974), comments to "A Visit to Red River and the Saskatchewan, 1861, by Dr. John Rae," *The Geographical Journal*, 140(1):6; her full articulation of the end of the commons is found in Irene M. Spry, "The Tragedy of the Loss of the Commons in Western Canada," in Ian A. L. Getty and Antoine S. Lussier, *As Long as the Sun Shines and Water Flows: A Reader in Canadian Native Studies* (Vancouver: UBC Press, 1983), 203–223.

territory."[9] What differed perhaps among the Young Dogs was a role they had taken on of regulating and controlling the trade-oriented pemmican economy in a specific western outpost.[10] John Rae in 1861 noted how Young Dogs in the South Branch areas were stopping the Métis from killing "the buffalo for food, without levying a heavy fine for every animal they kill," which in turn forced outsiders to join large groups of Hudson's Bay Company (HBC) hunters to obtain supplies of fresh meat or pemmican.[11] Cowie and Traill, as well as Archibald Campbell, the chief trader at Touchwood Hills, were all contending with this new warrior society that placed limits on the smaller bison commons, and organized to their profit the exchanges of pemmican, fat, and dried meat collected there. By 1868, Cowie traveled with the Young Dogs and saw them make special demands on outsiders exporting traded food stuffs. Once outsiders traded tons of meat products and wanted to quit the hunt, the Young Dogs took what the indignant Isaac Cowie called "export duties" paid in trade goods.[12]

Not only, then, were such groups forming new identities, but they also did so within the market economy itself. Either from within more closely circumscribed territories, or now assembling in large numbers to force their way into more congested "commons" areas, Native leaders and often multiethnic cooperatives gained new leverage to control these resources and raise prices to their own benefit. Ironically, they profited from the shrinking limits of the last bison ranges in western Canada. This advantage, however, was perhaps sustained only until the early 1870s when the final "danse macabre" of chaotic competition, robe hunting, whiskey trading, and violence overwhelmed the last of the pemmican trade.[13] This last chapter examines the changing dynamics of group hunts, their increasing size and cooperative nature, and the opportunities and finally reduced options the changing buffalo commons presented to western plains hunters.

---

[9] Edwin Thompson Denig, in J. N. B. Hewitt, ed., *The Assiniboine*. Bureau of American Ethnology No. 46 (Washington, DC: Smithsonian Institution, Canadian Plains Research Center, 2000), 477.

[10] See the description of a brigade from Fort Ellice, beyond the Moose and Woody Mountains, in a region "burned off the grass to such an extent that it was necessary to travel one hundred and sixty miles to the more distant hills before we sighted the first band of buffalo,' in Mae Atwood, ed., *In Rupert's Land: Memoirs of Walter Traill* (Toronto: McClelland and Stewart, 1970), 54.

[11] "A Visit to Red River and the Saskatchewan, 1861, by Dr. John Rae," 11.

[12] Cowie, *The Company of Adventurers*, 230–231.

[13] Peers uses the term *danse macabre* to describe the last years. See *The Ojibwa of Western Canada*, 181.

Outfitting for the Distant Hunting Territories

It was undoubtedly in the 1850s and 1860s, when their larger needs for consumer goods and credit advances prompted Métis and now Cree and Assiniboine bands to undertake quite amazing journeys to hunt buffalo. Abraham Salois, a prominent Métis freeman who supplied Fort Edmonton in the 1860s, is likely a good example of the now credited hunter. Hired at first as an "interpreter," Salois switched roles to that of buffalo hunter and finally trader among the Cree in long-distance forays from the post. As he organized larger expeditions, his credit expanded at Fort Edmonton. In 1866, he was more than £34 in debt, one of the most indebted of all the post's bison hunting specialists and traders. Much of his debt went to supply his family: blankets, silk handkerchiefs, shawls and worsted hose, scarlet cloth, twenty-one yards of hair ribbon, dessert knives, table spoons, and one pair of girl's shoes.[14] John Foster has made the point that a critical turning point in the buffalo hunt was when Métis hunters like Salois had to hunt more intensively to maintain their new, "artificial" needs created in the new western market economy.[15]

Massive hunts formed in the 1850s, organized by brigades that had their own formidable victualling requirements. Among the expeditions leaving Fort Edmonton, Abraham Salois led a contingent of 30 horse-drawn sleds to a hunting camp reporting 100 cows killed for the fort. It was a return trip of two weeks. Eventually some 46 horses were dispatched to the camp. However, the clerk was unable to account for its disappointing returns. Instead of 110 cows returning, he estimated 62, in total weighing 18,600 lbs. Explaining the waste of some 48 animals, the clerk belied that at least "some of this has been sold by the hunters to the freemen, who it seems are hard up for grub."[16]

In 1863, Salois' fall trade among the Cree extended some ten days' distance, when he returned with twenty-one carts loaded with forty-two animals of "fresh meat," the "meat beginning to spoil." En route his party had been harassed by the Blackfoot. Two days after returning, Salois was leading "hired freemen" for another trip. Many engaged to freight the thirty horses and carts. Even the HBC clerks were allowed

---

[14] HBCA. "Salois, Abraham," in Fort Edmonton Accounts, 1866, B. 60/d/165.
[15] John E. Foster, "The Metis and the End of the Plains Buffalo in Alberta," in John E. Foster, Dick Harrison, and I. S. MacLaren, eds., *Buffalo* (Edmonton: University of Alberta Press, 1992), 61–78.
[16] HBCA. January 29, 1855, Fort Edmonton Journals, B.60/a/29a.

"on a pleasure trip to see a little of the trade with the Indians" so regular and vital this activity had become. Salois aimed again to reach the Cree, now distanced seventeen days, on that occasion fetching more than 21 carts of provisions weighing 16,534 lbs. pemmican and 7,000 lbs. dried meat.[17]

These large, long-distance hunts required vast investments of labor and energy. They became movable feasts on the plains, as Métis had to displace contingents as "an army," the *Nor'-Wester* reported of a Metis summer hunt organizing to go to the Souris. In 1860, some 950 carts assembled for one event. There were 500 men, 600 women, and 680 children. Its hunting impact was enormous. Beyond what the group needed for commercial product, the newspaper learned that the entire contingent needed "two or three thousand fat carcasses" to come and go from the excursion. The first run, about sixty miles from the boundary line, killed 1,300 buffalo, then its carts drove on to the Sand Hills close to the Little Souris, where another 1,000 were killed. Small pockets of herds were then taken here and there. But, a final hunt was again needed by the very end of the season on the Missouri Coteau, to get animals "which were still wanting to fill the carts."[18] Beyond their daily requirements were the needs of the "few thousand" dogs that accompanied the brigade "for the purpose of being fattened for the winter."[19]

One wonders at the overall efficiency of these last hunts. One gargantuan summer hunt in 1860 included more than 900 persons, with 533 carts, 2,332 guns, 10 revolvers, and 21,000 ball for the muskets. It killed some 1,151 bulls, 1,893 cows and 226 calves. The take-home for market: 1,964 bags of pemmican, 2,329 bales of dried meat, 15,120 lbs. of marrow fat, and 9,600 pounds of tallow.[20] These group hunts were about two-thirds larger than Métis hunts organizing at the same time from Fort Edmonton.[21] How many thousands of animals were killed just for the subsistence of a 1863 summer hunt is not known. It extended from Red River south to Pembina and was out for a six-week excursion. The entire brigade comprised 1,200 people, with 800 carts. They encountered the first "immense herds of buffalo" feeding at the

---

[17] HBCA. September 25–27, 1863, Fort Edmonton Journals, B.60/a/33.
[18] "The Summer Hunt," *The Nor'-Wester*, August 14, 1860.
[19] Ibid.
[20] "Account of the White Horse Plain Hunters," *The Nor'-Wester*, August 28, 1860.
[21] HBCA. The Freemen arriving from the plains on August 2–4, 1864 left 92.5 bags pemmican, 4,305 lbs. of dried meat, 2,225 lbs. of hard grease, and 900 lbs. of pounded meat. August 2–4, 1864, Fort Edmonton Journals, B.60/a/34.

Grand Coteau, where in the opening race 1,000 animals were killed. The weather was "so excessively hot most of this time that although great numbers of buffalo were slaughtered, much of the meat was spoiled before it was used."[22]

In the case of these Métis, party size and distance to the hunt required large amounts for their traveling allowance alone.[23] In the 1870s, Métis formed super-camps to coordinate an increasingly competitive hunt in now violent territories. As Father Jean-Marie Lestanc, an Oblate priest accompanying one camp to as far as Fort Benton in Montana, reported, hunters had encountered perhaps 3,000 bison since leaving the Wood Mountain region. He estimated that no fewer than 15,000 animals were needed to fill their camp, this in a season before real pemmican making began.[24]

The population increase in British territories made its ongoing wild meat consumption unsustainable. Long-distance hunts were still feeding the stomachs of Red River citizenry, particularly in years when crops were rather "scrimpy."[25] This became completely unwieldy when the settlement's population grew to some 10,000 people by 1870. The *Nor'Wester* pushing for the region's annexation by Canada, criticized the buffalo hunter community for its waste, profligate consumption, and "living for the moment" behavior. It also estimated, likely without much exaggeration, the community's heavy meat diet was responsible for the killing of some half a million bison a year.[26]

Although there were certainly independent hunters in the market by the 1860s, the pemmican trade, now moving into a smaller and more distant commons, was increasingly commanded by prominent Métis hunters who could wield the capital necessary to undertake such adventures.

---

[22] "Running the Buffalo," *Nor'Wester*, September 11, 1862, 2.

[23] So, in the case of 1,780 people (men, women, and children) on one hunt in summer, "one scarcely wonders on being told that two or three thousand fat carcasses would barely serve them in food until they got home." This seems to have been the case. Having killed more than 3,000 bison over a number of days, they still needed to return to the Grand Coteau "to hunt the buffalo which were still wanting to fill the carts." "The Summer Hunt," *Nor'Wester*, August 14, 1860, 2.

[24] Centre du Patrimoine, St. Boniface, Lestanc to Taché May 22, 1871, *Taché Papers*, T8837.

[25] The Red River newspaper reported the "return of the green meat hunters, returning with a lot of cow meat. "We are happy to hear of such. Our grain crop is rather scrimpy this year." "Buffalo Hunt," *Nor'Wester*, November 1 1861.

[26] The most succinct critique of the buffalo hunt, still supporting Red River as "uncivilized" and "unbecoming," was offered in "The Plain Hunting Business," *Nor'Wester*, November 15, 1860, 2–3.

In the case of Métis, difficult economics were contributing toward some of this consolidation. They were most aggrieved in Red River, now so distanced from the hunt that its merchant capital was stretched to the limit.[27] Agricultural failure and grasshopper scourges (the massive 1868 famine being an important example) hit the colony to keep propelling the meat purchases, however distant they were undertaken. As Joseph James Hargrave, writing to the *Montreal Herald and Daily Commercial Gazette*, said in spring 1869, there were generally poor prospects for the French "half-breed" population, now numbering some 5,000, who still, it seemed, "depend almost entirely on the chase for the means of livelihood." But this seemed inconceivable to Harvgrave now that herds had "so far fled to the westward as to beyond the reach of Red River hunters."[28]

Many of those taking part in the caravans to the west, if not wintering for extended periods in *hivernants* robe-making quarters, were accompanying merchants whose capital had to be managed with care by 1868 and 1869. With the transfer of territories to Canada announced largely without warning, and the administrative control passing from the HBC to the Canadian government, economic uncertainty worsened. Throughout the summer of 1869, as the Métis held fast with a provisional government to negotiate their political rights and guaranteed land tenure in the new regime, the transfer coincided with a particularly bad turn in the pemmican trade. Drought and fire plagued the North Saskatchewan, prompting more long-distance hunting excursions to reach the last of the herds to the south. The HBC, too, added to uncertainty by adopting in 1869 the Canadian dollar as its reference medium, having always reckoned its Red River "dollar" to the sterling.[29] Meanwhile, traders who had maintained a book value on provisions in sterling had usually bartered with Native traders in the old "made beaver" standard. Now, in 1868 they were ordered to shift to the "money way," and traders found

---

[27] See Gerhard Ens, "Metis Ethnicity, Personal Identity and the Development of Capitalism in the Western Interior: The Case of Johnny Grant," in Theodore Binnema, Gerhard J. Ens, and R. C. Macleod, eds., *From Rupert's Land to Canada: Essays in Honour of John E. Foster* (Edmonton: University of Alberta Press, 2001), 169–171; on the political backdrop to the resistance, see Gehard Ens (1994), "Prologue to the Red River Resistance: Pre-Liminal Politics and the Triumph of Riel," *Journal of the Canadian Historical Association*, 5:111–123.

[28] September 18, 1869, J. M. Bumsted, ed., *Reporting the Resistance: Alexander Begg and Joseph Hargrave on the Red River Resistance* (Winnipeg: University of Manitoba Press, 2003), 33.

[29] HBCA. See Standing Orders, B.239/k/2, for 1839 (sterling values rated according to Red River dollars at 4/3 d); in 1840 (4/9 d), 1841 (4/9 d).

the new system bewildering and Native hunters resented it significantly.[30] The more fundamental issue, however, was the Canadian-American tariff, which would apply to Rupert's Land with the transfer: this was potentially disastrous to merchants given the sizable transborder commerce to St. Paul, and need of Red River merchants and suppliers to access American goods and markets. The HBC, readying for the tariff, ordered its posts to raise prices to pay for it, and be sure to raise them on stock in hand so that enterprising free traders, settlers, and even missionaries might not engross old stock at lower prices and sell them at an advantage. Proactively inflating the prices on its goods, then, the London committee admitted that the policy might be unpopular and "(s)ales might be adversely affected for a time," but the company was willing to apply it if only to discourage opportunism and ready the country for an overall higher cost of living.[31]

For Métis traders, these years of higher costs made the pemmican trade more risky from a financial perspective. Profits really awaited only the truly enterprising. Norbert Welsh began his trading from Red River with some ten carts and fifteen horses in 1862. He carried a typical, wide assortment of HBC fare from tobacco, tea and sugar, shot, HBC blankets, cottons, axes, and knives, "and alcohol, lots and lots of alcohol," he said, the latter having come to support much of the robe and pemmican trade.[32] On his return, Welsh felt the need to join other caravans, traveling with some 150 carts, representing some 30 families and led by Gabriel Dumont and four "sub-officers." Despite taking a considerable mark up on the goods traded for robes (they passed hands for as little as a pound of tea and a quarter pound of sugar each), the costs of long-distance excursions undercut profits. Welsh wound up $50 in debt to A. J. G. Bannatyne, one of the larger creditors in Red River. Bannatyne, however, encouraged Welsh by underwriting his next western excursion with more capital. Welsh now took $300 in debt to carry more goods. Bannatyne's confidence eventually proved well placed. Despite the massive distance to the upper Saskatchewan (typically a month of travel), the hunt in the last territories was gaining a greater pace and Welsh, buying comparatively lower in the oversupplied field conditions, could sell high back at Red River. There, the HBC buying in wholesale,

---

[30] Isaac Cowie, *The Company of Adventurers*, 306–307.
[31] HBCA. Macintosh Letter, 1869, Governor of Rupert's Land, Correspondence Inward, 1869–1872, D.10/1.
[32] Mary Weekes, *The Last Buffalo Hunter* (Toronto: Macmillan, 1945), 16.

offered 25 cents/lb., allowing Welsh to earn $1,175 from his pemmican sales alone.[33]

Only a few individuals could manage these long-distance hunts, however. They required an investment into security, leadership over large numbers, and a rock hard discipline over travel provisioning. For those who could carry it all off, profits returned. One of these hunters, John Andrew Kerr, estimated that a Red River cart could transport 800 lbs. of provisions, and that a single family in the 1870s was traveling with about a dozen, meaning that the male head was commandeering up to 10,000 lbs. of provisions a year. Anything less was likely not worth the trouble.[34] In Kerr's case, after his group reached St. Laurent, the "law of the plains" now held and was observed strictly by the camp to discourage "law breaking" loners who might hunt independently and disburse the herds. Marie Rose Smith remembered the large scale of these last hunts. Her father Urbain Delorme, a prominent trader in Red River, took part in a large caravan in 1868. He himself seems to have led no fewer than forty Red River carts, probably representing a final weight of provisions of some 32,000 lbs.[35]

Once reaching the commons, whatever was left of them, traders traveled in groups for self-protection. Greater challenges awaited those actually doing the hunting. The times favored strong leadership and individuals with extraordinary powers of personal influence. Within Native hunting parties, only a handful of chiefs could wield the influence needed to contain and organize ever-larger hunting parties. Given the consensual nature of band decision making, only a few could rise to occupy such a vital and difficult role in the bison hunt. Many of them used their personal qualities, diplomatic skills, reputations as warriors or hunters, and unquestioned "medicine" power to draw together sufficiently large parties and keep them together in the stressful, uncertain marches far into contested territories.

The movement toward mass, coordinated hunting is perhaps best seen in the life of Maskepetoon (Broken Arm), chief of the Rocky Mountain Cree, diplomat, warrior, and provisioner from the 1850s to his death in 1869. Born in the first decade of the century within the western slopes of the Rockies at a time of recently inflamed Blackfoot–Cree warfare,

---

[33] Weekes, *The Last Buffalo Hunter*, 71–73.
[34] John Andrew Kerr, "Hunting Bison on the Plains," *Winnipeg Tribune Magazine* Saturday, June 23, 1934, 3–4.
[35] Doris MacKinnon, "Métis Pioneers: Isabella Hardisty Lougheed and Marie Rose Delorme Smith," PhD dissertation, History Department, University of Calgary, 2012, 285–291.

Maskepetoon had begun, by the 1840s, to better organize Cree camps for bison hunting within the reduced and now violent bison commons to the south.[36]

The upriver Cree and Mountain Cree worked well with Maskepetoon and other "Methodist" Cree. The Methodist missionaries, since Robert Rundle's work in the 1840s, had made an impact on the western Cree and mountain Stoney people many years before. These camps had many reasons to find ways to coordinate larger hunting alliances. They certainly had increasingly different interests than their brethren downriver. The Cree in the lower reaches of the Saskatchewan attempted to control the shrinking herds on the plains to the south of the Saskatchewan from Fort Carlton. These Cree benefited from the state of war with the Blackfoot because it preserved the massive neutral territory that sprawled to the east of the South Branch and reduced interlopers in their own hunting grounds. Downriver Cree also used the hostilities to continue their horse raiding among the Blood, Blackfoot, and Peigan, an important means of replacing their constantly winter-killed herds.

By contrast, the upriver Cree, Beaver Hills people, the Mountain Cree, and Stoney (Nakota) along the eastern slopes of the Rockies, among whom Maskepetoon's influence grew, required great cohesion to travel together farther to the herds and manage them in their migration to the parkland areas. They also had much to gain from diplomacy and seasonal agreements with the Blackfoot. These parkland people lived, after all, in much more difficult circumstances, especially in the 1860s when the bison hunt failed more regularly (see Figure 6.1) and they found themselves farther distanced from the herds. The hunt was clearly moving southward, and Cree pounding locations were relocating accordingly, regularly as far as the Battle and Red Deer Rivers. Maskepetoon's personal qualities and the reputation of his *atayohkanuak*, the spirit helper that protected him in warfare and gave him favor in the hunt, proved key

---

[36] On Maskepetoon, see Hugh A. Dempsey, *Maskepetoon: Leader, Warrior, Peacemaker* (Victoria: Heritage House, 2010); on Maskepetoon's role in developing Methodist ties across bands in the eastern slopes, see my "The Methodists' great 1869 Camp meeting and Aboriginal Conservation Strategies in the North Saskatchewan River Valley," *Great Plains Quarterly*, **29**(1):3–28 (Winter 2009). Maskepetoon's work with Robert Rundle is found in *The Rundle Journals, 1840–1848*, provided by the introduction by Gerald M. Hutchinson, Hugh A. Dempsey, ed. (Calgary: Historical Society of Alberta, 1977). A good overview of the Methodist missionaries is provided by Hugh A. Dempsey, introduction, *Heaven Is Near the Rocky Mountains: The Journals and Letters of Thomas Woolsey* (Calgary: Glenbow Museum, 1989), v–xxiv.

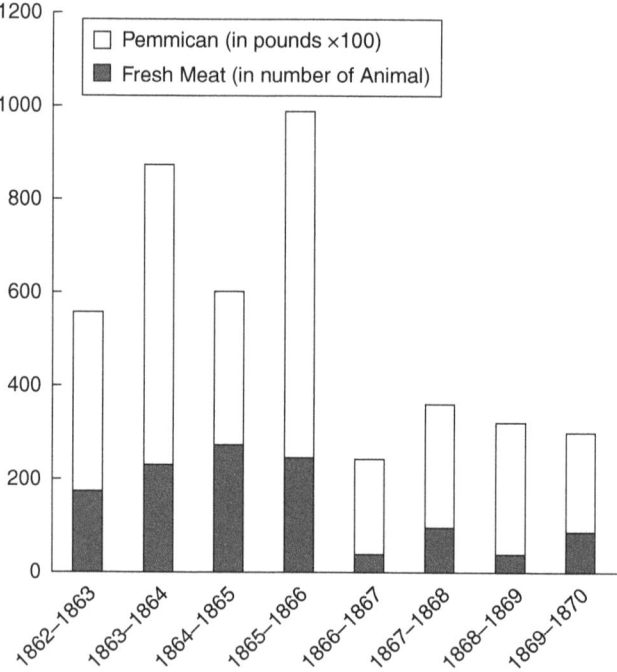

Figure 6.1. Fresh meat and pemmican production, Fort Edmonton, 1860s (compiled from HBCA, B.60 Journals).

in that respect. His influence allowed him to coordinate large numbers of plains and wood Cree to manage herd movements, and, most importantly, broker peace with the Blackfoot in the new pounding locations to the south. The Cree leader's abilities impressed missionary John McDougall who, in 1865, accompanied one of Maskepetoon's camps and saw firsthand the chief's influence among large numbers of hunters, in this case wood and plains Cree, many of them now of a "Methodist" affiliation (and moving hundreds of miles deep within Blackfoot territory). Maskepetoon told McDougall "what the camp's movements were to be, and that there was to be an immense gathering of several camps for the holding of the annual festival and 'Thirst Dance' of the 'pagan' Cree. He also told me that the buffalo were coming northward and westward, and we should move slowly to give them a chance to come in; that the plain Crees who were coming up country to join us were behind the herd of buffalo."[37]

---

[37] Quoted in Colpitts, "The Methodists' Great 1869 Camp Meeting," 17.

It took extraordinary management skills to stay current of the location and movement of bison to such an extent. Runners would have carried messages between camps. Leaders would have deliberated when they could. Maskepetoon, meanwhile, used his influence to broker numerous deals with the Blackfoot over shared or overlapping pound locations. His signature protocol was the use of a hat, a British officer coat, a British flag, and a syllabic bible in hand, with which he met Blackfoot, often on foot and completely alone. His display of courage on such occasions raised his esteem both among Cree followers and the Blackfoot themselves, the latter often agreeing to at least winter peace agreements while Cree and Blackfoot pounded bison near to each other. In many cases, these winter peace agreements had to be brokered, given that warfare between parties would effectively disperse the herds from pounds to everyone's detriment. In the past, especially during periods of mild "killing" winters where Blackfoot, Cree, and Assiniboine camps had to converge to overlapping territories, these seasonal agreements had allowed for quite extraordinary moments when even erstwhile enemies shared the reduced resources, joined each others' camps, pounded together, exchanged food, and traded together during these temporary winter periods of peace.[38]

In the last decades of the bison hunt, Cree following Maskepetoon gained some of their cohesion by a common affiliation with the network of upriver Methodist missions that had been established first in the 1840s, but reinvigorated in the 1850s and 1860s at Whitefish Lake, Victoria Mission, and Pigeon Lake. Some of these Cree and Stoney became close adherents to the religion; others were baptized in mass Methodist events. The extent of Methodist influence and its actual meaning among these western groups is not certain. Maskepetoon's own life suggests the complexity of such conversion. He waited until

---

[38] HBCA. The extraordinarily mild winters between 1829 and 1832, reported at Fort Piegan, Rocky Mountain House, and Fort Edmonton seems to have caused a large convergence of Blackfoot speaking camps toward Assiniboine and Cree pounding locations near Carlton House and the Neutral Hills. Fort Pitt employees learned "the Blackfeet + Crees are in sight of each other + Continually visiting each other + all is peace so far among them [but?] do not wish to be in a full Camp. Fort Pitt Journals, June 19, 1830, B.165/a/1; by January 1831, however, the camps had fused, were sharing food (see January 18, 1831), and even visiting Fort Pitt to trade together (see January 20, 1831). Some of the Beaver Hill Cree accompanied their Blackfoot poundmaking camps on war parties the next spring (September 15 and 16, 1831). See Fort Pitt Journals, B.165/a/1 and 2); and the same winter peace agreements were made in winter 1831/32, see February 4, 1832.

he was fifty-eight years of age, twenty-five years after meeting Robert Rundle, before agreeing to being baptized (with the name Abraham Wood), alongside his wife Sussewisk (Sarah). Whether they accepted the Methodist's faith or whether, likely in the case of Maskepetoon, Methodism "affirmed the qualities, attitudes and beliefs that he already possessed," as Hugh Dempsey suggests,[39] these Cree tended to employ Christian ritual and their camps closely coordinated themselves around the network of missions in Cree and Stoney territories to develop, in turn, terrifically cohesive hunting cooperatives.

Concurrently, the Roman Catholic missions enjoyed a large following, seeing wider connections made between "Catholic" Cree at St. Albert, lower on the Saskatchewan at Fort Carlton, later St. Laurent, and at Île-à-la-Cross, an important Cree–Métis Catholic mission. Many of these "Catholic" Cree joined each other at missions and traveled together as single minded catechists. Often, they allowed Catholic priests, such as Fathers Albert Lacombe, Constantin Scollen, or others to accompany their hunting camps. In the midst of the bison hunt, the priests erected chapel tents, provided mass, baptized, and administered the sacraments. One important meeting place for Catholic adherents was at *Matabes ku te weyak* (or Atapeskuteweyak), the Cree word for "the prairie which comes out of the river," a key entry point to the great plains herds still accessible across the North Saskatchewan River after 1864. A small mission was built there, St. Paul-des-Cris, later St. Paul des Métis (now Brassau, Alberta), which, though deserted most of the year, became hectic with camps coming together to organize their summer hunts. Here, "Catholic" hunters met the priests, attended mass, and many converted with or without rejecting their traditional spiritual worldviews. In 1868, the mission site received Okimasis, or Le Petit Chef, soon known as Sweet Grass, one of the more influential Catholic adherents in the West (receiving the name Abraham after his baptism in 1870).[40] The priests, though often remarking on the harmony of these Catholic adherents, were nevertheless often dismayed by the tumultuous arrival of the "Whitefish" or "Protestant" Cree, some of them grouped in camps of Maskepetoon.

The Protestant or Catholic affiliation of these groups likely indicated not so much religious conversion as political alliances that facilitated large hunting blocks to form and negotiate places in the smaller bison commons. Places such as St. Paul-des-Cris, for that reason, were likely

---

[39] Hugh Dempsey, *Maskepetoon*, 187.
[40] Colpitts, "The Methodists' Great 1869 Camp Meeting," 10.

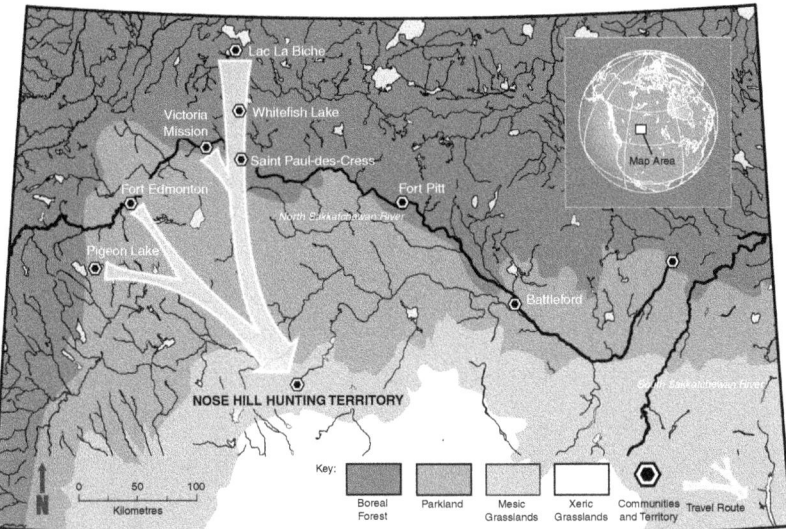

Figure 6.2. The 1869 "Methodist" hunt to Nose Hill (map by Shawn Mueller, 2010).

the negotiating place for groups dividing up territories or joining up for coordinated action in Blackfoot territory.

The cohesion afforded in such mission affiliation is perhaps best seen in 1869, when just before his killing by Blackfoot in a peace embassy, Maskepetoon helped Methodists organize a summer hunt that year to Nose Hill country (Figure 6.2). Although the Methodists understood this great "camp meeting" on the plains in terms of an open-air meeting in the Methodist tradition, where the Holy Spirit might bring revival to the land (and the hunt raise provisions for the missions), for the native participants, the organization had likely very different meanings and purposes. It was undoubtedly forming up as a defensive war party, moving into the peripheries of Blackfoot territories to Nose Hill territory and using large numbers for both self-defense and effective bison running. By the time that the hunt actually left for the plains, Maskepetoon with members of his own family on a diplomatic mission had been killed by the Blackfoot party led by Many Swans near the Bow River. A large number of the Cree on the Nose Hill hunt were anxious to seek out Blackfoot to take their revenge.[41]

---

[41] Maskepetoon's killing is recounted in oral history, see Hugh Dempsey, *The Amazing Death of Calf Shirt and other Blackfoot Stories, Three Hundred Years of Blackfoot History* (Saskatoon: Fifth House, 1994), 69.

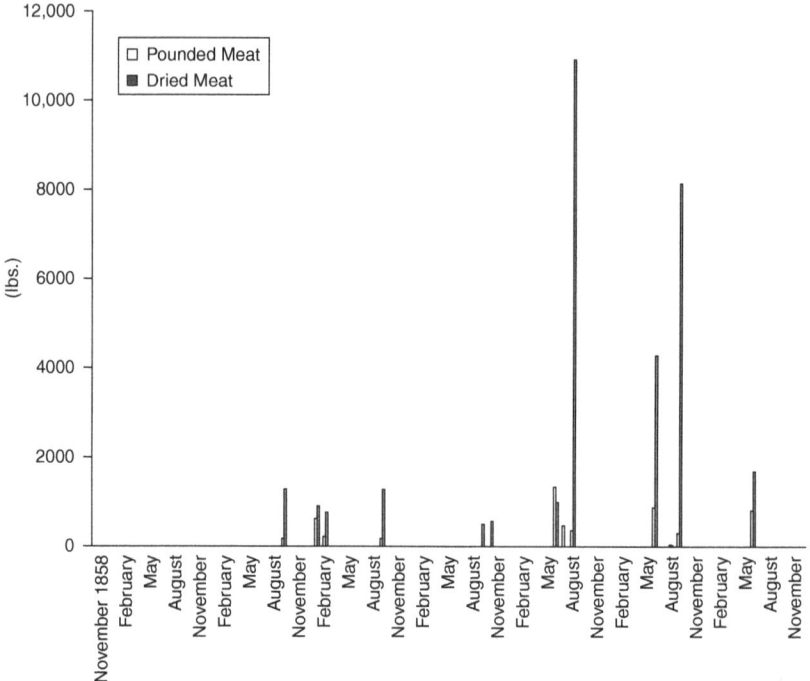

Figure 6.3. Métis pounded and dried meat trades, Fort Edmonton, 1858–1865, in pounds (compiled from HBCA, B.60 Journals).

When it left the various mission sites on the North Saskatchewan to join up in stages, the hunt, accompanied by Methodist missionaries John and George McDougall, Peter Campbell, and Henry B. Steinhauer, eventually involved many hundreds – if not up to a thousand – Cree, Stoney, and country-born Metis mission adherents from Whitefish Lake, Fort Edmonton, Victoria, Pigeon Lake, and Lac La Biche missions. It was also joined by Catholics from Saint Paul-des-Cris. As the Methodists moved southward, Catholic priests from that mission had also set off. They included the new priest J.-J. Dupin and the veteran missionary Constantine Scollen, the latter a fluent Cree speaker. The party met up with Cree Catholic adherents from farther down the Saskatchewan and, likely for the sake of larger numbers, the party joined briefly the Methodists in the field. While in camp, both Catholic and Protestant Cree maintained their quite separate affinities. The Cree from the North Saskatchewan attended the Methodist services; some were baptized. They abstained from hunting on the Sabbath. The Cree from downriver camped separately, took Catholic sacraments, hunted on Sunday, and

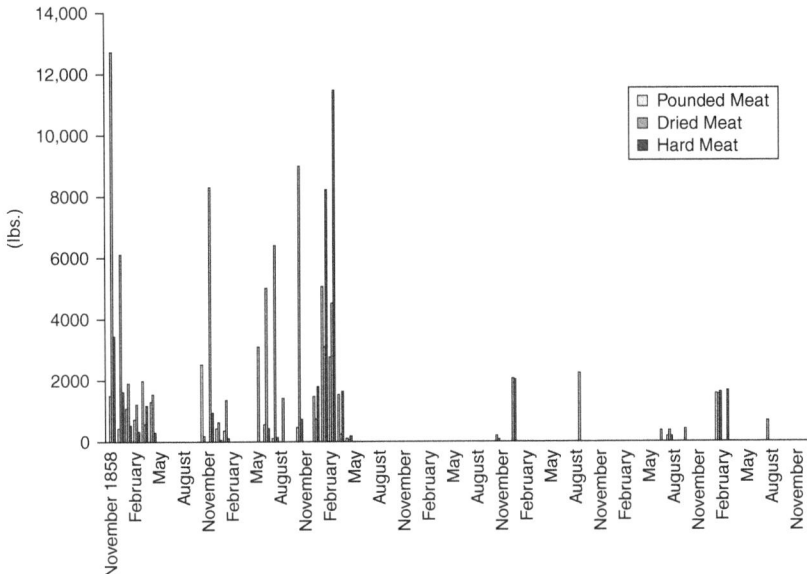

Figure 6.4. Niitistapi, Nakota, and Cree trade, Fort Edmonton, 1858–1863, in pounds (compiled from HBCA, B.60 Journals).

gave their children to Scollen for baptism. The great Methodist camp event ended in August, lasting fifty-one days. Within view of Blackfoot war parties, the camp's large numbers served its key purpose, giving the party license to travel without incident. One of the Methodist missionaries believed that about 5,000 bison were slaughtered, with about 120,000 lbs. of provisions returning to the missions, not counting the amounts eaten in camp and in transit.[42]

The Changing Ojibwa World and Hunting Cooperatives in the 1860s

The 1860s saw a notable, widespread movement into larger assemblies, amalgamations, and cooperatives. Their hunting for Fort Edmonton still divided between Métis summer pemmican trading, and Cree, Assiniboine and Blackfoot still selling from winter pounds (Figures 6.3, 6.4, and 6.5). All the same, many native groups now organized summer hunts on horseback. Multiethnic cooperatives assembled for these long distance and high risk bison hunts. As Milloy characterized them,

[42] Colpitts, "The Methodists' Great 1869 Camp Meeting," 4–5.

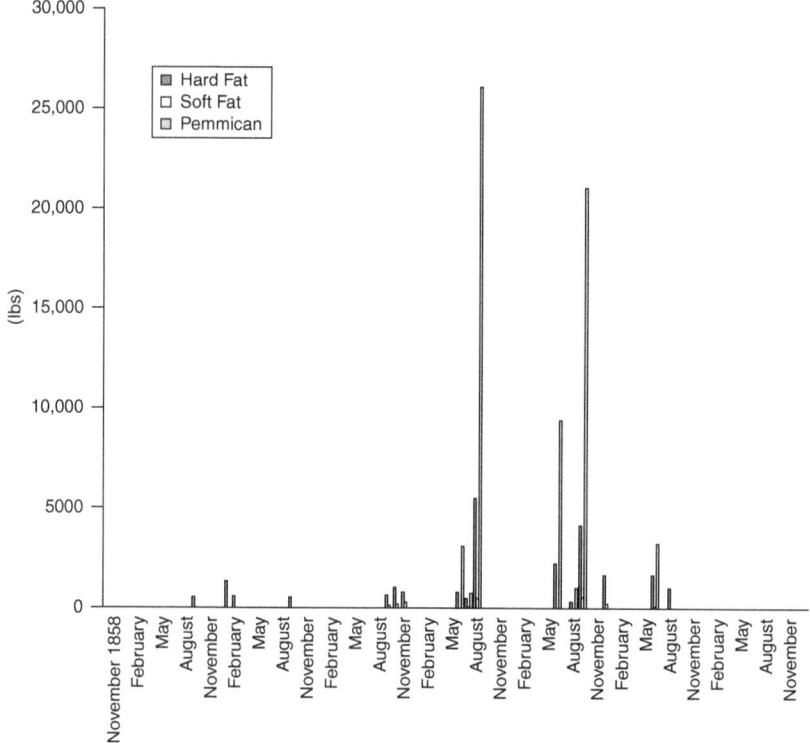

Figure 6.5. Métis fats and pemmican trades, Fort Edmonton, 1858–1863, in pounds (compiled from HBCA, B.60 Journals).

they constituted "heavily armed migrations."[43] Now that bison were more distant, and well within contested, overlapping territories of hunters, Methodist guide and interpreter Peter Erasmus remembered in 1870 joining one Cree camp and that "we had to travel more than thirty miles further south before we spotted buffalo." These longer distances required complex and coordinated politics; larger hunting parties needed to meet first to elect a leader of a contingent of fifty tents or more. If they were big, it would make "it highly improbable that we would be attacked."[44] Father Léon Doucet found that in 1870 his Métis purposely met at key points to regroup into a larger camp when they crossed over the North Saskatchewan for fear of "marauding" Blackfoot

[43] John S. Milloy, *The Plains Cree: Trade, Diplomacy, and War, 1790–1870* (Winnipeg: University of Manitoba Press, 1988), 114–115.
[44] Peter Erasmus, *Buffalo Days and Nights* (Calgary: Glenbow-Alberta Institute, 1976), 182; Colpitts, "The Methodists Great 1869 Camp Meeting," 8–9.

and, now "being numerous and well armed, we had nothing to fear from our enemies."[45]

Plains Cree, Assiniboine, and Ojibwa of the Winnipeg Steppe were forming large hunting cooperatives, often headed by powerful warrior societies, to access bison distanced in the west. Fort Ellice, in such circumstances, saw the formation of large hunts at least by 1866. Isaac Cowie, at Qu'Appelle, Archibald Macdonald at Fort Ellice, and William Trail at Egg Lake were now required to use horses and carts to go out and meet hunters in these large contingents. By this point, fall hunting was nonexistent or frequently busting in the Fort Ellice environs. Ojibwa such as Mosquito and Sons, and Misaquat, both long-time Fort Ellice hunters, returned now only from summer hunting well beyond the Wood Hills. Those not going, such as Kesikomay, had only the option of "hanging around about starving without means of getting off," in Keiskomay's case likely because he did not have enough horses. Those remaining nearby during winter were now frequently in terrible straits or needing subsistence provided by the forts. Ojibwa, for instance, remaining in the environs of Fort Ellice and arriving to the post in February 1867 starving, "without a bite to eat," were likely quite typical by that point.[46]

Very different circumstances awaited those who invested the time and effort to travel west. In 1865, William McKay and Willie Traill accompanied a long-distance hunt, and brought as many carts as they could get their hands on. McKay ended up with only twelve carts, but "had I had 50 I could have had them all loaded." Traill, by August in 1865, returned to the Fort Ellice area with an astounding 50,000 lbs. of pemmican from these returning, large hunts.[47]

In 1868, one hunt forming in the environs of Fort Ellice is fortuitously well documented in a variety of trade records. Both that post's traders and those of the Egg Lake outpost supplied the event with goods and later accompanied it to trade pemmican on the spot. There were important reasons as to why this and other large cooperatives were forming by that point. The lands to the east of Fort Ellice had been, simply put, overhunted and trapped. The Ojibwa by now faced greater uncertainty and many were in various states of seasonal want and dependency on the

---

[45] Provincial Archives of Alberta, Oblate Collection Léon Doucet Diary, July 24, 1874, 9, Doucet Journal 1868–1890, o.m.i., 71.220, item 62382, Box 151.
[46] HBCA. See October 19, 1866, October 31, 1866, and February 24, 1867 *Fort Ellice Journal*, B.63/a/9.
[47] *Fur Trade letters of Willie Traill, 1864–94*, 47, 52.

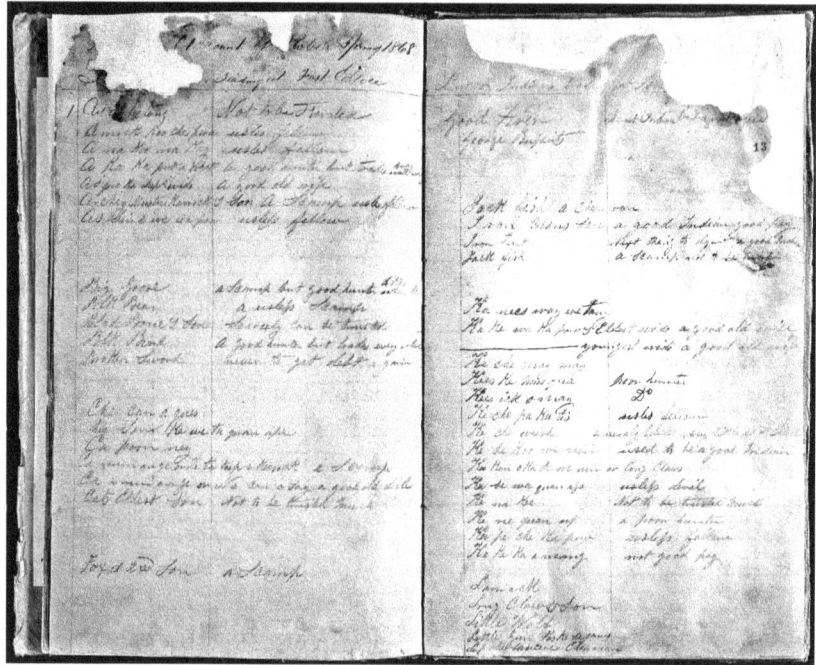

Figure 6.6. McKay's Character Book at Fort Ellice, 1868 (Source: HBCA).

fur posts of the steppe for food and trade goods.[48] As Ojibwa territory was progressively thinned of other wildlife and furbearers to hunt, the bison herds also receded farther to the west. The range of choices for these people became more "circumscribed," to use the phrase employed in some studies of Ojibwa dependency.[49]

This does not mean that all bands in the region were dependent on the fur trade. A glimpse of conditions can be gained by examining an intriguing Character Book written by Fort Ellice master, William Mckay, in 1868 (Figure 6.6). That it still exists is something of a miracle of

---

[48] There is debate about just how dependent the Ojibwa were. See Laura Peers, *The Ojibwa of Western Canada*, 194–195 and her point at odds with those who argued that the Ojibwa were in a desperate strait by this point: See A. J. Ray, "Periodic Shortages, Native Welfare, and the Hudson's Bay Company, 1670–1930," in Kenneth S. Coates and William R. Morrison, eds., *Interpreting Canada's North: Selected Readings* (Toronto: Copp Clark Pitman, 1989), 94–112; Friesen's views are summarized: "By a sleight-of-hand, it must have seemed, these Ojibwas had exchanged the autonomy of a hunting-gathering band for employee status and food." *The Canadian Prairies: A History* (Toronto: University of Toronto Press, 1987), 130.

[49] Introductory remarks in Kerry Abel and Jean Friesen, eds., *Aboriginal Resource Use in Canada: Historical and Legal Aspects* (Winnipeg: University of Manitoba Press, 1991), 7; for the context and concerns of Ojibwa treaty-makers see Jean Friesen, "Grant Me Wherewith to Make My Living," ibid., 141–155.

history: it was unearthed, surprisingly well preserved, just after WWI in a burnt-out log in the foundations of the old Fort Ellice by a farmboy.[50] Written in the post's accounts for 1868, McKay created the character book for the use of his successor to arrive in 1870. Its notes provide something of a "credit rating" for the many Ojibwa, Cree, and Sioux visitors to the post, that is, how much credit to extend them in trade goods.[51] Six pages in length, the table names ninety-seven Native and twenty-eight Métis hunters. Their characterizations range from "not to be trusted," "a good old wife," "a good hunter but trades little," to "a good hunter but trades everywhere," to "a useless scamp." These Indian "blotters" were to give a trader's "opinion of the Indian, for the guidance of his successor," as Isaac Cowie, a trader in the Fort Ellice area, noted for these years.[52] William McKay seems to have taken a hand in writing another lengthy list of the "gratuities given" to nearby Egg Lake hunters that year, containing another forty-eight names and characterizations.[53]

The blotter's great value is in hinting at the environmental changes to the region, such as the comment made of Ke se koo we weish, an Ojibwa, who "used to be a good Indian," but apparently did not have the means to be one now. Indeed, reading the Fort Ellice journals alongside the account reveals Ke se Koo we weish having as early as 1859 arriving to Fort Ellice "starving" and by 1865 arriving with furs to clear debts, but afterward not much more.[54] But, the credit ratings are a bit counterintuitive with respect to an individual's good or poor prospects. Much like the way credit card companies now profit most from extending credit

---

[50] HBCA. The character book, or blotter, is written within the Fort Ellice accounts for 1868–1869. A note on its provenance was provided by HBC archivist Angus McKay, who received the book in 1937 from an area farmer who said it was found in the old Fort Ellice foundations by a boy working on his farm nearby. See Fort Ellice Accounts, 1868–69, B.63/d/11.

[51] To date, thirty-four of the names have been confirmed Ojibawe, with some Cree derivations. My thanks to Louise Guimond, Ojibwa translator, for her assistance in this project. Many of the others, however, are difficult to transcribe and identify. Many are likely Siouan, Cree, and some even Chipewyan.

[52] See his description of Indian debt books, which "Could show himself as a great hunter by the furs he produced, or a man of many wives by the amount of pemmican and dried meat, buffalo robes and dressed leather, which were the result of their labours, for their lord and master stooped not to such laborious industries. .... at the head of the page opposite his name the officer previously in charge of a post, upon being transferred, was in duty bound to leave his experience and opinion of the Indian, for the guidance of his successor in office." Isaac Cowie, *The Company of Adventurers: A Narrative of Seven Years in the Service of the Hudson's Bay Company during 1867–1874 on the Great Buffalo Plains* (Toronto: William Brigs, 1913), 230–231.

[53] HBCA. See, Gratuities Given, 1868, Egg Lake Accounts, B.62/d/1.

[54] HBCA. Fort Ellice Accounts, 1866–1868, B.63/d/11.

to those in difficult circumstances, the HBC understood the "best" customers to be those willing to work but were dependent in some ways on its goods and, especially, its food stores. This was certainly the case in the Fort Ellice area among Ojibwa, whose lands the fur company had helped impoverish through decades of game and furbearer trading.

By matching the individuals characterized in the account to their earlier visits to the post, their relative, declining position becomes clearer. Those rating "well" in the HBC traders' view tended to be those most dependent on its food stores by the later era. Many of them had once brought furs and provisions to trade, but by the 1860s, now visited the post with only furs and often, to obtain pemmican paid for in small furbearers. Fort Ellice's pemmican was now hauled by the company into the steppe from more distant bison hunts. By contrast, many of those earning the poorest credit rating were those still having robust opportunities in game hunting, usually outside the region. Among these were individuals who joined cooperatives to make the difficult journeys into distant Blackfoot territories to hunt bison. For instance, Good Firer was a prominent plains Cree who frequently arrived with massive amounts of pemmican. But because his food surpluses gave him greater autonomy from the company, he earned a guarded rating accordingly. The opposite held true for Sha paw we tung, an Ojibwa whose winter bandlets usually hunted the Moose Mountain area. He had a positive credit rating, but it was also based on a long history of trading first foodstuffs, and later, almost exclusively furs, at Fort Ellice. By the later period, Sha paw we tung's family was likely taking much of its trade in food in his impoverished area of present-day Manitoba. Similar dependency is seen in the longstanding relationship of the Pipestone River Ojibwa, Wa way se ca paw (The Murderer), from 1859 onward, whose family faced frequent bouts of starvation and whose furs likely paid for post provisions in these difficult years. Wa way se ca paw earned a "good pay" rating by McKay. Wa way se ca paw was likely Neshecabow (Desjarlais) whom Isaac Cowie described wintering at the Fort Qu'Appelle area, a Métis who retained much of his Ojibwa identity.[55] The same can be said of "a good Indian," Mis a quat. Very poor plains hunting had left him, with time, trading furs not for goods but post provisions to survive upon (Figure 6.7).

Many of those joining cooperatives likely had greater confidence and collective clout than they had in the environs of company posts like Fort

---

[55] See Isaac Cowie's description of "Wah-ween-shee-cap-po," used by Devine in her analysis of the case of Nishecabo Desjarlais, in *The People Who Own Themselves*, 137.

Name	McKay's Characterization (appearing in Fort Ellice Account, 1866–68, B.63/d/11)	Recorded Arrivals to Fort Ellice (Drawn from Fort Ellice Journals, 1793–1868 (B.63/a/1–10)
Sha paw we tung (Ojibwa)	"good pay"	26 Aug 1858 with sons with provisions; 22 Jan 1859 with meat; 26 April 1859; 25 Dec 1862; 12 Mar 1863 "starving"; 16 April 1863 with meat of beaver and ducks; 17 Apr 1863; 1 Jun 1863; 30 Oct 1865 with furs; 1 Mar 1866 with sons and furs; 28 Oct 1866 with two sons and furs
Wa way se ca paw "The Murderer" (Ojibwa-Métis)	"good pay"	17 Jan 1859; 23 Feb 1859 sent furs; 25 Dec 1862; 17 Jan 1863 3 wives from Pesqu and Murderer tent arrived "starving"; 23 Jan 1863 wife and family arrived "starving" ; 23 Oct 1865 with furs; 24 Apr 1867 with furs
Mis a quat (Ojibwa)	"a good Indian"	31 Oct 1866 from Plains empty handed; 17 Dec 1866 with furs; 13 Feb 1867 with furs
Good Firer (Cree)	Smart Indian but a great liar	2 Apr 1864 ; 29 Nov 1864 "has nothing" ;16 Dec 1864; 19 April 1865; 27 Sept 1865 (with pemmican); 27 Aug 1866 (with pemmican and robes); 18 Oct 1866 (with pemmican)

Figure 6.7. Excerpts from McKay's Character Book, cross referenced with recorded visits to Fort Ellice (Source: HBCA Fort Ellice Accounts and Journals).

Ellice. In 1868, a massive conglomeration of Ojibwa, Plains Cree, and Assiniboine joined together to go west toward Cypress Hills. Eventually, the hunt numbered between 2,500 and 3,000 participants. The Young Dogs, the Cree–Assiniboine warrior society, now aggressively controlled the hunting territories to the southeast of the South Branch. Members of the Young Dogs led the large party. This made sense, given that it would be hunting, making pemmican, and trading with HBC directly in the Young Dogs' claimed territories. When McKay, Isaac Cowie, and Egg Lake trader, Willie Traill, set off to trade on the spot they found themselves frequently harassed, physically intimidated and then charged "export duties" by the Young Dogs. (No wonder that the Young Dog members who did trade at Fort Ellice tended to be disparaged as bad credit risks, and at Egg Lake extended very little credit at all).[56]

The 1868 bison hunt, though coming to blows with Blackfoot, had large enough numbers that it turned a great success. Willie Traill's Egg Lake accounts indicate that he traded massive provision stores in the field from the large camps assembled together. So did Isaac Cowie from Qu'Appelle. So successful was the hunt that, as they returned home, Ojibwa and Cree passing by Fort Ellice traded even more quantities directly to the traders. They provided some 3,980 lbs. of pemmican, 1,992 lbs. of dried meat, 202 lbs. of pounded meat, and 349 lbs. of grease on their first arrival in order to pay off their debts.

The same hunters went on to sell stock for what amounted to the post's discretionary surpluses, which, in turn, were used to feed other Ojibwa, now displaced Sioux, Cree, and other plains people providing furs to the post. In these trades, the post undoubtedly surpassed the district's assigned quotas and went on to build up reserves that underwrote the difficult winter bandlet hunting nearby. In 1869, for instance, the post traded "such abundance" that notwithstanding "the huge drain upon us in feeding our Cree friends for so many months on pemmican and dried meat [the following winter], there still remained when the hunt failed in the fall of 1870."[57] Through such large scale purchases, post clerks underwrote the gifts of food or food sales they made to fur hunters.[58] In turn, it was not uncommon for Fort Ellice clerks to find "wood Indians now would make no hunts without a supply of provisions from us," as one trader pointed out by 1874.[59] The well-stocked fort was in the position to move supply to a constellation of small "wood" posts, such as Egg Lake and Riding Mountain. In the case of the latter, Ojibwa

---

[56] The Egg Lake accounts contain a valuable account of "Indian Gratuities" listing fifty-two mostly Ojibwa recipients, many of them appearing in the Fort Ellice character book. HBCA. Egg Lake Accounts, 1868 B.62/d/1.

[57] Cowie, *A Company of Adventures*, 415.

[58] HBCA. When provisions prices jettisoned upwards, this practice was discouraged and traders told to limit themselves "to the acquisition of a sufficiency of provisions for the requirements of each post in district and any surplus beyond this is looked upon as so much stock available to trade now ... and swell the pelt returns off the station, so that no matter what quantity of provisions are collected during the plains hunting season, it is all got rid of during the progress of the outfit and the general business profits as little in reality by a successful provisions trade as it will by the reverse." See Fort Carton District Report, 1875, 2, B.27/e/7.

[59] HBCA. Fort Ellice District Report, 1874, B.63/e/11.

Ending the Pemmican Era 243

in those badly overhunted territories were supported by 3,000 to 4000 lbs. of pemmican over a single winter – continuing to trap for the company at the same time.[60]

Native hunters earned provisions by trading furs or by selling their labor to the posts directly. Debt servitude was common in these uncertain times. A myriad of informal work arrangements, many never recorded, were obviously agreed on between Fort Ellice clerks and Ojibwa. In 1864, Sa paw we tang, (who once in 1863 and twice in 1865 arrived "starving" to the post) left one of his sons at Fort Ellice to fulfill some type of debt servitude; when he retrieved him afterwards, they went off given one bag of pemmican, in debt.[61] Wa Way sing's son, too, was engaged by 1863. When Wa way sing had finished trading three buffalo skins, eight muskrats, and one mink "for his debt," William McKay "gave to Horse Fall [the son] his liberty to go off with his father."[62] Earlier in the winter, one of Way wa sing's wives was in a work contract with the post to cut dog wood at a rate of five beaver skins in goods, while "she has already cut 50 loads ... and she is cutting more for the same price," McKay noted, pleased by the bargain.[63]

These labor arrangements were critical to the post's economy. In 1863, when Nee cho koon appe brought two otters to the post, he also retrieved "all of his family that was about the fort for most of the winter," the same day when the Murderer, one of the longest standing Ojibwa traders with the Red River settlement, facing his own difficult circumstances in the woods, sent one of his wives and two children to "remain at the fort," undoubtedly working for their own subsistence while there.[64]

In such circumstances, the larger cooperatives forming to travel far to the west provided much needed leverage to people otherwise under the heel of the HBC. They offered Ojibwa a means to further autonomy in environmentally impoverished home territories, and, certainly, a greater power in bargaining. For instance, beginning on the 25th of July in 1868, camps from the large hunt were returning; on this occasion, the prominent Ojibwa, Pesqua, one of the bandlet heads who participated and Che

---

[60] Cited in Peers, *The Ojibwa of Western Canada*, 194.
[61] HBCA. Fort Ellice Journals, January 2, 1865, B.63/a/8.
[62] HBCA. Fort Ellice Journals, March 9, 1863, B.63/a/6.
[63] HBCA. Fort Ellice Journals, January 25, 1863, B.63/a/7.
[64] HBCA. Fort Ellice Journals, on Nee cho koon appe, see January 23 and 29, 1863, B.63/a/7; on Wa way sing's deal, see March 9, 1863, B.63/a/6; and the case of Sa paw we tang's sons paying off debt, January 2, 1865, B.63/a/8; Cowie is quoted by Peers, *The Ojibwa of Western Canada*, 200.

can e que's son (likely Ke we ta quan ape) were the first to arrive "with a little leather," and undoubtedly relating details of the camp coming up behind them. The next day, Cats Son and Pet wa wa quan asso's brother arrived "ahead of the big party," for horses and carts. "They are pretty well loaded," the post journal recorded. Over the next few days, first five horses with carts, then seven more horses were dispatched to aid the party's arrival. On August 3, the bandlet heads arrived with their large contingent and "made long speeches." The speeches were not recorded. The journal only noted that among those arriving were those paying off their debts directly from this hunting excursion: Cam a mungee (Can a mingee), Oh ka nen sens, Mus a quat, and his brother, Mis a pay's widow (either the elder or younger, perhaps both were likely there), Cat's son, Kennekess, Que we senses (or Little Boy) and his son-in-law, and Young Pheasant. Interestingly, some retained "good" credit ratings: Que we sense, Mis a quat, and at least Mis a pay's youngest widow all rated well in the Character Book. But McKay wrote damning notes about Cat's Eldest son, "Not to be trusted," Ca num an ye (also known as Ta tat up e keesick), "a scamp." Through Cowie's description, at least one of the Ouk-an-nay-sic family, all "splendid hunters ... of fine fur," had taken up with the Young Dogs Warrior society. Yellow Head (Ozaawishtigwaan), conspicuously rated "not to be trusted much" in the account book was well known by Fort Ellice traders. He had threatened Isaac Cowie and other HBC employees during the excursion, exacted tributes, and kept Métis traders under virtual house arrest in their tents to stop them from leaving camp with foods that should be taxed by the Young Dogs.[65]

The long distances of these hunts not only leveraged Ojibwa power at a time when their relative position in the trade was in decline, but they also increased their bargaining power, as these cooperatives effectively controlled access to the last herds. McKay seems to have extended better rates to the cooperative returning to trade these large quantities of pemmican. He gave them 4 d/lb. for pemmican and dried meat – and was trading hairless summer buffalo skins (amounting to leather) at 6 shillings.[66] He really had to. These groups were largely controlling supply and, for that reason, were able to force the HBC to raise prices. One clear example had already occurred in 1865, when Archibald

---

[65] The description of the hunt is best provided by Isaac Cowie, who accompanied it, see chapter XVIII, *Company of Adventurers*, 297–307; for the Young Dog's regulation of the trade, Ibid, 305–308.
[66] HBCA. Fort Ellice Journals, August 1, 1868, B.63/a/10.

McDonald, the factor at Fort Ellice, was demanded to attend a council of Cree, Assiniboine, and Ojibwa chiefs, who were organizing these long-distance hunts. The camp leaders represented almost the totality of hunters reaching the last of the herds. To his consternation, the leaders demanded better pay for their provisions. Facing a formidable united front, Macdonald had no option but to raise the value of pemmican from 3 d to 4 d /lb., fat from 2 to 3 d /lb., and dried meat from 1.5 d to 2 d.[67]

The New Bison Commons

The Fort Ellice area cooperatives offered greater autonomy to Ojibwa, Cree, and Assiniboines facing the uncertainty of overtrapped and hunted out territories at home. More importantly, these hunters could use their sheer numbers to control access to the herds, and drive up price in the bargain. As multiethnic hunts drove farther west, they effectively broke apart the HBC's district system. By the late 1850s there was a move upward in price as a result. In 1866 Fort Ellice's journal writer noted the Métis nearby organizing their camps for western hunting but having to pay Assiniboine "as a kind of toll," the post writer stated. "They [the Assiniboine] succeeded in getting it, I believe."[68] If these groups were large enough, they could do that. One Ojibwa Chief, likely connected to a larger cooperative of Assiniboine and Cree in 1863 could not have said it more clearly to the Métis from Whitehorse Plains, en route to the Souris hunting grounds: "The chief was very saucy, and told them they must not go on his hunting ground – that he was master of the plains, the buffalo were his cattle, and the Halfbreeds must not kill them."[69]

But any advantages to Native people in a shrinking, ever smaller, bison commons were short lived. The hard bargaining they won in the mid-1860s was lost in their collapsing position between 1871 and 1877. During this period herds were often below the 49th parallel.[70] Hunters as a collective were now pressed into close proximity. Beginning in 1868–1869, US and Canadian Métis were filling *hivernants* settlements

---

[67] Mae Atwood, ed., *In Rupert's Land: Memoirs of Walter Traill* (Toronto: McClelland and Stewart, 1970), 65.
[68] HBCA. The "Indians demanded 20 quarts of liquor from the freemen as a kind of toll." Fort Ellice Journals, 1865–1867, June 3, 1866, B.63/a/9.
[69] "Return of the Hunters," *Nor'Wester*, October 28, 1863, 2.
[70] See Gerhard Ens, "The Border, The Buffalo, and the Métis of Montana," in Sterling Evans, ed., *The Borderlands of the American and Canadian Wests: Essays on Regional History of the Forty-ninth Parallel* (Lincoln: University of Nebraska Press, 2006), 139–154.

in the Wood Mountain area. By 1870, as Hogue has pointed out, the overall Métis population in the area grew again by about a thousand people when Joseph Laverdure led some 100 families from the Dakotas and Red River to Wood Mountain.[71] In the ensuing years, Métis from Montana and Red River continued to move into the region. In addition, Métis hunters and traders from the North Saskatchewan moved first to the buffalo hunting parishes of St. Laurent, and then south to the small buffalo site and parish of Qu'Appelle. From there they took a place in the summer ranges or joined *hivernants* quarters.

The transborder flux in the early 1870s was now not lost on American, and then Canadian, authorities trying now to firm up the boundary. In 1871, the US military raided and burned out the Métis settlement at Frenchman's Creek with the view that Métis were selling liquor and ammunition to Sioux, with whom the Métis had established a long-standing truce and trading relationship. During these years, Yankonnai, Gros Ventre, as well as Siksika, were pressing into Piikani and Crow territory to hunt. The HBC, facing Métis and American free traders in the field, carried guns, ammunition, and alcohol in larger quantities to secure robes, but especially, some share of the provisions. The Sioux Wars in the United States finally brought Lakota fragments north into British territory, and in large councils they attempted to gain entry into the region. Siksika, Piikani, Kainai, and Assiniboine, whom the Lakota met, or sent messages to, were not, however, interested in allowing Sioux into their territories.[72] Concerns over cross-border hunting and British ammunition being traded by Métis became acute in the aftermath of Little Big Horn. "British Indians" and Métis camps after 1876 faced quite continual US Army harassment.[73]

Much of the change in the commons was due to a momentous diplomatic development. The bloody spate of revenge killings by Cree in the aftermath of Maskepetoon's assassination, the onslaught of the 1870 small pox epidemic and, finally, the horrific routing of the Cree at the Battle of the Belly River, provided the impetus in 1871 for Cree and Blackfoot to settle their differences and join in peace. There were now

---

[71] Michel Hogue, "Between Race and Nation: the Creation of a Métis Borderland on the Northern Plains." From Benjamin H. Johnson and Andrew R. Graybill, eds. *Bridging National Borders in North America: Transnational and Comparative Histories*, 63.

[72] David G. McCrady, *Living with Strangers: The Nineteenth Century Sioux and the Canadian-American Borderlands* (Norman: University of Oklahoma Press, 2006), 60–64.

[73] See Michel Hogue (Winter 2002), "Disputing the Medicine Line: The Plains Cree and the Canadian-American Border, 1876–85," *Montana The Magazine of Western History*, 52:2–17,

Ending the Pemmican Era 247

fewer reasons for large and self-defended parties to form. In June 1871, Father Léon Doucet, just after the peace between Cree and Blackfoot, saw a massive camp of 180 tents form at Round Butte, en route to the last of the herds, heavily supported by carts to return provisions to the North Saskatchewan.[74] But, this was not to continue as a practice. Smaller parties and independent hunters were also breaking up and attacking herds in small forays. Both Isaac Cowie and John McDougall believed that the Blackfoot–Cree peace of 1871 accelerated the end of the northern herds in that respect: "The hunters were no longer compelled to band together in large camps for self-protection and to regulate the hunting of the buffalo, especially by preventing bands of straggling hunters driving them about." Now in the peace "each hunter became a law to himself and these individuals became scattered all over the plains." They "drove the animal about so incessantly as to give them no time to fatten."[75]

Oblate priests accompanying hunters by that point believed that not only the last herds had shrunk, but in their continual hunting in smaller territories, especially of cows for robes and fatty meat, herds were unbalanced in numbers of male over female. Animals were also seriously underweight. Jean-Marie Lestanc, accompanying the still large summer Métis hunts in the 1870s (requiring numbers to now muscle their way into Piikani and Gros Ventre territories in Montana), reported animals of an "extraordinary skinniness" near the Milk River, "hardly having good marrow."[76] When his hunters did run bison, in small bands, he saw "nothing but skinny animals on the racks."[77] By spring, his camp almost starved and then it moved into the last summer hunting territory between the Cypress Hills and the Little Rocky Mountains of north-central Montana (now in the northern area of the Belknap Indian Reservation). In such circumstances, and given its needs, the camp finally made the decision that it was "necessary to give the animals of the prairie time to fatten" before hunting them, so skinny had they become.[78]

Certainly there were conservation efforts in these straightened circumstances. Norbert Welsh and his Native wife were careful not to kill buffalo

---

[74] Provincial Archives of Alberta, Edmonton June 1871, Diary of Leon Ducet PAA omi, 71.220 Item 6382, Box 151, 20–23.
[75] Quoted in Colpitts, "The Methodists' Great 1869 Camp Meeting," 19.
[76] Centre du Patrimoine, St. Boniface, Lestanc from Milk River, May 16, 1871, *Taché Papers*, T8746.
[77] Ibid., T8746.
[78] Centre du Patrimoine, St. Boniface from Grand Prairie along the White River a good journey in direction of the Cypress Mountain, April 25, 1871, T8709.

for their robes without using their flesh in these years. It was his wife who insisted that "since we were going to make a living hunting buffalo, she did not want me to kill more than we could dry and pack."[79] Their concerns likely grew as western nations, from the Assiniboine, to Cree, to the western Sioux, were conscious of the herds' quick destruction around them. Another Métis, Marie Rose Smith, said that Métis camps in the 1860s were careful to use the meat of animals that were killed for their robes. She seems, however, to have remembered a time when herds were so thin that there was little excess to waste. Indeed, she also remembered the Métis hunts reviving Cree organization to share the kills equally among all parties now that there were so few animals left. She called this tradition "Minis-a-wak."[80]

But growing competition moved most hunters to kill far beyond their immediate needs now that they saw so many rivals in the same fields. Even if one party conserved animals for the long term, nothing restrained other hunters, and the same game left by one group might not be there the following season. Whatever conservation he practiced, Welsh himself saw carcasses everywhere taken only for their robes. In 1874, the robe trade rapidly escalated to such a point where individual hunters were taking 300 to 400 robes a year, the greater toll more than implying waste. Blackfoot found their hands tied in dealing with interlopers, especially Métis entering their territories in large enough numbers. The Blackfoot claimed that when "Indians kill an animal they sit down around it and eat it. The Metis destroy great numbers...."[81] The Métis, in turn, claimed that the Blackfoot were the real wasters, especially between the Milk and Marias in the 1870s, when bison were being killed in such numbers for their robes only that a cart had to "swing from side to side to avoid running over fallen animals." The Métis, in these camps, were said to be following a law that unless it was diseased," the animals killed "had to be eaten. This rule, by the early 1870s, seems to have been shared by some of the Cree, "due to the preaching of Father Lacombe who taught that it was a sin to waste buffalo meat." Rose Smith remembered it that way and that "The Blackfeet were the real wasters."[82]

[79] Mary Weekes, *The Last Buffalo Hunter*, 83; on native perceptions of the end of the bison era, see Jeffrey Ostler (Winter 1999), "'They Regard Their Passing as Wakan': Interpreting Western Sioux Explanations for the Bison's Decline," *Western Historical Quarterly*, 30(4):475–497.
[80] Cited in Marie Rose Smith, "I Remember," Unpublished manuscript [ca. 1940] Marie Rose Smith Fonds, Glenbow Archives, M1184.
[81] "Canada and the Sioux," *Winnipeg Daily Free Press*, September 25, 1876, 2.
[82] Marie Rose Smith, "I Remember."

In 1874, the Red River newspaper, *The Nor'Wester*, agreed that the last of the bison needed to be saved, if only to preserve the Native populations in the west still dependent on them for food. The briefly appointed police commissioner Colonel George Arthur French believed that the new peace in the West between Cree and Blackfoot, and the rampant robe hunt, now unleashed an unrelenting "war on cows," so that five out of six animals remaining in the herds were males, "and extermination is imminent unless legislation in the interests of the Indians speedily takes place."[83] Jean-Marie Lestanc, an Oblate who arrived in 1870 at Fort Qu'Appelle, found the various nearby *hivernant* camps in want, bison "scarce" and the only animals seen were bands of skinny bulls, "not worth the effort" of hunting. "There are many who would want to have today the cows that they left on the prairie last winter."[84] Now with only one cow killed to that date in October, and it skinny, many must have been dissuaded from using restraint when opportunity presented itself. Throughout the following winter, Wood Mountain *hivernants* subsisted only on a little flour, bison having completely vanished from their wintering shelter.[85] Difficult searches scattered camps from Wood Mountain to White River in present-day Montana, Porcupine River, the Sweet Grass Hills and Cypress Hills. Lestanc wondered at just how far the Métis would continue traveling west, now that they were only a short ride out of Benton.[86]

The fear that animals would not be there the following season applied as equally to animals being left to fatten for other hunters' benefits. There could not be much forbearance in these circumstances. After 1872, when remnants of herds returned to Wood Mountain, they set about a short-lived frenzy of bloody overhunting – camps such as those at St. Joseph "passed the winter in abundance" in 1872 as a result.[87] The problem at centres like St. Florent (Qu'Appelle), Carlton and the new

---

[83] Canada and the Sioux," *Winnipeg Daily Free Press*, September 25, 1876, 2.
[84] Centre du Patrimoine, St. Boniface, Il y en a bien qui voudraient avoir aujourd'hui les vaches qu'ils ont laissées sur la prairie l'hiver dernier," Lestanc to Taché, October 10, 1870, *Taché Papers*, T8045-47.
[85] Centre du Patrimoine, St. Boniface, March 21, 1871, Lestanc from Wood Mountain to Taché, T8570.
[86] Centre du Patrimoine, St. Boniface, Lestanc, at Fort Benton, to Taché. May 22, 1871, *Taché Papers*, T8838.
[87] Centre du Patrimoine, St. Boniface, See Lestanc Letters, January 15, 1872, T9863; and May 3, 1872, T10302; I am using the term as explored by Arthur McEvoy, *The Fisherman's Problem: Ecology and Law in the California Fisheries, 1850–1980* (Cambridge: Cambridge University Press, 1986).

mission of St. Laurent was that there were too many hunters converging on these last territories. In 1872, when regional pemmican prices were now soaring – Winnipeg prices for pemmican were now at 12 cents/lb. – St. Florent residents were happy at Qu'Appelle to find the animals had "had the stupidity of approaching our lake, and all hurried themselves to go meet them." The Métis produced provisions in such "abundance" that their overhunting actually drove down price in their own local: pemmican sold at only 8 cents/lb., making merchandise purchased by the Métis that year, ironically, "very dear."[88] The winter of 1873 was so devastating, that the Métis faces were said to be "shining" with fat, and horses were being picked up for the robes in quantities "such as I've never before seen."[89] "Swimming in abundance," the Métis at Wood Mountain and White River had, despite the priest's pleading, followed their "detestable habit" of making "great, considerable waste of animals and meat."[90] Father André, from Fort Carleton, saw his own Métis congregants heading out after the herds in summer. "The future is hardly bright for our winters. Their prairie life will end and the animals will disappear, and, the Métis will become victims of their own improvidence and laziness...."[91] When Bishop Taché tried to encourage the end of Métis nomadicism, Lestanc understood that only the bison's destruction would bring an end to the wandering hunting life and wintering robe camps, when "our poor people," he said, would finally "take up the hoe and the plough." "They know it, they swear by it, and submit to the consequences of their great folly" of hunting these last animals, he said in 1874, but "they cannot do otherwise."[92]

Red River prices grew so high that pemmican attracted more traders and any attempt to organize mass hunts and apply the so-called "law of the plains" utterly failed. As early as spring 1864, freemen at Fort Edmonton had tried to bring order to the more congested summer hunt when they met in "a great assembly" "for the purpose of establishing some laws and regulations amongst themselves...."[93] There is no evidence that they succeeded. Helped by the recently appointed Father

[88] Centre du Patrimoine, St. Boniface, Lestanc from St. Florent Mission to Taché, July 28, 1872, *Taché Papers*, T10709.
[89] Centre du Patrimoine, St. Boniface, February 25, 1873, *Taché Papers*, T11653.
[90] Centre du Patrimoine, St. Boniface, March 31, 1873, *Taché Papers*, T11789.
[91] Centre du Patrimoine, St. Boniface, André to Taché, August 12, 1873, T12491–T12494.
[92] Centre du Patrimoine, St. Boniface, Lestanc to Taché, April 6, 1874, T14076–T14077.
[93] HBCA. *Fort Edmonton Journal*, March 30, 1864, B.60/a/34.

André, the Métis at the buffalo hunting parish of St. Laurent struck laws. The missionary even wrote up a "code" for the bison hunt in 1874, applying many of the principles of Native mass hunts and the former brigades to the new situation. John Andrew Kerr, who was living at St. Laurent at that point, knew of these laws.[94]

But these cooperatives could not contend with the bison's changing location and the entry of new hunters who may or may not have been disciplined by the same hunting rules. In 1876, a remarkable surge occurred as bison, almost in their death throe, broke free from their southwestern haunts and moved to the northeast. "Immense herds of buffalo were passed on the other side of Qu'Appelle," a recently appointed NWMP officer noted. It was likely no coincidence that the herds, moving into territory where they had not been seen for years, were hunted intensively: "Great numbers of Crees and half-breeds are out on the hunt," the officer reported, "the latter destroying the animals in their usual reckless and unthrifty fashion."[95] Another witness thought it was remarkable to see buffalo, for years restricted to the xeric territories to the west, now as far as the Touchwood Hills. So close were they that the Treaty 1 area Indians were mostly away from their reserves, "absent buffalo hunting."[96]

The eastward shift, though leaving Blackfoot parties in difficulty, allowed for a fantastic spoil of pemmican. The HBC at Qu'Appelle, where traders were returning in early fall, was on hand to purchase as much as possible. During the summer, W. J. McLean purchased an astounding 6,000 bags of pemmican and "hundreds" of bales of dried meat. The tempo of the hunt was itself a spectacle, "the rash advance of the buffalo this summer has brought sad havoc into their ranks," the *Winnipeg Daily Free Press* reported. The unexpected bounty meant that "consequentially enormous quantities of the meat have been cured" and while the more easterly bands taking part had laid by "ample supplies" for present and future requirements, their surpluses ruined the price in the Qu'Appelle trades, which the HBC was certain to have taken advantage of.[97]

During these years, the HBC indeed took advantage of the free-for-all. Where too many hunters worked against each other, the excessive stock on hand cheapened price considerably. With pemmican in the entire region soaring in price, huge profits could be made, especially when pemmican was hauled to hungry Winnipeg. The HBC, too, was

---

[94] John Andrew Kerr, "Hunting Bison on the Plains," 3–5.
[95] "Intelligence from the North-West," *Winnipeg Daily Press*, September 29, 1876.
[96] "Indians of the North-West," *Nor'Wester*, May 27, 1876.
[97] "Interesting Letter from Qu'Appelle," *Daily Free Press*, October 12, 1876.

most concerned that it could not get a reliable stock for its transport system, still tied to pemmican as an energy source. At Qu'Appelle Lakes in 1874, Métis attempted to gather their numbers into a single, hunting cooperative, one tied to explicit territorial claims. So adamant were they that traders feared for their lives. Edmond McKay told the Lieutenant Governor at Fort Garry that if a police or military force was not sent to the Northwest in the context of such movements, he would remove his wife and children and for their safety install them in Manitoba. He reported the Métis forming their own council to pass laws, and at a meeting at the church, Pierre Delorme, one of the hunters elected to the council, had "made a violent speech, calling upon the people to resist any attempt to interfere with their lands...."[98] By that year, Sioux migrants into the Fort Ellice environs threw white settlers and the post itself into panic; and, with alcohol rushing into the Cypress Hills hunt, the news of the massacre there committed by Benton wolfers against Assiniboine, hastened the dispatch of NWMP officers.

The Qu'Appelle Metis assembly, meanwhile, was stopping Native hunters from moving into their "territories" by the time the police were arriving. Within a year, at St. Laurent, the HBC squared off against the Métis cooperative forming around Father André's authority. Gabriel Dumont, as the elected "warden" of the plains, was able to seize the goods of one Primeau, who, according to the investigator into the affair, had been outfitted by goods by the HBC to go ahead of the larger assembly and gather provisions.[99] The HBC was also having difficulty with the likes of Robert Smith, a private trader, located on the "best spot" in the Qu'Appelle settlement, and able to get the first people who arrived from the hunt. He considered himself lucky to buy pemmican at a comparatively low rate of 6 cents/lb. (dried meat 5) in 1876.[100]

As early as 1874, a HBC district manager, Lawrence Clarke, lamented the quicksand the HBC now found itself. Despite a prosperous rise in fur trapping, most of it was coming from Métis no longer buffalo hunting at

---

[98] Provincial Archives of Manitoba, Memorandum of conversation with Edward McKay, May 19, 1873, No. 165, Alexander Morris Papers, MG 12 B1 Box 1.

[99] Provincial Archives of Manitoba, It was the Shoal Lake Constable of the NWMP who investigated Dumont's fining of $25 of Primau and the charge he made against the HBC G. A. French to Indian Commissioner, August 17, 1875, No. 1085 Letter from G. A. French in Alexander Morris Papers, MG 12 B1 Box 1, Provincial Archives of Manitoba.

[100] Provincial Archives of Manitoba, Robert Smith to John Schultz, September 27, 1876, John Schultz Files John Schultz Files MG 12 E1 Box 15, No. 7532. MG 12 B1 Box 1.

all. The posts of the Upper Saskatchewan barely sealed 148 pemmican bags of the 250 assigned them, and since almost all of it had come from trades over great distance, it was shockingly high in price (the Oblates recorded pemmican now rated at a shilling a pound at Fort Carlton). Fearing for the survival of the company's "intricate" transport system, Clarke bemoaned the "trap-hazard manner of doing business to depend entirely upon the resources of one provisions centre for the equipment of our whole carrying trade." While he pointed to the fact that "requisitions for country provisions getting to be very large, while the resources of the country are diminishing in the same ratio, and the demand for pemmican is, apart from our own wants, yearly in the increase,"[101] he expressed his fears for the future. He was also concerned for the free traders hiving at Fort Carlton. Many were vying with each other to grab up the smaller supplies. One mean little individual, Stoddard by name, was "determined to build up a business in the country" and "cast his goods broadest amongst the Freemen at almost any price; has lent them horses and carts free of cost to trade for him, and given them other advantages which we cannot pretend to offer." Clarke went on to say that "his object is to get all the pemmican possible at almost any price into his hands when he fancies that he can oblige us to purchase it from him at his own rates or starve our trade and reduce us impotent."[102]

Perhaps it is not surprising that in summer 1875, it was Clarke who precipitated a region-wide panic when he wrote Alexander Morris, the lieutenant-governor of Manitoba, to inform him that the Métis at Carlton had "assumed to themselves the right to enact laws, rules and regulations ... of a most tyrannical nature." He named none other than Gabriel Dumont as the "president of this government" and urged Morris to send a police force to his area of the country. Clarke had already suggested to his superiors that the pemmican trade should be completely monopolized for the company's transport system, even if that meant taking food out of the mouths of regional Native populations. Now Clarke urged police protection and "nothing but prompt action will save the country from an outbreak."[103]

News of the St. Laurent Métis then reached the public. "Trouble in the North-West,"[104] was how William Luxton described it in his *Winnipeg*

---

[101] HBCA. Report of G. Clark, Fort Carlton 1874, 3, B.27/e/5, Carlton House Reports on District, 1815–1875.
[102] Ibid., 6.
[103] George Stanley, "The Half-Breed 'Rising of 1875,'" *Canadian Historical Review*, 399.
[104] "Trouble in the North-West," *Winnipeg Daily Press*, July 21, 1875.

Daily Free Press. Given that only a few years previously Louis Riel had formed his provisional government to stop the transfer of the territories before political rights could be worked out, Luxton was not above giving wider circulation of the alarming "rumors" of a "Half breed Rising." Winnipeg's newspaper readers must have been more than disconcerted that there were, apparently, "10,000 Crees on the Warpath!" and "M. Louis Riel again to the Front!"[105]

The police arrived shortly to investigate. But they learned of nothing untoward about the Métis who were seemingly trying to control the hunt from its completely chaotic turn. The police dismissed Clarke for fear-mongering.[106]

By 1876, the *Winnipeg Daily Free Press* advanced a less radical issue, that of "the Protection of the Buffalo," in which the newspaper urged a close season to allow herd populations to recover, and preserve the animal as a source of food for Native people.[107] The Northwest Territory council's ordinance, then, passed in 1877 and one of the first in North America, went on to its reading before the House of Commons under the representation of western Senator and Red River scion John Shultz. Shultz estimated that the yearly slaughter was about 160,000 animals in British territory, and that the dangerously unbalanced sex ratio was leading the animal to its extinction.[108] The ordinance created a closed season in the very months when robe hunting was pursued (mostly fall and winter), and gave Native hunters but not Métis robers freedom to hunt. It also explicitly prohibited selective butchery and practices of killing bison only for sport or only for the tongue. But by leaving the summer months open, the ordinance allowed hunting for pemmican to continue, seemingly, right down to the very last animal.

Group Hunts, Multilateral Treaties

Between 1872 and 1875, plains Cree pressed the Canadian government to sign treaty in light of the rapidly changing conditions. They wanted treaties similar to those offered to Manitoba Lakes Ojibwa and Cree, the North-West Angle Saulteaux, and steppe Ojibwa. In these years, the HBC was barely keeping up its provision system; after the transfer, it

[105] Ibid.
[106] George Stanley, "The Half-Breed 'Rising of 1875," *Canadian Historical Review*, 399.
[107] "Protection of the Buffalo," *The Daily Free Press*, October 16, 1876.
[108] "Preservation of the Buffalo," *The Daily Free Press*, April 5, 1877.

was able to move away from its earlier obligations to Native people who now fell under the responsibility of the federal government. In many respects, pemmican supplies simply could not support the first treaty Indians in the West. This was acutely felt at Egg Lake, where Ojibwa had by the 1860s grown increasingly dependent on HBC food stores in return for furs, and only to find in the 1870s treaty era that support dwindling. Archibald McDonald, who at Fort Ellice had seen knives drawn at his house against him, now heard that a certain Ojibwa family had drawn them again at Egg Lake. He believed that a military force should be organized to defend the west and keep the peace on the plains now that food was becoming a widespread problem. In 1874, Egg Lake post was pillaged. Both at Egg Lake and Touchwood Hills, McDonald reported that Native rebels "have drawn knives and gone to the Company's people" in search of food. Thomas McKay (soon losing his life as an Indian instructor in the Riel Rebellion) had used his pistols and threatened to shoot ransacking and desperately hungry local hunters before throwing them out of the post. After McKay left for Fort Pelly, the group returned, scuffled with the two men in the post and "helped themselves to a bag of flour, a piece of pemmican less than half a bag and some lbs of sugar..."[109] Donald Smith, the new commissioner of the HBC, pointed out that these parties were "very different from what they were under the rule of the H.B.Co. and they are every year getting more unmanageable which is no fault of ours. Thousands of pounds of provisions are yearly spent on Indians at this place. About these very felons now threaten this place." The lieutenant-governor had once instructed not to give in to their demands, but "it is very easy from a person in his position at Fort Garry to give orders not to give anything to a lot of wild and starving savages."[110]

The Cree faced even greater stress in their hunting territories of the western Assiniboine and Qu'Appelle Valleys. They demanded a new relationship be struck with the Canadian government, or rather, the Queen, now that the HBC had transferred its territories.[111] As John Tobias has

---

[109] HBCA. Donald Smith to Morris, 6 March 1873, Alexander Morris Papers, No. 128, MG 12 B1, Box 1.
[110] Ibid.
[111] See John L. Tobias (1983), "Canada's Subjugation of the Plains Cree, 1879–1885," *Canadian Historical Review*, LXIV(4):21; on the treaty process in Canada, see Richard Price, *The Spirit the Alberta Indian Treaties* (Edmonton: University of Alberta Press, 1999); Sarah Carter, Walter Hildebrand, and Dorothy First Rider, *The True Spirit and Original Intent of Treaty 7* (Montreal: McGill-Queen's University Press, 1996); and Treaty 6 in Western Canada, see Arthur J. Ray, Jim Miller, and Frank Tough,

pointed out, Cree adopted two strategies in these years, to use treaties four (Qu'Appelle), five (Fort Pitt and Carlton), and six (the Saskatchewan) to protect the bison hunt from interlopers and outside hunters, and secure support for agriculture. Two Saskatchewan River Cree, Big Bear, and Little Pine, and an Assiniboine-Cree leader, Piapot, sought to use treaty provisions to safeguard their people now that the herds were in free fall decline. They wanted treaty promises for agricultural training, farming equipment, seed, and instructors, and, also important, to have a single, massive, hunting reserve set aside to straddle the last of the buffalo territories along the US–Canadian border. By 1876, when Big Bear met with Treaty Commissioner Alexander Morris, he was able to secure a promise that the government would regulate the bison hunt from outsiders. Morris was likely aware of the movement within the Northwest Territories council to pass the buffalo ordinance that year.[112] These three individuals led perhaps half of the Treaty 4 and 6 Indians with them to Cypress Hills to hunt the last bison.

When the three found the government lax in its protection of bison, they sat in council with Blackfoot and Teton Sioux led by Sitting Bull to organize the bison hunt now broiling along the western sections of the US–Canadian border. Their plans to organize the bison hunt, unsuccessful in the long term, especially given the longstanding animosities of Blackfoot and Sioux, nevertheless stoked fear in the Northwest of an Indian uprising in the making, with Battleford and Fort Benton papers carrying news of an Indian "confederacy" forming around the last bison hunting territories.[113]

Black Bear and Little Pine moved their Cree followers, with many of the Assinboine–Cree from Qu'Appelle, south into Montana. With bison now vacant from Canadian territory, the Canadian government wielded rations as a carrot-and-stick incentive to move treaty Indians into assigned, small reserves, and punish those whose poorly supported agricultural works, or movement onto other reserves or hunting territories,

---

Bounty and Benevolence: A History of Saskatchewan Treaties (Montreal: McGill-Queen's University Press, 2000), 32–44; Robert J. Talbot, *Negotiating the Numbered Treaties: An intellectual and Political Biography of Alexander Morris* (Saskatoon: Purich Publishing, 2009); Brian Titley, *The Indian Commissioners: Agents of the State and Indian Policy in Canada's Prairie West: 1873–1932* (Edmonton: University of Alberta Press, 2009). There are important views offered by James (Sa'ke'j) Youngblood Henderson, *Indigenous Diplomacy and the Rights of Peoples: Achieving UN Recognition* (Saskatoon: Purich, 2008), 21–23.

[112] Tobias, "Canada's Subjugation of the Plains Cree," 523.
[113] Ibid., 525.

was considered a threat.[114] But, in the meanwhile, Piapot, Black Bear, and other leaders effectively coordinated their response to the treaty process largely in consideration of the proven effectiveness of joint, cooperative hunting in the era of declining herds.

Their strategy was not restricted to the western plains Cree. Ojibwa bison hunters were similarly organizing their treaty demands and negotiations around the collective strength and profits leveraged formerly in the era of effective long-distance hunting. Pasqua, then, who had already taken treaty but found himself in 1875 with Chief Kah wah kah tose (the Poor Man) at Fort Qu'Appelle just after the summer bison hunt, for instance, took time to demand help from the Indian commissioner, especially in the form of agricultural implements.[115] Another familiar name at Fort Ellice, Wa-wa-se-cap-pot, te (Wa-wa-se-ka-pa-taw) was also by 1874 following up on the treaty his people had signed with communications to Alexander Morris. It was within a large, mixed hunt near the Cypress Hills where the last of the herds were to be found in 1876, that Little Child, Little Black Bear, Blade Bone, and other Cree and Saulteaux wrote that "we see with our own eyes that the buffalo are gradually dying and being killed off." Within such a large gathering, these hunters were preparing for the future, that "It will be only a year or two before we can not make our living by the chase."[116] Indeed, most of the prominent participants of the later treaties had refined multilateral diplomacy and joint organization in the era of long-distance, large-scale bison hunts.

Conclusion

By November 1879, there seemed not to be a single bison still standing above the Red Deer River,[117] and any sizeable herd had effectively disappeared from Canadian territory. That year, the HBC trader

---

[114] See James Daschuk's description of the carrot-and-stick rationing policies of the federal government in these years. *Clearing the Plains: Disease, Politics of Starvation and the Loss of Aboriginal Life* (Regina: University of Regina Press, 2013), 94–111.

[115] Provincial Archives of Manitoba, Letter from Pasqua and Kah wah kah tose, September 14, 1875, No. 1110. Alexander Morris Papers, MG 12 B1 Box 1.

[116] Provincial Archives of Manitoba, Ojibwa and Cree Chiefs' Letter to Liard, April 20, 1876, No. 1247, Alexander Morris Papers, MG 12 B1 Box 1, and Letter from Wa-wa-se-cap-po, te to Commissioner, November 4, 1875, No. 1149.

[117] Colonel Richardson at Battleford reported in 1879 that he had never seen any bison in the three years there. See "The Buffalo," *Winnipeg Free Press*, December 2, 1879. For references to "no buffalo north of the line." "North-Western Notes," ibid., November 29, 1879.

H. M. Robinson noted the soaring market price on pemmican, "procured with difficulty" for 1 shilling and 3 pence, when formerly it could be had for 2 pence. He thought "some new provision must be found to take the place of the old... This is a fact which threatens to revolutionize in manner the whole business of the territory."[118] There were many ways that company officials and western settlers were coping with this revolutionary change. In many fur trade territories, the company switched back to the dietary basics of wild rice, with a few strips of bacon, apportioned as a daily ration to each man in its employ. The HBC encouraged boreal forest hunters to supply deer meat and fat to produce deer pemmican; in the north, caribou was hunted more intensively.

The greatest change, however, was in the shift to a completely new energy regime. By the mid-1870s, railway building in the Mississippian valley had made obsolete the great riverboat fleets and their crews. Some of that technology was sold off at a bargain to the HBC, and the first steamboat, the *Northcote*, was transported in sections north on the existing Minnesota rail link to Red River, barged across the lakes via the narrows, and then reassembled on the Saskatchewan River.[119] With great fanfare in 1874, the first Saskatchewan service was moving goods direct from Red River to Fort Carlton via steamship; by then, Cumberland House was no longer the carryover point to Athabasca. Instead, Carlton was sending goods overland via Green Lake. In 1875, the "immense transfer of goods from York Factory to Norway House, and of furs to York Factory [was] done away," as one observer pointed out.[120] Immediately, about 130 to 140 mostly Ojibwa labourers regularly employed on York boats to Norway House, were laid off. Another forty or fifty Dene on the Mackenzie Brigades were also no longer needed. By the end of the decade three steamboats, one in the Mackenzie, now operated. The use of steam now strengthened the company's hand. It could ship goods

---

[118] H.M. Robinson, *The Great Fur Land: Or Sketches of Life in the Hudson's Bay Territory* [1879] (Toronto: Coles, 1972), 165.

[119] Innis discusses the adoption of Mississippian technology between 1874 and 1877 and the new steamboat service, Harold Innis, *The Fur Trade in Canada*, 343–344. On the urgent need for steamboats, see Frank Tough, *'As their natural resources fail': Native Peoples and the Economic History of Northern Manitoba, 1870–1930* (Vancouver: UBC Press, 1996), 52–55. Daschuk offers an important observation of the HBC's difficulty delivering goods on early steamboats and the greater efficiency of I. G. Baker's Benton supply into the territories, often of corrupt Indian ration goods. *Clearing the Plains*, 128–129.

[120] Provincial Archives of Manitoba, Letter No. 981 April 6, 1875, PAM, Alexander Morris Papers, MG 12 B1 Box 1.

once a year comfortably and do away with most of the ungainly and labor intensive York boat system.

Perhaps more than the transport service, however, was the shock to the provisioning system within the plains and parkland. The posts' discretionary surpluses ended. At Fort Carlton, its extra food stores were virtually evaporated during the meager summer trade in 1875. Whatever the post got was expensively procured and quickly dispensed for "all the starving wretches for miles round; who have little or nothing to give in return for their food supplies," reported the HBC's district inspector, G. Clarke. He understood the grave situation at hand and advocated that all pemmican in the area be directed to supporting the company's transport, that in no uncertain terms that "I can see no way to put an end to this state of affairs until you have a protective force in the country, and an Indian can be treated as any other mendicant."[121]

Although the end of the buffalo era was soon marked by a chaotic turn in Indian affairs, and plains people quickly declined into indigence in an unfamiliar transitional economy, there were nevertheless legacies of the buffalo hunt. Plains tribes, after all, had coordinated massive multiethnic camps to access the shrinking herds and gain greater advantages in the market. Their leadership and diplomatic skills undoubtedly had been honed in this last period of the pemmican era. Plains people approached and made demands in treaty negotiation based on this hard-earned experience. The subsequent treaty era, unfolding in a world now bereft of bison, was shaped by the expectations of plains hunters who, as they had with the HBC, demanded both "bounty and benevolence" from the federal government in the settlement era.[122]

Whether they received that, of course, was another matter altogether. The exchange relations and provisions trading once underpinning British colonization were now swept away with the region's rapid settlement, agricultural improvement, and new economic realities.

---

[121] HBCA. Report of G. Clark, Fort Carlton 1874, 5, B.27/e/5, Carlton House Reports on District, 1815–1875.

[122] The expression frames the study of Arthur J. Ray, Jim Miller and Frank Tough, *Bounty and Benevolence: A History of Saskatchewan Treaties* (Montreal and Kingston: McGill-Queen's University Press, 2002).

CONCLUSION

Appropriately, it was in Winnipeg where the first historical assessment of the pemmican era was undertaken. Isaac Cowie provided a vivid recounting of personalities and features of the fur trade era in the 1860s. His published narrative, *Company of Adventurers*, appeared in 1913 in a period still heady with Manitoba boosterism and just before the great financial crash occurred the same year. The Toronto publisher William Briggs had helped float the book's printing from Cowie's earlier newspaper serial descriptions by raising a massive subscription among many of Cowie's close friends, retired fur traders, territorial and city politicians, and a wide assortment of representatives, all mixed up in what might be termed the booster period in Manitoba and Territorial history. They included grain brokers in Calgary and real estate agents in Winnipeg. Even Calgary's obstreperous newspaperman, Bob Edwards, chipped in for its publication. Many of the book's investors dated their arrival to western Canada before or shortly after the transfer of territories to Canada.[1]

Cowie's narrative stood sharply at odds with the world modernizing in Manitoba. Commerce, lines of transportation, and human relations had all been rewired by 1913. Winnipeg was the great gateway and bustling commercial entrepôt for the "Last Best West." Street trolley lines unraveled down chaotic and muddy streets. Immigration boomed from Department of Interior western land promotions. British investment heightened expectations of settlement, improvement, and, more importantly for the Wheat Boom in full swing, transport infrastructure. Better wheat crosses, too, were being adapted to the northern latitudes. Canada No. 1 Northern was garnering premium prices on international markets. And the roadways, streets, and railway terminals from the plains were

---

[1] See preface and patrons listed in Isaac Cowie, *Company of Adventurers: A narrative of Seven Years in the Service of the Hudson's Bay Company during 1867–1874* (Toronto: William Brigs, 1913).

converging on Winnipeg's Exchange District to divert something of a sloshing deluge of wheat in and out of the city like the waters of the Assiniboine and Red Rivers had once flushed with the raw commodities in the fur trade.[2]

Cowie probably was quite astounded at how different this new period was from the old. Only forty years before, pemmican had served as a critical energy source for fur trade society, with very different exigencies and economic consequences. Bison meat had, in that period, circulated as a key exchange commodity, fully commercialized but still embedded in a mixed up middle ground of European and Native economies.

Canadian prairie history must grapple in some way with its pemmican past. The social ordering, and, in the case of the Hudson's Bay Company (HBC), its explicitly British class orientation, its values and economy, and, finally, its transport networks and post systems, all shaped the settlement period, territorial administration, town building, and emerging tradition in law enforcement. Any complete understanding of the Western Canadian experience should begin with fur trade society and its food ways.

This book has attempted to do that. It has explored the makings and eventual destruction of a "pemmican empire," one that shaped power relations and society in many portions of the British West. In the ideal climatic conditions of the Northern Great Plains, particularly in the periodic, if only stochastic superabundance produced in winter bison pounds, Native people and Europeans established the beginnings of factory pemmican production based upon the market economy. The unfolding bioregional history was driven by the sharper seasonality of winter and summer temperatures in the higher latitudes of the Northern Great Plains. Harsh winter fattened herd animals there and moved them, but not always, within predictable winter shelter to become a shared, movable feast for natives and newcomers. When a market hunt developed in summer, now to satiate growing demands by companies, the same climatic characteristics were just as significant; the comparatively lower maximum high summer temperatures in pemmican-making territories allowed hunters to handle, render, and transport fats, to create surpluses of such a massive quantity that they could be sold by the ton on the

---

[2] The image of wheat forming a deluge through Winnipeg's new commercial districts is offered by Jim Blanchard, *Winnipeg, 1912* (Winnipeg: University of Manitoba Press, 2005), 213–219.

market. Although this summer hunt was wasteful, and the vicissitudes of hot July temperatures could sometimes see whole hunts go rancid in the fly-buzzing noise of a prairie inferno, the summer hunt nevertheless could ably support the nearby market in the seemingly limitless bison commons.

The caloric wealth of bison fats provided energy to expand commerce and nourish settlement society. Pemmican itself might have transmogrified in its recent past. It changed from the stuff used traditionally by Native eaters, the rich, marrowy "sweet" pemmican, into the bulky and waxy bricks supporting York and canoe brigades. In the settler era, missionaries ate "toro"; settlers sliced it from sausage-shaped bundles and experimented with its flavors; they mixed it with raisons, salt, pepper, and no end of spices; floured it; made it into bannocks; or fried it as rubbaboo. But, if frontiers create their unique societies at least in part by their environments, it surely holds in the case of the Pemmican Empire. There it became, as Henry Rice observed in 1870, "a difficult matter to tell at all times exactly where the half-breed ends and the white man or Indian begins; correspondingly difficult is it to tell where the buffalo terminates and the pemmican begins."[3]

In the case of the northern latitudes of the Great Plains, Western Canadian history was shaped by the arguably unique relationship of Native people with newcomers around food. The food market created by the HBC was, of course, distorted profoundly in 1821, after which date the HBC was in the position to suppress prices and keep pemmican products to at least a quarter of their inflated value at the time of the monopolization. Many Native and Métis hunting strategies developed to find a better place in that market, search for alternative ones, or, more simply, produce larger amounts of product. The HBC controlled price by organizing a district buying system and quotas that effectively pitted all Native hunters and Métis together in the same market. Monopsony advantages allowed the company to purchase its primary energy source for the fur trade elsewhere and advance the "sinews" of British power and future colonization, especially its transport networks in and out of the prairie region. But at plains posts, managers also capitalized on suppressed food prices to purchase far more than they required and stockpile for discretionary transactions. These could then be used liberally – company directors, of course, would say improvidently – by the end of the season to sustain the hunt in rapidly overhunted areas. The

---

[3] Henry M. Rice (reprinted 1981), "Pemmican," in *the Minnesota Archaeologist,* **40**(2):96.

icehouse and "victualling shed" imparted to a post a princely position, then, in the aboriginal world.

Many of these advantages derived from a single decision made in 1810, when the HBC came very close to divesting itself of the trade to instead supply independent traders who would deal with native trappers themselves "on their own account." In the end the company's committee, following the lead of Andrew Colville, continued the ancient and, many thought, outmoded factor tradition into the modern world.[4] Hence, the factor trade survived the amalgamation of companies in 1821 and, in fundamental ways, divided the nature of the market that expanded on the Saskatchewan and Missouri, like two forks in a road. Despite the rapid expansion of the American Fur Company, already having seventeen posts in the Upper Mississippi Country by 1826, and the Columbia and Cheyenne American Fur Companies expanding northward as well, their business was inherently competitive and cutthroat. As a result, plains people in the American West faced a far different market. As this book has argued, on the British buffalo frontier, the monopolized trade after 1821 remained harnessed to the credit, management, and markets of the London metropolis. Native people there faced one buyer, were offered one price, and one company held most of the cards.[5]

This was not a peaceable kingdom by any means. It was also not completely one-sided, especially on the plains where food was concerned. Whatever advantages the HBC enjoyed, the provisions trade was always tilted in some manner towards the ultimate power of the provisioners: Native people and Métis could eat their food instead of trading it, after all. The leverage of this power was noted by George Simpson who lamented in 1839 that the company still had to "accommodate ourself to the waywardness and obstinacy of our intractable providers. We hope, nevertheless, to succeed in putting our provisions and fur hunters on the same footing."[6] That never happened. Bison hunters were a difficult lot to deal with, as Alexander Henry the Elder perhaps first noticed in 1776 among Assiniboine in the Winnipeg Steppe. Provisioners made demands on traders even when monopoly conditions dampened price mechanisms on the plains, setting there a unique relationship between the "company"

---

[4] Colville's retrenchment policy is described by E. E. Rich, ed., *Colin Robertson Letters* xxi–xxiii. I am also benefiting from discussions arising from Scott Stephen's paper on retrenchment at the Rupert's Land Colloquium, Winnipeg, Manitoba, May 2012.
[5] E. E. Rich, *The Hudson's Bay Company*, Vol. II (London: Hudson Bay Record Society, 1959), 519.
[6] George Simpson Report on 1839 to London Committee, D.4/106, fol. 31.

and native people. If there was any posturing and expectation of Native negotiators at the time of the treaties with the Canadian government, it was their presumption to claim the Queen's "bounty and benevolence" from her very hand, undoubtedly with the food stocks, surpluses and obligatory gifting they had grown to expect, and demand, on a frontier established with pemmican trading.

The treaty era was shaped in other ways by the exigencies and experience of the pemmican trade. The last twenty years of bison hunting was organized by prominent native leaders who shared handsome benefits. In the parkland areas, the warfare in bison territories necessitated that headmen of extraordinary personal qualities, talent, and perceived spiritual power step forward to gather otherwise autonomous bands onto a concerted war footing, or, by the 1860s, to coordinate multiethnic bison hunting into distant and dangerous territories. There is no doubt that leaders who so ably negotiated the interests of their followers in the last decades of the bison commons perfected techniques of multilateral diplomacy in these great bison concordats – Wood and Mountain Cree with Plains Cree, Assiniboine, with Ojibwa and Métis (members of the always close "Iron Alliance), and the Siksika, Aitsina, Kainai, and Tsuu T'ina. They brought the same multilateralism to Carlton and Blackfoot Crossing in 1876 and 1877, two of the most important locales in Western Canadian history, where Treaties No. 6 and 7, respectively, were worked out. Moreover, their approach to dealing with the British Crown was essentially the same: drawing outlier camps together to develop a coherent position of strength. A pertinent lesson of the bison hunt in the 1860s was that only through cooperatives and multilateral entities could the market really profit provisioners. Only then could the bison, now reduced to smaller territories, really feed the people.

The other element of this frontier was a close relationship based on food exchange. Even when they sold it as a trade commodity, traders invested food with meanings and obligations as it changed hands. Fur trade posts handling bison food products struck a very different society on the plains. For one thing, only a quasi-market orientation occurred among Cree, Assiniboine, and Blackfoot for most of their historical contact with Europeans. Until the end of the era, they continued to negotiate their wants and needs within the market by integrating their food trades inside their traditional seasonal rounds. Their band life and relationships around food reciprocity and food sharing, then, remained robust. Even as they invested greater labor into traded food and eventually sold ready-made pemmican to the market, food was never traded exactly like other animal commodities in the market economy expanding elsewhere in British and American frontiers.

In many respects, central to all of their decision making was the environment itself. Native hunters and Métis provisioning specialists negotiated their entry into the market through the realities of winter and summer climate marking the northern latitudes of the Great Plains. Winter seasonality provided ideal circumstances, usually, within pounding areas; summer weather allowed commercial hunters to expand their fat rendering and pemmican making in the hottest months of the year. Although the nature of the market in these territories tied the hands of opportunists, especially as their needs increased and plains warfare intensified, they could nevertheless bid their time, in their own way, within the market enveloping them. It is clear that the district quota system of the HBC cheapened provisions prices for half a century. Native hunters in effect were forced to play against each other in the British market for bison foodstuffs. There was little recourse, indeed, in such circumstances except for hunters to raise production or search for alternative markets. But in each of its unfolding phases, the "commons" confronted its human exploiters with new decisions, opportunities, and challenges.

For most of the pemmican era, Europeans and Native people struck a compromise on what had once been an ideal, softer, fatty fare. Europeans ate trade pemmican that was much harder in saturated fats than Native people preferred. But there was much back fat, too, changing hands, and that was always a complement in the Native World. Indeed, the closer the relations, the sweeter the pemmican. Sweet varieties of pemmican (albeit at double the price) accrued at fur posts and, whatever the vagaries of market forces, it continued to cement native–newcomer relations. This, then, was the complex nature of the Pemmican Empire, and a bioregional history based on food exchange that provided its nourishment.

FUR TRADE FOOD GLOSSARY

Beat Meat – Meat that has been sufficiently dried to allow it to be pounded into chunks and strips often loaded in a coarse state into bags for trade. "Men employed to pound the course beat meat" (Hudson's Bay Company Archives (hereafter HBCA) Carlton House Journals, May 13, 1819, B.27/a/8).

Bladder – This was the bladder of the bison. It often carried water, but, in trade, bone greases, hence, the Métis termed them *vessies de graisse de moëlle* (Belcourt Letter, 1845, 51). Before being filled, the bladder was inflated to artificially distend its capacity, usually to hold about 5 to 6 lbs. of marrow fat and/or bone "grease." A bison bladder expands to about 8″ × 5″ and resembles very much a balloon when full of air. Although the stomach or "paunch" was used for other purposes, bladders were sometimes also called PAUNCHES ("I send out three ... a few tongues, four panches..." (Library and Archives Canada (hereafter LAC).Anonymous Letter, January 15, 1809 *Selkirk Papers, Series B,* 80). Hunters were sure to save bison bladders after a kill: "They then washed them well, blew them up like a balloon and dried them. Later the grease was poured in through a birch bark funnel and then the mouth of the bladder was tied to seal it." (Marie Rose Smith, "Eighty Years on the Plains," *Cattlemen* 21(1):31, June 1949, 4.)

Boiled Meat – A common means of preparing bison meat, in soups or, given its lean character, to soften it. "The country is so plentifull that the Canoes have always either fresh meat or Fowl for their Kettles." (John Macdonell's "The Red River," ca. 1797, in Wood and Thiessen, eds., *Early Fur Trade on the Northern Plains,* 86.)

Commensal – COMMISSARY FOOD SHARING – The principle of sharing out of one's "commissary" or around the table. Most pronounced in subarctic regions, the tradition of food sharing implies giving generously or equally from a common food supply, even those who might have been outsiders fusing only temporarily with a larger group.

Common Property – Food – A Métis expression, "Minis-a-wak," coming into use at the end of the bison era when food was scarce and hunts formed to kill animals to be shared equally within the entire camp. (Glenbow Archives (hereafter GA.) "Minis-a-wak," cited in Marie Rose Smith, "I Remember," Unpublished manuscript [ca. 1940] Marie Rose Smith Fonds, M1184.)

Custom of the Country – A fur trade term sometimes used to describe marriage, but also to describe the custom of food sharing at trading posts. Native hunters who provided food from posts came to expect reciprocation in times of need. Fur traders saw this as a reasonable expectation, the "custom of the country."

Custom of the Voyageur – Typically forming the diet of traveling voyageurs on the east side of Grand Portage. Alexander Mackenzie said at Grand Portage the "custom" consisted of Indian corn husked in alkali, then dried. One quart of the corn was boiled in a gallon of water with two ounces of "melted suet," a "wholesome, palatable food, and easy of digestion." (Mackenzie quoted in Harold Innis, *Fur Trade in Canada*, 224.) The custom usually included some supply of dried peas.

Dépouille – The two strips of fat found on either side of the bison's or moose's backbone. This could be roasted lightly, or dipped in grease and smoked slightly for taste and long-term preservation. It was considered a great delicacy: "those who we heard from yesterday waiting for me, with the Flesh of two very Fat Cow Buffaloes, whose depouilles were about two inches in thickness…" (Gough, ed. *Alexander Henry the Younger*, Vol. I, p. 31.) The dépouilles of the cow were almost always larger in diameter than the bull. Henry thought a bull with dépouilles of two inches in diameter, shot in 1806, was extraordinary, while "cows often had one to two inch diameter depouille, some known to have even three inches (p. 210). He found by early July bull bison and moose "beginning to get in good order. The moose had 1.5 inches of diameter around the rump, and the bulls 1 inch of depouille." (*Alexander Henry the Younger*, II, 453.) In Métis pemmican making, this luxury fat, for convenience sake, was used as a fat alternative to marrow, and stored in bladders. ("Ils font aussi fonder les dépouilles dont ils tirent la graisse qu'ils conservent dans les vessies." Centre du Patrimoine, St. Boniface, Archives (hereafter CP). Laflèche to Thomas Caron 1 June 1845 Arch. Dioc. De S.-B, 0917).

Dépouilles could also be derived from other animals: notably the very sweet back fat from bears in the autumn, and even raccoons that "are very fat, having depouilles from 2 to 3 inches thick and are excellent eating when stript of their fat and roasted." (Gough, *Journals of Alexander Henry the Younger*, I, 73.)

Dried Meat – Meat dried in the sun, sometimes with the aid of smoke or the heat of a fire. The preferred technique was to use sun over longer periods of time in order to achieve pleasing tastes and avoid the "fishy" taste that came from meat being too rapidly dried. Smoke was generally used to drive away flies, not cure meat. When meat was being dried for commercial purposes, women often lit fires underneath it on stages in order to accelerate the drying process. Fur traders sometimes used the expression "under bare poles" to designate the end of meat drying processes and the meat trade. (LAC. Alexander Macdonnel Letter to NWC Agents, March 13, 1816, *Selkirk Papers, Series A*, 9066). The Métis were said to go to camps to make dried meat "and also for a kind of recreation. Such a camp was called by the half- breeds of the north 'nick-ah-wah,' and to go into it was 'aller en nick-ah-wah'." (Charles Larpenteur, *Forty Years a Fur Trader*, 80.) Stefansson stated that if in rainy weather or in a hurry, Native people could dry meat over a "slow fire… suspended within the tepee and became smoked incidentally." In some areas of North America, he said that smoking was deliberate "most likely in places where the climate was damp." (Stefansson, *Not by Bread Alone* (Macmillan, 1946, 186.) The chief benefit of meat drying was not only to preserve it longer, but to reduce its bulk. Six pounds of fresh meat could usually be dried to one, allowing for its easier transport.

En Échafaud – To put fresh meat on stage during the winter, safely out of the reach of scavengers and dogs. "Chacun avait de grandes quantités de viandes fraîches en échafaud. Ces échafauds sont des plate-formes assez élevées de terre pour n'être pas à la portée des chiens." (CP. February 16, 1850, Letter to Dubuque Fonds George Antoine Belcourt, 0324/382/file 016.)

Éparer – Translated by fur traders as "Turning Out," was the slicing of meat in thin pieces to dry in the sun. "C'est ce que l'on appelle en termes du pays éparer." (CP. June 1, 1845, Laflèche to Thomas Caron, Arch. Dioc. De S.-B, 0916); the term with its French connotation came to generalize the butchery of the bison for the market: "L'on ouvre ensuite la peau sur le dos, et on la lève; après quoi l'on épare l'animal"

(Lettre du Pere Belcourt, 47). It likely had origins in the verb *Parer* with an older understanding of preparing meat for cooking such as "Parer de la viande." (See "Parer," Paul Robert, *Le Nouveau Petit Robert* Paris: Dictionnaire Le Robert, 1996, 1588.)

Fan – A dressed fawn skin used to carry some meats and fats. Because of its smaller size, a fan implied a certain capacity. It was rarely used as a term in the plains trade, however exceptions exist: "They keep it [fat] in doe-skins sewn together and which are called *Faons*." (*Tixier's Travels on the Osage Prairies*, 1844 ed. John Francis McDermott, 194–195.) A fan held the most precious fats that were given as gifts to esteemed guests. Hind, visiting Cree camp tents, was given fan skins of marrowfat: "they generally presented me with a choice piece of buffalo meat from a fat cow, or a small skin of marrowfat." (Hind Narrative, 1870, I, 347.)

Fat Bags – Usually calf skins doubled over, sewn together, and sealed with tallow; they carried hard fats, rendered tallow, or unrendered back fats and interior hard (leaf) fats such as rib fat or organ fats. The Métis called them *baskoyas*. The Cree, if they did not use bladders, would drip bone greases into bags called *oskanpimi;* the shoulder and rump fats were poured into bags called *sasipmanpimi* (used as frying grease) (Mandelbaum, *The Plains Cree* (2001)[1979] 58–59).

Folle Avoine – WILD RICE: "Altho I wished to be very saving of your folle Avoine for the ensuing season, still I am under the necessity of sending five men for as much as they can bring of it which will be at least three kegs each." (LAC. Donald Cameron to Dugald Cameron, November 26, 1814, *Selkirk Papers, Series A*, 8850.)

Grease – Fat derived from the most axial areas of the animal's body. These had the highest proportions of unsaturated fatty acid chains and the lowest melting points. Closer to the hoof, some marrow fats could run liquid at room temperature, although the marrow in the most axial portion of a bison foreleg can be quite substantial. Grease as a fur trade term denoted both marrow fats, extracted from the interior of the bone, and "grease" properly speaking, boiled out of crushed bone. Grease was considered the most delectable fat and most pleasing in the palette, since it did not leave an aftertaste. After the bones were crushed and boiled, "The grease was then poured off ready for use; this grease never turned hard or set. It is the nicest grease I have ever tasted... when needed [it] was poured out of the bladder onto a piece of pemmican or into a dish into which we could 'dunk' our bannock." (Marie Rose Smith,

"Eighty Years on the Plains," *Canadian Cattlemen* 21(1):31, June 1949, 4). Grease was given to esteemed guests: Hind was offered pounded meat and marrow fat by Qu'Appelle Valley Cree: "Birch bark dishes full of that nutritious but not very tempting food were placed on the ground before us and we were requested to partake of it. The Indians took a piece of the pounded meat in their fingers and dipped it into the soft marrow." (Hind Narrative, 1860, Vol. I, 341). Miles Macdonnel at Turtle River among Ojibwa in 1815 recorded "the most eldest man ... returned some time afterwards with my servant loaded with Buffalo tongues and a Cake of fat as a present...." (Miles Macdonnel's Journal, *Selkirk Papers*, Series A, 16959).

Grits – *See* Homony.

Half-Beat Meat – Dried meat only partially reduced for the sake of carrying in bags. References to "pemmican" in winter were sometimes of half-beat meat, carried in a semidried state, and used during that season often by joining it with fat carried in separate bags.

Half-Dried Meat – More commonly seen in the subarctic where winters were cold enough that meat could dry through wind action. The sunlight dries and marbles only the surface of the meat and allows the interior to stay fresh and preserved. It was considered a delicacy because of both its fresh qualities and the delicious marbling of its surface. To half-dry the meat, often two sides of a moose carcass would be hung over line and left a considerable period of time. Matthew Cocking made the distinction between what was "dried" meat at York Factory, and what was "half-dried" of this delicious sort at Cumberland House where moose meats were often traded; see E. E. Rich, ed., *Cumberland and Hudson House Journals 1775 1782*, Vol. I (London: The Hudson's Bay Record Society, 1951), 28.

Hard Fat – *See* Tallow.

Homony – (Sometimes called "Grits") made by the Mandan and Arikara of bison fat and ground corn: "After the meat, they offered us homony made of corn dried in the milk, mixed with beans, which was prepared with buffaloe marrow, and tasted extremely well." (Henry Brackenridge: *Views of Louisiana* (Cramer, Spear, and Eichbaum, 1814, 248). Among the Teton Sioux, Lewis and Clark reported that "the repast was served up to us ... to this were added, pemitigon, a dish made of buffaloe meat, dried or jerked, and then pounded and mixed raw with grease and a kind of ground potatoe, dressed like the preparation of Indian corn called hominy, to which it is little inferior." (Meriwether Lewis and William Clark, *History of the Expedition under the Command of Captains Lewis and Clark*, Vol. I. New York: J. Maxwell, 1814, 84.)

Hump or Bosse – Fatty folds of meat overlaying the vertical high spines of the vertebrae of the bison at the neck. The *Grosse bosse* was distinguished from the *Petite bosse*, which made up the much smaller anterior sirloin cap of the animal, also overlain in fat. "These fleeces, from a large animal, will weigh, perhaps, a hundred pounds each, and comprise the whole of the hump on each side of the vertical processes (commonly called the hump ribs) which are attached to the vertebra. The fleeces are considered the choice parts of the buffalo, and here, where the game is so abundant, nothing else is taken, if we except the tongue, and an occasional marrow bone." (John Kirk Townsend, *Narrative of a Journey Across the Rocky Mountains to the Columbia River*, George A. Jobanek, ed. Carvallis: Oregon State University Press, 1999, 35). As a delicacy meat, it often figured as a gifts between officers, bourgeois and men of esteem. In other settings, it was called ROIGNON (or Rognon in French) – (cited anonymous letter, January 15, 1809, 80 *Selkirk Papers, Series B*, 80), tied up with *maitres* or cords. The hump sometimes arrived on the bone: "they bring nothing but fresh and dried Provisions, Tongues and Ridge Bones in abundance." (*Journal of Alexander Henry the Younger*, II, 421); "The hump was a special tid bit, the unused muscle alternating with layers of fat, which constituted it a dish, if either boiled, fried or roasted, fit for a king." (Walter Bown Testimony, Appendix I, Vol. 21, *Journals of the Senate of Canada*, Select Committee on Natural Food Products of the North-West Territories, 1887, 111).

Pelu – Bison robe. The word originated in the Latin *Pilus* or hair, and became current in the era of robe hunting. "The money is the *pelu* paid at good market value" ("L'argent est le pelue payé à bon marché," Father Lestanc to Taché, March 21, 1871, Centre du Patrimoine, T-8570).

Pemmican (pe'mi kân) – Sometimes called "taureau" or "toro" given that it was often sewn in a pack made from bull hide. A loaf or cake composed of dried, pounded meat and hardened fat ("a côté de lui, il y avait une galette de toro..." Father Lestanc letter to Taché, September 12, 1870, Centre du Patrimoine, T7942). There were many variants:

Traditional, or *"fine," "sweet,"* – Heavier in soft (or marrow and bone) fats extracted as a gelatinous solid by twisting and cracking the bones, and/or pulverizing and boiling the calcaneous bone to extract "grease." The root words of pemmican contain the idea of bone marrow fats or "grease": in Cree, *pemitigan* (*he makes grease*) contains the root *pimme;* in Ojibwa *Pemetai,* Blackfoot, *Poomis,* and Siouan, *Wassna.* (Henry's "Short Dictionary," *Journal of Alexander Henry the Younger,* II 387.) The Blackfoot, for home consumption, made finer pemmican that used marrow fats. Hamilton, quoted in Wissler, suggested that for their own use, "The choicest cuts of meat are selected and cut into flakes and dried. Then all the marrow is collected and the best of the tallow, which are dissolved together over a slow fire to prevent burning. Many tribes use berries in their pemmican.... The meat is now pulverized to the consistency of mince meat; the squaws generally doing this on a flat rock, using a pestle.... A layer of meat is spread about two inches thick, the squaws using a wooden dipper, a buffalo horn, or a claw for this work. On this meat is spread a certain amount of ingredients made from the marrow and tallow, the proportion depending on the taste." (Clark Wissler, "Material Culture of the Blackfoot Indians," *Anthropological Papers of the American Museum of Natural History,* V, Part I, March 1910.)

Some sweet pemmican was mixed with berries and was considered a delicacy fit for gift-giving and diplomacy. The berry of choice was the service or June berry (*Amelanchier alnifolioa* Nutt.):"On the great Plains there is a shrub bearing a very sweet berry of a dark blue color, much sought after ... and as much as possible mixed to make Pemmecan." (David Thompson *Narrative,* Champlain Society, 1916, 434). The Crow served fine pemmican to Osborne Russel in 1834: "After an hours dumb conversation a dish of roasted Buffaloe tongues was set before me accompanied by a large cake made of dried meat and fruit pounded together mixed up with Buffaloc marrow." (Journal of a Trapper... by Osborne Russel.) It was fine pemmican that bourgeois and officers reserved for themselves: "Mr McKenzie lost a keg in which was put up some salted tongues and bosses and a quantity of particular made pemmican to which he is very partial." (LAC. Miles Macdonnel's Journal, July 6, 1815, *Selkirk Papers, Series A,* 17049). Stefansson said that pemmican makers filled bags with shredded "pounded" meat "lightly and fluffily ... somewhat as we fill a pillow with feathers" before pouring melted fats into it. (Stefansson, *Not by Bread Alone* (Macmillan, 1946), 186. Blackfoot sweet pemmican was sometimes made in the following way: jerky meat was placed on coals until their fats ran out and the meat turned dark brown; this was pounded into powder, then chokecherries were semidried to remove much of their moisture and pounded. Melted suet was added to the berries and pounded meat so that "egg-shaped balls" could be preserved in oiled cloth or bags. (Reginald and Gladys Laubin, *The Indian Tipi*. Norman: University of Oklahoma Press, 1989, 153.)

Trade or Voyageur Pemmican – Heavier in hard fats drawn from the back fat of the buffalo or its core body fats. In the early periods of the fur trade, trade pemmican could be made of 1/5 marrow; 4/5 hard fats. The more typical, however, was back fat only, so "others melting or Boiling back (Buffaloe) fat to put in the Pimican, all the women at work sewing Bags to put the Pimican into" (March 3, 1801 Archibald N. McLeod Diary, Fort Alexandria, Gates, ed., *Five Fur Traders of the Northwest*, 161). David Thompson later claimed pemmican fats used at Cumberland House were half-hard, half-soft, but, the "hard" in his case were derived from the hard interior fats balanced with only the softer subcutaneous back fats; there was likely no marrow fat in this concoction (Tyrell, ed., *David Thompson's Narrative of His Explorations in Western America, 1784–1812*, 434). With time, companies often switched simply to tallow for trade pemmican, as suggested by descriptions by the 1840s and 1850s. This likely coincided with the heavier hunt of summer weight bulls, which were rich in tallow fat.

The use of harder fats for trade pemmican increased its storage life and using *dépouille* rather than marrow fats balanced out the waxy quality of interior fats. The practice of using *dépouille* as a softer fat made pemmican tastier, as Alexander Macdonnel suggested at Qu'Appelle in February 1816: his post had traded "two thousand odd depoules, which will make our teaureaux of a most excellent quality." (LAC. Letter to NWC Agents, March 13, 1816, *Selkirk Papers, Series A*, 9066).

Seed or "loaf" Pemmican – Was made with berries or other additives. "...on their way back they found John Scart collecting some herbs to boil with Pemmican...." (LAC. May 25, 1815, Winnipeg Journals, B.235/a/3). In the later pioneer period, *Loaf* pemmican was favored by new settlers who sometimes used berries, flour, salt, and even sugar as a means of making it more palatable. There is some indication that *Bread* pemmican corresponded to regular pemmican; *Flavored, Holiday*, and *Cake* pemmican corresponded to *Loaf*. (CP. Vilhjalmur Stefansson letter, February 25, 1944, to John C. West, Bison File 1.2/49). Hewgill "rejoiced" in these pioneer alterations including "curried pemmican," "rushou pemmican stewed in onion," and pemmican shredded "very fine, mixed with flour, baking powder, pepper and salt and then making bannocks of it. These could always be warmed up by placing them in front of the fire when you arrived in camp." (L. F. Hewgill, "Making Pemmican," *In the Days of Pioneering*, March 1, 1894, Centre du Patrimoine, St. Boniface.) *Pioneer loaf pemmican* was usually made in ten to twenty pound sacks for easier use, "shaped in rolls so when the pemmican was cut the slices were round," (Whyte Museum Archives (hereafter WMA). Eleanor Luxton, unpublished manuscript, "Latch String Out,"ca. 1955, Lux/II, 123–124).

Winter Pemmican – Made of bags of half-dried meat often with fat only coarsely mixed within it or not included at all. Given the difficulty of fully drying meats in some winter conditions, grease was carried separately and added later. When it was mixed with fat, winter pemmican, by necessity, had a very short storage life. W. F. Wentzel by 1807 described Beaver [Indians] producing "Taureau or Piimecan" which was "tolerably good when mixed up with grease." (W. F. Wentzel to Roderic McKenzie, March 27, 1807, in Masson, *Les Bourgeois du Nord-Ouest*, 90; and personal communication with Stephen Greyeyes, September 2011.) A lot of winter pemmican, for that reason, was likely manufactured only for the spring and early summer, not long-term use (Vilhjalmur Stefansson, *The Fat of the Land*, 1957), 193–194).

Fish Pemmican – John Cameron in 1826 described Ojibwa making sturgeon pemmican: "They cut up [sturgeon flesh] in flakes and dry over a low fire, after which they pound the dried flakes between stones until it becomes like a kind of sponge; this with the oil they gather; affords them a rich and substantial food of which they are very fond." (Quoted in Victor Lytwyn *Muskekowuck Athinuwick*. University of Manitoba Press, 2002, 234.) Salmon pemmican was terrifically popular in the plains trade, and the product made specifically at the Dalles on the Columbia, considered a delicacy (Theodore Stern, *Chiefs and Traders: Indian Relations at Fort Nez Perces* (1993, 18–33).

Wasna – A type of pemmican favored among the Dakota as "a sort of pemmican or mincemeat" made with heavy proportions of dried wild cherries or chokecherries(*Prunus virginiana L.*). *Wasna* of this type was a favorite dish especially along the Missouri. See Thomas W. Haberman, "Floral analysis of an historic pemmican sample," *Newsletter of the South Dakota Archaeological Society* 9(3), 1979, 9–11. The word, too, was Siouan for *grease*, Wasna, and signified pemmican among Siouan groups.

Yokeg*, or *Nokeg*, or *Hoke, – A Northeastern Algonquian traveling cake used similarly as pemmican for travel food but made from large kernel corn, dried, and pounded into powder. This "journey cake" became known in English as "Johnny cake." It was mixed with water before being eaten. (Reginald and Gladys Laubin, *The Indian Tipi*. Norman: University of Oklahoma Press, 1989. 157.)

Piece Meat – "Piece" was usually 90 lbs. in weight. A "piece of dried meat" was a common exchange commodity; when referred to by traders "piece meat" was fresh and usually stored on ice or in frosty winter sheds. Robert Goodwin, at Brandon House, "the pieces of meat I cannot weigh yet owing to ye snow laying upon it" (HBCA, B.22/a/6, March 4, 1799).

Piled Meat – Referred to by Charles Chaboillez, 1797, 281: "The Former made a Present of Twenty Pieces Dryed Meat Six Bladders Grease, Six Fans Pilld Meat...." (Hickerson, "The Journal of Charles Jean Baptiste Chaboillez, 1797–98," in Harold Hickerson, *Ethnohistory* 1959, 307, footnote 70), suggests piled meat could have been dried meat of the buffalo rolled into balls, without tallow. However, in this case, Chaboillez was more likely referring to "half beat" meat not fully dried and used as a winter staple.

Pounded, or Powdered Meat – Beat meat further dried and pounded into a fine, powder state, often to be carried in bags. Fat was often poured into pounded meat to create pemmican. "Pounded meat" appearing in the record was often in fact dried meat pounded into shreds with a wooden maul, stored in bags and "suspended within the tepee or warehouse." (Stefansson, *Not by Bread Alone*. Macmillan, 1946, 186).

Quart de Lodge – At Fort Vermillion, Henry said the *Quart* was twenty animals, including the twenty hides needed to make pemmican bags. "This [is] called making their *Quart de Lodge*, and each man is obliged to put twenty Animals upon the stage. And haul the same number in to the Fort.... Each man must also raise Buffalo hides sufficient to make 20 Pemmican Bags, for which purpose their woman generally go with them to make their *Quart de Lodge* where they also have the advantage of getting the Tallow and other offals of the Buffalo..." (*Journal of Alexander Henry the Younger*, II, 418). The completion of each hunter's *quart* usually followed with a dance at the post to celebrate. Given that the fort's hunters were lodged four families per cabin, the total per lodge by the end of the season was eighty bags. At Fort Vermillion that equated 560 bags.

Rubaboo – Usually denoted pemmican fried with flour (see A. F. Chamberlain, "The Life and Growth of Words in the French Dialect of Canada," *Modern Language Notes*, **9**(3), March 1894, 139–140).

Ruchagan – Pemmican cut into chunks and added to grease to increase its palatability and, likely, its total caloric energy value; alternatively, dried buffalo meat mixed with fat. So, "Indians are all Employed in drying of Meat and Making Ruhigan…" (Anthony Henday, May 1755 B.239/a/40, in Barbara Belyea, ed., *A Year Inland*, 180). The Ojibwa were eating unheated "Ruchagan" in the 1780s: "They [Ojibwa] are in such a hurry to return home" that they had a little fat "which they mix with Ruahaggan and eat while they paddle" (HBCA. John Sutherland's Journal, June 16, 1785, Gloucester House Journals, B.78/a/15). In the fur trade era, pemmican was often fried in grease, considered a delectable alternative than eating it hard. In the pioneer period, ruchagan could constitute a heavy soup in which pemmican was boiled with potatoes and onions. (*Manitoba Pageant* "the Buffalo" by Harwell Bowsfield, Spring 1965, 23). Since beat meat was often carried separate and mixed with fat while traveling, traders sometimes called beat meat "ruahigan" (as did Brandon House Journals, February 1, 1797, listing "2000 lb Beat Meat or Ruahigan" in one of its trades with Ojibwa, HBCA, B.22/a/4).

Salt Meats and Tongues – Solar salt derived from natural alkali sources in the west was used for pickling and preserving meats. Salt meats were commonly made at posts as an alternative to dried meats: "Employed in salting Tongues, little Bosses & tripes" (LAC. Miles Macdonnel's Journal, April 2, 1813, *Selkirk Papers*, Series A, 16842). These were generally stored in 100-lb. kegs of "salted meat." The salting process was really a pickling: "Employed the Piper to provide stuff for making large tubs for salting meat." (LAC. Miles Macdonnel's Journal, February 9, 1814, *Selkirk Papers*, Series A, 16881). Salting preserved the best traded meat. When traveling to winter camps, traders directed representatives to "load their sleighs with the best, as we want it to salt for headquarters [York Factory]." They returned, indeed, with 100 tongues, "some boss and other meats." (HBCA. Fort Edmonton Journals, February 8, 1829, B.60/a/26). The same went to a Blackfoot pound: "our men are desired to bring the best of the buffalo meat as we require some to salt for Y[ork] F[actory]." (HBCA. Fort Edmonton Journals, February 26, 1829, B.60/a/26). Archibald McLeod put tongues in salt ten days, then hung them to dry (Archibald N McLeod's Journal, March 3, 1801, Gates, ed., *Five Fur Traders of the Northwest*, 178). Salt was critical for preserving bison tongues for market after the HBC began enlarging sales in London after 1821. Tongues were pickled in barrels and shipped by the hundred. Like cod fish, they needed desalination before preparation: "before boiling they [the bison tongues] should be soaked for 20 to 30 hours in cold water" (William Smith letter to Wm. Day & Co., London, November 4, 1822, *Minutes of Council: Northern Department of Rupert Land*, 20). The Northern Council ordered fifteen kegs of salt from Norway House and five from Cumberland House that year to be furnished to Colin Robertson at Edmonton House, "*for Tongues*" (Footnote 1, *Minutes of Council: Northern Department of Rupert Land*, 20).

Sans Dessein – Without interest, in Native trade traditions usually of consumable products given as a gift with an expected return in the future. Food gifts were given with an expectation of reciprocation, and reaffirmed or created fictive kin relations.

Sinew – The threadlike tendon usually taken from each side of the back of the animal from the shoulder to the thigh, dried with all meat removed. "It's very fine for making thread for sewing, even used for violin strings. It's so strong you can strip it as fine as you like or make the strings as coarse as you like." (Marie Rose Smith, "Eighty Years on the Plains," *Canadian Cattlemen* 21(1):31, June 1949, 4.)

Starvation – Discourse of starvation that elicited food as gifts from traders. Though there were certainly cases of actual starvation, Native people also employed a discourse of starvation to gain better terms on trade or gifts of food. (Mary Black-Rogers, 1986. "Varieties of 'Starving': Semantics and Survival in the Subarctic Fur Trade, 1750–1850." *Ethnohistory* 33:4.) The strategic claim to starvation affected not only the food trade, but also other trades, especially furs and skins. It was one of the opening, important, bids in relationships of reciprocity. The term "Bungee" or "Pungee" used by HBC traders to describe Ojibwa comes from the Ojibwa term "give us a little," used frequently in first encounters (see Lytwyn, *Muskekowuck Athinuwick* 45).

Tallow – Any of the fats derived from the axial portions of the animal, including the organ (sometimes referred to as "kidney") fat, those very hard and lining the intestines and stomachs, and the flaky portions that came out of the very marbled muscle. Some of the subcutaneous fats could also constitute the hard fat, collected in bags and traded. These were later cut down by traders and rendered.

In summer, tallow was collected often from bulls taking the interior core (leaf) fats around the organs, and especially the kidneys. In fall, tallow was created from often cows' back fats which, still axial in relation to the core of the animal, were largely saturated. The large bull shot in 1806 Henry believed "would have produced near one hundred weight of tallow from his inside only." (*Journal of Alexander Henry the Younger*, I, 210). Tallow could also be reduced from back fat, losing about ¼ of its weight in the rendering. Tallow fats became more unsaturated as an animal aged and lost their stability, attaining a greasier, less palatable, and lower value in trade. "Now I have found out about these matters myself. I had first to learn the difference between tallow fat or suet and market fat or lard, between tender meat and hard meat, packed in bladders in which Indians bring it to us, and whether the dried strips of flesh were cut from a cow or an ox." (*Journal of Rudolph Friederich Kurz*, J. N. B. Hewitt, ed., Bureau of American Ethnology Bulletin 115. Washington, DC: Smithsonian Institution, 1937, 240–241.) Tallow, more carefully rendered and barrelled became a part of the summer bison hunt, with exports to the London market as part of the HBC's annual returns. Bison tallow made for excellent candles. In the 1870s on the North Saskatchewan, "Several pieces of cotton wick were suspended in a row from a slender stick. This wick came in balls seven to fifteen pence in price from England and were brought out by the Hudson's Bay Company. The [bison] tallow had to be rendered and well strained to make certain that it was clean." Dipped in the hot tallow, the wicks were suspended in a wooden frame. Annie McDougall, wife of trader David McDougall, missed the hard fat of bison for candle making after the herds disappeared, when pioneers had to switch to quicker-burning cattle tallow candles, called *bitches*. (Eleanor Luxton, unpublished manuscript, Latch String Out, ca. 1955, Whyte Museum Archives, Lux/II, 130–131.

Taureau – A bull hide prepared as a skin (*en parchemni*, as was often said) by being stretched between usually hickory pegs, its interior scraped with a sharp bone or metal tool, and then allowed to dry. Its hair was mostly removed by a heavy comb. The parchment was usually cut in half and sewn with sinew to make a bag, usually holding about 90 lbs. of pemmican. The term was used interchangeably with *parflêche*, often designated a bag of pemmican: Alexander Henry the Younger: 1806 "Four Torreaux per Canoe and one for passengers" (Vol. I, 184). The taureau was described in shape by David Thompson: "closely packed in a bag of about thirty inches in length, by near twenty inches in breadth, and about four inches in thickness which makes them flat, the best shape for stowage and carriage" (David Thompson *Narrative*, Champlain Society, 1917, 434). It was likened to a pillow in size and shape: "ils mettent dans des sacs de peau de la forme et un peu plus grand qu'une taie d'oreillers" (CP. Lafleche a Thomas Caron 1 juin 1845 Arch. Dioc. De S.-B, 0917). Taureaux could also be called "parchments" given that they were made from a leather: "the men attending Indians of yesterday. Brot parchment leather for Pimtcon…" (HBCA. Robert Goodwin, in *Brandon House Journals*, February 17, 1795, B.22/a/2.) In the pioneer era, some hides were scraped clean and dried as robes, others were left untanned for buckskin thongs, bindings for carts or halters for the horses. Poor skins were cleaned and left as mats on which pemmican was mixed. Taureau bags, meanwhile, were "filled and sewn up two little ears were left on the sides, to toss the sacks up into the carts more easily." (Eleanor Luxton, unpublished manuscript, "Latch String Out," ca. 1955, Whyte Museum Archives, Lux/II, 123.)

Vache Grass[e] – Fat cow beef. "This was a glorious sight for my people who had been anxiously expecting to feast on Vache Grass, for some days past" (*Journal of Alexander Henry the Younger*, I, 31.)

BIBLIOGRAPHY

Archives

Alberta Provincial Archives, Edmonton, Alberta
American Fur Company Papers, Missouri Historical Society, Microfilm collection
Archives, Centre du Patrimoine, St. Boniface, Winnipeg, Manitoba
Glenbow Archives, Calgary, Alberta
Library and Archives Canada, Ottawa, Ontario
Hudson's Bay Company Archives, Winnipeg, Manitoba
Manitoba Provincial Archives, Winnipeg, Manitoba
McCord Archives, McCord Museum, Montreal, Quebec
McGill Rare Books Library, Montreal, Quebec
Montana State Historical Archives, Helena, Montana

Published Primary Sources

"A Visit to Red River and the Saskatchewan, 1861, by Dr. John Rae," in Irene Spry, ed., *The Geographical Journal* 140(1):1–17, February 1974.
"Letter de M. Belcourt," November 25, 1845," in *Letter from the Secretary of War Transmitting Report of Major Wood*, Ex. Doc. No. 51. 1st. Sess., 31st Cong. Washington, DC: 1850, 47–48.
"Letter from the Secretary of War, Report of Major Wood, Relative to His Expedition to Pembina Settlement," March 19, 1850, 1st Sess., 31st Cong. House of Representatives, Ex. Doc. No. 51.
"Select Committee on Natural Food Products of the North-West Territories," 1887, Appendix 1. *Journals of the Senate of Canada* Session 1887, 21, Ottawa: Maclean, Roger and Co., 1887.
"The Fort Benton Journal, 1854," and "The Fort Sarpy Journal, 1855–1856," in *Contributions to the Historical of Montana*, Vol. 10, 1940. Boston: J. S. Canner and Company, 1966.
"The Journal of Charles Jean Baptiste Chaboillez, 1797–98," in Harold Hickerson, ed., *Ethnohistory* 1959:265–316.
Allan, Joel Asaph. *A History of the American Bison*. Washington, DC: Government Printing Office, 1877.

Anonymous, "Robert Kennicott," *Transactions of the Chicago Academy of Sciences*, 1:133–226, 1867.
Atwood, Mae, ed. *In Rupert's Land: Memoirs of Walter Traill.* Toronto: McClelland and Stewart, 1970.
Bumsted, J. M., ed. *Reporting the Resistance: Alexander Begg and Joseph Hargrave on the Red River Resistance.* Winnipeg: University of Manitoba Press, 2003.
Caitlin, George. *Letters and Notes on the North American Indians*, Michael Moody, ed. New York: Clarkson N. Potter, 1975.
Coues, Elliott, ed. *The Personal Narrative of Charles Larpenteur, 1833–1872*, Part I. Minneapolis: Ross & Haines, 1962.
Cowie, Isaac. *Company of Adventurers: A Narrative of Seven Years in the Service of the Hudson's Bay Company during 1867–1874.* Toronto: Wiliam Briggs, 1913.
Davies, K. G., ed. *Peter Skene Ogden's Snake Country Journal 1826–27.* London: The Hudson's Bay Record Society, 1961.
Dempsey, Hugh A., ed. *The Rundle Journals, 1840–1848.* Calgary: Historical Society of Alberta, 1977.
Dempsey, Hugh A., ed. *Heaven Is Near the Rocky Mountains: The Journals and Letters of Thomas Woolsey.* Calgary: Glenbow Museum, 1989.
Denig, Edwin Thompson. *Five Indian Tribes of the Upper Missouri.* John C. Ewers, ed. Norman: University of Oklahoma Press, 1961.
   The Assiniboine. J. N. B. Hewitt, ed. Bureau of American Ethnology No. 46. Washington, DC: Smithsonian Institution, Canadian Plains Research Center, 2000.
Erasmus, Peter. *Buffalo Days and Nights.* Calgary: Glenbow-Alberta Institute, 1976.
Fitzgerald, James Edward. *An Examination of the Charter and Proceedings of the Hudson's Bay Company, with Reference to the Grant of Vancouver Island.* London: Trelawney, 1849.
Fleming, R. Harvey, ed. *The Minutes of Council: Northern Department of Rupert Land.* Toronto: The Champlain Society, 1940.
Gates, Charles M., ed. *Five Fur Traders of the Northwest.* St. Paul: University of Minnesota Press, 1933.
Gough, Barry M., ed. *The Journal of Alexander Henry the Younger, 1799–1814*, Vols. 1 and 2. Toronto: The Champlain Society, 1988.
Gunn, Donald. *History of Manitoba: From Its Earliest Settlement to 1835.* Ottawa: Maclean, Roper and Co., 1880.
Hargrave, Joseph James. *Red River.* Alton: Friesen, 1977 [1871].
   Red River Settlement. Montreal: John Lovell, 1871.
Harmon's Journal 1800–1819, new edition with Foreword by Jennifer S. H. Brown. Surrey: Touchwood Editions, 2006.
Henry, Alexander (the Elder). *Travels and Adventures: In Canada and the Indian Territories.* Edmonton: M. G. Hurtig Ltd., 1969.
Hewitt, J. N. B., ed. *Journal of Rudolph Friederich Kurz.* Bureau of American Ethnology Bulletin 115. Washington, DC: Smithsonian Institution, 1937.
Hind, Henry Youle. *Narrative of the Canadian Red River Exploring Expedition of 1857, and of the Assiniboine and Saskatchewan Exploring Expedition of 1858*, Vols. I and II. London: Longman, Green, 1860.

Hornaday, William Temple. *The Extermination of the American Bison* [1889]. Washington, DC: Smithsonian Institution, 2002.
James, Edward, ed. *A Narrative of the Captivity and Adventures of John Tanner (US Interpreter at the Saut de Ste. Marie): During Thirty Years among the Indians in the Interior of North America.* New York: G.&C.&H. Carvill, 1830 [1956].
Johnson, Alice M., ed. *Saskatchewan Journals and Correspondence: Edmonton House 1795-1800; Chesterfield House, 1800-1802.* London: The Hudson's Bay Record Society, 1967.
Kerr, John Andrew. "Hunting Bison on the Plains." *Winnipeg Tribune Magazine* Saturday, June 23, 1934, 3-4.
Lamb, W. Kaye, ed. *Voyages from Montreal*, in *The Journals and Letters of Sir Alexander Mackenzie.* Cambridge: Cambridge University Press, 1970.
Maximilian, Prince of Wied. *Travels in the Interior of North America, 1833-34*, in Reuben Gold Thwaites, ed., *Early Western Travels, 1746-1846.* New York: AMS Press, 1966.
McDermott, John Francis, ed., trans. Albert J. Salvan. *Tixier's Travels on the Osage Prairies.* Norman: University of Oklahoma Press, 1940, 2007.
McKenzie, Roderic. "Réminiscences," in L. R. Masson, *Les bourgeois de la Compagnie du Nord-Ouest*, Vol. I. New York : Antiquarian Press, 1960.
Morton, Arthur S., ed. *The Journal of Duncan M'Gillivray of the North West Company at Fort George on the Saskatchewan, 1794-5.* Toronto: Macmillan, 1929.
Munro, K. Douglas, ed. *Fur Trade Letters of Willie Traill, 1864-1893.* Edmonton: University of Alberta Press, 2006.
Palliser, John. *Solitary Rambles and Adventures of a Hunter in the Prairies.* Edmonton: M. G. Hurtig, 1969.
Report of the Proceedings Connected with the Disputes between the Earl of Selkirk and the North-West Company at the Assizes, Held at York in Upper Canada, October, 1818. Montreal: James Lane & Nahum Mower, 1819.
Rice, Henry M. (reprinted). "Pemmican." *The Minnesota Archaeologist* 40(2):96, 1981.
Rich, E. E., ed. *Colin Robertson's Correspondence Book, September 1817 to September 1822.* Toronto: Champlain Society, 1939.
Rich, E. E. *Cumberland House Journals and Inland Journal 1775-1782*, Vols. I and II. London: Hudson's Bay Record Society, 1951.
Robinson, H. M. *The Great Fur Land: Or Sketches of Life in the Hudson's Bay Territory* [1879]. Toronto: Coles, 1972.
Ross, Alexander. *The Red River Settlement: Its Rise, Progress, and Present State.* London: Smith, Elder & Co., 1856.
Ross, Helen E., ed. *Letters from Rupert's Land, 1826-1840: James Hargrave of the Hudson's Bay Company.* Montreal and Kingston: McGill-Queen's University Press, 2009.
Russell, Osborne, *Journal of a Trapper: Or Nine Years Residence among the Rocky Mountains Between the Years of 1834 and 1843.* L. A. York, ed. Boise, ID: Syms-York, 1914.
Smith G. Hubert, and Wood, W. Raymond, eds. *The Explorations of the La Vérendryes in the Northern Plains, 1738-43.* Norman: University of Nebraska Press, 1980.

Tyrell, J. B., ed. *Journals of Samuel Hearne and Philip Turnor between the Years 1774 and 1792*. Toronto: Champlain Society, 1934.
Umfreville, Edward, *The Present State of Hudson's Bay*. London: Charles Stalker, 1790.
Wallace, W. Stewart, ed. *Documents Relating to the North West Company*. Toronto: Champlain Society, 1934.
Weekes, Mary. *The Last Buffalo Hunter*. Toronto: Macmillan, 1945.

Secondary Articles, Books, and Theses

Abel, Kerry, and Jean Friesen, eds. *Aboriginal Resource Use in Canada: Historical and Legal Aspects*. Winnipeg: University of Manitoba Press, 1991.
Albers, Patricia C. "Changing Patterns of Ethnicity in the Northeastern Plains 1780–1870," in Jonathan D. Hill, ed., *History, Power, and Identity: Ethnogenesis in the Americas, 1492–1992*, 1–110. Iowa City: University of Iowa Press, 1996.
Allen, C., and Ian Keay, "Bowhead Whales in the Eastern Arctic, 1611–1911: Population Reconstruction with Historical Whaling Records." *Environment and History*, 12:89–113, 2006.
Alvard, Michael. "Good Hunters Keep Smaller Shares of Larger Pies." *Behavioral & Brain Sciences*, 27(4):560–561, August 2004.
Anderson, Fred, *Crucible of War: The Seven Years' War and the Fate of Empire in British North America 1754–1766*. New York: Vintage Books, 2001.
Arthur, George W. "An Introduction to the Ecology of Early Historic Communal Bison Hunting Among the Northern Plains Indians." Archaeological Survey of Canada Paper No. 37. Ottawa: National Museums of Canada, 1975.
Ball, Timothy. "Climatic Change, Droughts and the Social Impact: Central Canada, 1811–20, a Classic Example;" and "The Year without Summer: Its Impact on the Fur Trade and History of Western Canada," in C. R. Harington, ed., *The Year without Summer: World Climate in 1816*. Ottawa: Canadian Museum of Nature, 1992.
Barbour, Nicolas. *Fort Union and the Upper Missouri Fur Trade*. Norman: University of Oklahoma Press, 2002.
Barsh, Russell Lawrence, and Chantelle Marlor, "Driving Bison and Blackfoot Science." *Human Ecology*, 31(4):571–593, December 2003.
Belich, James. *Replenishing the Earth: The Settler Revolution and the Rise of the Anglo-World, 1783–1939*. Oxford: Oxford University Press, 2009.
Bellyea, Barbara. *Dark Storm Moving West*. Calgary: University of Calgary Press, 2007.
Binford, Lewis R. *Nunamiut Ethnoarchaeology*. New York: Academic Press, 1978.
Binford, Lewis R., and Jack B. Bertram. "Bone Frequencies – And Attritional Processes," in Lewis R. Binford, ed. *For Theory Building in Archaeology: Essays on Faunal Remains, Aquatic Resources, Spatial Analysis, and Systematic Modeling*, pp. 77–153. New York: Academic Press, 1977.
Binnema, Theodore. "Old Swan, Big Man, and the Siksika Bands, 1794–1815." *Canadian Historical Review*, 77(1):1–32, March 1996.
   Common and Contested Ground: A Human and Environmental History of the Northwestern Plains. Norman: University of Oklahoma Press, 2001.
Blanchard, Jim. *Winnipeg, 1912*. Winnipeg: University of Manitoba Press, 2005.

Bleakney, J. Sherman. *Sods, Soil, and Spades: The Acadians at Grand Pré and Their Dykeland Legacy*. Montreal: McGill-Queen's University Press, 2004.

Bliege Bird, Rebecca L., and Bird, Douglas W. "Delayed Reciprocity and Tolerated Theft: The Behavioral Ecology of Food Sharing Strategies." *Current Anthropology*, 38:297–321, 1997.

Blurton Jones, N. G. "A Selfish Origin for Human Food Sharing: Tolerated Theft." *Ethology and Sociobiology*, 5(1):1–3, 1984.

Brink, J. W. "Fat Content in Leg Bones of *Bison bison*, and Applications to Archaeology." *Journals of Archaeological Science*, 24:259–274, 1997.

Brooks, James F. *Captives and Cousins: Slavery, Kinship, and Community in the Southwest Borderlands*. Chapel Hill: University of North Carolina Press, 2002.

Brown, Jennifer. *Strangers in Blood: Fur Trade Company Families in Indian Country*. Vancouver: UBC Press, 1980.

Brown, Jennifer. "Fur Trade as Centrifuge: Familial Dispersal and Offspring Identity in Two Company Contexts," in Raymond J. Demallie and Alfonso Ortiz, eds., *North American Anthropology: Essays on Society and Culture*, 119–217. Norman: University of Oklahoma Press, 1994.

"Partial Truths: A Closer Look at Fur Trade Marriage," in Theodore Binnema, Gerhard J. Ens, and R. C. Macleod, eds., *From Rupert's Land to Canada: Essays in Honour of John E. Foster*, 59–80. Edmonton: University of Alberta Press, 2001.

Brown, Stanley P., Wayne C. Miller, and Jane M. Eason. *Exercise Physiology: Basis of Human Movement in Health and Disease*. Baltimore: Lippincott Williams & Wilkins, 2006.

Bruce, E. L. "The Canadian Shield and Its Geographic Effects." *Geographic Journal*, 16:230–239, 1939.

Bryce, George. *The Remarkable History of the Hudson's Bay Company*. London: Samson Low Marston, 1910.

Bumsted, J. M. *Fur Trade Wars: The Founding of Western Canada*. Winnipeg: Great Plains Publications, 1999.

Bunn, Henry T. "Hunting, Power Scavenging, and Butchering by (Hadza) Foragers and by Plio-Pleistocene *Homo*, in Craig B. Stanford and Henry T. Bunn, eds. *Meat-Eating and Human Evolution*, 199–218. Oxford: Oxford University Press, 2001.

Burnett, John. *Plenty and Want: A Social History of Diet in England from 1815 to the Present Day*. London: Thomas Nelson, 1966.

Campbell, Marjorie Wilkins. *The North West Company*. Toronto: Macmillan, 1957.

Carlos, Ann M., and Frank D. Lewis. *Commerce by a Frozen Sea: Native Americans and the European Fur Trade*. Philadelphia: University of Pennsylvania Press, 2010.

Carter, Sarah, Walter Hildebrand, and Dorothy First Rider. *The True Spirit and Original Intent of Treaty 7*. Montreal: McGill-Queen's University Press, 1996.

Clark, Nancy, Cato Coleman, Kerri Figure, Tom Mailhot, and John Zeigler. "Food for Trans-Atlantic Rowers: A Menu Planning Model and Case Study." *International Journal of Sport Nutrition and Exercise Metabolism*, 13:227–242, 2003.

Clarke, John. *The Ordinary People of Essex: Environment, Culture, and Economy on the Frontier of Upper Canada*. Montreal and Kingston: McGill-Queen's University Press, 2010.

Clarke, Margaret L., "Reconstituting the Fur Trade Community of the Assiniboine Basin, 1793–1812." MA thesis, University of Winnipeg, 1997.

Clow, Richmond, "Bison Ecology, Brulé and Yankton Winter Hunting, and the Starving Winter of 1832–33." *Great Plains Quarterly*, 15:259–270, Fall 1995.

Collins, E. J. T. "Dietary Change and Cereal Consumption in Britain in the Nineteenth Century." *Agricultural History Review*, 23(2):97–115, 1975.

Colpitts, George. *Game in the Garden: A Human History of Wildlife in Western Canada to 1940*. Vancouver: UBC Press, 2001.

"Moose-Nose and Buffalo Hump: The Amerindian-European Foo Exchange in the British North American Fur Trade to 1840," in Diane Kirkby and Tanja Luckins, eds., *Dining on Turtles: Food Feasts and Drinking in History*, 64–81. Basingstoke, UK: Palgrave Macmillan, 2007.

"'Victuals to Put into our Mouths': Environmental Perspectives on Fur Trade Provisioning Activities at Cumberland House, 1775–1782," in Gregory P. Marchildon, ed. *The Early Northwest*, 125–146. Regina: Canadian plains Research Center, 2008.

"The Methodists' Great 1869 Camp Meeting and Aboriginal Conservation Strategies in the North Saskatchewan River Valley." *Great Plains Quarterly*, 29(1): 3–28, Winter 2009.

Conaty, Gerald T. "Economic Models and Blackfoot Ideology." *American Ethnologist*, 22(2): 403–412, May 1995.

Corbin, Annalies, and Bradley A. Rodgers. *The Steamboat Montana and the Opening of the West: History, Excavation and Architecture*. Gainesville: University Press of Florida, 2008.

Cronan, William. *Nature's Metropolis: Chicago and the Great West*. New York: W. W. Norton, 1992.

Crowther, Gillian. *Eating Culture: An Anthropological Guide to Food*. Toronto: University of Toronto Press, 2013.

Danz, Harold P. *Of Bison and Man*. Niwot: University Press of Colorado, 1997.

Dary, David. *Frontier Medicine: From the Atlantic to the Pacific, 1492–1941*. New York: Alfred A. Knopf, 2008.

Daschuk, James. "A Dry Oasis: The Canadian Plains in Late Prehistory." *Prairie Forum*, 34(1):1–29, 2009.

Daschuk, James, and Greg Marchildon. IACC Project Working Paper No. 7 Climate and Aboriginal Adaptation in the South Saskatchewan River Basin, A.D. 800–1700, April 15, 2005.

Daschuk, James. *Clearing the Plains: Disease, Politics of Starvation, and the Loss of Aboriginal Life*. Regina: University of Regina Press, 2013.

de Moor, Tine. "Avoiding Tragedies: A Flemish Common and Its Commoners under the Pressure of Social and Economic Change during the Eighteenth Century." *Economic History Review*, 62:1–22, 2009.

Dempsey, Hugh A. *The Amazing Death of Calf Shirt and other Blackfoot Stories, Three Hundred Years of Blackfoot History*. Saskatoon: Fifth House, 1994.

Maskepetoon: Leader, Warrior, Peacemaker. Victoria: Heritage, 2010.

Denevan, William M. "The Pristine Myth: The Landscape of the Americas in 1492." *Annals of the Association of American Geographers*, 82(3):369–85, 1992.
Devine, Heather. *The People Who Own Themselves: Aboriginal Ethnogenesis in a Canadian Family, 1660–1900*. Calgary: University of Calgary Press, 2004.
— "Oeconomy must now be the order of the day." George Simpson and the Reorganization of the Fur Trade to 1826," in Michael Payne, Donald Wetherell, and Catherine Cavanaugh, eds. *Alberta Formed: Alberta Transformed*, Vol. I, 161–178. Edmonton: University of Alberta Press, 2006.
Dick, Lyle. "The Seven Oaks Incident and the Construction of a Historical Tradition, 1816 to 1970." *Journal of the Canadian Historical Association*, 2(1):91–113, 1991.
Dobak, William A. "Killing the Canadian Buffalo, 1821–1881." *Western Historical Quarterly*, 27:39–48, Spring 1996.
Dorsey, George A. and Alfred L. Kroeber, *Traditions of the Arapaho*. 45–47. Lincoln: University of Nebraska Press, 1997.
Driver, Jonathan C. "Meat in Due Season: the timing of Communal Hunts," in Leslie B. Davis and Brian O. K. Reeves, eds. *Hunters of the Recent Past*, 11–33. London: Unwin Hyman, 1990.
Drouard, Alain, "Reforming Diet at the End of the Nineteenth Century in Europe," in Peter Lumnel Atkins and Derek J. Peter Oddy, eds. *Food and the City in Europe Since 1800*, Abingdon: Ashgate, 2008.
Ehrlich, Clara, "Tribal Culture in Crow Mythology." *The Journal of American Folklore*, 50(198) 307–408, October–December 1937.
Emerson, Alice Marie. "Archaeological Implications of Variability in the Economic Anatomy of *Bison bison*." PhD thesis, Washington State University, 1990.
Ens, Gerhard J. "Prologue to the Red River Resistance: Pre-Liminal Politics and the Triumph of Riel." *Journal of the Canadian Historical Association*, 5:111–123, 1994.
— "Fatal Quarrels and Fur Trade Rivalries: A Year of Living Dangerously on the North Saskatchewan, 1806–07," in Michael Payne, Donald Wetherell, and Catherine Cavanaugh, eds., *Alberta Formed: Alberta Transformed*, Vol. I, 133–159. Edmonton: University of Alberta Press, 2005.
— "The Border, The Buffalo, and the Métis of Montana," in Sterling Evans, ed., *The Borderlands of the American and Canadian Wests: Essays on Regional History of the Forty-ninth Parallel*, 139–154. Lincoln: University of Nebraska Press, 2006.
— "The Battle of Seven Oaks and the Articulation of a Metis National Tradition, 1811–1849," in Nicole St.-Onge, Carolyn Podruchny, and Brenda Macdougall, eds., *Counters of a People: Metis Family, Mobility, and History*, 93–119. Norman: University of Oklahoma Press, 2012.
— "Métis Ethnicity, Personal Identity and the Development of Capitalism in the Western Interior: The Case of Johnny Grant," in, Theodore Binnema, Gerhard J. Ens, and R. C. Macleod, eds., *From Rupert's Land to Canada: Essays in Honour of John E. Foster*, 169–171. Edmonton: University of Alberta Press, 2001.
— *Homeland to Hinterland: The Changing Worlds of the Red River Metis in the Nineteenth Century*. Toronto: University of Toronto Press, 1996.

Epp, Henry, and Ian Dyck. "Early Human-Bison Population Interdependence in the Plains Ecosystem." *Great Plains Research: A Journal of Natural and Social Sciences*, 325–326, 2002.

Faragher, John Mack. "The Custom of the Country: Cross-Cultural Marriage in the Far Western Fur Trade," in Lillian Schlissel, Vicki L. Ruiz and Janice Monk eds., *Western Women: Their Land, Their Lives*, 199–220. Albuquerque: University of New Mexico Press, 1988.

Farr, William. "'When we were first paid,': The Blackfoot Treaty, the Western Tribes, and the Creation of the Common Hunting Ground, 1855." *Great Plains Quarterly*, 21(2):131–154, Spring 2001.

Feeney, Robert E. *Polar Journeys: The Role of Food and Nutrition in Early Exploration*. Fairbanks: University of Alaska Press and American Chemical Society, 1997.

Ferguson, Theresa A. "Wood Bison and the Early Fur Trade," in Patricia A. McCormack, and R. Geoffrey Ironside, eds., *The Uncovered Past: Roots of Northern Alberta Societies*, 63–79. Circumpolar Research Series No. 3. Edmonton: Canadian Circumpolar Institute Press, 1993.

Fisher, Robin. *Contact and Conflict: Indian-European Relations in British Columbia, 1774–1890*. Vancouver: UBC Press 1992.

Flores, Dan. "Bison Ecology and Bison Diplomacy." *History* 78:465–485, September 1991.

— *The Natural West: Environmental History in the Great Plains and Rocky Mountains*. Norman: University of Oklahoma Press, 2003.

Forkey, Neil. *Shaping the Upper Canadian Frontier: Environment, Society and Culture in the Trent Valley*. Calgary: University of Calgary Press, 2003.

Foster, John E. "The Metis and the End of the Plains Buffalo in Alberta," in John E. Foster, Dick Harrison and I. S. MacLaren, eds. *Buffalo*, 61–78. Edmonton: University of Alberta Press, 1992.

— "Wintering, the Outsider Adult Male and the Ethnogenesis of the Western Plains Métis," in Patrick C. Douaud, ed., *The Western Métis: Profile of a People*, 91–103. Regina: Canadian Plains Research Centre, 2007 (1994).

Foster, Martha Harroun. *We Know Who We Are: Métis Identity in a Montana Community*. Norman: University of Oklahoma Press, 2006.

Fowler, William F. Jr. *Empire at War: The French and Indian War and the Struggle for North America 1754–1763*. New York: Walker and Company, 2005.

Friesen, Gerald. *The Canadian Prairies: A History*. Toronto: University of Toronto Press, 1987.

Gayton, Don. *The Wheatgrass Mechanism: Science and Imagination in the Western Canadian Landscape*. Saskatoon: Fifth House, 1990.

Giraud, Marcel. *The Metis in the Canadian West*, Vols. I and II. George Woodcock, trans. Edmonton: University of Alberta Press, 1986.

Gluek, Jr. Alvin C. "Industrial Experiments in the Wilderness: A Sidelight in the Business History of the Hudson's Bay Company." *The Business History Review*, 32:423–433, Winter 1958.

Göktepe, A. Salim. "Energy Systems in Sport," in Centre of Excellence Defence Against Terrorism, Ankara, ed., *Amputee Sports for Victims of Terrorism*, 24–

31. NATO Science for Peace and Security Series, Vol. 31, Amsterdam: IOS Press, 2007.
Goldring, Philip. "MacKintosh, William." in Vol. VII, *Dictionary of Canadian Biography*, 567–568. Toronto: University of Toronto Press, 1988.
Gordon, Bryan H. C. "Of Men and Herds in Canadian Plains Prehistory." Archaeological survey of Canada, Paper No. 84, National Museum of Man Mercury Series, Ottawa: National Museums of Canada, 1979.
Gough, Barry. *Gunboat Frontier: British Maritime Authority and Northwest Coast Indians, 1846–1890*. Vancouver: UBC Press, 1984.
Grigg, David, "The Nutritional Transition in Western Europe." *Journal of Historical Geography*, 21(3):247–261, 1995.
Grove, Richard H. *Green Imperialism: Colonial Expansion, Tropical Island Edens and the Origins of Environmentalism, 1600–1860*. Cambridge: Cambridge University Press, 1995.
Gurven, Michael. "The Evolution of Contingent Cooperation." *Current Anthropology*, 47(1):185–192, February 2006.
Haack, Steven C. "'This must have been a grand sight': George Bent and the Battle of Platte Bridge." *Great Plains Quarterly*, 30(1):3–20, Winter 2010.
Hackett, Paul, Weley Allen-Arave, Kim Hill, and Magdalena Hurtado, "'It's a Wonderful Life': Signaling Generosity among the Ache of Paraguay." *Evolution and Human Behavior*, 21:263–282, 2000.
Hackett, Paul. *A Very Remarkable Sickness: Epidemics in the Petit Nord 1670 to 1846*. Winnipeg: University of Manitoba Press, 2002.
"Historical Mourning Practices Observed among the Cree and Ojibwa Indians of the Central Subarctic." *Ethnohistory*, 52(3) Summer, 2005, 503–532.
Hämäläinen, Pekka. "The First Phase of Destruction: Killing the Southern Plains Buffalo, 1790–1840." *Great Plains Quarterly*, 21(2):101–104, Spring 2001.
"The Rise and Fall of Plains Indian Horse Cultures." *Journal of American History*, 90(3):833–862, December 2003.
The Commanche Empire. New Haven: Yale University Press, 2008.
Hames, Raymon. "Reciprocal Altruism in Yanömamo Food Exchange," in Lee Cronk, Napoleon Chagnon, and William Irons, eds., *Adaptation and Human Behavior: An Anthropological Perspective*, 397–416. New York: Aldine de Gruyter, 2000.
Hamilton, Henry E. *Incidents and Events in the Life of Gurdon Saltonstall Hubbard 1802–1886*. The Newberry Library, 1902 [Graff 1997].
Hammond, Lorne. "Marketing Wildlife: The Hudson's Bay Company and the Pacific Northwest, 1821–1849," in David Freeland Duke, ed., *Canadian Environmental History: Essential Readings*, 203–222. Toronto: Canadian Scholars' Press, 2006.
Hargreaves, Mark, and Lawrence Spriet, eds. *Exercise Metabolism*, 2nd ed. Champaign, IL: Human Kinetics, 2006.
Harris, R. Cole, ed. *Historical Atlas of Canada: From Beginning to 1800*, Vol. I. Toronto: University of Toronto Press, 1987.
Hawley, John A., and Will G. Hopkins. "Aerobic Glycolytic and Aerobic Lipolytic Power Systems." *Sports Medicine*, 19(4):240–250, 1995.

Helm, June. "'Always with them either a feast or a famine' Living off the Land with Chipewyan Indians, 1791–92." *Arctic Anthropology*, 30(2):46–60, 1993.
Henderson, James (Sa'ke'j) Youngblood. *The Mikmaw Concordat*. Halifax: Fernwood Publishing, 1997.
Indigenous Diplomacy and the Rights of Peoples: Achieving UN Recognition. Saskatoon: Purich, 2008.
Henning Bohn, and Robert T. Deacon. "Ownership Risk, Investment, and the Use of Natural Resources." *American Economic Review*, 90:526–549, June 2000.
Hildebrandt, Walter, and Brian Hubner. *The Cypress Hills: An Island by Itself*. Saskatoon: Purich, 2007.
Hindle, Gordon Bradley. *Provision for the Relief of the Poor in Manchester, 1754–1826*. Manchester: Oxford University Press, 1975.
Hogue, Michel. "Disputing the Medicine Line: The Plains Cree and the Canadian-American Border, 1876–85." *Montana the Magazine of Western History*, 52:2–17, Winter 2002.
"Between Race and Nation: The Creation of a Métis Borderland on the Northern Plains," in Benjamin H. Johnson and Andrew R. Graybill, eds., *Bridging National Borders in North America: Transnational and Comparative Histories*, 59–87. Durham, NC: Duke University Press, 2010.
Hurtado, Albert L. "When Strangers Met: Sex and Gender on Three Frontiers," *Frontiers: A Journal of Women Studies*, 17:52–75, 1996.
Intimate Frontiers: Sex, Gender and Culture in Old California. Albuquerque: University of New Mexico Press, 1999.
Iacovetta, Franca, Valerie J. Korinek, and Marlene Epp, eds. *Edible Histories, Cultural Politics: Towards a Canadian Food History*. Toronto: University of Toronto Press, 2012.
Innis, Harold A. "Peter Pond and the Influence of Capt. James Cook on Exploration in the Interior of North America." *Transactions of the Royal Society of Canada*, 3rd Ser. Section II 131–137, 1928.
Peter Pond: Fur Trade and Adventurer. Toronto: Irwin and Gordon, 1930.
The Fur Trade in Canada: An Introduction to Canadian Economic History, new edition. Toronto: University of Toronto Press, 1999.
Innis, Robert Alexander. *Elder Brother and the Law of the People: Contemporary Kinship and Cowesses First Nation*. Winnipeg: University of Manitoba Press, 2013.
Isaac, G. "Food-Sharing and Human Evolution: Archaeological Evidence from the Plio-Pleistocene of East Africa." *Journal of Anthropological Research*, 34:311–325, 1978.
Isenberg, Andrew. *The Destruction of the Bison: An Environmental History, 1750–1920*. Cambridge: Cambridge University Press, 2000.
Jablow, Joseph. *The Cheyenne in Plains Indian trade Relations 1795–1840*. Monographs of the American Ethnological Society No. 19. Seattle: University of Washington Press, 1966.
Jacquin, Philippe. *Les Indiens Blancs: Français et Indiens en Amérique du Nord (XVIe–XVIIIe siècle)*. Montreal: Libre Expression, 1996.
Jennings, John. *The Canoe: A Living Tradition*. Toronto: Firefly Books 2002.
Johnson, Dennis F. *York Boats of the Hudson's Bay Company: Canada's Inland Armada* Saskatoon: Fifth House, 2006.

Kehoe, Alice B. "The Function of Ceremonial Sexual Intercourse among the Northern Plains Indians." *Plains Anthropologist*, 15(48):99–103, 1970.
Kehoe, Thomas F. *The Gull Lake Site: A Prehistoric Bison Drive Site in Soutwestern Saskatchewan*. Publications in Anthropology and History No. 1. Milwaukee Public Museum, 1973.
Kiple, Kenneth F. *A Movable Feast: Ten Millennia of Food Globalization*. Cambridge: Cambridge University Press, 2007.
Krech, Shepard III. "On the Aboriginal Population of the Kutchin." *Arctic Anthropology*, 15(1):89–104, 1978.
III. *Ecological Indian: Myth and History*. New York: W. W. Norton, 1999.
Lai, Ping, and Nancy C. Lovell. "Skeletal Markers of Occupational Stress in the Fur Trade: A Case Study from a Hudson's Bay Company Fur Trade Post." *International Journal of Osteoarchaeology*, 2:221–234, 1992.
Lambert, Estelle V., David P. Speechly, Steven C. Dennis, and Timothy D. Noakes. "Enhanced Endurance in Trained Cyclists during Moderate Intensity Exercise Following 2 Weeks Adaptations to a High Fat Diet." *European Journal of Applied Physiology*, 69:287–293, 1994.
Landals, Alison. "Horse Heaven: Change in Late Precontact to Contact Period Landscape Use in Southern Alberta," in Brian Kooyman and Jane H. Kelley, eds., *Archaeology on the Edge: New Perspectives from the Northern Plains*, 231–262. Calgary: University of Calgary Press, 2004.
Lansing, Michael. "Plains Indian Women and Interracial Marriage in the Upper Missouri Trade, 1804–1868." *Western Historical Quarterly*, 31(4):413–433, Winter, 2000.
Lappage, Ronald S. "The Physical Feats of the Voyageur." *Canadian Journal of the History of Sports*, 15(1):30–37, May 1984.
Licht, Daniel S. *Ecology and Economics of the Great Plains*. Lincoln: University of Nebraska Press, 1997.
Lippincott, Isaac, "A Century and a half of Fur Trade at St. Louis." *Washington University Studies*, III, Part II (No 2), 221–259, April 1916.
Listenfelt, Hattie. "The Hudson's Bay Company and the Red River Trade," in *Collections of the State Historical Society of North Dakota*, Vol. IV, 1913.
Losey, Timothy C., and Gabriella Prager, "A Consideration of the Effects of the Demise of Bison on the Subsistence Economy of Fort Victoria: A Late 19th Century Hudson's Bay Post." *Canadian Archaeological Association Bulletin*, No. 7:162–182, 1975.
Lott, Dale F. *American Bison: A Natural History*. Berkeley: University of California Press, 2002.
Lovell, Nancy C., and Aaron A. Dublenko. "Further Aspects of Fur Trade Life Depicted in the Skeleton." *International Journal of Osteoarchaeology*, 9:248–256, 1999.
Lutz, John Sutton, ed. *Myth & Memory: Stories of Indigenous-European Contact*. Vancouver: UBC Press, 2007.
Lutz, John Sutton, *Makúk: A New History of Aboriginal-White Relations*. Vancouver: UBC Press, 2008.
Lytwyn, Victor P. *The Fur Trade of the Little North: Indians, Pedlars and Englishmen East of Lake Winnipeg, 1760–1821*. Winnipeg: Rupert's Land Research Center, 1986.

Muskekowuck Athinuwick: Original People of the Great Swampy Land. Winnipeg: University of Manitoba Press, 2002.

Macdougall, Brenda. *One of the Family: Metis Culture in Nineteenth-Century Northwestern Saskatchewan.* Vancouver: UBC Press, 2010.

Macdougall, Brenda, and Nicole St-Onge, "Rooted in Mobility: Métis Buffalo-hunting brigades." *Manitoba History,* 71:21–32, Winter 2013.

Mackie, Richard. *Trading Beyond the Mountains: The British Fur Trade on the Pacific, 1793–1843.* Vancouver: UBC Press, 1997.

MacKinnon, Doris. "Métis Pioneers: Isabella Hardisty Lougheed and Marie Rose Delorme Smith." PhD dissertation, History Department, University of Calgary, 2012.

MacLeod, Margaret, and W. L. Morton. *Cuthbert Grant of Grantown.* Toronto: McClelland Stewart, 1974.

Malainey, M. E., R. Przybylski, and B. L. Sherrif. "One Person's Food: How and Why Fish Avoidance May Affect the Settlement and Subsistence Patterns of Hunter-Gatherers." *American Antiquity,* 66(1):141–161, January 2001.

Malainey, M. E., R. Przybylski, and B.L. Sherriff, "One Person's Food: How and Why Fish Avoidance May Affect the Settlement and Subsistence Patterns of Hunter-Gatherers." *American Antiquity,* 66(1):141–161, 2001.

Malainey, M. E., and Barbara L. Sherriff, "Adjusting Our Perceptions: Historical and Archaeological Evidence of Winter on the Plains of Western Canada." *Plains Anthropologist,* 41(158):333–357, 1996.

Mandelbaum, David G. *The Plains Cree: An Ethnographic, Historical, and Comparative Study.* Regina: Canadian Plains Research Center, 1979.

Marchand, Philip. *Ghost Empire: How the French Almost Conquered North America.* Toronto: McClelland and Stewart, 2005.

Martin, Paul S., and Christine R. Szuter, "War Zones and Game Sinks in Lewis and Clark's West." *Conservation Biology,* 13(1) 36–45, 1999.

Massie, Merle. *Forest Prairie Edge: Place History in Saskatchewan.* Winnipeg: University of Manitoba Press, 2014.

McArdle, William D., Frank I. Katch, and Victor L. Katch. *Essentials of Exercise Physiology,* 3rd ed., Vol. I. Baltimore: Lippincott, Williams & Wilkins, 2006.

McCrady, David, G. *Living with Strangers: The Nineteenth Century Sioux and the Canadian-American Borderlands.* Norman: University of Oklahoma Press, 2006.

McEvoy, Arthur. *The Fisherman's Problem: Ecology and Law in the California Fisheries, 1850–1980.* Cambridge: Cambridge University Press, 1986.

McKenna, John, Anne Marie O'Hagan, James Power, Michael Macleod, and Andrew Cooper. "Coastal Dune Conservation on an Irish Commonage: Community-based Management or Tragedy of the Commons?" *The Geographical Journal,* 173:157–169, June 2007.

McLeod, Neal. "Plains Cree Identity: Borderlands, Ambiguous Genealogies, and Narrative Irony." *The Canadian Journal of Native Studies,* 20(2):437–454, 2000.

— *Cree Narrative Memory: From Treaties to Contemporary Times.* Saskatoon: Purich Publishing, 2007.

McNeill, J. R. *Something New Under the Sun: An Environmental History of the Twentieth Century World.* New York: W. W. Norton, 2000.
McNeill, W.H. "How the Potato Changed the World's History." *Social Research,* LXVI(1):67–83, 1999.
Mendelsohn, Robert. "Property Rights and Tropical Deforestation." *Oxford Economic Papers,* New Ser., 46:750–756, October 1994.
Mercer, Alison. "Half-Hitches, Dressed Leather, and Nice Easy Long Strides: Métis Horsemanship in the Mounted Buffalo Hunt." Honours thesis, Department of History, University of Calgary 2007.
Meyer, David, and Henry T. Epp. "North-South Interaction in the Late Prehistory of Central Saskatchewan." *Plains Anthropologist,* 38(142):321–340, November 1990.
Milloy, John S. *The Plains Cree: Trade, Diplomacy and War.* Winnipeg: University of Manitoba, 1990.
Mintz, Sidney W., and Christine M. Du Bois. "The Anthropology of Food and Eating." *Annual Review of Anthropology,* 31:99–119, 2002.
Morgan, Lewis Henry, *The Indian Journals, 1858–62.* Ann Arbor: University of Michigan Press, 1959.
Morgan, R. Grace. "Beaver Ecology/ Beaver Mythology." PhD thesis, University of Alberta, 1991.
Morin, E., "Fat Composition and Nunamiut Decision-making: A New Look at the Marrow and Bone Grease Indices." *Journal of Archaeological Science,* 34:69–82, 2007.
Morse, Eric W. *Freshwater Saga: Memoirs of a Lifetime of Wilderness Canoeing in Canada.* Toronto: University of Toronto Press, 1987.
Fur Trade Canoe Routes of Canada: Then and Now. Toronto: University of Toronto Press, 1989.
Morton, A. S. *A History of the Canadian West to 1870–71.* Toronto: University of Toronto Press, 1973.
Morton, W. L. *Manitoba: A History.* Toronto: University of Toronto Press, 1967.
"The Battle at the Grand Coteau, July 13 and 14, 1851." [1859–60], reprinted in Antoine S. Lussier and D. Bruce Sealey, eds., *The Other Natives: The Métis,* 52–53. For an overall descriptions, see Garrett Wilson, *Frontier Farewell: The 1870s and the End of the Old West,* 123–132. Regina: Canadian Plains Research Center, 2007.
Muldrew, Craig. *Food, Energy and the Creation of Industriousness: Work and Material Culture in Agrarian England, 1550–1780.* Cambridge: Cambridge University Press, 2011.
Murton, James. *Creating a Modern Countryside: Liberalism and Land Resettlement in British Columbia.* Vancouver: UBC Press, 2007.
Noakes, T. D. "Physiological Models to Understand Exercise Fatigue and the Adaptations that Predict or Enhance Athletic Performance." *Scandinavian Journal of Medicine & Science in Sports,* 10:123–145, 2000.
Nute, Grace Lee. *Voyageur.* Minnesota Historical Society, 1987.
O'Riordan, Terence. "Straddling the 'Great Transformation': The Hudson's Bay Company in Edmonton during the Transition from the Commons to Private Property, 1854–1882." *Prairie Forum,* 28(1):1–26, Spring 2003.

Ostler, Jeffrey. "'They Regard Their Passing As Wakan': Interpreting Western Sioux Explanations for the Bison's Decline." *Western Historical Quarterly*, 30(4):475–497, winter 1999.
— "'The Last Buffalo Hunt' and Beyond: Plains Sioux Economic Strategies in the Early Reservation Period." *Great Plains Quarterly*, 21(2):115–130, Spring 2001.
Otter, Chris. "The British Nutrition Transition and its histories." *History Compass*, 10/11(818) [812–825]: 2012.
Pannekoek, Fritz. "The Historiography of the Red River Settlement, 1830–1868." *Prairie Forum*, 6(1):75–85, 1981.
Peck, Trevor Richard. "Bison Ethology and native Settlement Patterns during the Old Women's Phase on the Northwestern Plains." PhD thesis, University of Calgary, 2001.
Peck, Trevor R., and J. Rod Vickers. "Buffalo and Dogs: The Prehistoric Lifeway of Aboriginal People on the Alberta Plains, 1004–1005," in Michael Payne, Donald Wetherell, and Catherine Cavanaugh, eds., *Alberta Formed: Alberta Transformed* Vol. I, 55–79. Edmonton: University of Alberta Press, 2006.
Peers, Laura. *The Ojibwa of Western Canada, 1780–1870*. Winnipeg: University of Manitoba Press, 1994.
Perren, Richard. *Taste, Trade and Technology: The Development of the International Meat Industry Since 1840*. Surrey, UK: Ashgate, 2006.
Perry, Richard J. "The Fur Trade and the Status of Women in the Western Subarctic." *Ethnohistory*, 26(4):363–375, 1979.
Pilcher, Jeffrey M. *Food in World History*. New York and London: Routledge, 2006.
Pilcher, Jeffrey M. ed. *The Oxford History of Food History*. New York: Oxford University Press, 2012.
Podruchny, Carolyn. *Making the Voyageur World: Travelers and Traders in the North American Fur Trade*. Lincoln: University of Nebraska Press, 2006.
Potyondi, Barry. *In Palliser's Triangle: Living in the Grasslands, 1850–1930*. Saskatoon: Purich Publishing, 1995.
Price, Richard. *The Spirit the Alberta Indian Treaties*. Edmonton: University of Alberta Press, 1999.
Pritchard, James. *In Search of Empire: The French in the Americas, 1670–1730*. Cambridge: Cambridge University Press, 2004.
Pyne, Stephen J. *Awful Splendour: A Fire History of Canada*. Vancouver: UBC Press, 2007.
Quigg, J. Michael. "Bison Processing at the Rush Site, 41TG346, and Evidence for Pemmican Production in the Southern Plains." *Plains Archaeologist*, 42(159):145–161, February 1997.
Rannie, W. F. "'Awful Splendour': Historical Accounts of Prairie Fire in Southern Manitoba Prior to 1870." *Prairie Forum*, 26(1):17–46, Spring 2001.
Ray, Arthur J. "Competition and Conservation in the Early Subarctic Fur Trade." *Ethnohistory*, 25(4):347–357, 1978.
— "The Northern Great Plains: Pantry of the Northwestern Fur Trade, 1774–1885." *Prairie Forum*, 9:263–280, 1984.

"Periodic Shortage, Native Welfare, and the Hudson's Bay Company." 1670–1930," in K. Coates and W. Morrison, eds., *Interpreting Canada's North: Selected Readings*, 94–112. Toronto: Copp Clark Pitman, 1989.

"Some Conservation Schemes of the Hudson's Bay Company, 1821–1850: An Examination of the Problems of Resource Management in the Fur Trade," in Larry M. Dilsaver and Craig E. Colten, eds., *The American Environment: Interpretations of Past Geographies*, 33–49. Lanham, MD: Rowman & Littlefield, 1992.

Indians in the Fur Trade: Their Role as Trappers, Hunters, and Middlemen in the Lands Southwest of Hudson Bay, 1660–1870. Toronto: University of Toronto Press, 1998.

Ray, Arthur J., Jim Miller, and Frank Tough. *Bounty and Benevolence: A History of Saskatchewan Treaties*. Montreal: McGill-Queen's University Press, 2000.

Reeves, Brian O. K. "Communal Bison Hunting on the Northern Plains," in L. B. Davis and B. O. K. Reeves, eds., *Hunters of the Recent Past*, 169–170. London: Unwin, Hyman, 1990.

Scheiber, Laura L. "Bison Economies on the Late Prehistoric North American High Plains." *Journal of Field Archaeology*, 32(3):297–313, 2007.

Rich, E. E. *A History of the Hudson's Bay Company 1670–1870*, Vol. I and II. London: Hudson Bay Record Society, 1959.

Richards, John F. *The Unending Frontier: An Environmental History of the Early Modern World*. Berkeley: University of California Press, 2003.

Ritchie, Leslie. "'Expectations of Grease & Provisions,': The Circulation and Regulation of Fur Trade Foodstuffs." *Eighteenth-Century Life*, 23(2):124–142, 1999.

Roe, F. G. "Buffalo and Snow." *Canadian Historical Review*, 17:125–146, 1936.

The Indian and the Horse. Norman: University of Oklahoma Press, 1955.

The North American Buffalo: A Critical Study of the Species in its Wild State, 2nd. ed. Toronto: University of Toronto Press 1970.

Salisbury, Neil. "The Indians' Old World: Native Americans and the Coming of Europeans" *The William and Mary Quarterly*, 3rd ser., 53(3):435–568, July 1996.

Sharrock, Susan. "Cree, Cree-Assiniboines, and Assiniboines: Interethnic Social Organization on the Northern Plains." *Ethnohistory*, 21:95–122, 1974.

Sherow, James E. "Workings of the Geodialectic: High Plains Indians and Their Horses in the Region of the Arkansas River, 1800–1870." *Environmental History Review*, 16:61–84, Summer 1992.

The Grasslands of the United States: An Environmental History. Santa Barbara: ABC Clio, 2007.

Simmons, I. G. *Changing the Face of the Earth: Culture, Environment, History*, 2nd ed. Oxford: Blackwell, 1996.

Skinner, Claiborne A. "The Sinews of Empire: The Voyageurs and the Carrying Trade of the *Pays d'en Haut*, 1681–1754." PhD dissertation, University of Illinois at Chicago, 1991.

Regional Perspectives on Early America: The Upper Country: French Enterprise in the Colonial Great Lakes. Baltimore: Johns Hopkins University Press, 2008.

Sleeper-Smith, Susan. "Women, Kin and Catholicism: New Perspectives on the Fur Trade." *Ethnohistory*, 47(2):423–452, Spring 2000.

Sloan, W. A. "The Native Response to the Extension of the European Traders into the Athabasca and Mackenzie Basin, 1770–1814." *Canadian Historical Review*, LX(3): 281–299, 1979.

Smith, Brian J. "The Historical and Archaeological Evidence for the Use of Fish as an Alternate Subsistence Resource among Northern Plains Bison Hunters," in Kerry Abel and Jean Friesen, eds., *Aboriginal Resource Use in Canada: Historical and Legal Aspects*, 35–49. Winnipeg: University of Manitoba Press, 1991.

Smyth, David. "The Niititapi Trade: Euroamericans and the Blackfoot Speaking Peoples to the Mid-1830s." PhD dissertation, Department of History, Carleton University, 2001.

Speth, John D., and Katherine A. Spielmann. "Energy Source, Protein Metabolism, and Hunter-Gatherer Subsistence Strategies." *Journal of Anthropological Archaeology*, 2: 1–31, 1983.

Sprenger, Herman G. "The Métis Nation: Buffalo Hunting vs. Agriculture in the Red River Settlement (Circa 1810–1870)," in Antoine S. Lussier and D. Bruce Sealey, eds., *The Other Natives: The Métis*, Vol. I: 1700–1885, 158–178. Winnipeg, Manitoba: Manitoba Metis Federation, 1978.

Spry, Irene M. "The Great Transformation: The Disappearance of the Commons in Western Canada," in Richard Allen, ed., *Man and Nature on the Prairies*, 21–45. Regina: Canadian Plains Research Center, 1976.

"The Tragedy of the Loss of the Commons in Western Canada," in Ian A. L. Getty and Antoine S. Lussier, eds., *As Long as the Sun Shines and Water Flows: A Reader in Canadian Native Studies*, 203–223. Vancouver: UBC Press, 1983.

Stanford Craig B., and Henry T. Bunn, eds., *Meat-Eating & Human Evolution*. Oxford: Oxford University Press, 2001.

Stanley, George. "The Half-Breed 'Rising of 1875." *Canadian Historical Review*, 17(4):399–412, 1936.

Stefansson, Vilhjalmur. *Not by Bread Alone*. New York: Macmillan and Company, 1946.

The Fat of the Land. New York: Macmillan Company, 1957.

Stern, Theodore. *Chiefs and Chief Traders: Indian Relations at Fort Nez Perces, 1818–1855*. Eugene: University of Oregon Press, 1993.

Stunden Bower, Shannon. *Wet Prairie: People, Land and Water in Agricultural Manitoba*. Vancouver: UBC Press, 2011.

Sunder, John E. *The Fur Trade in the Upper Missouri, 1840–1865*. Norman: University of Oklahoma Press, 1965.

Swagerty, William R. "Marriage and Settlement Patterns of Rocky Mountain Trappers and Traders." *Western Historical Quarterly*, 11:159–180, April 1980.

Talbot, Robert J. *Negotiating the Numbered Treaties: An Intellectual and Political Biography of Alexander Morris*. Saskatoon: Purich Publishing, 2009.

Terrell, John Upton. *Furs by Astor*. New York: William Morrow & Company, 1963.

Titley, Brian. *The Indian Commissioners: Agents of the State and Indian Policy in Canada's Prairie West: 1873–1932*. Edmonton: University of Alberta Press, 2009.

Tobias, John L. "Canada's Subjugation of the Plains Cree, 1879–1885." *Canadian Historical Review* LXIV(4):519–548, 1983.
Tough, Frank. *'As their natural resources fail': Native Peoples and the Economic History of Northern Manitoba, 1870–1930*. Vancouver: UBC Press, 1996.
Turkel, William J. *The Archive of Place: Unearthing the Pasts of the Chilcotin Plateau*. Vancouver: UBC Press, 2007.
Vale, Thomas. "The Pre-European Landscape in the United States." *Fire, Native Peoples and the Natural Landscape*, Thomas Vale, ed. Washington, DC: Island Press, 2002.
Van Kirk, Sylvia. *Many Tender Ties: Women in Fur-Trade Society in Western Canada, 1670–1870*. Winnipeg: Watson & Dwyer, 1980.
Verbicky-Todd, Eleanor. "Communal Buffalo Hunting among the Plains Tribes." Archaeological Survey of Alberta Occasional Paper NO. 24, 1984. Edmonton: Alberta Culture Historical Resources.
Vernon, James. *Hunger: A Modern History*. Cambridge, MA: The Belknap Press of Harvard University Press, 2007.
Vibert, Elizabeth. "The Contours of Everyday Life: Food and Identity in the Plateau Fur Trade," in Carolyn Podruchny and Laura Peers, eds., *Gathering Places: Aboriginal and Fur Trade Histories*, 119–148. Vancouver: UBC Press, 2010.
Vickers J. Rod, and Trevor R. Peck. "Islands in a Sea of Grass: The Significance of Wood in Winter Campsite Selection on the Northwestern Plains," in Brian Kooyman and Jane H. Kelley, eds., *Archaeology on the Edge: New Perspectives from the Northern Plains*, 95–124. Calgary: University of Calgary Press, 2004.
Vrooman, Nicholas C.P. *"The Whole Country was … 'One Robe.'"* Helena: Drumlummon Institute, 2012.
Webb Hodge, Frederick, ed. "Pemmican." Smithsonian Institution Bureau of American Ethnology, Bulletin No. 30, *Handbook of American Indians North of Mexico*, Vol. II., 223–224. Washington, DC: Smithsonian Institution, 1912.
Weist, Katherine. "Beasts of Burden and Menial Slaves: Nineteenth Century Observations of Northern Plains Indian Women," in Patricia Albers and Beatrice Medicine, eds., *The Hidden Half: Studies of Plains Indian Women*, 29–52. Lanham, MD: University Press of America, 1983.
Weltfish, Gene. *The Lost Universe*. New York: Basic Books, 1965.
Wentworth, Edward N. "Dried Meat: Early Man's Travel Ration." *Agricultural History*, 30(1):2–10, 1956.
West, Elliott. *The Contested Plains: Indians, Goldseekers, and the Rush to Colorado*. University Press of Kansas, 2000.
Whelan, Mary K. "Dakota Indian Economics and the Nineteenth-Century Fur Trade." *Ethnohistory*, 40(2):256–273, Spring 1993.
White, Richard. *Roots of Dependency: Subsistence, Environment, and Social Change among the Choctaws, Pawnees, and Navajos*. Lincoln: University of Nebraska Press, 1983.
   "Are You an Environmentalist or Do You Work for a Living?" in William Cronan, ed., *Uncommon Ground: Rethinking the Human Place in Nature*, 171–185. New York: W. W. Norton, 1996.
Wilson, Garrett. *Frontier Farewell: The 1870s and the End of the Old West*. Regina: Canadian Plains Research Center, 2007.

Winterhalder, Bruce. "Intragroup Resource Transfers: Comparative Evidence, Models and Implications for Human Evolution, in Craig B. Stanford and Henry T. Bunn, eds., *Meat-Eating and Human Evolution*, 279–301. Oxford: Oxford University Press, 2001.

Wischmann, Lesley. *Frontier Diplomats: Alexander Culbertson and Natoyist-Siksina' Among the Blackfeet.* Norman: University of Oklahoma Press, 2004.

Wissler, Clark. "Material Culture of the Blackfoot Indians." *Anthropological Papers of the American Museum of Natural History*, V, Part I, March 1910.

Wolf, Eric. *Europe and the People without a History.* Berkeley: University of California Press, 1997.

Worster, Donald. "Doing Environmental History," in *The Ends of the Earth: Perspectives on Modern Environmental History*, 289–307. Cambridge: Cambridge University Press, 1988.

  Under Western Skies: Nature and History in the American West. Oxford: Oxford University Press, 1992.

Wynn, Graeme. *Canada and Arctic North America: An Environmental History.* Santa Barbara: ABC-Clio, 2007.

Young, Emily. "State Intervention and Abuse of the Commons: Fisheries Development in Baja California Sur, Mexico." *Annals of the Association of American Geographers*, 91:283–306, 2001.

INDEX

Aitsina, 63, 119
Albany
    Fort, 25
    House, 19, 26–28, 38, 129
    River, 25
alcohol, 38, 39, 76, *See* brandy
    high wines, 38
    use in the fur trade, 38–41
amalgamation
    of Hudson's Bay Company and North West Company, 149
American Fur Company, 15, 55, 55n.108, 71n.35, 75n.46, 175, 187, 201, 202n.39, 203, 203n.46, 208n.64, 212n.78, 213n.79, 263, 281
Arctic
    Ocean, 2, 15, 46, 57
Arikara, 22
Assiniboine
    bison hunt, 51
    poundmakers, 105
    River, 14, 20, 22, 39, 41, 56, 59, 61, 75, 80
    territory, 17
    tribe, 17, 28, 41, 59–61, 151
    valley, 21, 103
Athabasca
    brigades, 151
    district, 14, 16, 56, 128
    expedition, 131
    furs, 129
    Lake, 43, 56
    River, 41, 43, 46
    valley, 117
Auld, William, 132

bateaux, 20, 27, 84, 129
bear, 69

beaver, 45
    Beaver Creek, 20, 211
    Beaver tribe, 47
    George Simpson and conservation program, 150
bison, 18, 47
    bison-human-beaver nexus, 64
    conservation, 15, 151
    dépouille, 89, 95
    fats, 89–93
    herds, 2, 17, 18, 22, 89–93
    hunt, 18
    North American plains species (Bison bison), 9, 49, 62
    overkill, 5
    pounds, 77
    Rughaghan, 9
    summer hunt, 89–93, 122–126
    Utah herds collapse, 74
    wood subspecies (Bison bison athabascae), 9, 43
Blackfoot, xii, 7, 11–12, 14, 18, 22, 63–64, 151
    Painted Feather, 117–118
    provisions market, 113–120
    territory, 17
    trade with Europeans, 115
    war with the Cree, 132
Blood
    River, 42
Brandon House, 20, 28, 38
    gift giving, 78–79
    sacking of by Métis and Nor'Westers, 143
    summer hunting, 121
    summer scarcity, 122
brandy, 38–41, 80, 110–111, 121
    journey brandy, 38, 39
Bryce, George, 100

Caledonia
  territory, 16
Canadian Shield, 14, 19, 22, 25, 34, 42, 61
canoe
  birchbark, 27, 30, 103
  voyageurs, 29–32
Canton, China
  Pacific coastal trade, 129
caribou, 48
Carlton House
  fall in trade, 135
  pemmican provisions, 134
Chaboillez, Charles, 79–80
Chipewyan, 44–48, 52
  territory, 43
Chouteau, Pierre, 150
Cocking, Matthew, 49, 52
Coltman Commission, 137, 140, 144
Columbia
  River, 150
  territory, 16
conservation, 187
conservation programs, 150
Cree, 7, 14, 17, 18, 28, 36, 41, 59–61, 149–151
  decline of influence, 113–114
  pemmican, 8
  poundmakers, 105
Crow, 114, 116
Culbertson, Alexander, 58
Cumberland House, 22, 49, 56
  bison supply, 102
  hunting camps, 120
  pemmican preparation, 96

deer, 47, 69
Delorme. *See* François Enos
Dene, 14, 47–48
Detroit, 28, 34, 35

elk, 47, 75
endosomatic energy regime, 22, 29
epidemics, 148
Ermatinger, Edward
  pemmican trade in the late nineteenth century, 99
exosomatic energy regime, 30

Fidler, Peter, 34, 45–46, 63, 134
  and pemmican wars, 86

competition with the North West Company, 142
HBC expansion into the Athabasca district, 131
Métis as "New Nation", 101
relationship with Red River colonists, 130
Flathead, 114
food exchange
  anthropology, 105–106
  Native groups, 106–107
Fort Augustus, 82, 113
  relationship with Blackfoot, 116–118
Fort Carlton, 18
  pemmican provisions, 142
Fort Daer, 123, 141
  rationing, 135
Fort des Prairies
  western Manitoba, 51
Fort Edmonton, 17, 22, 40, 75, 82, 113
  aggressive pemmican purchasing, 142
  and scarcity of pemmican supplies in 1813, 120
  besieged by Tsuu-Tsina and Cree, 118
  promise to supply pemmican to Red River colony, 135
Fort Ellice, 17, 20, 62n.14, 97, 98n.121, 152, 154, 154n.15, 192, 211, 219, 222n.10, 237–243, 238f. 6.6., 241t. 6.7., 244–245, 252, 255, 257
Fort George, 21n.7, 56, 56n.111, 68, 69n.31, 84, 108, 108n.30, 108n.33, 109, 115, 116, 116n.60, 116n.61, 283
Fort Peigan, 118
Fort Pitt, 82
Fort Vancouver, 149
Fort Vermillion, 56, 82
François Enos (et Hémault *dit* Delorme), 137
Frobisher, Benjamin, 42
Frobisher, Joseph, 42
Frobisher, Thomas, 42
fur trade, xi, 3, 12, 25, 41–44
  diet and caloric intake of fur traders, 21–41
  energy regime, 29–31
  Hudson's Bay Company, 15
  northern, 19
  reliance on pemmican, 21–22
  subarctic, 6, 13

Gloucester House, 27, 52
Goodwin, Robert, 60
    food exchange at Brandon House, 84
    meat consumption at Brandon House, 108
    pemmican procurement, 97
    prices at Brandon House, 110
Grand Portage, 36, 43, 53, 55, 56
Grant, Cuthbert
    Seven Oaks Massacre, 144
Grant, Peter, 32
Great Lakes, 31
    St. Lawrence – Great lakes Corridor, 34
Green River, 149
Gros Ventres, 114–115, 119

Harmon, Daniel, 61, 71
Helm, June, 45
Henderson, Jacob, 78
Henry, Alexander the Elder, 42, 76
    trading with Ojibwa, 36
Henry, Alexander the Younger, 41, 60, 61, 95
    and Blackfoot, 116–119
    food consumption at Pembina post, 108
    organization of summer hunts, 123–124
    pemmican preparation, 95
    pemmican provisions, 88, 97
    Red River colonists, 135
    use of guns among the Ojibwa, 112
    views on Métis, 126
    women at fur posts, 95
Hillier, William, 128
Hind, Henry Youle, 2
Horse Wars, 114
Hudson Bay
    territory, 2, 13, 15, 25, 102, 129
Hudson's Bay
    Company, 2, 14–16, 18

Illinois Country, 35
Innis, Harold, 44
Iron Alliance
    of northern plains people, 124
Isbister, Joseph, 27

James Bay, 19, 25, 27, 36, 39, 48, 129
    post, 14
    transport supply, 102
Jarvis, Edward, 27–28

Jollycoeur, 82

Kanai, 117
Kootenay, 114, 116, 119
Kurtz, Rudolph Friedrich, 148

L'Homme à Calumet
    a.k.a. Day Light, The Horns and Iron Shirt, 119
La Jérémy, 41
La Vérendrye, Pierre Gaultier, 41
Lac La Pluie, 36, 53
    and pemmican treaty, 141
Lagodimière, 135
    service to Red River colony, 137
Lake of the Woods, 36
Lake Ouinipique, 24
Lake Superior, 36
Lewis and Clark, 93, 119
Longoore, John, 49
Lord Selkirk, 15, 104n.12, 105n.16, 129, 136, 139
    pemmican production, 105
    Selkirk settlement, 100, 144

Macdonald, Alexander, 126
Macdonell, John, 61, 68
Macdonell, Miles, 124, 134
    and Selkirk settlers, 127
    food purchasing program, 135
    hiring of hunters, 137
    Pemmican Proclamation, 136–137, 139
McKay, Donald, 20, 29, 36–40
    use of brandy in Red River area, 120
McKay, John
    conditions at Brandon House, 110–113
    pemmican purchases at Qu'Appelle, 142
    relationship with Ojibwa and Assiniboine, 78
Mackenzie
    territory, 16
Mackenzie, Alexander, 47, 53
Manchester House, 22
Mandan, 22, 60, 78, 114
    Indian trade networks, 103
Manitoba, 19–21, 22, 27, 41, 102, 152
    fur trading posts, 52
    Lake, 62
    Steppe, 107
Marten Falls, 26, 27
Maugenest, Germain, 26

Maximilien, the Prince of Wied
  witness to pemmican use among Native peoples, 93
McEachern, Hector, 138
McVicar, John, 138
Métis, 12, 14, 16–18, 149–154
  and pemmican wars, 127
  freemen, 126, 138
  intensive bison hunts, 100
  mock hunts, 144
  Seven Oaks Massacre, 144
  summer hunt, 92, 152
  Upper Mississippi, 60
M'Gillivray, Duncan, 20, 56, 68
  complaints concerning Siksika, 115
  food requirements at Fort George, 108
  plains foods, 99
  price of pemmican, 109–110
Miles, Robert Seaborne, 33
Minnesota, 60, 62, 87
Mississippi
  Upper Mississippi, 20
Missouri, 8
  bison butter, 10
  Upper, 12, 150
monopsony, 15, 151
Montagne à la Bosse, 59, 143
moose, 44, 45, 48–49, 69, 75
  meat, 49

Naubunoitouog
  "Man with one Ear, 123
Nor'wester. *See* Chaboillez, Charles; North West Company
North Dakota, 62
  Devil's Lake, 60
North West Company, 14, 48
  amalgamation with XY Company, 125
  and pemmican trade, 105
  attempt to build South Branch house, 133
  payments and wages, 137
  pemmican treaty, 140–141
  pemmican war and HBC, 143
  resentment toward Red River colonists, 129
Norway House, 131, 152

Ojibwa, 17, 25–26, 29, 36, 42, 52, 59, 152
  Captain Quinquehanea, 77
  Gavion Bouche, 80

Saulteaux, 114
Osnaburgh House, 28

Pacific
  coastal trade, 149
  HBC campaign, 150
  Ocean, 46, 57
Palliser, John, 133
  sweet pemmican, 10
parkland, 14, 59, 60, 65, 70–72, 100
  belts, 22
  convergence model, 70–72
  ecotone, 6, 70, 84
Passongab (the Murderer), 122
Pawnee
  hunting territories, 74
Peace River, 47, 145
pemmican, 1
  as national dish, 1
  empire, 7, 8
  energy source, 7–8
  factory production, 97
  jerky, 8
  mythology, 11–12
  prices, 7–8, 109–111, 140–141, 143
  Proclamation, 104
  Ruchagan, 87
  storage and production at trading posts, 87–89
  sweet pemmican, 10–11
  trade pemmican, 99
  treaty, 140–141
  violence, 100–102
  wars, 15
pemmican wars, 102, 127
Piikani, 113, 117, 118–119
  massacre of by Rocky Mountains Kootenay, 131
plains tribes
  bison hunt, 63–66
polyethnic mixing
  in Manitoba, Minnesota and North Dakota, 124
Pond, Peter, 41, 42, 44, 46
Postes de l'Ouest, 41
pounds, 14, 51, 61, 64, 66–70, 109
  areas, 15
  in Red and Assiniboine Valleys, 120
  makers, 84, 102, 108, 115
  pricing strategies, 110
  winter, 46, 59, 115, 122

Pruden, John, 85
  Carlton House, 134
  pemmican preparation, 96
  pemmican procurement, 142
  tribal warfare, 132

Qu'Appelle, 20, 25
  pemmican provisions, 104
  valley, 126
Qu'Appelle, 18

Rainy Lakes, 28, 36
Ray, Arthur, 71
  meat consumption at Pemibina post, 109
Red River, 1, 14, 20, 25, 41, 59, 74, 80, 81
  brigades, 151
  colonists, 141
  colony, 15, 16, 34, 122
  food scarcity, 130
  Granite, 1
  pemmican, 97
  post, 56
  valley, 14, 17, 19, 22, 103
Red River cart, 124, 135, 228
Rice, Henry M., 1, 3, 197, 215, 215n.86, 262
Robertson, Colin, 137
Rocky Mountains, 22–25, 113
Rupert's Land, 2, 9n.20, 15, 19n.2, 23n.12, 28n.24, 77n.53, 100, 108, 145, 147, 148, 151, 183, 188, 190, 199, 227, 263n. 4

Saskatchewan, 20, 67, 75, 103
  North Saskatchewan catchments, 14
  pemmican, 97
  River, 22, 40, 41, 48–49, 60, 102, 113, 129, 131
  River valley, 14, 17, 96, 109, 119
  south-central, 114
  watershed, 91
Saulteaux, 149
Semple, Robert, 143–144
Seven Oaks Massacre, 15, 100–101, 137
  Selkirk settlement, 100
Siksika, 64, 113, 115
Simpson, George, 16, 149, 150, 151, 153, 154, 158, 159, 179, 187, 189, 190, 207, 214, 263
  development of HBC polices, 149–151

Sioux
  Siouan Dakota, 22
  territory, 60
Skene, Peter Ogden, 149
Slave
  Lake, 45, 48
  River, 43, 46
Snake, 114, 149
Souris, 14, 22, 59, 83, 93, 143, 169, 175, 196, 224, 245
St. Laurent, 18, 195, 228, 232, 246, 250, 251, 252, 253
St. Lawrence
  valley, 20, 29
St.-Lazaar, 20
Stefansson, Viljalmur, 47
Sun dance, 121
Sutherland, James, 19, 27, 37, 78–79
Sutherland, John, 19–20, 52, 58, 80
  provisions at Brandon House, 110

taboos
  against eating fish, 65
  against killing beaver, 64, 115
Tanner, John, 123–124, 126
tobacco, 33, 143
  as gift, 80, 110–111, 116
  trade, 76–77, 116
tragedy of the commons, 4, 4n.9, 292
transport and transportation, 15, 27, 32, 102, 124, 135, 184, 185, 228

Umfreville, Edward, 67

voyageurs, 2, 14

Winnipeg
  Lake, 25, 36, 39, 41–42, 48, 56, 62, 102, 128
  River, 39, 56
  steppe, 22, 29, 60–61, 72, 129
Worster, Donald, 6, 7n. 16

Yankton Sioux, 114
York
  boat, 15, 38
  boats and crews, 32–33
  Factory, 102, 128–129, 132, 140
york boat, 2, 27, 32, 103, 114, 151, 184, 185, 190, 258, 259, *See* transport and transportation

Other Books in the Series (*continued from page iii*)

Mark Elvin and Tsui'jung Liu *Sediments of Time: Environment and Society in Chinese History*
Richard H. Grove *Green Imperialism: Colonial Expansion, Tropical Island Edens and the Origins of Environmentalism, 1600–1860*
Elinor G. K. Melville *A Plague of Sheep: Environmental Consequences of the Conquest of Mexico*
J. R. McNeill *The Mountains of the Mediterranean World: An Environmental History*
Theodore Steinberg *Nature Incorporated: Industrialization and the Waters of New England*
Timothy Silver *A New Face on the Countryside: Indians, Colonists, and Slaves in the South Atlantic Forests, 1500–1800*
Michael Williams *Americans and Their Forests: A Historical Geography*
Donald Worster *The Ends of the Earth: Perspectives on Modern Environmental History*
Samuel P. Hays *Beauty, Health, and Permanence: Environmental Politics in the United States, 1955–1985*
Warren Dean *Brazil and the Struggle for Rubber: A Study in Environmental History*
Robert Harms *Games Against Nature: An Eco-Cultural History of the Nunu of Equatorial Africa*
Arthur F. McEvoy *The Fisherman's Problem: Ecology and Law in the California Fisheries, 1850–1980*
Alfred W. Crosby *Ecological Imperialism: The Biological Expansion of Europe, 900–1900, Second Edition*
Kenneth F. Kiple *The Caribbean Slave: A Biological History*
Donald Worster *Nature's Economy: A History of Ecological Ideas, Second Edition*

Lightning Source UK Ltd.
Milton Keynes UK
UKHW011051091019
351267UK00001B/61/P